Verifiable Programming

C.A.R. Hoare, Series Editor

BACKHOUSE, R.C., *Program Construction and Verification*
DEBAKKER, J. W., *Mathematical Theory of Program Correctness*
BARR, M and WELLS, C., *Category Theory for Computing Science*
BEN-ARI, M., *Principles of Concurrent and Distributed Programming*
BIRD, R. and WADLER, P., *Introduction to Functional Programming*
BORNAT, R., *Programming from First Principles*
BUSTARD, D., ELDER, J. and WELSH, J., *Concurrent Program Structures*
CLARK, K. L. and McCABE, F. G., *Micro-Prolog: Programming in logic*
CROOKES, D., *Introduction to Programming in Prolog*
DAHL, O-J., *Verifiable Programming*
DROMEY, R. G., *How to Solve it by Computer*
DUNCAN, E., *Microprocessor Programming and Software Development*
ELDER, J., *Construction of Data Processing Software*
ELLIOTT, R. J. and HOARE, C. A. R., (eds.), *Scientific Applications of Multiprocessors*
GOLDSCHLAGER, L. and LISTER, A., *Computer Science: A modern introduction (2nd edn).*
GORDON, M. J. C., *Programming Language Theory and its Implementation*
GRAY, P. M. D., KULKARNI, K. G. and PATON, N. W., *Object-Orientated Databases*
HAYES, I, (ed), *Specification Case Studies*
HEHNER, E. C. R., *The Logic of Programming*
HENDERSON, P., *Functional Programming: Application and implementation*
HOARE, C. A. R., *Communicating Sequential Processes*
HOARE, C. A. R., and JONES, C. B. (eds), *Essays in Computing Science*
HOARE, C. A. R., and SHEPHERDSON, J. C. (eds), *Mathematical Logic and Programming Languages*
HUGHES, J. G., *Database Technology: A Software engineering approach*
HUGHES, J. G., *Object-orientated Databases*
INMOS LTD, *Occam 2 Reference Manual*
JACKSON, M. A., *System Development*
JOHNSTON, J., *Learning to Program*
JONES, C. B., *Systematic Software Development using VDM (2nd edn).*
JONES, C. B. and SHAW, R. C. F. (eds), *Case Studies in Systematic Software Development*
JONES, G., *Programming in occam*
JONES, G. and GOLDSMITH, M., *Programming in occam 2*
JOSEPH, M., PRASAD, V. R. and NATARAJAN, N., *A Multiprocessor Operating System*
KALDEWAIJ, A., *Programming: The Derivation of Algorrithms*
KING, P. J. B. *Computer and Communication Systems Performance Modelling*
LEW, A., *Computer Science: A mathematical introduction*
MARTIN, J. J., *Data Types and Data Structures*
McCABE, F. G., *High-Level Programmer's Guide to the 68000*
MEYER, B., *Introduction to the Theory of Programming Languages*
MEYER, B., *Object-oriented Software Construction*
MILNER, R., *Communication and Concurrency*
MORGAN, C., *Programming from Specifications*
PEYTON JONES, S. L., *The Implementation of Functional Programming Languages*
PEYTON JONES, S., and LESTER, D., *Implementing Functional Languages*
POMBERGER, G., *Software Engineering and Modula-2*
POTTER, B., SINCLAIR, J., TILL, D., *An Introduction to Formal Specification and Z*
REYNOLDS, J. C., *The Craft of Programming*
RYDEHEARD, D. E. and BURSTALL, R. M., *Computational Category Theory*
SLOMAN, M. and KRAMER, J., *Distributed Systems and Computer Networks*
SPIVEY, J. M., *The Z Notation: A reference manual*
TENNENT, R. D., *Principles of Programming Languages*
TENNENT, R. D., *Semantics of Programming Languages*
WATT, D. A., *Programming Language Concepts and Paradigms*
WATT, D. A., WICHMANN, B. A., and FINDLAY, W., *ADA: Language and methodology*
WELSH, J. and ELDER, J., *Introduction to Modula 2*
WELSH, J. and ELDER, J., *Introduction to Pascal (3rd edn).*
WELSH, J. ELDER, J. and BUSTARD, D., *Sequential Program Structures*
WELSH, J. and HAY, A., *A Model Implementation of Standard Pascal*
WELSH, J. and McKEAG, M., *Structured System Programming*
WIKSTRÖM, Å., *Functional Programming using Standard ML*

Verifiable Programming

Ole-Johan Dahl
Department of Informatics
University of Oslo, Norway

Prentice Hall
New York London Toronto Sydney Tokyo Singapore

First published 1992 by
Prentice Hall International (UK) Ltd
66 Wood Lane End, Hemel Hempstead
Hertfordshire HP2 4RG
A division of
Simon & Schuster International Group
© Ole-Johan Dahl, 1992

Printed and bound in Great Britain by
Dotesios, Trowbridge, Wilts.

Library of Congress Cataloging-in-Publication Data

Dalh, Ole-Johan, 1931-
    Verifiable programming / Ole-Johan Dahl.
        p.   cm. — (Prentice Hall international series in computer science)
    Includes bibliographical references.
    ISBN 0-13-951062-1
    1. Computer programs–Verification. I. Title. II. Series.
QA76.76.V47D34   1992
005.1'4–dc20

British Library Cataloguing in Publication Data

Dahl, Ole-Johan
    Verifiable programming.
I. Title
005.1

ISBN 0-13-951062-1

1 2 3 4 5 96 95 94 93 92

Contents

To my wife

Preface

This book is a result of a research activity at the Department of Informatics, University of Oslo, on "Program Specification and Verification", in continuous interaction with a slowly developing student course on the same topic. The activity goes back to the first half of the 1970's and has Simula 67 as one of its starting points, [6], [3]. The other main conceptual inputs have been the program logic developed by C.A.R. Hoare, in this book called "Hoare Logic", see e.g. [17], and the technique of type specification by generator induction, as developed by J.V. Guttag and J.J. Horning, [15]. The first published result of the research activity occurred in 1977, [7], which is an early forerunner of the present work.

The author is greatly indebted to many colleagues for cooperation and feedback. First and foremost of them is Olaf Owe, who has contributed very substantially to the research as well as to the actual text of the book. Thanks are also due to Dag F. Langmyhr who has contributed to the research and to the preparation of this text, to Stein Krogdahl and Bjørn Kirkerud, who have provided helpful criticism and suggestions, to Neelam Soundararajan, The Ohio State University, who helped prevent a couple of embarrassing mistakes, and to Zhenjia Lei, The University of Xi'an, who provided useful feedback on an early version of the manuscript. Several anonymous referees have contributed very substantially to the quality of the text. Finally, thanks are due to Tony Hoare for accepting the present work for publication at a fairly early stage of its development.

University of Oslo   Ole-Johan Dahl
November 14, 1991

ix

Chapter 1

Introduction

A user of computers whose programming experience is limited to making small programs, using simple and well documented programming tools, may be convinced that programming is easy: just tell the computer what to do, then it does it for you. It is only after having tried his hand at something slightly larger than toy size that he may realize that there is more to programming than just explaining to a computer what to do. This book is primarily intended for readers who know, from personal experience, that programming is in fact *very difficult*.

There are many sources of difficulties. Here are a few:

- *Conceptual difficulties*: in the planning of a computer system, say an interactive information system of some kind, you have to achieve complete understanding of the purpose of the system. In order to acquire it you may have to interact with people from different user groups with different professional backgrounds and perhaps different and conflicting requirements. In the design of the system you have to use specialized concepts suitable for the task. If you are lucky you can learn useful concepts by reading books or talking to colleagues. If not, you have to make up your own vocabulary, in such a way that it can be explained to other people, so they can understand what you are talking about.

- *Documentation*: in order to realize your system you will have to make use of software tools prepared by others: certainly a programming language, and probably other tools such as a system "package" to get information to and from interactive graphic devices. The former is perhaps a well described and well tested standard product, but the latter may be the first version of a program system under development in some company. A user manual is provided in order to enable a person to use the package without having to dig into the details of the code (he might not even be allowed access to the code for reasons of copyright!). But the document may be difficult to understand, not sufficiently precise, incomplete, and may even be incorrect. So, countless hours are spent in guesswork, trial, and retrial.

- *Documenting*: it is more difficult than one might think to produce precise, complete, correct, and easily readable documentation of software tools. Even having somehow established a suitable precise vocabulary, there is the difficulty of keeping the documentation up to date as the system develops over time. Improving the code usually takes priority for practical reasons; there is no point in improving the manual if the system does not function as well as intended.

- *Program readability*: program texts are not in general self explanatory. They describe in detail what is supposed to happen, but not the reason for these actions in a larger context. Anybody who has tried to understand programs written by others has experienced this kind of difficulty, and perhaps you have had a hard time understanding your own programs from a week ago because you had not bothered to include the right explanatory comments.

- *Modularization*: a good way to construct complicated systems is to use well designed modules as building blocks. Actually, it is the *only* way for any non-trivial digital system, if you consider that it will ultimately consist of elements of electronic circuitry. But even taking a good "high level" programming language as the conceptual basis, program modularization will be essential for the design of life-sized systems. Unfortunately, it is not easy to design good modules, or even to know in advance what good modules are, except that they will somehow facilitate your programming task.

- *Volume of reasoning*: the human mind does not seem to be well equipped for dealing accurately and dependably with large numbers of details. Good modularization can help, but even so, the volume of reasoning that goes into the construction of any real software system is likely to be enormous. For that reason logical errors are difficult to avoid.

- *Volume of program text*: even the task of writing text on a keyboard becomes difficult when the volume is large, because the requirements of accuracy are very high when writing instructions to a machine. A well designed programming language helps by providing syntax checking and other consistency checks, and so do syntax driven editors. But there is always room for such clerical mistakes as choosing the wrong variable or writing $<$ instead of $>$. Such errors are sometimes more difficult to locate than "interesting" logical ones.

Software engineering is a practical discipline concerned with matters of economy: software must adapt to the available hardware with efficient usage of storage space and computing time, it must exploit equipment operating concurrently, compensate for the unreliability of transmission lines, and so forth. These aspects contribute very much to the complexity of programs.

One tries to combat some of these difficulties by defining standards of program documentation, by focusing on program structure, and by identifying modularization techniques. Thus, "structured programming" and "object orientation" are some of the catch words of software engineering. "High level" and "abstract" programming are terms which point to the importance of using program modules to establish levels of abstraction, by implementing problem oriented concepts using machine oriented mechanisms.

Efficiency considerations may call for the use of a procedural, also called *imperative*, programming language. Then it is essential to decompose the total state space into manageable pieces, corresponding to program modules of reasonable size, such as procedures, data types, object classes, and other kinds of "packages". Thus, one important aspect of object orientation is to limit the data access to the components of one object at a time.

For the design of a module to be successful the external module specification must be *simpler* than the sum of the implementation details. The simplification may be obtained by hiding details, but more often by a complete reinterpretation of the module as a more "abstract" entity. To use a familiar example, bit strings together with certain operations on them are seen as integers with associated arithmetic operations. The important point in this connection is that integers have very simple properties, expressed as algebraic laws which are independent of representational details. This same principle must be applied much of the time, more or less explicitly and formally, in order to achieve simplification. It is therefore necessary that software designers have tools for the definition of abstract concepts. Such tools must be helpful to users who are not highly trained mathematicians.

This book attempts to contribute to the art of programming in two main ways:

1. By focusing on program *verifiability* and techniques of program verification through reasoning about the program text. Verifiability in this sense is a good measure of many aspects of program quality.

2. By identifying a style of "abstract" formal concept definition, useful for the specification of and reasoning about programs, and which lends itself to mechanized reasoning.

Program verification consists of showing, by reasoning about the program text, that the program fulfils its purpose, as stated in an "external specification". Thus, a verifiable program is necessarily documented by stating its purpose, otherwise verification would be meaningless. In order for a life-sized program to be verifiable in a practical way, it must be structured in terms of manageable and carefully specified modules. In order to facilitate verification, certain reasoning hints are in general necessary for each piece of program, such as loop invariants and other key comments. When included in the program text such additional information provides essential "internal documentation" which, together with module specifications, can make the program easier to understand as well. The documentation may be in the form of explanations in prose or it may be expressed more formally.

By looking at techniques of formal program verification the reader can get a feel for the "amount" of reasoning required. Even if actual formal verification is not intended, however, it is believed that the idea of constructing programs that are easy to verify may lead to a change of programming attitudes, and a resulting improvement in program quality.

As already mentioned, large volumes of reasoning represent a serious obstacle to achieving programs that are internally consistent in all details and correct with respect to their external specifications. It would seem that the only really effective way to attack the problem of volume is to enable the computer to do most of the work involved in the verification. For that purpose we have to provide *formalized* specifications, and techniques for the writing of formal specifications therefore become important.

Our starting point is predicate calculus and standard axiomatic techniques. But we identify a sublanguage of so-called "generator inductive" definition of data types and associated functions. This style of definition can be seen as an applicative programming language, and as such is a better tool for trained programmers than are non-constructive techniques. The definitions are suitable for automatic term rewriting, which is a useful technique for formula simplification as well as for semi-mechanized proof construction.

In chapter 2 notations and standard laws of propositional calculus (i.e. Boolean algebra) and predicate calculus are surveyed. Most of the chapter is devoted to proof techniques that are useful for manual as well as mechanized proof construction.

Chapter 4 provides a comprehensive account of so-called Hoare logic, which is a formal system of logic for procedural programs. Chapter 3 is a short, informal introduction to this kind of reasoning. Central concepts are preconditions and postconditions of programs or pieces of program, and invariants. It is argued that the identification of such state assertions should go hand in hand with the development of the program. In this way the program verification may be prepared for in advance, and there will be a better chance of producing a correct program. An external specification of a piece of program is either a pair of pre- and postconditions or a so-called "effect function" which specifies the final state (the outputs) in terms of the initial state (the inputs).

In chapter 5 the main topic is "abstract" data types. The principle of *generator induction* is used for the definition of data types and associated functions, as well as for proof purposes. Several aspects of specification languages are discussed, including the concept of parameterized type modules. A number of standard concepts are defined, useful for reasoning about programs, including a small tool kit of operators on *sequences* (such as arrays, files, and sequences in time). Finally, the notion of type *simulation* is introduced. An abstract type, designed for easy reasoning, may be replaced in a program by another type designed for execution efficiency, provided proofs are given that the latter type formally simulates the former. Alternatively, the former type may be seen as an *abstract specification* of the latter.

In the final chapter we return to the paradigm of procedural programs and develop a concept of *object classes* as a procedural analogy of the applicative notion of data types. Thus, whereas a typed "value", such as the integer 3, is an immutable piece of data, a class object is a data structure, potentially of large volume, which is modifiable incrementally by procedural operators. A class may, however, be specified abstractly by a data type which represents the set of possible states of objects of the class. Consequently, each object may be regarded as a program variable of that type. For reasons of efficiency class objects are accessed and manipulated through *pointers*. A programming style is identified, which may be enforced by (mainly) textual checks, such that object pointers are transparent logically. Finally, a rather more complicated program logic is sketched in case these rules have to be violated for reasons of efficiency.

The book is primarily intended for programmers who feel the need for new perspectives on their work. No knowledge of mathematics is required, beyond familiarity with elementary aspects of functions, sets, and relations. Some familiarity with logical (Boolean) operators is advantageous. Some of the topics discussed, however, may be of a more specialist nature. Among the more advanced are the topic of well-definedness of expressions, which is discussed in several subsections, the treatment of "many-to-one generator bases", as well as more language oriented topics such as function overloading. A non-specialist reader may choose to skip such discussions, at least during a first reading.

Chapter 2

First Order Predicate Logic

In documenting programs and expressing specifications we need a language for stating conditions on inputs and expressing properties of results as well as describing intermediate states of computation. First order predicate calculus is a standard tool of expression that is useful for these purposes. It is a simple yet powerful formal language with a precise semantics. Furthermore, reasoning about formulas in predicate calculus can to a certain extent be mechanized. This is important when dealing with specifications and programs of more than toy size.

2.1   The Formula Language

Our version of the first order predicate language is a strongly typed functional language with a specific list of types, typed variables, and typed functions for each application. A type may be taken to represent a *set of values*. We indicate that a variable x is of type T by writing $x:T$. Thereby the variable is restricted to range over values of the type T. A function f is characterized syntactically by its *profile* or *signature*, which is specified by writing

$$f :\ T_1 \times T_2 \times \cdots \times T_n \longrightarrow T$$

where $n \geq 0$ is the number of arguments of f, its "arity", $T_1, T_2, \ldots, T_n$ are the argument types, and T is the type of the function value, called the *range* or *codomain* of f. A function of arity zero is called a *constant*. The list of argument types of a non-constant function is called its *domain*. A non-constant function can only be applied in a meaningful way to argument values of the types indicated in its domain. In the sequel we use the term "profile" for any single syntactic characterization of a function, such as the one given above; it is useful to reserve the term "signature" to mean a *set of profiles*.

7

Any well-formed expression has an associated type. An expression is well-formed and of type T if it is either

- a variable of type T, or
- a function application $f(e_1, e_2, \ldots, e_n)$ ($n \geq 0$, parentheses omitted if $n=0$), where each argument e_i is a well-formed expression of type T_i, $i = 1, 2, \ldots, n$, and f has the profile $T_1 \times T_2 \times \cdots \times T_n \longrightarrow T$.

Thus, the type of a functional expression is equal to the codomain of the main operator. It is required that argument types match the domain of the applied function. We extend the set of well-formed expressions by allowing other traditional notations, such as infix notation, writing e.g. $a + b > c$ rather than $> (+(a,b), c)$. We also allow such expressions as $a = b < c$, meaning $(a = b)$ and $(b < c)$, and similar usage of other binary infix relational operators.

Although the type checking inherent in the concept of well-formed expressions is a purely syntactic device, it has a very important semantic consequence: any expression of type T can only have a *value of type* T, whatever (legal) values are assigned to the variables occurring in e (given that the functions occurring in e are properly defined semantically). This implies that expressions which are not well-formed are semantically meaningless, and by excluding them from the language, using a mechanical type checking device, a large class of user mistakes are prevented.

For the remainder of this book there is a permanent assumption that any expression considered shall be well-formed.

We assume that the type *Bool* (shorthand for Boolean) is defined, which stands for the set of truth values, as well as the following standard functions, called logical constants and operators. The sign ˆ is used to indicate operand positions for prefix, infix, and other "mixfix" notations.

$$
\begin{array}{lll}
\mathbf{t} & : \longrightarrow Bool & \text{(the truth value "true")} \\
\mathbf{f} & : \longrightarrow Bool & \text{(the truth value "false")} \\
\neg\hat{\ } & : Bool \longrightarrow Bool & \text{(negation)} \\
\hat{\ } \wedge \hat{\ } & : Bool \times Bool \longrightarrow Bool & \text{(conjunction, logical and)} \\
\hat{\ } \vee \hat{\ } & : Bool \times Bool \longrightarrow Bool & \text{(disjunction, logical or)} \\
\hat{\ } \Rightarrow \hat{\ } & : Bool \times Bool \longrightarrow Bool & \text{(implication)}
\end{array}
$$

The operators are listed in the conventional order of precedence. Thus, for instance $\neg x \vee y \wedge z$ means $(\neg x) \vee (x \wedge y)$. We assume that the reader is acquainted with these operators from their use in programming languages. However, for the sake of completeness we list their truth value tables, and useful algebraic properties are shown in the following subsections.

$\neg$	t	f
	f	t

$\wedge$	t	f
t	t	f
f	f	f

$\vee$	t	f
t	t	t
f	t	f

$\Rightarrow$	t	f
t	t	f
f	t	t

Notice that the expression $A \Rightarrow B$ means exactly the same as $\neg A \vee B$, which is true if A is false or if B is true. Some readers may feel that it would be wrong to regard "A implies B" as a true statement if A is false. But it is a useful convention. This is illustrated by the expression $x < 5 \Rightarrow x < 6$, which ought to be true for any integer x. (Try the values 4, 5, and 6 !)

The following operators are included for every type T (including *Bool*).

$$\hat{\ } = \hat{\ } : \qquad T \times T \longrightarrow Bool \qquad \text{(equality)}$$
$$\hat{\ } \neq \hat{\ } : \qquad T \times T \longrightarrow Bool \qquad \text{(inequality)}$$
$$\textbf{if } \hat{\ } \textbf{ then } \hat{\ } \textbf{ else } \hat{\ } \textbf{ fi} : Bool \times T \times T \longrightarrow T \quad \text{(alternative selection)}$$

The equality and inequality operators bind more strongly than those above. Notice that they apply to operands of all types, including Booleans. It is useful, however, to include an alternative equality operator $\Leftrightarrow$ for Booleans, which means the same as $=$, but binds less strongly than all the operators mentioned above. The **if**-operator is fully parenthesized, with **if** and **fi** as opening and closing brackets, respectively; therefore it needs no specification of binding precedence. Also the **if**-operator may be applied to Boolean operands. The following equalities hold, for $x, y, z : Bool$, using $\Leftrightarrow$ as the main operator in order to save parentheses.

$$x = y \Leftrightarrow (x \Rightarrow y) \wedge (y \Rightarrow x)$$
$$\textbf{if } x \textbf{ then } y \textbf{ else } z \textbf{ fi} \Leftrightarrow x \wedge y \vee \neg x \wedge z \Leftrightarrow (x \Rightarrow y) \wedge (\neg x \Rightarrow z)$$

2.1.1 Propositional calculus

The propositional calculus deals with expressions of type *Bool*, traditionally called *formulas*. The formulas of propositional calculus consist exclusively of Boolean operators, constants, and variables. It follows from the definition tables that the the following standard transformation laws hold for the operators $\neg$, $\wedge$, and $\vee$ (for variables $x, y, z : Bool$):

$\neg\neg x \Leftrightarrow x$		(double negation)
$x \wedge y \Leftrightarrow y \wedge x,$	$x \vee y \Leftrightarrow y \vee x$	(commutativity)
$x \wedge (y \wedge z) \Leftrightarrow (x \wedge y) \wedge z,$	$x \vee (y \vee z) \Leftrightarrow (x \vee y) \vee z$	(associativity)
$x \wedge x \Leftrightarrow x,$	$x \vee x \Leftrightarrow x$	(idempotence)
$x \wedge (x \vee y) \Leftrightarrow x,$	$x \vee x \wedge y \Leftrightarrow x$	(absorption)
$x \wedge (y \vee z) \Leftrightarrow x \wedge y \vee x \wedge z,$	$x \vee y \wedge z \Leftrightarrow (x \vee y) \wedge (x \vee z)$	(distributivity)
$\neg(x \wedge y) \Leftrightarrow \neg x \vee \neg y,$	$\neg(x \vee y) \Leftrightarrow \neg x \wedge \neg y$	(de Morgan's laws)

For the implication operator the following transformation laws are useful. Those of the last two lines are perhaps less obvious intuitively than many of the other rules.

$$x \Rightarrow y \Leftrightarrow \neg x \vee y \Leftrightarrow \neg y \Rightarrow \neg x, \quad \neg(x \Rightarrow y) \Leftrightarrow x \wedge \neg y$$
$$x \Rightarrow y \wedge z \Leftrightarrow (x \Rightarrow y) \wedge (x \Rightarrow z), \quad x \Rightarrow y \vee z \Leftrightarrow (x \Rightarrow y) \vee (x \Rightarrow z)$$
$$x \wedge y \Rightarrow z \Leftrightarrow (x \Rightarrow z) \vee (y \Rightarrow z), \quad x \vee y \Rightarrow z \Leftrightarrow (x \Rightarrow z) \wedge (y \Rightarrow z)$$
$$x \Rightarrow (y \Rightarrow z) \Leftrightarrow x \wedge y \Rightarrow z \Leftrightarrow y \Rightarrow (x \Rightarrow z)$$

In addition, the following transformation rules are useful for formula simplification:

$$x \wedge \mathbf{t} \Leftrightarrow x, \quad x \wedge \mathbf{f} \Leftrightarrow \mathbf{f}, \quad x \vee \mathbf{t} \Leftrightarrow \mathbf{t}, \quad x \vee \mathbf{f} \Leftrightarrow x$$
$$\mathbf{t} \Rightarrow x \Leftrightarrow x, \quad \mathbf{f} \Rightarrow x \Leftrightarrow \mathbf{t}, \quad x \Rightarrow \mathbf{t} \Leftrightarrow \mathbf{t}, \quad x \Rightarrow \mathbf{f} \Leftrightarrow \neg x$$

The validity of all these rules may be verified easily by trying out all combinations of values, $\mathbf{t}$ and $\mathbf{f}$, for the variables which occur, and using the definition tables above to check that the equalities hold in all cases. This is a general proof technique, called *proof by truth table*. Any formula of propositional calculus whose value is $\mathbf{t}$ in all cases is called a *tautology* (of propositional calculus).

Most tautologies are valid in a very strong sense to be explained later, even if the variables stand for general Boolean expressions which may not always be *well-defined*, i.e. having a defined value. In particular, this is true for all the transformation rules listed above. Some tautologies, however, such as $x \vee \neg x$ depend explicitly on the fact that there are only two truth values. This formula cannot be regarded as true if we have to reckon with a third possibility that x is neither true nor false, but *ill-defined*, i.e. *has no value*. The equations above involving the **if**-operator are further examples of tautologies of the propositional calculus which cannot be generalized to the case of ill-defined component formulas.

2.1.2   First order predicate calculus

Predicate calculus deals with formulas which may contain variables and subexpressions of types other than *Bool*. Functions with codomain *Bool* and arguments of other types are traditionally called *relations* or *predicates*. Hence the term "predicate calculus". The formula language of predicate calculus contains two important logical operators in addition to those mentioned above: the universal and existential quantifiers, $\forall x$ and $\exists x$, where x stands for any variable.

Let P be a formula and T a type. Then

$$\forall x : T \bullet P \qquad \text{(read: for all (T-values) } x, \ P)$$

expresses the idea that P holds for *all* values of x ranging over the type T. Also, the idea that P holds for *some* value of x in T is expressed by:

$$\exists x : T \bullet P \qquad \text{(read: there exists (a T-value) } x \text{ such that } P)$$

Our syntax for quantifiers, $\forall x : T \bullet$ and $\exists x : T \bullet$, is somewhat more complicated than the traditional mathematical notation, owing to the fact that our formula language is fully typed. In a context where typing is not an important issue, however, we sometimes cheat by omitting the type part "$:T$" of quantifiers. Syntactically a quantifier is a unary (prefix) operator which binds less strongly than all other logical operators, except $\Leftrightarrow$. The operand of a quantifier is called its *scope*. This expression is also the scope of the variable introduced in the quantifier.

EXAMPLE 2.1

$\forall x : T \bullet P \Rightarrow P' \Leftrightarrow Q \wedge \exists y : U \bullet R \Rightarrow R'$ is to be understood as $(\forall x : T \bullet P \Rightarrow P') \Leftrightarrow (Q \wedge \exists y : U \bullet (R \Rightarrow R'))$. Thus, the scope of the universal quantifier is $P \Rightarrow P'$ and that of the existential one is $R \Rightarrow R'$.

$\sqcap$

As an aid to intuition it may be useful to regard a universally quantified formula, $\forall x \bullet P$, as a kind of *generalized conjunction*, $(P_1 \wedge P_2 \wedge \cdots)$, with one term for every possible value of the quantified variable (often an infinite number). In the same way an existentially quantified formula may be seen as a generalized *disjunction*, $(P_1 \vee P_2 \vee \cdots)$.

Consider the formula $\forall x \bullet x > 0 \Rightarrow y \leq x$, where x and y are integer variables. It asserts something about y, but nothing about x. In fact the formula is equivalent to $y \leq 1$. We express the different roles of x and y by saying that x is a *bound* variable (bound by the quantifier), whereas y is said to be *free*. The name of a bound variable is irrelevant, as long as it does not conflict with the free variables in its scope. Thus, using the name z in place of x makes no difference:

$$\forall x \bullet x > 0 \Rightarrow y \leq x \quad \Leftrightarrow \quad \forall z \bullet z > 0 \Rightarrow y \leq z$$

The free occurrences of a variable x in a formula P are exactly those which are outside the scope of any x-quantifier inside P. These occurrences are bound by the quantifier Qx in the formula Q$x \bullet P$ where Q stands for $\forall$ or $\exists$. Or, looked at differently: these occurrences of the free variable x are reinterpreted as occurrences of a bound variable x introduced by the quantifier Qx for its scope. A formula without free variables is said to be *closed*.

The term *first order* predicate calculus alludes to the fact that the quantifiers introduced above only apply to variables ranging over "first order values", such as truth values and integers, and not to "second order" entities such as functions and types. Higher order calculi exist, but they are outside the scope of this book. The first order calculus is sufficiently expressive for our purposes.

Quantified formulas are subject to the following transformation rules. Many of them are analogues of rules listed in the last subsection, and all of them are valid in the same strong sense. The letters P and Q stand for arbitrary formulas, and R stands for a formula without free occurrences of the variable x:

$$\forall x \bullet R \Leftrightarrow R,$$
$$\forall x \bullet \forall y \bullet P \Leftrightarrow \forall y \bullet \forall x \bullet P,$$
$$\forall x \bullet (P \wedge Q) \Leftrightarrow (\forall x \bullet P) \wedge \forall x \bullet Q,$$
$$\forall x \bullet (P \vee R) \Leftrightarrow (\forall x \bullet P) \vee R,$$
$$\forall x \bullet (P \Rightarrow R) \Leftrightarrow (\exists x \bullet P) \Rightarrow R,$$
$$\forall x \bullet (R \Rightarrow P) \Leftrightarrow R \Rightarrow \forall x \bullet P$$
$$P \vee \forall x \bullet P \Leftrightarrow P,$$
$$\neg \forall x \bullet P \Leftrightarrow \exists x \bullet \neg P,$$

$$\exists x \bullet R \Leftrightarrow R$$
$$\exists x \bullet \exists y \bullet P \Leftrightarrow \exists y \bullet \exists x \bullet P$$
$$\exists x \bullet (P \vee Q) \Leftrightarrow (\exists x \bullet P) \vee \exists x \bullet Q$$
$$\exists x \bullet (P \wedge R) \Leftrightarrow (\exists x \bullet P) \wedge R$$
$$\exists x \bullet (P \Rightarrow Q) \Leftrightarrow (\forall x \bullet P) \Rightarrow \exists x \bullet Q$$
$$P \wedge \exists x \bullet P \Leftrightarrow P$$
$$\neg \exists x \bullet P \Leftrightarrow \forall x \bullet \neg P$$

Notice that a universal quantifier distributes over $\wedge$, but not in general over $\vee$ and $\Rightarrow$, and *vice versa* for existential quantifiers. A succession of universal quantifiers such as $\forall x : T \bullet \forall y : T \bullet \forall z : U \bullet$ is abbreviated as follows: $\forall x, y : T, \; z : U \bullet$, and similarly for existential ones.

2.1.3   Syntactic operators

We introduce a syntactic function $\mathcal{V}$: expression $\longrightarrow$ variable set,   whose value is the set of variables occurring free in a given expression. This function may be defined in a step by step manner by the following defining equations (the symbol $\triangleq$ stands for "is defined equal to"):

$$\mathcal{V}[c] \triangleq \emptyset$$
$$\mathcal{V}[x] \triangleq \{x\}$$
$$\mathcal{V}[f(e_1, e_2, \ldots, e_n)] \triangleq \mathcal{V}[e_1] \cup \mathcal{V}[e_2] \cup \cdots \cup \mathcal{V}[e_n], \;\; n > 0$$
$$\mathcal{V}[\forall x \bullet P] \triangleq \mathcal{V}[\exists x \bullet P] \triangleq \mathcal{V}[P] - \{x\}$$

Here c stands for a constant, x for a variable, P for a formula, f for a function (including logical operator, except quantifier), and $e_1, e_2, \ldots, e_n$ stand for expressions. The notation $f(e_1, e_2, \ldots, e_n)$ stands for an application of the given function or operator, regardless of the syntactic form of the application, infix or otherwise.

Remark

> Step by step definitions like the above are said to be *inductive*. The function $\mathcal{V}$ is said to be defined *by induction on syntactic structure*, which means that it is defined directly for atomic items (variables and constants), whereas for compound ones the definition is in terms of the same function applied to component items. Notice that the concept of well-formed expressions was defined using a similar technique.

We also need a syntactic operator for substituting expressions for free variables in formulas and other expressions. The notation

$$P_e^x \qquad \text{(read: } P \text{ with } e \text{ for } x\text{)}$$

where P and e are expressions and x a variable (e and x being of the same type) is used to represent the result of replacing each free occurrence of x in P (if any) by e. If there are conflicts between free variables in e and bound variables in P, the latter must be systematically renamed in the substitution process. Parentheses enclosing e are understood to be added if necessary. P^x_e is said to be an *instance* of P obtained by *instantiating* the (free) variable x to e.

EXAMPLE 2.2

The following formula is a theorem in the theory of natural numbers (non-negative integers).

$$\forall y \bullet (\forall x \bullet y \le x) \Rightarrow y = 0$$

Since the theorem is of the form $\forall y \bullet P$, P^y_e should hold for arbitrary type correct, expression e. Let e be the expression x, which by definition contains a single free occurrence of the variable x. Then naïve substitution would give the result

$$(\forall x \bullet x \le x) \Rightarrow x = 0, \text{ equivalent to } x = 0$$

which is not a universally true formula. A correct result is obtained by renaming the bound variable x:

$$(\forall x' \bullet x \le x') \Rightarrow x = 0$$

□

EXAMPLE 2.3

Let T be a type with the finite value set $\{a_1, a_2, \ldots, a_n\}$. Then we may use the substitution operator to formalize the connection between quantification over T and the corresponding propositional operators:

$$\forall x : T \bullet P \quad \text{is the same as} \quad P^x_{a_1} \wedge P^x_{a_2} \wedge \cdots \wedge P^x_{a_n} \quad (\text{or } \bigwedge_{i=1}^{n} P^x_{a_i}), \text{ and}$$

$$\exists x : T \bullet P \quad \text{is the same as} \quad P^x_{a_1} \vee P^x_{a_2} \vee \cdots \vee P^x_{a_n} \quad (\text{or } \bigvee_{i=1}^{n} P^x_{a_i})$$

□

The notation $P^{x_1, x_2, \ldots, x_n}_{e_1, e_2, \ldots, e_n}$ is used to denote the result of the simultaneous substitution of e_i for the free occurrences of x_i, $i = 1, 2, \ldots, n$. It is meaningful only if $x_1, x_2, \ldots, x_n$ are distinct variables.

The substitution operator satisfies the following lemmas, in which x and y denote lists of distinct variables, e and d denote corresponding lists of expressions, and $\equiv$ stands for syntactic equality. If l is a list, the notation $\{l\}$ stands for the set of elements occurring in l. The lemmas express important properties of the substitution operator used in the sequel. Notice the side conditions; they indicate that some of the properties are less obvious than one might perhaps think:

$$
\begin{aligned}
\mathcal{V}[E_e^x] &= (\mathcal{V}[E] - \{x\}) \cup \mathcal{V}[e] & &\text{for } \{x\} \subseteq \mathcal{V}[E] & &(2.1)\\
E_x^x &\equiv E & & & &(2.2)\\
E_e^x &\equiv E & &\text{for } \{x\} \cap \mathcal{V}[E] = \emptyset & &(2.3)\\
(E_d^x)_e^y &\equiv E_{d_e^y,e}^{x,\,y} & &\text{for } \{x\} \cap \{y\} = \emptyset & &(2.4)\\
(E_d^x)_e^y &\equiv E_{d_e^y}^x & &\text{for } \{y\} \subseteq \{x\} & &(2.5)\\
(E_y^x)_x^y &\equiv E & &\text{for } \{y\} \cap (\mathcal{V}[E] - \{x\}) = \emptyset & &(2.6)
\end{aligned}
$$

The first lemma follows from the fact that all free variable occurrences in e remain free in E_e^x, and that all free occurrences of x-variables in E are removed. The fourth lemma expresses that the occurrences of y-variables in E_d^x consist of those in E itself and those in the copies of d's which replace occurrences of x's in E, provided that the lists x and y are disjoint. The last lemma expresses the fact that opposite substitutions cancel out if and only if the second substitution only changes variable occurrences that were changed by the first one.

A notation of the form M_e^x is said to be a *meta-expression*. Its "value" is an expression in the formula language which is the result of applying a certain textual operation to the expression denoted by M. The letter M here stands for another meta-expression, possibly a *meta-variable* ranging over formula language expressions. Notice that M_e^x indicates a substitution in the expression represented by M, not a substitution in M itself. So, for instance, in $(E_y^x)_x^y$ the outer substitution does not act on the superscript of the inner one.

EXAMPLE 2.4
$$
((i+j+k)_{h,i}^{i,j})_{i,j}^{h,i} = (h+i+k)_{i,j}^{h,i} = (i+j+k), \text{ whereas}
$$
$$
((i+j+k)_{k,i}^{i,j})_{i,j}^{k,i} = (k+i+k)_{i,j}^{k,i} = (i+j+i)
$$

$\square$

2.2   Formal Reasoning

A *proof* is a sequence of reasoning steps designed in order to convince the reader about the truth of some formula, called a *theorem*. In order to be convincing the proof must lead from *axioms* which are obviously true (or at least agreed upon to be true) to the theorem, by reasoning steps which make sense individually. Mathematicians have studied elementary steps for reasoning within given formal languages, and they have arrived at a notion of *formal proof*. This notion is interesting to us for two reasons:

- As a very solid basis of what constitutes a correct proof. To be sure, formal proofs are much too detailed and tedious to be generally useful. Still, a convincing human-to-human proof might take the form of an argument that a formal proof *exists*, provided that the reasoning is in terms of a formal language, or even that a formal proof *would* exist if the notions discussed were formalized to a sufficient degree.

- Formal proofs written out in full are mechanically checkable, and, as we shall see, in many cases and to some extent they may also be constructed mechanically. In other words, reasoning about formalized concepts can be partly automated. Now, programming languages certainly are formal, and given tools for formalized system specification and program documentation, a kind of interactive, computer aided program verification would be feasible, as would computer aided reasoning about the specifications themselves. The role of the computer would be to guarantee extreme reliability of reasoning, and at the same time alleviate the tedium associated with formal proofs.

Much of the challenge in program development and verification consists of the formulation of such concepts as data types and functions suitable for expressing problem and system specifications, as well as other kinds of program documentation. The actual proofs required for the verification of well structured and well documented programs tend to be simple and uninteresting mathematically, whereas the volume of reasoning can be enormous. These facts indicate that the work involved is better suited for computers than for humans, to the extent that it can be mechanized.

In this section we take a look at formal reasoning in terms of first order predicate logic. We use a style of reasoning inspired by so-called "natural deduction", as defined by Prawitz [28]. It is expressed, however, in terms of a suitable version of "sequent calculus" developed by Gentzen [11]. We also present another, more mechanistic proof style and recommend a mixture of the two for manual proof construction, as in the following worked example.

Our starting point is the following piece of annotated program, which could be the body of a loop for zero-ing an array A, indexed from 1 to N ($N > 0$) using the program variable k as a counter. We assume that the variable i below belongs to the type of "positive integers":

$$\{\forall i \bullet i < k \Rightarrow A[i] = 0\}$$
$$A[k] := 0$$
$$\{\forall i \bullet i \leq k \Rightarrow A[i] = 0\}$$

The annotation consists of a *precondition* and a *postcondition*, both enclosed in braces, which characterize the state at two points in the loop. We would like to prove that the latter holds after the assignment statement provided that the former holds prior to it. The following proof, however trivial, illustrates the kind of reasoning typically involved in program verification. It is also simple enough that we can follow the reasoning in very small steps. Clearly, what must be proved is that the precondition plus what is achieved by the assignment statement imply the postcondition.

Prove $(\forall i \bullet i < k \Rightarrow A[i] = 0) \wedge A[k] = 0 \Rightarrow \forall i \bullet i \leq k \Rightarrow A[i] = 0$

The validity of this formula is quite obvious, at least to a trained eye. After all, the first conjunct of the antecedent expresses that $A[i] = 0$ for all indices i less than k, and according to the second conjunct $A[k]$, too, is equal to zero. So, obviously, $A[1] = A[2] = \cdots = A[k] = 0$, which is what the consequent asserts. However, by developing a proof slowly and systematically we demonstrate a technique of proof construction and reasoning which has very wide applicability. The proof will consist of reasoning steps which are elementary in the sense that each step is exclusively concerned with a single operator occurrence.

Notice that the program variable k should be interpreted as an ordinary free variable in the present context, representing an unspecified integer in the range 1 to N, and the array A may be regarded as a function from index values to element values.

Proofs are usually presented by forward reasoning, starting with appropriate axioms and ending with the theorem. This does not tell the reader much about how the proof was *constructed*. The structure of a proof is, however, to a certain extent determined by that of the formula to be proved, and for that reason it may be a good strategy to work *backwards* through the proof, starting with the theorem. Each step in the backward construction will be to replace one proof obligation by one or more simpler obligations.

In particular, the last elementary reasoning step in the proof can be associated with the main operator of the formula, in our case an implication sign. In the style of natural deduction we may prove an implication by *assuming* that the antecedent is true and then prove the consequent. Thus, the first step in our proof construction is to replace the given sentence by the following one:

Assuming $(\forall i \bullet i < k \Rightarrow A[i] = 0) \wedge A[k] = 0$
prove $\forall i \bullet i \leq k \Rightarrow A[i] = 0$

Notice that we take this whole sentence as our new proof obligation (not only the last formula). We may now turn our attention to the assumption, which is a conjunction. It is sometimes more practical to have two separate assumptions:

Assuming $\forall i \bullet i < k \Rightarrow A[i] = 0$ **and** $A[k] = 0$
prove $\forall i \bullet i \leq k \Rightarrow A[i] = 0$

Returning to the the formula to be **proved**, the main operator is a universal quantifier. A general strategy for proving a universally quantified formula is to take away the quantifier and try to prove the formula with a free variable instead (possibly retaining the old variable name). If the proof succeeds we have managed to show that the formula holds for an *arbitrary* (type correct) value of that variable, which is good enough. It must be required, however, that no assumption restricts the value of the variable, otherwise it is not arbitrary. In our case we choose to introduce a new variable j in order to avoid confusion with the bound variable i occurring in the first assumption. (It should be interpreted as representing an integer in the range 1 to N.)

Assuming $\forall i \bullet i < k \Rightarrow A[i]=0$ **and** $A[k]=0$
prove $j \leq k \Rightarrow A[j]=0$

Again the theorem is an implication, so we introduce another assumption.

Assuming $\forall i \bullet i < k \Rightarrow A[i]-0$ **and** $A[k]=0$ **and** $j \leq k$
prove $A[j]=0$

The next step could be to make use of an axiom stating that $\leq$ means $<$ or $=$. Substituting equals for equals we get:

Assuming $\forall i \bullet i < k \Rightarrow A[i]=0$ **and** $A[k]=0$ **and** $j < k \vee j = k$
prove $A[j]=0$

Rather than having an assumption in the form of a disjunction, say $P \vee Q$, we may consider the case that P is true and the case that Q is true and prove our theorem in both cases. (If they are both true either proof will do.) We may retain the other assumptions (or those which are actually needed):

Assuming $\forall i \bullet i < k \Rightarrow A[i]=0$ **and** $A[k]=0$ **and** $j < k$
prove $A[j]=0$

Assuming $\forall i \bullet i < k \Rightarrow A[i]=0$ **and** $A[k]=0$ **and** $j = k$
prove $A[j]=0$

It would be possible to continue the process of backward proof construction until all our proof obligations are of the form

Assuming ... **and** P **and** ... **prove** P

which can be taken as carried out by definition. Thus, at that point a proof of the original formula has been completed, consisting of all the sentences constructed. However, a more natural proof may result by directly carrying out the last two proof obligations, reasoning *forwards* from the assumptions that we have introduced.

Thus, in the first proof the theorem follows in two elementary steps. In the first step we note that $j < k \Rightarrow A[j]=0$ must be a valid consequence of the first assumption, since the implication is assumed to hold for any value of the bound variable i. The theorem then follows from this and the third assumption, by a rule of reasoning often called "*modus ponens*", identified a couple of millennia ago by Aristotle: if P and Q are assertions about something, no matter what, and you know that P implies Q, and that P holds, then you are entitled to conclude that Q holds as well. In our case P is $j < k$, and Q is $A[j] = 0$.

In the second proof the theorem follows from the second and third assumptions by substituting equals for equals in the former.

2.2.1   Sequent calculus

We introduce a shorthand notation for sentences such as those given above:

$$P_1, P_2, \ldots, P_n \vdash Q$$

called a *sequent*, or sometimes a *subsidiary deduction*. To the left of the turnstile ($\vdash$) is the *assumption part* of the sequent, in which a set (possibly empty) of assumptions are listed in arbitrary order, and to the right is the *theorem part*. In our version of the sequent concept the latter is a single formula. A sequent is not an expression in the formula language, but a meta-expression which makes a statement *about* the constituent formulas. The interpretation is that the truth of the theorem part, Q, *follows from* the truth of all assumptions, $P_1, P_2, \ldots, P_n$. In particular, a sequent without assumptions $\vdash P$ asserts that the formula P is provable.

Our notion of formal proof is a set of proof lines, each of which is a sequent. The proof may be seen as a tree with certain trivial sequents as leaves and the main theorem sequent as the root. (The latter often has an empty assumption part.) The tree structure is such that each internal node is a consequence of its immediate descendant nodes according to given *rules of inference*. Notice that sequents are usually interpreted as statements of fact, but in the process of *constructing* a proof tree, starting with the theorem, it is useful to read them as commands, as we did above.

We now introduce a notation for describing inference rules (also called *proof rules* or *deduction rules*):

$$\frac{S_1; \; S_2; \; \ldots; \; S_n}{S}$$

which is interpreted as follows: given sequents of the forms $S_1, S_2, \ldots, S_n$ ($n \geq 0$), the *premises*, we may infer a sequent of the form S, the *conclusion*. The "sequent forms", usually called sequent *schemas*, are expressed using meta-variables and other meta-expressions denoting formulas. For instance, the proof rule *modus ponens* may be described as follows using meta-variables P and Q (disregarding assumption parts):

$$\frac{\vdash P \Rightarrow Q; \; \vdash P}{\vdash Q}$$

In the following the letters P, Q, R, x, t, Γ, possibly decorated, are meta-variables. P, Q, R denote formulas, x denotes a variable in the formula language, t an expression of the same type as that of x, and Γ denotes a list, possibly empty, of mutually distinct formulas.

We first consider proof rules which deal with the sequent concept as such, independently of the formula language details. Collectively they define a version of *sequent calculus*, SC.

$$\text{RFL}: \quad P \vdash P \qquad\qquad \text{TRN}: \quad \frac{\Gamma_1 \vdash P;\ \Gamma_2, P \vdash Q}{\Gamma_1 \cup \Gamma_2 \vdash Q}$$

$$\text{AI}: \quad \frac{\Gamma_1 \vdash P}{\Gamma_1 \cup \Gamma_2 \vdash P} \qquad\qquad \text{VI}: \quad \frac{\Gamma \vdash P}{\Gamma_t^x \vdash P_t^x}$$

Figure 2.1: Rules for sequent calculus, SC.

The notion of logical consequence expressed by a sequent is a relation between (lists of) formulas which is clearly reflexive as well as transitive. The purpose of the rules RFL and TRN is to express these facts. RFL may be seen as an inference rule with zero premises; it therefore expresses that any sequent of the form $P \vdash P$ holds and may occur as a leaf node of a proof tree. TRN expresses a generalized concept of transitivity, which reduces to the standard one if Γ_1 is a singleton list and Γ_2 is empty. Thus, given the sequents $R \vdash P$ and $P \vdash Q$, we may conclude $R \vdash Q$. (In the case where both assumption lists are empty TRN may be understood as a *"modus ponens"* on the meta-level, the sequent of the second premise playing the role of an implication.) The notation $\Gamma_1 \cup \Gamma_2$ stands for a list of all formulas occurring in Γ_1 or in Γ_2, duplicates deleted. Thus, additional assumptions in either premise must be propagated to the conclusion.

The rule AI permits the introduction of additional assumptions, or the deletion of redundant ones during backward proof construction. In this way it is expressed that redundant assumptions do not harm a logical consequence. Redundancy in sequents is sometimes needed in order to make proofs hang together.

The role of free variables in a sequent is expressed by the rule VI for variable instantiation. The logical consequence expressed by a sequent $\Gamma \vdash P$ is supposed to hold for *arbitrary* (type correct) values of any free variable x. Therefore validity must be preserved by the instantiation of x to any expression t of the same type as x. Notice that all free occurrences of x in the entire sequent must be similarly instantiated; this indicates that they all are supposed to stand for the same quantity. This means that we are entitled to regard those assumptions which have free occurrences of x as restrictions enforced on a free x in the theorem part.

It should be noted that our use of the symbol $\vdash$ is slightly different from the traditional use in predicate calculus, as for instance in [29]. In this tradition the assumptions are interpreted as closed formulas implicitly quantified universally. That is not the case in a sequent.

EXAMPLE 2.5

We may obtain an instance of VI as follows. Instantiate Γ to the single formula $v \neq 0$ and P to $v/v = 1$. Now instantiate x to v and t to $a+b$. Then Γ_t^x becomes $(v \neq 0)_{a+b}^v$, which is the formula $a+b \neq 0$, and in a similar way P_t^x becomes $(a+b)/(a+b) = 1$. Thus, VI shows that the sequent $a+b \neq 0 \vdash (a+b)/(a+b) = 1$ may be inferred from $v \neq 0 \vdash v/v = 1$ by instantiating v to $a+b$.

Notice that we have used the term "instantiate" for the meta-variables Γ, P, x, t, as well as the variable v of the formula language. The substitution notation, on the other hand, is *only* used to express instantiation of formula language variables.
□

All four SC rules must hold in any formal logic based on (our version of) sequent calculus. In addition, one needs rules explaining how to reason about the logical operators of a given formula language. Notice that assumptions represented by Γ's in the premises of TRN and AI play no other role in an inference step than being propagated to the conclusion. In the sequel inference rules are abbreviated, as in the traditional style of "natural deduction" rules, by not mentioning such assumptions. As a compensation we need the following general convention of inference rule application:

- If the actual premises of an inference step have assumptions not mentioned in the (abbreviated) rule, the consequence must *inherit all of them*.

The following are abbreviated versions of the rules TRN, AI, and VI, respectively:

$$\text{TRN}' : \quad \frac{\vdash P; \ P \vdash Q}{\vdash Q} \qquad \text{AI}' : \quad \frac{\vdash P}{\Gamma \vdash P} \qquad \text{VI}' : \quad \frac{\Gamma_x \vdash P}{(\Gamma_x)_t^x \vdash P_t^x}$$

where Γ_x in rule VI' stands for the list of all those assumptions which contain free occurrences of x (any others will be inherited unchanged and need not be mentioned).

2.2.2   Natural deduction

In figure 2.2 we list a complete set of proof rules for predicate calculus with the following logical operators: $\neg, \wedge, \vee, \Rightarrow, \forall, \exists$, as well as the logical constant $\mathbf{f}$ (taking $\mathbf{t}$ as an abbreviation for $\neg \mathbf{f}$). The system resembles one given by Prawitz [28] for "natural deduction", ND. It consists of rules for the introduction (I) and elimination (E) of logical operators in the theorem parts of sequents.

The asterisk ($*$) marking the rules $\forall$I and $\exists$E indicates that there is a restriction on free occurrences of x in the actual sequents. Thus, any free x in P, in the premise of $\forall$I, should represent an arbitrary type correct value; *therefore there must be no assumption for the premise containing free x* (cf. the informal proof above). The restriction on the use of $\exists$E concerns the second premise and is explained below.

$$\wedge\text{I}: \quad \frac{\vdash P;\ \vdash Q}{\vdash P\wedge Q} \qquad\qquad \wedge\text{E}: \quad \frac{\vdash P\wedge Q}{\vdash P} \text{ or } \frac{\vdash P\wedge Q}{\vdash Q}$$

$$\vee\text{I}: \quad \frac{\vdash P}{\vdash P\vee Q} \text{ or } \frac{\vdash Q}{\vdash P\vee Q} \qquad \vee\text{E}: \quad \frac{\vdash P\vee Q;\ P\vdash R;\ Q\vdash R}{\vdash R}$$

$$\Rightarrow\text{I}: \quad \frac{P\vdash Q}{\vdash P\Rightarrow Q} \qquad\qquad \Rightarrow\text{E}: \quad \frac{\vdash P\Rightarrow Q;\ \vdash P}{\vdash Q}$$

$$\forall\text{I}: \quad \frac{\vdash P}{\vdash \forall x\bullet P} \quad (*) \qquad\qquad \forall\text{E}: \quad \frac{\vdash \forall x\bullet P}{\vdash P_t^x}$$

$$\exists\text{I}: \quad \frac{\vdash P_t^x}{\vdash \exists x\bullet P} \qquad\qquad \exists\text{E}: \quad \frac{\vdash \exists x\bullet P;\ P\vdash Q}{\vdash Q} \quad (*)$$

$$\mathbf{f}\text{I}: \quad \frac{\vdash P;\ \vdash \neg P}{\vdash \mathbf{f}} \qquad\qquad \mathbf{f}\text{E}: \quad \frac{P\vdash \mathbf{f}}{\vdash \neg P}$$

$$\neg\text{E}: \quad \frac{\vdash \neg\neg P}{\vdash P}$$

Figure 2.2: Rules for natural deduction, ND

The rules denote elementary steps of reasoning which, although very small, seem to correspond fairly well to what we do when reasoning informally. Some of the rules have in fact been used in the above proof development: $\Rightarrow$I and $\forall$I, used for backward proof construction, and $\forall$E and $\Rightarrow$E, used for forward reasoning. Notice that $\Rightarrow$E is identical to *modus ponens*. $\vee$E describes a kind of "proof by cases", i.e. case P or case Q, one or both of which must hold. $\mathbf{f}$E describes another useful proof strategy: proof by contradiction, and $\mathbf{f}$I shows how to arrive at a contradiction. Clearly, $\mathbf{f}$I will only be used to derive a conclusion with a non-empty list of assumptions.

$\exists$E can perhaps best be understood as a generalization of $\vee$E, since an existentially quantified formula is a kind of generalized disjunction, and the variable x of the assumption P in the second premise is free, denoting an arbitrary type-correct value. Thus, given that x ranges over a finite value set $\{a_1,\ldots,a_n\}$, the $\exists$E rule could be written as follows, where the list (possibly empty) of additional assumptions for the second premise has been made explicit:

$$\frac{\vdash P_{a_1}^x \vee \cdots \vee P_{a_n}^x;\ \Gamma, P_{a_1}^x \vdash Q;\ \ldots;\ \Gamma, P_{a_n}^x \vdash Q}{\Gamma \vdash Q}$$

Notice that the last n premises all follow from $\Gamma, P \vdash Q$ by the SC rule $\vee$I, *provided that x does not occur free in Q nor in any of the additional assumptions Γ*

for that sequent. (Assumptions with free x for the first premise would be harmless, however.) This is the restriction on the use of ∃E which is indicated by the asterisk.

In addition to the ND rules proper the four SC rules are included by definition. It turns out that TRN, AI, and VI, though useful, are superfluous in the context of ND (cf. exercise 2.7); RFL, however, is essential for providing trivially valid start nodes. Sequents which may be derived from trivial ones using the proof rules of ND, are said to be *derivable* in ND. We mainly use ND to derive ultimately a sequent with an empty assumption part. A formula P is a *theorem* by ND if and only if the sequent ⊢ P is derivable in ND.

A formula is said to be *valid* if it is true for arbitrary values of its free variables, if any, and for arbitrary interpretation of function symbols. ND has the following very important properties:

- It is *sound*, i.e. only valid formulas in the predicate calculus are theorems by ND.
- It is *complete*, i.e all valid formulas in the predicate calculus are theorems by ND.

Theorems of the predicate calculus as such, i.e. those provable without additional rules or axioms, are called *tautologies of predicate calculus*. If we leave out the four rules dealing with quantifiers, the remaining system is complete for the propositional calculus.

Notice that validity is a *semantic* concept; it relates to the meaning of formulas. On the other hand, formal derivation of theorems is like a game with strings of symbols, which have no other meaning than what is prescribed in the mechanistic rules of the game. It is a strange and wonderful fact that a formal system like ND can be sound and complete for the whole of predicate calculus. It shows that logical reasoning in a fairly general sense can be mimicked mechanistically and to some extent automated. It is outside the scope of this book to prove soundness and completeness of formal proof systems. The interested reader is referred to standard textbooks of mathematical logic such as [29] or [16].

EXAMPLE 2.6
The proof tree of figure 2.3 is a formalization of a fragment of the informal proof at the beginning of section 2.2.
□

The ND system has the desirable property that many proofs can be given a very perspicuous structure. Starting with well chosen trivial sequents, elimination rules are used to break down the theorem parts into smaller constituents, as in example 2.6. These constituents are in turn combined to form the final theorem, or necessary intermediate ones, using introduction rules. At the same time the assumptions inherited from the trivial start sequents are thrown off, so that no sequent has any redundant assumptions.

$$\forall i \bullet i < k \Rightarrow A[i] = 0 \vdash \forall i \bullet i < k \Rightarrow A[i] = 0$$

$$\Big| \, \forall \mathrm{E}$$

$$\forall i \bullet i < k \Rightarrow A[i] = 0 \vdash j < k \Rightarrow A[j] = 0 \qquad j < k \vdash j < k$$

$$\Big| \Rightarrow \mathrm{E}$$

$$\forall i \bullet i < k \Rightarrow A[i] = 0, \ j < k \vdash A[j] = 0$$

Figure 2.3

EXAMPLE 2.7

The proof of the tautology $(A \vee B \Rightarrow C) \Rightarrow (A \Rightarrow C)$ of propositional calculus comes out nicely in ND:

$$A \vdash A$$

$$\Big| \, \vee \mathrm{I}$$

$$A \vee B \Rightarrow C \vdash A \vee B \Rightarrow C \qquad A \vdash A \vee B$$

$$\Big| \Rightarrow \mathrm{E}$$

$$A \vee B \Rightarrow C, \ A \vdash C$$

$$\Big| \Rightarrow \mathrm{I}$$

$$A \vee B \Rightarrow C \vdash A \Rightarrow C$$

$$\Big| \Rightarrow \mathrm{I}$$

$$\vdash (A \vee B \Rightarrow C) \Rightarrow (A \Rightarrow C)$$

Figure 2.4

□

It may be noted that the interpretation of the tree in figure 2.4 depends on the interpretation of A, B, and C. If they are Boolean variables, the tree is a formal proof of a formula. We might also take them to be meta-variables which stand for arbitrary formulas; in that case the tree is a *proof schema*. Any proof schema can be instantiated to a proof by substituting actual formulas for the occurring meta-variables.

There are two main difficulties in the construction of proofs in ND: one has to hit on the right trivial sequents to start off the proof, and some theorems need proof by contradiction in ways that are not at all obvious. For instance, the proof of the simple tautology $A \vee \neg A$ is a puzzle which requires three applications of the contradiction principle, and the result, shown in figure 2.5, does not look very "natural" either. (Notice that the tree really contains two identical leaf nodes.

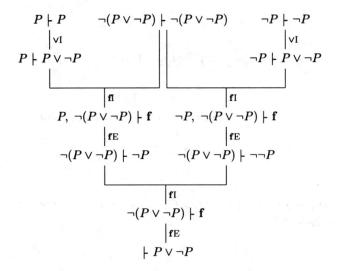

Figure 2.5: Proof of $P \lor \neg P$.

One does not, however, bother to write down the sequent more than once. The same would apply to identical subtrees of more than one node.)

2.2.3   Proof construction

As we have seen already it may be easier to work backwards than forwards when constructing proofs, starting with the theorem we want to prove. It turns out, however, that only a few of the ND rules are useful for backward proof construction. For instance, the rule ∨E for proof by cases does not specify how to get the formulas P and Q for given R, nor do ⇒E or fI give us any clue as to what the formula P might be. And if the desired theorem is a disjunction, both alternative ∨I rules require one of the disjuncts to be provable by itself, which is not very likely in general.

Ideally any rule for backward construction should satisfy the following criteria (in addition to being sound):

1. It should show explicitly how the premises must look for any given conclusion sequent of the right form.

2. The premises should hold whenever the conclusion holds; otherwise they might not be provable, even if the conclusion is.

3. Each premise should have a shorter proof than the conclusion (provided some suitable choice strategy is followed during backward construction), otherwise the construction process might not terminate for provable sequents.

The set of rules, shown in figure 2.6, corresponds to the ND set, but is designed for backward proof construction, BPC. All rules satisfy requirement 2, and most of them satisfy 1 and 3 also. (A∀, and T∃ do not, whereas T¬ and, A¬ satisfy all requirements except number 1.) A typical rule represents the "introduction" (by forward reasoning!) of the main operator, of either the theorem part (T) or a chosen assumption (A).

$$\text{T}\wedge:\ \dfrac{\vdash P;\ \vdash Q}{\vdash P\wedge Q} \qquad\qquad \text{A}\wedge:\ \dfrac{P,Q \vdash R}{P\wedge Q \vdash R}$$

$$\text{T}\vee:\ \dfrac{\overline{P} \vdash Q}{\vdash P\vee Q}\ \text{ or }\ \dfrac{\overline{Q} \vdash P}{\vdash P\vee Q} \qquad \text{A}\vee:\ \dfrac{P \vdash R;\ Q \vdash R}{P\vee Q \vdash R}$$

$$\text{T}\!\Rightarrow:\ \dfrac{P \vdash Q}{\vdash P\Rightarrow Q} \qquad\qquad \text{A}\!\Rightarrow:\ \dfrac{\overline{P} \vdash R;\ Q \vdash R}{P\Rightarrow Q \vdash R}$$

$$\text{T}\neg:\ \dfrac{P \vdash \overline{Q}}{Q \vdash \neg P} \qquad\qquad \text{A}\neg:\ \dfrac{\overline{Q} \vdash P}{\neg P \vdash Q}$$

$$\text{T}\forall:\ \dfrac{\vdash P^x_{x'}}{\vdash \forall x\bullet P}\ \ x'\text{ fresh} \qquad \text{A}\forall:\ \dfrac{P^x_t,\ \forall x\bullet P \vdash Q}{\forall x\bullet P \vdash Q}$$

$$\text{T}\exists:\ \dfrac{\vdash P^x_t \vee \exists x\bullet P}{\vdash \exists x\bullet P} \qquad\qquad \text{A}\exists:\ \dfrac{P^x_{x'} \vdash Q}{\exists x\bullet P \vdash Q}\ \ x'\text{ fresh}$$

Figure 2.6: Rules for backward proof construction, BPC.

The rules T∧, T⇒, and T∀ are (nearly) identical to the corresponding I-rules of ND, and A∃ corresponds to ∃E. Notice that the restrictions which have to be enforced on forward application of ∀I and ∃E can be circumvented by variable renaming (if necessary) when constructing proofs backwards. The side condition requires that the chosen variable does not occur free anywhere in the actual conclusion sequent. The rules T⇒, T∀, A∧, and A∨ were all used for backward construction in the informal example at the beginning of the present section.

For backward proof construction it is practical to handle negation through a meta-operator. Thus, the notation $\overline{P}$ stands for adding or removing an outermost negation operator, in such a way that double negation is avoided. Furthermore, it is to be understood that the rules T¬ and A¬ have $\dfrac{P \vdash \mathbf{f}}{\vdash \neg P}$ and $\dfrac{\vdash P}{\neg P \vdash \mathbf{f}}$ as respective special cases. Thus, an assumption $\overline{\mathbf{f}}$ (i.e. **t**) is to be regarded as empty. Thereby the sequent $\vdash \mathbf{t}$ holds trivially. BPC does not, like ND, require unnatural use of proof by contradiction. For instance, $P\vee\neg P$ follows by a single application of T∨.

Application of any BPC rule, except T∃ and A∀ (we return to them), is entirely mechanical, provided that all additional assumptions in an actual sequent, i.e. those not mentioned in the conclusion of the relevant rule, are propagated to *every premise*. However, in general this results in the construction of sequents containing redundant assumptions, so that the resulting proofs are likely to be unnecessarily complex. Furthermore the SC rule AI will be needed for completeness. Another possibility which is sometimes more convenient (especially with automated proof systems, see section 2.2.4 below) is to redefine the notion of trivial sequents to be all sequents of the form $\Gamma \vdash P$, where the assumption list Γ either contains P, or contains Q and $\neg Q$ for some formula Q.

EXAMPLE 2.8
We illustrate this proof technique by showing a proof of the tautology of example 2.7 constructed using BPC rules backwards. (Another three proof steps, using A¬ and AI, are needed if all leaf nodes must be of the form $P \vdash P$.)
□

$$\neg C,\ A,\ \neg A \vdash B$$
$$\Big|_{\text{T}\vee}$$
$$\neg C,\ A \vdash A \vee B$$
$$\Big|_{\text{A}\neg}$$
$$\neg(A \vee B),\ A \vdash C \qquad C,\ A \vdash C$$
$$\Big|_{\text{A}\Rightarrow}$$
$$A \vee B \Rightarrow C,\ A \vdash C$$
$$\Big|_{\text{T}\Rightarrow}$$
$$A \vee B \Rightarrow C \vdash A \Rightarrow C$$
$$\Big|_{\text{T}\Rightarrow}$$
$$\vdash (A \vee B \Rightarrow C) \Rightarrow (A \Rightarrow C)$$

Figure 2.7

Notice that, although each backward rule application is fully deterministic, there is room for choice in selecting the object formula in each step from among the assumptions and the theorem part of the current sequent. Unwise choice may lead to proofs which are more complicated than necessary; for instance, working on semantically redundant assumptions leads to entirely useless proof steps.

When constructing proof trees manually, applying BPC rules backwards, it is sufficient to include only non-redundant assumptions in premises. Even so, simpler and more natural proofs can often be obtained by mixing backward use of BPC with forward reasoning in ND, from assumptions accumulated during backward construction (formally from trivial sequents based on such assumptions). *This is therefore our recommended mode of work for doing manual proofs.* For instance, the proof of example 2.7 may be obtained by backward construction in two steps followed by forward reasoning. See also figure 2.10 below.

The rules A∀ and T∃ are not constructive as they stand, nor is the premise "simpler" than the conclusion. The way to instantiate a universally quantified assumption depends in a non-trivial way on the conclusion sequent. It may even happen that several different instances of the same assumption are needed in a proof; therefore, in rule A∀ the quantified assumption has to be propagated to the premise sequent in addition to the instance. Sooner or later, however, the quantified assumption becomes redundant in a successful proof; it is known that a finite number of well chosen instances are sufficient if the given sequent is provable at all. In a similar way it may happen that several alternative instances of an existentially quantified theorem must be given in a proof. Therefore, in rule T∃ the second disjunct of the premise is needed in general, but will eventually become redundant in a successful proof. The following example makes this point. (See also exercise 2.6(2) p. 35, where two instances of a universally quantified axiom are needed.)

EXAMPLE 2.9

Let R be a binary relation over some type T, $R : T \times T \longrightarrow Bool$.   Not having any semantic information about R we may still prove that the formula $\exists z : T \bullet R(x,z) \Rightarrow R(z,y)$ holds for arbitrary $x, y : T$. The proof follows by instantiating z to x and y obtaining $R(x,x) \Rightarrow R(x,y)$ and $R(x,y) \Rightarrow R(y,y)$, respectively. Now, if $R(x,y)$ is true the former implication holds, and if it is false then the second one holds. Thus, one of the two must hold, although we do not know which one. Backward construction of the proof of figure 2.8 is now simple. Redundant assumptions have not been propagated.

□

In order to "get rid of" the main operator, i.e. the outermost quantifier, of a universally quantified assumption or an existentially quantified theorem part through a single backward rule application, in analogy with the other BPC rules, one would have to introduce all necessary instances at once. Thus the following rules are possible alternatives to T∃ and A∀. They satisfy requirement 2 (p. 24), provided that the instance set is chosen judiciously for each given conclusion sequent:

$$\text{T}\exists' : \quad \frac{\vdash P^x_{t_1} \vee ... \vee P^x_{t_n}}{\vdash \exists x \bullet P} \ (n > 0) \qquad \text{A}\forall' : \quad \frac{P^x_{t_1}, ..., P^x_{t_n} \vdash Q}{\forall x \bullet P \vdash Q} \ (n > 0)$$

Notice that a given sequent, together with its proof tree, may occur as a subtree at several places in a proof. That explains why the ND rule ∀E is sufficient for obtaining more than one instantiation of a universally quantified theorem part by forward reasoning. It is less obvious that ∃I is sufficient for forward reasoning even if alternative instances are required, but it does follow using the ∨E rule, cf. exercise 2.8 p. 36.

$$R(x,y),\ \neg R(x,y) \vdash R(y,y)$$
$$\Big|\, \text{T}\Rightarrow$$
$$\neg R(x,y) \vdash R(x,y) \Rightarrow R(y,y)$$
$$\Big|\, \text{A}\neg$$
$$\neg((R(x,y) \Rightarrow R(y,y))) \vdash R(x,y)$$
$$\Big|\, \text{AI, T}\Rightarrow$$
$$\neg((R(x,y) \Rightarrow R(y,y))) \vdash R(x,x) \Rightarrow R(x,y)$$
$$\Big|\, \text{T}\vee$$
$$\vdash (R(x,x) \Rightarrow R(x,y)) \vee (R(x,y) \Rightarrow R(y,y))$$
$$\Big|\, \text{AI, T}\vee$$
$$\vdash (R(x,x) \Rightarrow R(x,y)) \vee (R(x,y) \Rightarrow R(y,y)) \vee \exists z : T \bullet R(x,z) \Rightarrow R(z,y)$$
$$\Big|\, \text{T}\exists$$
$$\vdash (R(x,x) \Rightarrow R(x,y)) \vee \exists z : T \bullet R(x,z) \Rightarrow R(z,y)$$
$$\Big|\, \text{T}\exists$$
$$\vdash \exists z : T \bullet R(x,z) \Rightarrow R(z,y)$$

Figure 2.8

2.2.4 Automated proof construction

It turns out that the mathematical insight needed in order to select useful instantiations can be mechanized. In fact the only potentially useful variable instances are terms of the right type built up of those free variables and functions, including constants, which occur in the given sequent. (If only bound variables and no constants occur for some type, an artificial constant of that type may have to be introduced.) Although there may be infinitely many such terms in general, it is possible to search in such a way that those actually needed in the proof will necessarily be found sooner or later. There are ways of speeding up the search, see e.g. [4], but we shall not pursue that topic any further here. Referring to our informal example it was fairly easy to see that a useful instance of the assumption $\forall i \bullet i < k \Rightarrow A[i] = 0$ could be obtained by instantiating i to the free variable j. Notice also that the two instantiations needed in example 2.9 are the only possible ones unless new free variables or functions are introduced.

Given a systematic way of selecting potentially useful instantiations mechanically, proofs of all provable sequents of predicate calculus may be constructed automatically using BPC backwards. The choice between the different proof steps possible at any one time is largely arbitrary, but certain scheduling rules must be added in order to secure termination of the construction process. This is due to the fact that four of the BPC rules do not satisfy requirement 3 above: T$\neg$, A$\neg$, T$\exists$ and A$\forall$. Specifically, application of the former two must be suitably restricted in order to prevent cycling, for instance applying T¬ only with the "empty" assumption **t**, and A¬ only for atomic Q and non-atomic P. The latter two may lead to infinite fruitless instantiation, unless they have lowest priority and are applied in "fair" order. Proper scheduling will guarantee successful termination for any provable start sequent. For an invalid sequent the construction either terminates with an incomplete proof tree, i.e. one with illegal leaf nodes, or, if repeated instantiations occur, it may go on for ever. In the former case the formula has been disproved; in the latter there is no general way to get an answer about the truth of the given formula.

It is difficult to determine mechanically whether given proof steps contribute to a proof or not (except after a proof has actually been found). Therefore proofs constructed mechanically often contain large numbers of useless proof steps. This is a major difficulty in the design of efficient proof generators.

2.2.5 Predicate logic with equality

We extend the BPC system to cater for *predicate logic with equality* by adding the following rules for the equality operator.

$$\text{TEQ}: \quad \frac{\vdash P^\alpha_{t'}; \ \vdash t=t'}{\vdash P^\alpha_t} \qquad\qquad \text{AEQ}: \quad \frac{P^\alpha_{t'} \vdash Q; \ \vdash t=t'}{P^\alpha_t \vdash Q}$$

$$\text{B}=: \quad \frac{P \vdash Q; \ Q \vdash P}{\vdash P=Q} \qquad\qquad \text{EAX}: \quad \vdash \forall x \bullet x=x$$

TEQ and AEQ express substitution of equals for equals, and B= essentially serves to identify Booleans with truth values. EAX is an axiom expressing the reflexive property of equality. Notice that the equality operator of B= is restricted to Boolean operands, whereas those of the other rules may have operands of any type.

Application of TEQ or AEQ for backward proof construction means to replace one or more occurrences (not necessarily all) of a term t in the conclusion by t', where t and t' are the left and right hand sides of a given equation. The variable α occurring in these rules can be thought of as a mechanism for pointing out those occurrences of t which are to be replaced.

There are two alternative ways of treating axioms formally:

1. either as extensions to the formal system, i.e. as inference rules without premises,
2. or as explicit assumptions for each theorem (after universal quantification of free variables, otherwise they become restrictions on these variables!).

For manual proof construction we recommend the former, which implies that axioms are allowed to occur as leaf nodes in proof trees, and that ND rules are used to draw conclusions from them. For that reason we identify axioms (as well as theorems) in this book by prefixing them by $\vdash$. We have felt no need to identify explicitly the formal system underlying each instance of (semi-)formal reasoning. The set of available axioms should in each case be sufficiently clear by context, as well as additional inference rules, such as rules of induction for given data types.

EXAMPLE 2.10
The detailed formal proofs shown in figure 2.9 demonstrate that equality, as interpreted in our extended (combined) system, is symmetric and transitive. Since it is also reflexive, it is an equivalence relation. Clearly, any formula of the form $x = y \Rightarrow f(\ldots, x, \ldots) = f(\ldots, y, \ldots)$ is also easy to prove, which shows that equality is a so-called *congruence relation*. (For each non-trivial proof line the premises and the proof rule used to obtain it are identified. Thereby the structure of the proof tree is exhibited.)

□

$$
\begin{array}{lll}
1. & \vdash \forall x \bullet x = x & \text{(axiom)} \\
2. & \vdash y = y & (1, \forall \text{E}) \\
3. & x = y \vdash x = y & \text{(trivial)} \\
4. & x = y \vdash y = x & (2,3, \text{TEQ with } y = \alpha \text{ as } P) \\
5. & \vdash x = y \Rightarrow y = x & (4, \text{T}\Rightarrow) \\
\end{array}
$$

$$
\begin{array}{lll}
1. & y = z \vdash y = z & \text{(trivial)} \\
2. & x = y \vdash x = y & \text{(trivial)} \\
3. & x = y, \; y = z \vdash x = z & (1,2, \text{TEQ with } \alpha = z \text{ as } P) \\
4. & x = y \wedge y = z \vdash x = z & (3, \text{A}\wedge) \\
5. & \vdash x = y \wedge y = z \Rightarrow x = z & (4, \text{T}\Rightarrow) \\
\end{array}
$$

Figure 2.9

Figure 2.10, shows the complete formal proof of the example given on pp. 16–17 (written in the usual forward direction). It is clear that the proof, once written down, can be checked mechanically; and in this case a proof could have been generated automatically without exploring many blind alleys. However, the example also shows that detailed formal proofs are not in general practical for humans.

2.2.6 Equational logic

In *equational logic* all axioms are quantifier-free equations, and all reasoning is based on variable instantiation and the substitution of equals for equals. (A formula P which is not an equation can be turned into one by writing $P = \mathbf{t}$.) *Term rewriting* is a restricted form of equational logic where the axioms are only used as left-to-right rewrite rules. Thus, a system for term rewriting only contains TEQ and a

1. $\forall i \bullet i < k \Rightarrow A[i] = 0 \vdash \forall i \bullet i < k \Rightarrow A[i] = 0$ (trivial)
2. $j < k \vdash j < k$ (trivial)
3. $\forall i \bullet i < k \Rightarrow A[i] = 0 \vdash j < k \Rightarrow A[j] = 0$ (1, $\forall$E)
4. $\forall i \bullet i < k \Rightarrow A[i] = 0, \; j < k \vdash A[j] = 0$ (3,2, $\Rightarrow$E)
5. $A[k] = 0 \vdash A[k] = 0$ (trivial)
6. $j = k \vdash j = k$ (trivial)
7. $A[k] = 0, \; j = k \vdash A[j] = 0$ (5,6, TEQ)
8. $\forall i \bullet i < k \Rightarrow A[i] = 0, \; A[k] = 0, \; j < k \lor j = k \vdash A[j] = 0$ (4,7, A$\lor$)
9. $\vdash \forall m \bullet \forall n \bullet (m \leq n) = (m < n \lor m = n)$ (axiom)
10. $\vdash \forall n \bullet (j \leq n) = (j < n \lor j = n)$ (9, $\forall$E)
11. $\vdash (j \leq k) = (j < k \lor j = k)$ (10,$\forall$E)
12. $\forall i \bullet i < k \Rightarrow A[i] = 0, \; A[k] = 0, \; j \leq k \vdash A[j] = 0$ (8,11, AEQ)
13. $\forall i \bullet i < k \Rightarrow A[i] = 0, \; A[k] = 0 \vdash j \leq k \Rightarrow A[j] = 0$ (12, T$\Rightarrow$)
14. $\forall i \bullet i < k \Rightarrow A[i] = 0, \; A[k] = 0 \vdash \forall i \bullet i \leq k \Rightarrow A[i] = 0$ (13, T$\forall$)
15. $(\forall i \bullet i < k \Rightarrow A[i] = 0) \land A[k] = 0 \vdash \forall i \bullet i \leq k \Rightarrow A[i] = 0$ (14, A$\land$)
16. $\vdash (\forall i \bullet i < k \Rightarrow A[i] = 0) \land A[k] = 0 \Rightarrow \forall i \bullet i \leq k \Rightarrow A[i] = 0$ (15, T$\Rightarrow$)

Figure 2.10: Proof of informal example.

rule for instantiating free variables (combining $\forall$I and $\forall$E). Starting with a given formula each rewriting step consists in applying the instantiation rule forwards in order to obtain a useful instance of some axiom, and then performing a substitution in the formula using TEQ backwards. The proof of a formula succeeds when it has been transformed to $\mathbf{t}$.

If the axiom set satisfies certain "convergence" conditions which guarantee termination with a unique result, the whole rewriting process can be automated in a dependable way. Termination can be guaranteed if the right hand side of each axiom is in some suitable sense "simpler" than the left hand side. For instance, the rewrite rule $x + 0 = x$ satisfies this, but not the rule $x + y = y + x$. Clearly the latter can be applied infinitely often to any expression containing a plus operator.

EXAMPLE 2.11
In figure 2.11 we show a proof of the formula $m < m{+}1$ by term rewriting. The following equational axioms (rewrite rules) are assumed to be available: $\vdash \mathbf{t} \lor x \Leftrightarrow \mathbf{t}$, $\vdash x = x \Leftrightarrow \mathbf{t}$, and $\vdash x < y{+}1 \Leftrightarrow x = y \lor x < y$. The axiom instantiations are indicated using the substitution notation.
□

Notice that the technique of term rewriting can be applied to expressions of arbitrary type for the purpose of simplification or "symbolic evaluation". An important advantage in using term rewriting for automated proof construction, compared to the more general technique sketched earlier, is the high efficiency which can be obtained. We shall return to the use of term rewriting in chapter 5.

$$\vdash \mathbf{t}$$
$$\left|\ \vdash (\mathbf{t} \lor x \Leftrightarrow \mathbf{t})^x_{m < m}\right.$$
$$\vdash \mathbf{t} \lor m < m$$
$$\left|\ \vdash (x = x \Leftrightarrow \mathbf{t})^x_m\right.$$
$$\vdash m = m \lor m < m$$
$$\left|\ \vdash (x < y + 1 \Leftrightarrow x = y \lor x < y)^{x,\ y}_{m,\ m}\right.$$
$$\vdash m < m + 1$$

Figure 2.11: Proof by term rewriting.

2.2.7   Shortcuts

As already mentioned, formal proofs are too detailed to be practical for human use, and therefore a better proof style is to demonstrate that a formal proof exists. One simple way to do so is to omit details in a formal proof by making use of proven theorems ("lemmas") as if they were axioms. Obviously, if a proof tree has a lemma in a terminal node, a complete formal proof may be obtained by tacking on the proof tree for the lemma at that node.

Proven lemmas play a role in theorem proving comparable to that of verified program modules for program development. In order to implement computer assisted reasoning about specifications and programs as a practical mode of development work, one will need a well stocked library of lemmas in addition to reusable specification and program modules.

Another useful shorthand results from the introduction of *derived inference rules*. In order to formally derive an inference rule R of the form $\frac{S_1;\ S_2;\ ...;\ S_n}{S}$ a derivation tree (schema) must be constructed with the sequent schema S as its root and $S_1, S_2, \ldots, S_n$ as leaf nodes, possibly with trivial sequents and axioms, if any, in addition. Now any proof tree containing an inference step of type R is understood to be an abbreviation of the proof tree obtained by inserting the relevant instance of the R derivation tree connecting the premises of the R step with the conclusion.

EXAMPLE 2.12

Figure 2.12 shows a derivation of the rule $\dfrac{\vdash \neg(P \land Q)}{\vdash \neg P \lor \neg Q}$.

□

Both techniques mentioned above can be seen as ways of extending the very concept of formal proof. In practice, when writing down proofs meant for human readers one will leave out many of the "obvious" proof steps, without explicitly introducing compound rules and lemmas. After all, the goal in this case is to show that a proof exists, not to bore the reader with trivial detail.

$$
\begin{array}{lll}
1. & \vdash \neg(P \wedge Q) & \text{(premise)} \\
2. & P \vdash P & \text{(trivial)} \\
3. & Q \vdash Q & \text{(trivial)} \\
4. & P, Q \vdash P \wedge Q & (2,3, \wedge\text{I}) \\
5. & P, Q \vdash \mathbf{f} & (1,4, \mathbf{f}\text{I}) \\
6. & P \vdash \neg Q & (5, \mathbf{f}\text{E}) \\
7. & \vdash \neg P \vee \neg Q & (6, \text{T}\vee)
\end{array}
$$

Figure 2.12: Derivation of an inference rule.

2.2.8   Limitations

In spite of the fact that natural deduction is complete for the first order predicate calculus, there is an important theorem by Gödel which reveals incompleteness in the following sense: there exist mathematical structures of such complexity that no internally consistent axiom set for the occurring functions is strong enough to prove all true statements about these functions. Thus no consistent formal system can be complete *for such structures.* Gödel also showed that the structure of natural numbers with equality, addition, and multiplication is already too complex for a complete system to exist. Fortunately incompleteness in this sense has no practical consequences for the kind of reasoning relevant for program development.

In order to reason about functions defined recursively it is in general necessary to enrich the formal proof system by *induction rules.* Then automated techniques are no longer sufficient to generate proofs of all provable formulas, even in principle. Some mathematical intuition may then be needed in order to formulate provable auxiliary lemmas.

It must be noted that traditional formal logic is designed for reasoning with *total* functions and predicates, i.e. functions which have defined values for all type correct argument values. However, typical computer programs, which we intend to reason about in the following chapters, abound with partially defined ones. It is possible to design formal systems which cater explicitly for expressions which are not always well-defined, such as x/y or $A[i]$ for integers x, y, i and array A; but we may use the formal system as it is if we supplement proofs with some additional reasoning about well-definedness.

Let a well-defined formula C be a sufficient condition for a formula P to be well-defined, then we shall regard $C \wedge P$, as well as $C \Rightarrow P$, as well-defined formulas by taking the former as $\mathbf{f}$ and the latter as $\mathbf{t}$ if C has the value $\mathbf{f}$, although the subformula P may not in that case be well-defined. By extending the truth tables of the logical operators as follows, all transformation rules listed in section 2.1.1 are valid in the strong sense that the left and right hand sides are either well-defined and equal or both are ill-defined. The symbol $\perp$ stands for an ill-defined formula:

¬	t	f	⊥
	f	t	⊥

∧	t	f	⊥
t	t	f	⊥
f	f	f	f
⊥	⊥	f	⊥

∨	t	f	⊥
t	t	t	t
f	t	f	⊥
⊥	t	⊥	⊥

⇒	t	f	⊥
t	t	f	⊥
f	t	t	t
⊥	⊥	t	⊥

Quantifiers should be interpreted as generalized conjunctions or disjunctions with respect to well-definedness. Thus, $\forall x \bullet P$ is true if P is well-defined and true for all x, false if there is an x such that P is well-defined and false, and ill-defined otherwise. $\exists x \bullet P$ is true if there is an x such that P is well-defined and true, false if P is well-defined and false for all x, and ill-defined otherwise. With these interpretations the transformation rules of section 2.1.2 are strongly valid too.

Furthermore, the well-definedness of sequents is determined by interpreting commas separating assumptions as $\wedge$, and $\vdash$ as $\Rightarrow$. If we then insist that all axioms, $\vdash A$, and all trivial sequents, $P \vdash P$, of a proof are well-defined, and require that any variable instantiation preserves well-definedness of the sequent, then our formal first order logic (with equality) is complete and sound in the context of partial functions, in the sense that *a formula is provable if and only if it is well-defined and true for arbitrary values of free variables.*

With this approach nothing can be proved formally about a partial function for arguments outside its domain of definition. Notice that the rule RFL of sequent calculus must weakened by the side condition that its formula P be well-defined (for arbitrary values of free variables).

EXAMPLE 2.13

Taking $(x/y)*y = x$ and $z*0 = 0$ as axioms would lead to the invalid result $1 = 0$ unless precautions are taken. It would follow by instantiating x to 1, y to 0, and z to $1/0$. By guarding the first axiom with the condition $y \neq 0$ the inconsistency disappears. In this case it is sufficient also to prevent the instantiation of z to the ill-defined term $1/0$.

□

Proofs of strong equality may proceed in two phases: proof of equality assuming well-definedness of the left and right hand sides, and proof of equality of definedness conditions. We return to the topic of well-definedness several times in the following chapters. See in particular sections 4.3.2 and 5.2.1. Notice that the rules AEQ and TEQ preserve well-definedness, even if the substitution terms t and t' are not well-defined, provided that the equality $t = t'$ holds strongly. Cf. section 5.3.1.

Remark

The above is only one of many ways of dealing with ill-defined formulas, but probably the one closest to everyday intuition. In particular, the interpretation of the Boolean operators is such that tautologies are satisfied strongly, except those that depend on the assumption that there is no third Boolean value, such as $P \vee \neg P$ and $P \Rightarrow P$, which only hold strongly for well-defined P. Our interpretation of sequents implies that all ND rules are sound in the above strong sense, except $\forall$E where well-definedness of the conclusion must be required. This leads to what is sometimes called "WS-logic", where any assumption must be interpreted as **t** in those cases where it is not well-defined, i.e. "weakly", whereas an ill-defined theorem part must be interpreted as **f**, or "strongly". The drawback is the fact that the sequent $P \vdash P$ will be interpreted as $\mathbf{t} \vdash \mathbf{f}$ whenever P is ill-defined, which is inconsistent. The advantage is that nothing can be proved from ill-defined assumptions. A more thorough discussion of these points occurs at the end of section 4.3.2. See in particular exercise 4.5. See also [26].

Exercises

2.1   Prove the transformation rules of section 2.1.1.

2.2   Prove the tautologies
1. $x \wedge y \vee \neg x \wedge z \Rightarrow y \vee z$
2. $x \wedge y \vee \neg x \wedge z \Leftrightarrow (x \Rightarrow y) \wedge (\neg x \Rightarrow z)$

2.3   Prove the transformation rules of section 2.1.2 for well-defined P, Q, R.

2.4   Prove the following implications for well-defined P, Q (no equalities!):
1. $(\forall x \bullet P) \Rightarrow \exists x \bullet P$
2. $(\forall x \bullet P) \vee (\forall x \bullet Q) \Rightarrow \forall x \bullet P \vee Q$
3. $(\exists x \bullet P \wedge Q) \Rightarrow (\exists x \bullet P) \wedge (\exists x \bullet Q)$

2.5   Find the error in the following formal proof, where $x \in \mathcal{V}[P]$:

1. $P \vdash P$ (trivial)
2. $\exists x \bullet P \vdash P$ $(1, A\exists)$
3. $\exists x \bullet P \vdash \forall x \bullet P$ $(2, T\forall)$
4. $\vdash \exists x \bullet P \Rightarrow \forall x \bullet P$ $(3, T\Rightarrow)$

2.6   Prove the following theorems, given the axiom $\vdash x < y+1 \Leftrightarrow x = y \vee x < y$:
1. $\forall m \bullet \exists n \bullet m < n$
2. $\forall m \bullet m < (m+1) + 1$

2.7   Show that the SC rules TRN, AI, and VI are superfluous in ND by deriving them in ND, without using any of the three in the derivations.

2.8   Prove that BPC is *sound* by deriving each BPC rule using ND $\cup$ SC only. Prove also that BPC is *complete* by deriving each ND rule using BPC $\cup$ SC only. (We take it for granted that ND $\cup$ SC has both properties.) Hint: The derivation of TV (either alternative) in ND resembles the proof of $P \vee \neg P$ in ND.

2.9   Construct BPC-style rules, **Tif** and **Aif**, for the Boolean **if-then-else-fi** construct satisfying the requirements 1 – 3 above. Verify **Tif** and **Aif** by deriving rules obtained from them by replacing the if-construct, say **if** P **then** Q **else** R **fi**, by one of the equivalent formulas $(P \Rightarrow Q) \wedge (\neg P \Rightarrow R)$ and $P \wedge Q \vee \neg P \wedge Q$.

2.10   Prove $\forall x \bullet P \Leftrightarrow \forall y \bullet P_y^x$ and $\exists x \bullet P \Leftrightarrow \exists y \bullet P_y^x$ for well-defined P such that $y \notin \mathcal{V}[P]$. Prove also that none of the four implications is universally valid if $y \in \mathcal{V}[P]$.

Chapter 3

Programs and States

One of the main topics of this book is to reason about "procedural" or "imperative" sequential programs, i.e. programs written in traditional languages such as Pascal and Ada. Somewhat simplified, an imperative program defines a *state space* and a *pattern of actions* operating in the state space. The state space is defined through a collection of typed *program variables* which may be thought of as the coordinate axes of the state space; their values then define a point in the space called a *state*. When we look at a program as implemented on a computer the state space may consist of storage elements as well as peripheral devices, where the latter typically are represented by abstract variables in the form of sequences of inputs and outputs.

Notice that program variables are different from ordinary "mathematical" variables, in the sense that their values *change* as a result of executing parts of the program. In contrast, the purpose of an ordinary free variable is to stand for the same (unspecified) value throughout its textual scope.

Let the program variables be $x_1, x_2, \ldots, x_n$. Then the state space is the Cartesian product of the respective variable types, $T_1, T_2, \ldots, T_n$ (where each type stands for its associated value set), and a state σ is a corresponding n-tuple of values:

$$\sigma = (a_1, a_2, \ldots, a_n) \in T_1 \times T_2 \times \cdots \times T_n$$

The actions performed during a program execution consist of changing the current state by assigning new values to program variables. Each action takes place as the result of executing an imperative of the program, for instance an *assignment statement* of the form $x := e$, where x is a program variable, and e is an expression. The corresponding action consists of evaluating the expression and assigning the result as the new value of x. The old value of x is lost. The expression e may have free occurrences of program variables, in which case the value of e depends on the current state.

A program execution as a whole is a sequence of actions $A_1, A_2, A_3, \ldots$, causing transitions through a sequence of states $\sigma_0, \sigma_1, \sigma_2, \ldots$, possibly terminating in a final state σ_n, as shown in figure 3.1. The initial state, σ_0, represents input data

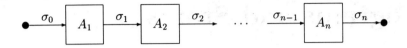

Figure 3.1

to the program and σ_n represents the results. The initial state may be different for different executions of the program, and so will the intermediate and final states. Assume for simplicity that the program is a linear sequence of assignment statements, $S_1; S_2; \ldots; S_n$, and consider a set of program executions such that the initial states satisfy some condition P_0. Since for every execution each action A_i, $i = 1, 2, \ldots, n$, is caused by the statement S_i we get the picture of figure 3.2, where

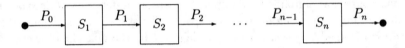

Figure 3.2

each P_i, $i > 0$, expresses properties of the states possible at the i'th stage. Thus σ_i satisfies the predicate P_i for $i = 1, 2, \ldots, n$, provided that P_0 holds for σ_0.

Interlude
The use of such terms as condition, requirement, assertion and relation is often sloppy in a technical sense. It is seldom clear whether they refer to *formulas* which are expressions of type *Bool*, or to *predicates* which are functions with codomain *Bool* and domains which usually contain other types.

Even the term predicate is sometimes misused. Thus, the "predicate" $x < 2y$ perhaps refers to a function p_1 with two arguments, such that $p_1(x, y) \triangleq x < 2y$. Using so-called λ-notation we may define that function more explicitly as

$$p_1 \triangleq \lambda x, y \bullet x < 2y \quad \text{(i.e. that function of } x \text{ and } y \text{ whose value is } x < 2y\text{)}$$

p_1 is not, however, the only predicate which may be associated with the formula $x < 2y$. Here are some others:

$$p_2 \triangleq \lambda x \bullet x < 2y$$
$$p_3 \triangleq \lambda y \bullet x < 2y$$
$$p_4 \triangleq \lambda x, y, z \bullet x < 2y$$

The variable y is free in p_2, whereas x is bound by the λ operator and identifies the single argument of p_2. Thus, the identity of the predicate p_2 depends on the value of the free variable y. Similarly p_3 depends on the free variable x. The predicate p_4 takes three arguments, but is a constant with respect to the last one.

Application consists of substituting argument expressions for λ-bound variables:

$$p_2(v) = (v < 2y)$$
$$p_3(2) = (x < 4)$$
$$p_4(5, 2, v) = p_1(5, 2) = (5 < 4) = \mathbf{f}$$

In general, $p \triangleq \lambda x \bullet P$ gives $p(e) = P_e^x$, where x is a list of distinct variables and e is a corresponding list of expressions.

In the sequel, whenever we use the term "predicate" for a formula P (or the term "function" for an expression e), we mean $\lambda x \bullet P$ (respectively $\lambda x \bullet e$), where x stands for $x_1, x_2, \ldots, x_n$, the list of all program variables. A state $\sigma = (a_1, a_2, \ldots, a_n)$ satisfies the predicate iff P_σ^x, i.e. $P_{a_1, a_2, \ldots, a_n}^{x_1, x_2, \ldots, x_n}$, holds.

We assume furthermore that *functions never have "hidden" arguments* as, for instance, p_2 and p_3 above. Then we may conclude that the value of any expression e can depend on, at most, the variables contained in the set $\mathcal{V}[e]$, i.e. those occurring free in e.

It may be useful to think of a predicate P (really $\lambda x \bullet P$, here we go!) as a *set of states*: the set of all those states that satisfy the predicate:

$$P \sim \{\sigma \bullet P_\sigma^x\}$$

It may even be convenient to make P play the role of a set in expressions. Thus, we sometimes write $\sigma \epsilon P$ for P_σ^x, $P \cap Q$ for $\lambda x \bullet P \wedge Q$, $P \cup Q$ for $\lambda x \bullet P \vee Q$, and $P \subseteq Q$ for $\forall x \bullet P \Rightarrow Q$. (Notice the quantifier! Which set expression corresponds to the predicate $\lambda x \bullet P \Rightarrow Q$?)

The symbol $\supset$ is often used to denote implication. Unfortunately, however, $P \supset Q$ indicates the wrong relationship if P and Q are thought of as sets of states. It is in order to avoid this source of confusion that we are using a different implication symbol in this book.

Notice the importance now of identifying the list of argument variables of a predicate. For instance, the predicate $\lambda x \bullet x = 0$ corresponds to a singleton set, whereas $\lambda x, y \bullet x = 0$ does not.

We say that a predicate P is *stronger than* a predicate Q (or equal) iff $P \subseteq Q$, meaning $\forall x \bullet P \Rightarrow Q$. Notice that $P \subseteq Q$ holds if $P \Rightarrow Q$ is *provable*: $\vdash P \Rightarrow Q$. We also say that $P \wedge Q$ is P *strengthened by* Q, and that $Q \Rightarrow P$ is P *weakened by* Q.

end of interlude

Figure 3.2 above may be generalized to arbitrary flow diagrams with branchings and cycles, whose arcs (connecting lines) are annotated with state predicates. Notice that the arcs of a flow diagram represent (sets of) states, whereas the nodes, or boxes, represent state transitions. Clearly, only the descriptions of the latter, the operations of the program, are relevant for its execution; however, it turns out that state predicates are generally of fundamental importance in order to understand programs and to reason about them.

J. von Neumann and H.H. Goldstine, in a report on the programming of electronic computers [25], dated as early as 1947, recommend using flow diagrams containing "assertion boxes" as well as "operation boxes". The former would contain assertions about the current state at indicated points of the diagram, of no consequence for the automatic execution of the program, but important for human readers in order to understand it. This idea, important from a practical as well as theoretical point of view, remained more or less unnoticed until 20 years later, when R.W. Floyd [10] showed how strict reasoning about the meaning of flow diagrams could be carried out, provided suitable assertions were associated with the arcs.

A predicate P associated with an arc A is intended to signify that *the state satisfies P whenever control passes along A.*

Then the predicate $\mathbf{t}$ (really $\lambda x_1, x_2, \ldots, x_n \bullet \mathbf{t}$) is an empty assertion, since all states satisfy it. The predicate $\mathbf{f}$, on the other hand, is not satisfied by any state, hence the assertion $\mathbf{f}$ on an arc means that control will never reach that arc. Notice that no associated predicate can assert that control *will* pass a given arc.

The flow diagram of figure 3.3 expresses a version of the Euclidean algorithm for computing the greatest common divisor, *gcd*, of one non-negative and one positive integer. (The example and its treatment owes much to the introductory example of [23].)

$a, b := e, f$ express the simultaneous assignment of the value of e to a and the value of f to b. The expressions x/y and $x \bmod y$ denote respectively the integer quotient and remainder obtained by dividing non-negative x by positive y.

We wish to show that the assertion on each arc is satisfied whenever control passes the arc, provided P_0 holds initially. A general technique for carrying out such a proof is as follows. For each node in the graph and every pair of incoming and outgoing arcs we prove that if the assertion on the former holds before the operation of the node, then the assertion on the outgoing arc must hold after the operation. As a result of these proofs the theorem follows by induction on the number of operations performed.

In our case P_1 obviously holds given P_0. In order to verify P_2 we note that both P_1 and P_5 imply $x \geq 0$, $y > 0$, and $gcd(x, y) = gcd(m, n)$. Thus P_2 must hold after the computation of the quotient q and the remainder r by integer division of x by y. On the YES branch after the test we know that x is a multiple of y, and thus $gcd(x, y) = y$. P_2 then gives $y = gcd(m, n)$. On the NO branch r is non-zero which, by P_2, gives $0 < r$ in P_4. The simultaneous assignment $x, y := y, r$ shows that what is true for y, r in P_4 must hold for x, y in P_5. $0 < r < y$ in P_4 therefore ensures $x > 0$ and $y > 0$ in P_5. In order to justify $gcd(x, y) = gcd(m, n)$ in P_5 we

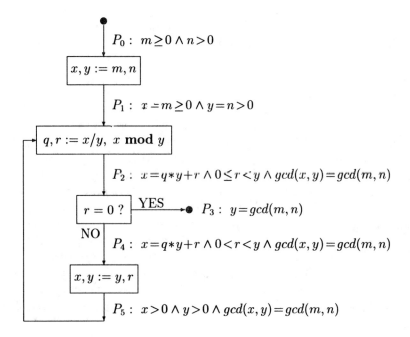

$P_0: \ m \geq 0 \wedge n > 0$

$x, y := m, n$

$P_1: \ x = m \geq 0 \wedge y = n > 0$

$q, r := x/y, \ x \ \textbf{mod} \ y$

$P_2: \ x = q*y + r \wedge 0 \leq r < y \wedge gcd(x, y) = gcd(m, n)$

$r = 0 \ ?$ YES $P_3: \ y = gcd(m, n)$

NO

$P_4: \ x = q*y + r \wedge 0 < r < y \wedge gcd(x, y) = gcd(m, n)$

$x, y := y, r$

$P_5: \ x > 0 \wedge y > 0 \wedge gcd(x, y) = gcd(m, n)$

Figure 3.3

must show that P_4 implies $gcd(y, r) = gcd(m, n)$. This follows by a mathematical argument which is the crux of the algorithm.

P_4 gives $x = q*y + r$. Thus, if y and r are both evenly divisible by an integer k, then so is x. Define a function producing the set of divisors of a given positive integer:

$$F(x) \triangleq \{k \bullet k \text{ divides } x \text{ evenly}\}$$

We have now seen that $F(y) \cap F(r) \subseteq F(x)$. But P_4 also gives $r = x - q*y$, which implies $F(x) \cap F(y) \subseteq F(r)$.

Intersection of the left and right hand sides of both inclusions by $F(y)$ gives

$$F(y) \cap F(r) \subseteq F(x) \cap F(y), \text{ and}$$
$$F(x) \cap F(y) \subseteq F(r) \cap F(y)$$

Consequently, $F(y) \cap F(r) = F(x) \cap F(y)$, which implies

$$gcd(y, r) = gcd(x, y) \ \ (= gcd(m, n) \text{ by } P_4)$$

It follows from all this that $y = gcd(m, n)$ whenever the algorithm terminates. So it does compute the greatest common divisor of m and n, for $m \geq 0$ and $n > 0$, *provided* control eventually reaches the YES branch of the test.

In order to demonstrate that this will in fact happen we need another kind of reasoning, one which shows that *progress* toward a goal is being made. In this example it is sufficient to show that the value of the variable y decreases with each execution of the loop: $y := r$ is the only assignment to y in the loop, it takes place each time, and P_4 asserts $r < y$. On the other hand, y remains positive throughout the execution of the program. Thus, the execution cannot go on for ever.

P_0 and P_3 together comprise an *external documentation* or *specification* of the program. They give information necessary for a user of the program: what is required of the input, and what will be achieved by the program. The other assertions comprise *internal* documentation, which contributes to explaining to a reader of the program *how* and *why* the algorithm works.

Not all the assertions $P_0 - P_5$ are equally important from a logical point of view: if e.g. P_2 is given, it turns out that all the others may be constructed by simple mechanical reasoning. P_2 is called a *loop invariant*, since it remains true every time around the loop. In general, in order to understand the result of a loop, and how it works, one needs information in addition to the program text itself. The loop invariant P_2 may look superfluous to one who already knows the principle of the Euclidean algorithm, but to one who does not, it provides essential and non-obvious information. From the point of view of program documentation P_0 and P_3 are important too, since they provide information essential to any user of the program.

Notice that the great majority of proof steps involved in our verification are quite trivial mathematically. This is typical of program verification. Nevertheless, *all* the steps are important for the correctness of the program, not only the mathematically interesting ones.

With good high level programming languages around, one prefers to use one of them, instead of the cumbersome notation of flow diagrams. An adequately documented program text for the Euclidean algorithm might look as follows, using a small programming language explained more fully in the next chapter. The program annotation is marked by being enclosed in braces. We use a **loop** construct, in which the loop test (the **while** clause) may be any one of the list of statements that forms the loop body. That gives more flexibility than the more standard **while-do** construct:

$$
\begin{aligned}
&\textbf{const } m, n : Int; \ \{m \geq 0 \ \wedge \ n > 0\} \\
&\textbf{var} \quad x, y : Int = m, n; \\
&\textbf{loop} \quad \{\textbf{const } q : Int = x/y; \} \\
&\qquad\qquad \textbf{const } r : Int = x \ \textbf{mod } y; \\
&\qquad\qquad \{x = q*y + r \ \wedge \ 0 \leq r < y \ \wedge \ gcd(x, y) = gcd(m, n)\} \\
&\textbf{while } r \neq 0; \\
&\qquad\qquad x, y := y, r \\
&\textbf{repeat} \\
&\{y = gcd(m, n)\}
\end{aligned}
$$

The state space is defined explicitly by variable and constant declarations. It consists of the program variables x and y, as well as the "program constants" m,n,q, and r. (Notice that program constants are variables in the mathematical sense!) The scope of q and r is the loop body: new constants q and r appear with each repetition. The constant q plays no role in the algorithm itself, it only occurs in the loop invariant. For that reason its declaration has been included in curly brackets, and thereby identified as part of the documentation so that it may be ignored during program execution (cf. section 4.8).

Two important remarks are due in connection with the techniques used above:

1. They are not likely to be applicable in a practical sense to life-sized programs, unless one is very careful with the program structure, because of the exorbitant amount of work involved. It is particularly important to compose large programs in such a way that only small parts of the total state space need be considered in detail at any point of the program. We therefore need programming languages with strong mechanisms for data hiding and data abstraction. Even so, mechanized aids to reasoning will be indispensable in practice.

2. State assertions should not be afterthoughts; they belong to the program design phase, as indicated by the following example. (It must be admitted, however, that old programming habits are difficult to change, and also non-trivial invariants are difficult to dream up, so sometimes new invariants are discovered along the way during off-the-cuff programming. When that happens, major program cleanup often results.)

Consider the problem of computing

$$y = e^x = \Sigma_{k=0}^{\infty} x^k/k!$$

for given $x : Real$ and with a given relative accuracy $\varepsilon : Real > 0$. With a little programming experience we see the outline of an iteration on variables $y, z : Real$ and $k : Int$ meaning, roughly, the current partial sum, term, and term number, respectively. We have not yet seen all the details clearly, but make a list of some plausible ways of initializing the variables:

$y := 0$ or maybe 1 or maybe $1 + x$
$z := 1$ or maybe x, and
$k := 0$ or maybe 1

Then there will be a loop containing assignment statements updating the variables:

$y := y + z$ or maybe $y + z * x/k$ or even $y + z * x/(k+1)$
$z := z * x/k$ or maybe $z * x/(k+1)$, and
$k := k + 1$

Now the task of writing down the program amounts to selecting of one out of the $3 \times 2 \times 2 \times 3 \times 2 = 72$ possible statement sets, many of which might seem reasonable, but only a few are correct. On top of this, many programming languages only cater for the updating of a single variable at a time, and since the result is not independent of the order of the latter three statements, there is an additional factor of 6 in the number of candidate programs. As every programmer will know, it takes accurate and systematic reasoning to arrive at a correct one. (Try to figure out the percentage of correct ones!)

A good programming strategy is to choose a suitable loop invariant *first*, e.g.

$$I: \quad y = \Sigma_{i=0}^{k} x^i/i! \ \wedge \ z = x^k/k!$$

which is one of several slightly different variants that could be used. If we now choose to initialize k to 1, then, in order to satisfy I, y and z must be initialized to $1+x$ and x, respectively. I now holds at the top of the loop and shows that the term z has already been included in the sum. Therefore z should be updated before y. In order to compute the next term we need the value $k+1$, which indicates that k should be updated first. We want to carry on summing until the absolute value of the last term added is less than $\varepsilon*y$. An acceptable program text could therefore be as follows, given x, ε, and a computer able to deal with exact real numbers:

```
const x, ε : Real;  {ε > 0}
var    k : Int = 1;
var    y, z : Real = 1+x, x;
loop   {y = Σᵏᵢ₌₀xⁱ/i! ∧ z = xᵏ/k!}
while abs(z) ≥ ε * y;
       k := k + 1;  z := z * x/k;  y := y + z
repeat
       {y = Σᵏᵢ₌₀xⁱ/i! ∧ abs(xᵏ/k!) < ε*y}
```

Unfortunately, computer representation of real numbers and operations on them generally involve rounding errors, which cause the equations of our assertions to be approximate only. The art of reasoning about rounding errors belongs to the science of numerical analysis, which is outside the scope of this book. We shall therefore avoid data of type *Real* in the following chapters, although the techniques discussed in chapter 4 do apply to programs with real numbers if idealized so that rounding errors would not occur. (Notice by the way that the loop above must terminate for a given range of inputs if the relative rounding errors are sufficiently small, because z approaches zero as k increases, and y will end up sufficiently near e^x to be positive.)

Exercises

3.1 An alternative way to demonstrate that the Euclidean algorithm must terminate could be to count the number of loop executions, and prove that this number is bounded by a constant. For that reason consider an embellished version of the flow diagram of figure 3.3 in which assignments to a counter k have been added to the top and bottom operations, respectively:

$$x, y, k := m, n, 0 \quad \text{and} \quad x, y, k := y, r, k+1.$$

Prove that the condition $k < n$ holds in the loop by strengthening the assertions $P_1, \ldots, P_5$ appropriately. Hint: Try to find an assertion which holds before the loop, which is provably maintained in the loop, and which implies $k < n$. The latter predicate is not quite strong enough by itself.

3.2 Construct a program for the exponential function with the same net effect as the one developed above, but based on an invariant asserting that $z = x^k / k!$ is the first term not yet included in the current sum y.

Chapter 4

Hoare Logic

As mentioned in the last chapter strict reasoning about large programs may imply the processing of an enormous volume of formulas. We try to combat that difficulty by imposing various kinds of *program structure*, provided for by our programming language:

1. A *functional (applicative) sublanguage* provides an implementation of the mathematical concepts of function definition and function application. The evaluation of a fully applicative expression has only one effect, that of computing the *value* of the expression (given that it is well-defined). The expression can therefore be thought of as a mathematical object denoting that value. It obeys the usual mathematical laws, in particular that of substitution: any two expressions denoting the same value may substitute for one another. In this way the intermediate states and state transitions during expression evaluation are abstracted away and, consequently, reasoning is greatly simplified. Unfortunately, for reasons of efficiency this degree of abstraction is not always feasible. It may then be necessary to resort to *procedural (imperative)* language features and to reason explicitly about states and changes of state.

2. *Structure in the large* is obtained by composing programs out of such modules as procedures (not necessarily functional), classes, and other kinds of "packages". Typically each module is concerned with only a small part of the total state space, and provided that its external properties are simpler than the sum of internal detail, the composition of programs (or bigger modules) is simplified. Simplification is achieved by:

   - operational abstraction, such as considering the net effect of a procedure, not the operational details and intermediate states,
   - data hiding, such as hiding away the local variables of procedures, and
   - data abstraction, by which complicated data objects may be reinterpreted as more "abstract" entities satisfying simple algebraic laws.

If a library of useful proven program modules is available, program development may be greatly simplified.

3. *Structure in the small* is provided for by control notations for branching and looping, as well as mechanisms for the grouping of data into records and arrays.

There is good reason to keep the use of the applicative and imperative features of a programming language well separated. In particular, the use of "functions" with side effects is detrimental to easy reasoning, because then the law of substitution is lost, and in general it becomes necessary to consider the operational details of expression evaluation. Changes of state are more easily dealt with in terms of explicit assignments and sequential composition of actions. A special logic devised by Hoare [17] provides a simple thought model for reasoning about imperative program texts.

The "Hoare Logic" is based on the idea of flow diagram annotation, but associates proof rules directly with the structural elements, so-called "phrases", of a program text. The theory is restricted to consideration of phrases which are basic or compound statements including statement lists, and which have a single entry (at the left) and a single normal exit (at the right). A corresponding annotated "flow diagram" for a phrase S is

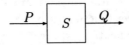

where P is called the *precondition* and Q the *postcondition* or *postassertion*. In [17] Hoare introduced corresponding logical formulas of the form $P\{S\}Q$. We prefer to include the annotation in braces, rather than the program text proper, and therefore write

$$\{P\}S\{Q\}$$

which we call a "Hoare sentence". Hoare sentences are considered to be new kinds of logical formulas, and interpreting state assertions as in the last chapter, the Hoare sentence above has the following meaning:

- *If the precondition P holds before an execution of the program phrase S, and the execution terminates normally, then the postcondition Q holds upon termination.*

Notice that we allow for the possibility that an execution of S would not terminate normally. This may happen e.g.

1. because control has entered an infinite loop, or

2. because an error situation has occurred, which resulted in program abortion.

It is important that mathematically meaningless operations, such as division by zero or the removal of an item from an empty list, should cause program abortion and not lead to normal termination with a spurious result. Abortion should also result if some internal capacity limit of the computing device is exceeded, such as the available amount of storage space, or the number of bits available to hold the result of an arithmetic operation on integers. Notice that in case 1 the program execution also exceeds a capacity limit, namely the available computation time. Some form of interruption will take place sooner or later, e.g. caused by the operating system or by the user. (In practice the same thing happens even with programs that would terminate normally given enough time, if the computation takes too long.)

If the Hoare sentence $\{P\}S\{Q\}$ is valid according to the above interpretation, we say that the program (-phrase) S is *partially correct* with respect to the specification consisting of the predicate pair (P, Q) or, alternatively, that (P, Q) is a valid *partial specification* of S.

Notice that Hoare sentences cannot be used to assert normal program termination. On the other hand, any precondition P for a program S, such that $\{P\}S\{\mathbf{f}\}$ holds, is a sufficient condition for abnormal behaviour of S. Then, by implication, $\neg P$ is a *necessary* condition for the normal termination of S.

If a precondition P guarantees both normal termination of S and the validity of a postassertion Q, then S is said to be *totally correct* with respect to (P, Q).

It is usually quite impractical to insist on total correctness proofs for life sized programs running on actual computers. It would be necessary to take into account all kinds of internal capacity limitations, and for programs written in a high level language many implementation details would have to be considered, such as the representation of data of built-in and user defined types, the implementation of procedures and functions, internal memory management, etc. When discussing criteria for normal termination of high level programs it is therefore necessary in practice to reason in terms of execution on an idealized machine with memory and processing capacities always sufficient for the task at hand.

Let S be a given high level ("abstract") program, and let S' be the implementation of S actually running on a given computer. We assume that S is defined in terms of constructively definable data and operations (which excludes infinite structures such as real numbers). Even so we cannot in general, for reasons just mentioned, achieve exact correspondence between the behaviour of S and that of S' for all legal inputs. We can and should, however, implement S in such a way that S' never behaves wrongly and then terminates normally. In other words all results produced by S' should be correct, i.e. exactly the same as those that would be produced by S, but we have to allow for the possibility that S' may fail to terminate normally more often than S would. This convention implies that *any partial correctness result for S will also hold for S'*, provided that the pre- and postconditions of S' can be expressed directly in terms of "abstract" concepts (cf. section 5.9):

$$\text{IMPL}: \quad \frac{\vdash \{P\}\,S\,\{Q\}}{\vdash \{P\}\,S'\,\{Q\}}$$

We therefore follow Hoare in dealing primarily with partial correctness, but we shall also consider certain kinds of additional reasoning that will guard against specific forms of abnormal behaviour.

Two formal languages are involved in a Hoare sentence $\{P\}S\{Q\}$:

- a formula language, FL, and

- a programming language, PL.

P and Q are formulas of FL, and S is a phrase in PL, in our treatment restricted to a statement or a list of statements.

FL is a typed first order language which caters for Boolean (*Bool*), integer (*Int*) and other types, some of which may be user defined. PL is an imperative (Pascal-like) programming language. A subset EE of FL, the set of "evaluatable expressions", is part of PL in the following sense: it contains those expressions which may legally occur as parts of executable statements. EE does not contain quantifiers and not necessarily all types and functions available in FL. On the other hand all types and functions implemented in PL are part of FL. We do not restrict ourselves to any uniquely defined programming language PL, but rather consider various constructs which are typical of imperative languages.

In the following we present a logic for reasoning about the partial correctness of programs—"Hoare Logic"—as an extension to an (unspecified) formal first order system with the formula language FL. The formulas of the extended system are either formulas of FL or Hoare sentences.

In order to apply partial correctness results for high level programs to the behaviour of an actual computer executing these programs, it must be assumed that the rule IMPL is valid. This requirement applied to arbitrary PL programs is a natural correctness criterion for the implementation of the high level programming language PL. In addition, one would require that PL program executions should terminate normally "as often as possible" on the given computer.

4.1   Mathematical and Linguistic Preliminaries

If we wanted to design a well founded metatheory for a formal Hoare Logic, proving properties such as soundness and aspects of completeness, we would need mathematical models of Hoare sentences, which in turn would have to be based on mathematically defined semantics of the programming language PL. We very briefly sketch one way of doing this.

Define any program statement (or list of statements) S as denoting a *relation* between a pair of states in some state space defined in advance. Let σ_1 and σ_2 be states. Then $\sigma_1|S|\sigma_2$ means that an execution of S starting in state σ_1 may terminate normally in state σ_2.

For an ordinary, deterministic programming language such relations are *functional*, i.e. correspond to functions, possibly partial. Thus, if S terminates normally when started in σ_1, there is exactly one state σ_2 such that $\sigma_1|S|\sigma_2$ holds, otherwise $\sigma_1|S|\sigma_2$ is false for all σ_2. However, since most of Hoare Logic works for non-deterministic languages as well, it is useful to have the relation concept as a basis. Anyway, input operations must be taken as non-deterministic, unless the expected input data are identified in preconditions.

EXAMPLE 4.1

Let the state space be $x = (x_1, x_2, ..., x_n)$ and $\sigma_1 = (a_1, a_2, ..., a_n)$. Then the formula

$$\sigma_1|x_k := e|\sigma_2$$

holds for $\sigma_2 = (a_1, ..., a_{k-1}, e_{\sigma_1}^x, a_{k+1}, ..., a_n)$, where $e_{\sigma_1}^x$ denotes the value of e evaluated in state σ_1, and given that e is well-defined in state σ_1 and the evaluation terminates normally.

□

It is possible to give similar definitions for all imperative constructs of a programming language (although some non-trivial mathematics is needed for defining constructs expressing repetition or recursion). Assume that this has been done. Then we may define

$$\{P\}S\{Q\} \triangleq \forall \sigma_1, \sigma_2 : T_1 \times \cdots \times T_n \bullet P_{\sigma_1}^x \wedge \sigma_1|S|\sigma_2 \Rightarrow Q_{\sigma_2}^x \qquad (4.1)$$

where the T's are the types of the program variables. Notice that occurrences of program variables in a Hoare sentence stand for components of σ_1 in the precondition and for components of σ_2 in the postcondition (and those of the program segment S are to be regarded as part of the name of a relation on states). Thus they are not to be regarded as free variables of the Hoare sentence as a whole. The definition shows that *Hoare sentences represent closed formulas*.

At this point we discontinue the discussion of mathematical foundations for Hoare logic; it is sufficient for our purpose that such foundations may be built. In the following sections we formulate axioms and proof rules of Hoare logic on the basis of informal reasoning. We do claim, although without proof, that these axioms and rules are consistent with the intended semantics of programs and that they are as complete for reasoning about programs as the underlying formal first order system permits (as well as preserving the soundness of the latter).

The reasoning about a program S is simplified to some extent if we know in advance the set of variables that exist outside S and which may be changed in an execution of S, as well as those whose (initial) values may have an influence on the resulting changes. For that purpose we introduce two syntactic functions:

$$\mathcal{V}, \mathcal{W} : \text{statement} \longrightarrow \text{variable set}$$

where $\mathcal{V}[S]$ is the set of (non-local) variables used in S, and $\text{W}[S]$ is the the set of those that may be assigned to in S, also-called the *out-variables* of S. The former is a natural extension of the function defined in section 2.1.3, giving the set of free variables of expressions.

We cannot expect the syntactically defined variable sets to match the semantic ones exactly; for the value of an expression may be independent of a variable x even if x occurs free in it, and an assignment $x := a$ does not change the value of x if it is already equal to a. We must, however, insist that the syntactic sets do contain all possibly relevant variables, otherwise our reasoning could be unsound, as we shall see. At the same time the sets should be as small as possible and easy to compute. This provides some important feedback to programming language design and programming style: Serious obstacles are e.g. pointer variables, dynamic binding of variables as in old-fashioned LISP, and the combined use of procedure name parameters and non-local variables, which is possible, for instance, in Algol/Simula.

In the sequel we apply the programming language convention that all variables are *introduced explicitly*, as declared program variables or program constants, or as formal parameters of a procedure, and that each variable has a uniquely defined *textual scope*. Only static variable binding is used. It follows that the accessible part, Σ_p, of the state space at a point p in a program is syntactically defined for any p, and that $\mathcal{V}[S] \subseteq \Sigma_p$ holds for any statement S at point p in a legal program. In fact, we could define $\mathcal{V}[S] = \mathcal{W}[S] = \Sigma_p$, but sharper reasoning is possible with smaller sets. The two syntactic functions will be defined along with the introduction of the various imperative constructs considered.

4.2   Program Independent Rules

The following rules express program independent properties of Hoare sentences. They are direct consequences of definition (4.1):

$$\text{CQL}: \quad \frac{\vdash P \Rightarrow P'; \ \vdash \{P'\}S\{Q\}}{\vdash \{P\}S\{Q\}} \qquad \text{(Left Consequence)}$$

$$\text{CQR}: \quad \frac{\vdash \{P\}S\{Q'\}; \ \vdash Q' \Rightarrow Q}{\vdash \{P\}S\{Q\}} \qquad \text{(Right Consequence)}$$

$$\text{CJ}: \quad \frac{\vdash \{P\}S\{Q_1\}; \ \vdash \{P\}S\{Q_2\}}{\vdash \{P\}S\{Q_1 \wedge Q_2\}} \qquad \text{(Conjunction)}$$

$$\text{DJ}: \quad \frac{\vdash \{P_1\}S\{Q\}; \ \vdash \{P_2\}S\{Q\}}{\vdash \{P_1 \vee P_2\}S\{Q\}} \qquad \text{(Disjunction)}$$

As we shall see many steps of partial correctness reasoning are fully mechanizable, in the sense that useful pre- and/or postconditions may be constructed automatically. Suppose we wish to prove $\{P\}S\{Q\}$, and suppose $\{P'\}S\{Q'\}$ could be verified mechanically. Then we may use the consequence rules backwards in order to identify what remains to be proved: $P \Rightarrow P'$ by CQL, and $Q' \Rightarrow Q$ by CQR. Thus, we have as the net result reduced the verification of S with respect to the partial specification (P, Q), by mechanical means, to the proof of two lemmas in ordinary first order logic. The formulas $P \Rightarrow P'$ and $Q' \Rightarrow Q$ are called *verification conditions*. The number of verification conditions that have to be proved in connection with the verification of a piece of program depends on the structure of the program, e.g. the number of loops.

The rules CJ and DJ indicate ways of performing incremental proofs. In particular, rule CJ is useful to accumulate additional reasoning in order to disprove specific abnormal behaviour.

For the sake of completeness we mention the following general axiom schemas:

TA : $\vdash \{\mathbf{t}\}S\{\mathbf{t}\}$
FA : $\vdash \{\mathbf{f}\}S\{\mathbf{f}\}$

TA expresses the fact that an empty precondition is sufficient to ensure an empty postassertion. FA says that control will not leave S normally if it does not enter S. (There is by definition only one point of entry!)

The following fairly trivial theorem schemas follow by the consequence rules:

TT : $\vdash \{P\}S\{\mathbf{t}\}$
FT : $\vdash \{\mathbf{f}\}S\{Q\}$

The following definitions are useful:

- Consider the following Hoare sentences for the same program: $\{P\}S\{Q\}$ and $\{P'\}S\{Q'\}$. The latter is said to be *stronger than or equal to* the former if the precondition P' is weaker than or equal to P, i.e. $\vdash P \Rightarrow P'$ (more states satisfy P'), and the postcondition Q' is stronger than or equal to Q, i.e. $\vdash Q' \Rightarrow Q$ (less states satisfy Q').
- A Hoare sentence is said to be *left maximal* if the precondition is the weakest possible for the given postcondition to hold whenever the given program segment terminates normally.

The consequence rules represent weakening, in the sense that the Hoare sentence premise in either case is stronger than or equal to the conclusion. In both of the rules CJ and DJ the conclusion is stronger than or equal to either of the premises. TA is left maximal, FA is left maximal for program segments which terminate normally for any initial state.

It will be seen that any valid Hoare sentence which cannot be strengthened is left maximal. But the converse does not hold in general. Example: $\{\mathbf{t}\}x := 0\{\mathbf{t}\}$ is left maximal, but the postcondition may be strengthened by $x = 0$.

Exercises

4.1   Derive the inverses of the rules CJ and DJ from the previous rules:

$$\text{ICJ}: \quad \frac{\vdash \{P\}S\{Q_1 \wedge Q_2\}}{\vdash \{P\}S\{Q_i\}} \quad (i \in \{1, 2\})$$

$$\text{IDJ}: \quad \frac{\vdash \{P_1 \vee P_2\}S\{Q\}}{\vdash \{P_i\}S\{Q\}} \quad (i \in \{1, 2\})$$

4.2   Show that the rules CCJ and DDJ are equivalent to CJ and DJ respectively (using the consequence rules):

$$\text{CCJ}: \quad \frac{\vdash \{P_1\}S\{Q_1\}; \ \vdash \{P_2\}S\{Q_2\}}{\vdash \{P_1 \wedge P_2\}S\{Q_1 \wedge Q_2\}}$$

$$\text{DDJ}: \quad \frac{\vdash \{P_1\}S\{Q_1\}; \ \vdash \{P_2\}S\{Q_2\}}{\vdash \{P_1 \vee P_2\}S\{Q_1 \vee Q_2\}}$$

4.2.1   Constancy and normal termination

Let the statement S and the state predicate P be such that variables which may be changed by S do not occur free in P: $\mathcal{V}[P] \cap \mathcal{W}[S] = \emptyset$. Then we say that P is *insensitive* to S. In that case the truth of P cannot be influenced by executing S, so that if P holds before an execution of S, it must hold after:

$$\text{CONS}: \quad \vdash \{P\}S\{P\} \quad \text{for} \ \mathcal{V}[P] \cap \mathcal{W}[S] = \emptyset \ \text{and} \ P \text{ well-defined.}$$

This axiom schema shows the benefit of knowing the sets $\mathcal{V}[P]$ and $\mathcal{W}[S]$. Clearly the sets should be as small as possible; but it is essential that they contain all relevant variables, otherwise the schema is unsound. For instance, let x be a variable changed by S and whose value may influence the truth of P. If x is not a member of both sets we may be able to prove, wrongly, the constancy of x over S. The reason for requiring the condition P to be well-defined is explained in section 4.3.2.

For given S and P, where P is insensitive to S, CONS is not in general left maximal; for instance, if S never terminates then an empty precondition, **t**, is good enough. In order to obtain a left maximal schema we have to introduce the necessary and sufficient precondition for the normal termination of S. Let t_S denote that condition (assuming that there is a way of expressing it in FL). Provided that the condition t_S can only depend on variables which occur in S, we may conclude: $\mathcal{V}[t_S] \subseteq \mathcal{V}[S]$.

If S is deterministic, then t_S may be expressed in a simple way using the mathematical model (4.1) of Hoare sentences (section 4.1), interpreting S as a relation between the initial and terminal states. Let $\mathcal{V}[S] = (x, y, \ldots, z)$. Then t_S holds in the current state if and only if there exists a terminal state for S:

$$t_S \;=\; \exists x', y', \ldots, z' \bullet (x, y, \ldots, z)|S|(x', y', \ldots, z')$$

Using the notation t_S we can formulate the following axiom schema:

TERM : $\vdash \{\neg t_S\} S \{\mathbf{f}\}$

From CONS and TERM we may deduce the following theorem schema by means of DDJ:

CT : $\vdash \{t_S \Rightarrow P\} S \{P\}$ for $\mathcal{V}[P] \cap \mathcal{W}[S] = \emptyset$ and P well-defined

This schema is left maximal. By that we mean that any Hoare sentence contained in the schema is left maximal.

Exercise

4.3 Prove the schema $\{P\} S \{P \wedge t_S\}$, given that both P and t_S are insensitive to S.

4.2.2 Auxiliary variables

For a given Hoare sentence $\{P\} S \{Q\}$ let z be the list of variables occurring free in P and/or Q but not in S.

$$\{z\} = \mathcal{V}[P, Q] - \mathcal{V}[S]$$

These are said to be *auxiliary variables* of the Hoare sentence.

EXAMPLE 4.2
In the sentence $\{x = x_0\}\; x := x + 1\; \{x = x_0 + 1\}$ the variable x_0 is an auxiliary one, used in the postcondition to refer to the value of the program variable x prior to the assignment.
$\square$

Some of the auxiliary variables of $\{P\} S \{Q\}$ may well be program variables declared in the environment of S, others may be variables introduced for the purpose of the Hoare sentence, and whose declarations we have not bothered to write down, such as x_0 of example 4.2. In either case they are to be regarded as part of the state space, at least in a formal, or "mythical" sense (section 4.8). This implies that they are to be regarded as universally quantified over their respective types, for the sentence as a whole, as specified by the mathematical model (4.1) of Hoare sentences. However, since their values are irrelevant to the behaviour of S the corresponding state components may be ignored and omitted from the state relation part of the model, after which the only occurrences of auxiliary variables in the model are those of P and Q.

It follows that auxiliary variables which occur only in the precondition or only in the postcondition may be quantified locally. Standard transformation rules (see sections 2.1.1 and 2.1.2) show that the local quantifiers should be existential in the precondition and universal in the postcondition.

$$\text{EXST}: \quad \frac{\vdash \{P\}S\{Q\}}{\vdash \{\exists z \bullet P\}S\{Q\}} \quad \text{for } \{z\} \cap (\mathcal{V}[S] \cup \mathcal{V}[Q]) = \emptyset$$

$$\text{UNIV}: \quad \frac{\vdash \{P\}S\{Q\}}{\vdash \{P\}S\{\forall z \bullet Q\}} \quad \text{for } \{z\} \cap (\mathcal{V}[P] \cup \mathcal{V}[S]) = \emptyset$$

The EXST rule can be seen as a generalization of the disjunction rule DJ of section 4.2. Assume that the variable list z ranges over the finite value (tuple) set $\{a_1, \ldots a_n\}$. Then the premise of EXST corresponds to the following list of premises, $\vdash \{P_{a_1}^z\}S\{Q\}; \ldots; \vdash \{P_{a_n}^z\}S\{Q\}$, and the conclusion corresponds to $\vdash \{P_{a_1}^z \vee \cdots \vee P_{a_n}^z\}S\{Q\}$. Notice that S and Q remain unaffected by the substitution on z since the variable does not occur (free) in either of them. In a similar way UNIV can be seen as a generalization of the conjunction rule CJ.

Since auxiliary variables are universally quantified, the validity of a Hoare sentence should be preserved by instantiation of auxiliaries, provided that the instantiating expressions are well-defined and their values are not changed by the program in question. For instance, $\{x = 10\}\ x := x + 1\ \{x = 11\}$ would be a valid consequence of the sentence of example 4.2.

$$\text{AUX}: \quad \frac{\vdash \{P\}S\{Q\}}{\vdash \{P_e^z\}S\{Q_e^z\}} \quad \text{for } \{z\} \cap \mathcal{V}[S] = \mathcal{V}[e] \cap \mathcal{W}[S] = \emptyset \text{ and } e \text{ well-def.}$$

We give a formal derivation of the AUX rule for the case that P and Q are well-defined.

1.	$\vdash \{P\}S\{Q\}$	(premise)
2.	$\vdash \{z = e\}S\{z = e\}$ for $\mathcal{V}[z,e] \cap \mathcal{W}[S] = \emptyset$, e well-def.	(CONS)
3.	$\vdash \{P \wedge z = e\}S\{Q \wedge z = e\}$	(1,2, CCJ)
4.	$\vdash Q \wedge z = e \Rightarrow Q_e^z$	(math.)
5.	$\vdash \{P \wedge z = e\}S\{Q_e^z\}$	(3,4, CQR)
6.	$\vdash \{\exists z \bullet\ P \wedge z = e\}S\{Q_e^z\}$ for $\{z\} \cap (\mathcal{V}[S] \cup \mathcal{V}[e]) = \emptyset$	(5, EXST)
7.	$\vdash P_e^z \Rightarrow \exists z \bullet\ P \wedge z = e$ for $\{z\} \cap \mathcal{V}[e] = \emptyset$	(math.)
8.	$\vdash \{P_e^z\}S\{Q_e^z\}$	(7,6, CQL)

The side conditions add up to those of AUX (because $\mathcal{W}[S] \subseteq \mathcal{V}[S]$), except for the additional requirement that no z should occur in e. The latter is easily circumvented by performing the instantiation in two stages, first replacing z by fresh variables. (The given proof may be generalized to arbitrary P and Q by first using the interpretation rule INTPR of section 4.3.2 and applying its inverse RPTNI as the last step.)

Exercise

4.4 Show that the rules UUNIV and EEXST are derivable, and that they may replace UNIV and EXST, assuming $i \notin \mathcal{V}S$:

$$\text{UUNIV}: \quad \frac{\vdash \{P_i\}S\{Q_i\}; \text{ for } i = 1, 2, \ldots, n}{\vdash \{\forall i \bullet 1 \le i \le n \Rightarrow P_i\}S\{\forall i \bullet 1 \le i \le n \Rightarrow Q_i\}}$$

$$\text{EEXST}: \quad \frac{\vdash \{P_i\}S\{Q_i\}; \text{ for } i = 1, 2, \ldots, n}{\vdash \{\exists i \bullet 1 \le i \le n \land P_i\}S\{\exists i \bullet 1 \le i \le n \land Q_i\}}$$

4.2.3 Type invariants

Consider a variable x of type T, e.g. introduced by a declaration **var** $v : T$. It is reasonable to assume that the variable always has a value of type T. This so-called type invariant may be expressed as $v \, \mathbf{isa} \, T$ in the formula language, which is thus a valid invariant throughout the scope of v. (See section 4.4.4 for a more thorough discussion.) Notice that the state component corresponding to v in the model (4.1) of Hoare sentences is a universally bound variable of type T.

If T is a "maximal" type (cf. section 5.6), such as *Int* of integers or *Bool* of Booleans, then the type invariant for v does not contribute semantic information beyond the type checking of expressions containing v. But the case where T is a subtype is different. For instance, consider a range type $\{a..b\}$, where $a, b : Int$, which is a subtype of *Int*. The type invariant $v \, \mathbf{isa} \, \{a..b\}$ is equal to $a \le v \le b$.

Type invariants may be freely introduced in pre- and postconditions. So, for backwards (top down) proof construction, in order to prove a sentence $\{P\}S\{Q\}$ it is sufficient to prove a "weaker" one obtained by strengthening the precondition and weakening the postcondition:

$$\text{TDTINV}: \quad \frac{\vdash \{v \, \mathbf{isa} \, T \land P\} \, S \, \{v \, \mathbf{isa} \, T \Rightarrow Q\}}{\vdash \{P\}S\{Q\}} \quad \text{for } v : T$$

Also, having proved a given sentence we may conclude a "stronger" one obtained by weakening the precondition and strengthening the postcondition. This provides a rule that is more directly useful for forward (bottom up) reasoning:

$$\text{BUTINV}: \quad \frac{\vdash \{P\}\; S\; \{Q\}}{\vdash \{v\,\mathbf{isa}\,T \Rightarrow P\}S\{v\,\mathbf{isa}\,T \wedge Q\}} \quad \text{for } v:T$$

It should be noted that the introduction of type invariants as indicated in these rules represents strengthening and weakening only in a syntactic sense. Actually, the premise and conclusion of either rule are equivalent semantically. This follows from the semantic model (4.1) of Hoare sentences and the fact that $\forall x:T\bullet P \Leftrightarrow \forall x:T\bullet x\,\mathbf{isa}\,T \Rightarrow P$. (See also the rule ∀SUBTY of section 5.6.)

A type invariant is permanent in the sense that it holds in all states of a computation, where "all states" are those which can exist between operations considered to be "atomic" at a given *level of abstraction*. For a typed programming language a level of abstraction may be defined as *a set of types and classes*, where the atomic operations are assignments of values to variables of these types, function applications, and update operations on class objects (chapter 6). At another, less abstract level the atomic operations associated with an "abstract" type (or class) may be represented or "simulated" by compound operations on structures of less abstract types, which means that the atomicity is more fine-grained. Cf. section 5.9.

Exercise

4.5   Prove the equivalence of TDTINV and BUTINV by the rules of Hoare logic.

4.3   Basic Mechanisms

The partial correctness properties of basic statements are described by axioms in the form of Hoare sentences. Conditions for normal termination are stated with respect to implementation on an *idealized computer,* i.e. one which by definition has sufficient capacity to perform a given finite task within an insignificant amount of time.

4.3.1   Doing nothing

We introduce two basic statements, **skip** and **abort**. They contain and affect no variables:

$$\mathcal{V}[\mathbf{skip}] \triangleq \mathcal{W}[\mathbf{skip}] \triangleq \mathcal{V}[\mathbf{abort}] \triangleq \mathcal{W}[\mathbf{abort}] \triangleq \emptyset$$

The **skip** statement terminates normally in all states, whereas **abort** never terminates normally:

$$t_{\mathbf{skip}} \triangleq \mathbf{t}, \qquad t_{\mathbf{abort}} \triangleq \mathbf{f}$$

The following axioms are direct consequences of respectively CONS and TERM of section 4.2.1. Both are left maximal:

SKIP : $\vdash \{P\}$ **skip** $\{P\}$ for P well-defined

ABORT : $\vdash \{\mathbf{t}\}$ **abort** $\{\mathbf{f}\}$

Since the **abort** statement never terminates normally it is partially correct with respect to any specification whatsoever. In fact the axiom ABORT, together with the consequence rules CQL and CQR, imply $\vdash \{P\}$**abort**$\{Q\}$ for arbitrary P and Q.

The statement is useful when programming consistency and capacity checks. When developing larger programs we may use **abort** statements to represent unfinished program segments. Thereby the program may remain partially correct throughout the development phase, producing valid results whenever it terminates normally.

It is useful to augment the **abort** statement by a string parameter, to serve as an "error message" informing the user of the reason for the program abortion.

4.3.2   Expression evaluation

In executable program text all occurring functions are *constructively defined*, which means that there is an algorithm for computing the value of any expression encountered during program execution, provided that the expression is *well-defined* in the sense that it actually has a value. (Notice that only quantifier-free expressions are allowed in executable program text.) We may therefore assume that the evaluation of any well-defined expression will terminate normally with the value of the expression, provided that the computation is performed by an idealized machine which evaluates expressions strictly in accordance with the function definitions.

We also assume that the evaluation of a well-defined expression e has no other effect than producing its value. Then, since no accessible program variable will be affected by the evaluation of e, the technique of evaluation employed is of no concern to the program logic. Otherwise the results of a program (terminating normally) might be sensitive to the sequencing of operations during expression evaluation, such as the order of subexpression evaluations under an arguments first strategy.

This absence of "side effects" is not usually enforced by traditional programming languages; however, in order to simplify the reasoning about programs, and in order to make programs insensitive to many implementation details, the use of side effects in function evaluation is strongly discouraged. *In the following we assume that the No Side Effects (NSE) convention is adhered to consistently.*

The logic of expression evaluation is made considerably more complicated by the facts that

1. partial functions occur, and
2. idealized computers do not exist.

Thus, it may happen that an evaluation of an expression e cannot lead to a correct value, either because e is mathematically ill-defined, i.e. has no value, or because imperfections of the computing instrument, such as capacity constraints, make it impossible to compute the correct value.

It is of fundamental importance for our confidence in a program that *it should never produce wrong results which could be mistaken for correct ones*. Instead, one should insist on some easily recognizable abnormal behaviour, such as program abortion, whenever correct results cannot be computed. We therefore introduce another very important programming principle, the AID convention:

- *Abort when Ill-Defined,* i.e. instead of executing operations which are wrong or meaningless when viewed at an appropriate level of abstraction.

In practice the abort statement will take a text parameter which is used to provide an explanatory "error message" as feedback to the programmer. Notice that error messages are most informative if they relate to an appropriate level of abstraction. For instance, the message "Customer table too large" is more useful than "Subscript out of bounds at hex B5A7D". The latter might be the ultimate result if the programmer did not bother to put in his own checks for customer table overflow (assuming that the programming language implementation provides automatic checking of array subscripts, if not there is no telling what might happen).

Partial functions

A function is said to be *partial* if there are type correct arguments such that no function value exists. Otherwise the function is said to be *total*. An application of a function is said to be *well-defined* if there is a function value for the given arguments, otherwise it is said to be *ill-defined*. An expression containing free variables is considered well-defined if and only if the outermost function application is well-defined for all possible type correct values of these variables.

The question now is what will happen as the result of trying to evaluate an ill-defined function application. With our constructive approach to function definition there is an easy answer to that question: *the evaluation does not terminate.* Thus, we may take non-termination as the operational equivalent of mathematical ill-definedness. Notice that if an ill-defined expression must be evaluated as part of the computation of a function value the former will not terminate, which means that the latter also becomes ill-defined.

EXAMPLE 4.3

The following is a definition of integer division on natural numbers (i.e. non-negative integers):

$$x/y \quad \triangleq \quad \textbf{if } x < y \textbf{ then } 0 \textbf{ else } ((x - y)/y) + 1 \textbf{ fi} \quad \text{(for } x, y : Nat)$$

The definition is *recursive* since the function being defined occurs within the right hand side. An evaluation algorithm based on this definition may nevertheless terminate, provided $y \neq 0$, because the numerator decreases with successive recursive applications, whereas the denominator remains unchanged, so $x < y$ must occur eventually. In the case of $y = 0$, however, the right hand side reduces to x/y, which means that any evaluation algorithm will cycle endlessly. Thus, the divide function is partial: it is well-defined if and only if the denominator is non-zero.

A natural number quotient is characterized by the facts that when multiplied by the denominator the result is equal to or less than the numerator, and the difference is strictly less than the latter, provided the latter is non-zero:

$$y \neq 0 \Rightarrow 0 \leq x - (x/y) * y < y$$

We prove that the function as defined has this property.

Case $x < y$: Then the result is 0 and the property follows.

Case $x \geq y$: Then the result is $((x - y)/y) + 1$, and we must prove $y \neq 0 \Rightarrow 0 \leq x - (((x-y)/y) + 1) * y < y$. However, since $0 \leq x - y < x$, we may assume inductively that the recursive application satisfies the desired property: $y \neq 0 \Rightarrow 0 \leq x - y - ((x-y)/y) * y < y$, which is equivalent to our proof obligation by properties of the operations $+, -,$ and $*$.

◻

Exercise

4.6 The above function does not correspond to ordinary division if we extend it to the domain of, possibly negative, integer arguments. Discuss the properties of the extended function.

Fortunately, the fact that ill-definedness leads to non-termination (for an idealized machine) means that the AID convention is automatically respected, at least in the sense that normal termination with a spurious result is prevented. However, an infinite computation producing no results is not very useful and provides little feedback to the programmer. (How long do we have to wait for results before guessing that our program is stuck somewhere? Shall we ever be certain?) If a reasonably simple sufficient condition for ill-definedness is known, it is more efficient and more informative to test for it in the program and cause immediate abortion with an appropriate error message when it holds. There is no difference between these two kinds of abnormal behaviour with respect to Hoare logic, since the postcondition **f** will be provable in both cases. We therefore modify our operational definition of ill-definedness as follows:

- *An expression is considered ill-defined if and only if its evaluation leads to abnormal program behaviour, i.e. abortion or non-termination.*

We also introduce the special expression $\perp$, pronounced "error" or "bottom", which by definition is type correct everywhere and mathematically ill-defined in all program states. Its evaluation leads to immediate program abortion. In example 4.4 below, the expression has been augmented by an "error message" to be reported back to the user in case of abortion at this point. This has no significance for the program logic.

EXAMPLE 4.4
Since immediate abortion is preferable to infinite computation, the following definition of natural number division is better than that of example 4.3. It has exactly the same properties with respect to well-definedness:

$$x/y \quad \triangleq \quad \textbf{if } y{=}0 \textbf{ then } \perp \text{ "zero division"}$$
$$\textbf{else if } x{<}y \textbf{ then } 0 \textbf{ else } ((x-y)/y){+}1 \textbf{ fi} \quad (\text{for } x,y : Nat)$$

Notice that this definition is "the same" under partial correctness as that in example 4.3, although its actual behaviour is quite different for zero denominator. Both behave abnormally in that case.

$\square$

Definedness conditions
In this subsection we shall show how definedness conditions may be formalized. Let e denote an arbitrary expression. Then d_e denotes the condition that e is well-defined. The well-definedness of e will depend on some or all of the variables free in e, $\mathcal{V}[d_e] \subseteq \mathcal{V}[e]$, and on properties of the functions occurring in e. d_e is not in general constructively defined, see below, and for that reason the notation should not be included in the programming language PL. We also regard it as a meta-expression outside the formula language FL, which may or may not denote a known formula. We may, however, assume that any definedness condition is itself *well-defined* whether known or not, $d_{d_e} = \textbf{t}$. Example: $d_{x/y}$ is known to stand for the expression $y \neq 0$.

The well-definedness condition of an expression e can be defined by induction on the structure of e, provided that definedness conditions are known for the constituent function applications.

Certain constants (so-called generators, see section 5.1) are well-defined by definition:

$$d_c \triangleq \mathbf{t} \qquad (c \text{ a constant generator})$$

Variables are ordinarily considered well-defined, whether free or bound:

$$d_x \triangleq \mathbf{t} \qquad (x \text{ a simple variable})$$

This is in agreement with the principle that formulas occurring in a formal proof should be well-defined, and in particular that variables are only instantiated as well-defined expressions, cf. section 2.2.8. An exception to this rule is given in section 5.2. Cf. also section 4.4.4.

The expression $\perp$ is ill-defined by definition:

$$d_\perp \triangleq \mathbf{f}$$

The well-definedness condition of a function application depends on the properties of the function, as well as on the well-definedness of the arguments. An application of a total function is well-defined for arbitrary well-defined (and type correct) arguments:

$$d_{e_1} \wedge d_{e_2} \wedge \cdots \wedge d_{e_n} \Rightarrow d_{f(e_1, e_2, \dots, e_n)} \qquad \text{(totality)}$$

A function f is said to be *strict in its i'th argument* if an application of f can only be well-defined if that argument is well-defined:

$$d_{f(e_1, e_2, \dots, e_n)} \Rightarrow d_{e_i} \qquad \text{(strictness in } i\text{'th argument, } 1 \le i \le n)$$

(Here and in the following $e_1, e_2, \dots, e_n$ are meta-variables which stand for expressions not necessarily well-defined.) A function is said to be *strict* if it is strict in all its arguments:

$$d_{f(e_1, e_2, \dots, e_n)} \Rightarrow d_{e_1} \wedge d_{e_2} \wedge \cdots \wedge d_{e_n} \qquad \text{(strictness)}$$

Thus, an application of a total and strict function is well-defined if and only if all arguments are well-defined. It follows from the operational representation of ill-definedness that strictness corresponds to implementing arguments as *parameters passed by value*. So-called lazy evaluation, however, as well as parameters passed by "name" in the old Algol sense, may be used to implement non-strictness. Most functions used in practice are strict.

For arbitrary function f let D_f be a total predicate over the same domain which expresses the definedness of f for well-defined type correct arguments. Thus, $D_f(x_1, \dots, x_n)$ is true if $f(x_1, \dots, x_n)$ is well-defined and otherwise false. D_f is called the *definedness predicate* of f.

It is not possible in general to determine the definedness predicate by constructive methods for arbitrary function f, say recursively defined. This is the notorious "halting problem" of algorithm theory, which has been proved unsolvable. However, for functions defined by so-called "terminating generator induction", TGI, as explained in section 5.2, definedness predicates may be derived constructively, as well as strictness properties.

For a strict function f the well-definedness condition of an application has the form

$$d_{f(e_1, e_2, \ldots, e_n)} \triangleq d_{e_1} \land d_{e_2} \land \cdots \land d_{e_n} \land D_f(e_1, e_2, \ldots, e_n)$$

EXAMPLE 4.5
The divide operator is a strict function, and since $D_{\widehat{/}}(x, y) = (y \neq 0)$, we get $d_{e_1/e_2} = (d_{e_1} \land d_{e_2} \land e_2 \neq 0)$.
□

It follows from section 2.2.8 that three of the standard logical operators should be non-strict in the following ways, and it is fairly obvious that the **if**-operator should be non-strict in the second and third arguments:

$$
\begin{array}{lll}
d_{e_1 \land e_2} & \triangleq & (d_{e_1} \land d_{e_2}) \lor (d_{e_1} \land \neg e_1) \lor (d_{e_2} \land \neg e_2) \\
d_{e_1 \lor e_2} & \triangleq & (d_{e_1} \land d_{e_2}) \lor (d_{e_1} \land e_1) \lor (d_{e_2} \land e_2) \\
d_{e_1 \Rightarrow e_2} & \triangleq & (d_{e_1} \land d_{e_2}) \lor (d_{e_1} \land \neg e_1) \lor (d_{e_2} \land e_2) \\
d_{\textbf{if } e_1 \textbf{ then } e_2 \textbf{ else } e_3 \textbf{ fi}} & \triangleq & (d_{e_1} \land \textbf{if } e_1 \textbf{ then } d_{e_2} \textbf{ else } d_{e_3} \textbf{ fi}) \lor \\
& & (d_{e_2} \land d_{e_3} \land e_2 = e_3)
\end{array}
$$

In the special case where all arguments of the **if**-operator are Boolean we choose to make it non-strict in the first argument as well, so that **if** e_1 **then** e_2 **else** e_2 **fi** is equal to e_2, even if e_1 is ill-defined. Thereby the following tautologies hold strongly:

$$
\begin{array}{lcl}
e_1 \land e_2 & \Leftrightarrow & \textbf{if } e_1 \textbf{ then } e_2 \textbf{ else f fi} \\
e_1 \lor e_2 & \Leftrightarrow & \textbf{if } e_1 \textbf{ then t else } e_2 \textbf{ fi} \\
e_1 \Rightarrow e_2 & \Leftrightarrow & \textbf{if } e_1 \textbf{ then } e_2 \textbf{ else t fi}
\end{array}
$$

Exercise

4.7 Use the definitions given above to show that all four operators are total functions. Show also that $d_{e_1 \land e_2}$ and $d_{e_1 \lor e_2}$ are well-defined expressions, given that d_{e_1} and d_{e_2} are well-defined, and given that the negation operator is total.

Non-constant functions which are non-strict in all arguments are not easy to implement efficiently by traditional means. Thus, in programming language implementations Boolean operators are usually strict in the leftmost argument. Then, if the leftmost argument is ill-defined evaluation leads to abnormal behaviour even if the expression as a whole is well-defined. However, if the operator behaves as the abstract one whenever the leftmost argument is well-defined, it is an *approximation* to the abstract one, see the following subsection.

Definedness conditions for quantified formulas may be derived in analogy with those for conjunction and disjunction:

$$d_{\forall x \bullet P} \triangleq (\forall x \bullet d_P) \vee \exists x \bullet d_P \wedge \neg P$$
$$d_{\exists x \bullet P} \triangleq (\forall x \bullet d_P) \vee \exists x \bullet d_P \wedge P$$

It is useful to distinguish between two forms of equality. The ordinary, implemented equals operator, $=$, is *strict*, i.e. meaningful only for well-defined arguments. We also define a "strong" equality operator, $==$, non-strict in both arguments. Its value is **t** if both arguments are well-defined and equal, or if both are ill-defined, otherwise the value is **f**. It is not implementable in its full generality as a function of its arguments (why not?); it can, however, be defined explicitly in terms of well-definedness conditions and strict equality:

$$e_1 == e_2 \triangleq d_{e_1} = d_{e_2} \wedge (d_{e_1} \Rightarrow e_1 = e_2)$$

It follows that $d_{e_1 == e_2}$ is equal to **t**. The strong equality will be used for the purpose of formal function definition (cf. section 5.2).

Exercise

4.8 Show that $d_e = \exists x \bullet x == e$ for any expression e and variable $x \notin \mathcal{V}[e]$.

Function approximation

The limitations of real computers often make it necessary to represent mathematically defined "abstract" functions by "concrete" implementations, which are functions behaving as the abstract ones only over part of their domains. Typically, data structures of potentially unlimited volume have to be embedded in memory structures of fixed sizes. Then operations that would require more than the available memory space for their correct completion must necessarily cause program behaviour which is different from that of an ideal machine.

Examples: the result of an arithmetic operation may be a number exceeding hardware capacity; a growing table may become too large to fit into an array of user defined size. During the evaluation of a recursive function application the volume of bookkeeping information and intermediate results typically increases with the recursion depth. If the available memory space is not sufficiently large the evaluation must fail in some way or other. Many implementation dependent capacity constraints, such as upper limits on the depth of recursion, are hard to specify in advance.

The AID convention should be a guiding principle with function implementation: never terminate normally except with correct results. In other words, the only way in which an implementation should be allowed to differ from the abstract function is by leading to *less well-defined applications*.

Let e and e' be expressions of the same type. e' is said to *approximate* e, $e' \sqsubseteq e$, if:

$$d_{e'} \Rightarrow d_e \wedge e' = e \qquad \text{(for arbitrary values of free variables)}$$

Thus, $e \sqsubseteq e$ and $\perp \sqsubseteq e$ hold for any expression e.

Now let f and f' be functions with the same domain and codomain. f' is said to be an approximation to f if any application of f' approximates the corresponding application of f:

- $f'(e_1, e_2, \ldots, e_n) \sqsubseteq f(e_1, e_2, \ldots, e_n)$, for arbitrary (type correct) argument expressions, not necessarily well-defined.

More specifically, f' is an approximation to f if:

- f' is less or equally defined, $D_{f'} \subseteq D_f$,
- f' is more or equally strict, $\neg d_{e_i} \wedge d_{f'(e_1, \ldots, e_n)} \Rightarrow d_{f(e_1, \ldots, e_n)}$, $i = 1, \ldots, n$, and
- well-defined applications of f and f' are equal for strongly equal arguments, $d_{f'(e_1, e_2, \ldots, e_n)} \Rightarrow f'(e_1, e_2, \ldots, e_n) = f(e_1, e_2, \ldots, e_n)$.

In general we must permit an approximating function f' to have arguments and/or function value of types different from those of f, such that the corresponding values are "concrete representations" of those of f. Thus, the definition of expression approximation, $e' \sqsubseteq e$, should be generalized to allow the value of e' to be a representation of that of e. Also the definition of function approximation should be modified accordingly. See section 5.9 for a discussion of these points. Here we only assume that such value representations are, in a suitable sense, *exact*. Operations on infinite structures such as real numbers are outside the scope of this book; we do not consider approximate value representation and associated "rounding" errors.

Let e and e' be variable-free expressions such that the latter is obtained from e by replacing functions by valid approximations (in a systematic way respecting the representation of argument values). Then, for practical purposes, we may conclude that $e' \sqsubseteq e$ holds. If both expressions are well-defined this follows from the exact representation assumption. In general, however, we have to assume that all occurring functions are *monotonic* with respect to well-definedness:

$$e' \sqsubseteq e \Rightarrow f(\ldots, e', \ldots) \sqsubseteq f(\ldots, e, \ldots) \qquad \text{(definedness monotonicity)}$$

Fortunately this is true for any implementable function. Indeed, if $f(\ldots, \perp, \ldots)$ is not strongly equal to $f(\ldots, e, \ldots)$, then the result depends on that particular argument, which means that the argument expression must be evaluated in order to obtain the result. But then the former application of f is necessarily ill-defined.

Exercise

4.9 Show that strong equality is not a monotonic function (with respect to approximation).

A function implementation developed according to the AID principle only terminates normally with correct results. It is thus an approximation to the given one in the sense defined. Assume now that the AID principle has been respected at all levels of abstraction in the development of an abstract program S, including the programming language implementation on a given computer. Then it follows from the the discussion above that *the actual program running on the computer is an approximation to S,* if both are seen as functions from input to output. This in turn implies that the rule IMPL identified at the beginning of the present chapter is indeed valid, and that the precondition on the input can be stated in abstract terms.

If the AID convention is not respected by a function implementation, it is necessary to restrict its area of safe application by identifying a sufficiently strong precondition, and one is obliged to prove that precondition for every actual application of the function, which may be impractical. It must also be assumed that a sufficient precondition can be found which is not prohibitively strong. This may be difficult in practice, and sometimes useful restrictions may not be expressible at all at the desired level of abstraction.

To demonstrate the last point, consider a data base implemented by recording the sequence of transactions applied to it: additions, deletions, etc. Then the use of memory space is not related to the abstract contents of the data base, but to the number of transactions, which is something one would want to abstract away.

Thus, the principle of abstraction in general breaks down unless the AID convention is followed at all lower levels. For instance, if a program execution could terminate normally in spite of violating hardware constraints, the results would surely be unpredictable in terms of the programming language. Thus the pertinent details of the language implementation could not be ignored when reasoning about the program. Notice that the same would be true, even if the AID convention is obeyed consistently, if one insists on providing sufficient conditions for normal termination, i.e. for total correctness reasoning about running programs.

Given that the AID convention is followed consistently, it may still be useful to identify preconditions for program components which are sufficient to ensure that specific function approximations do not cause abortion. Then one may be able to prove for a given program that abnormal behaviour will not occur for these reasons.

It would appear from the above discussion that implemented functions are generally less defined than the abstract ones, due to capacity constraints, but that is not always the case. Array subscripting is a counter example, given that the array fits into the available memory. The abstract operation is a partial function, ill-defined for subscripts out of bounds:

$$d_{A[i]} \triangleq d_i \wedge i \in A.ix$$

where $A.ix$ is the set of legal subscripts for the (one-dimensional) array A, usually an integer interval. For efficiency reasons, however, implementation is likely to be by a hardware mechanism well-defined over the entire memory space. So, unless the hardware provides checks for subscript arguments, software checks should be provided by the programming language implementation. In some programs the incurred run time overhead may be unacceptable, and therefore many language implementations provide an option for inhibiting subscript checking. However, the omission of such checks constitutes a violation of the AID convention, and thus in order to retain program reliability additional proofs about subscript values may be required.

Arithmetic operations on integers are normally implemented by hardware operations on digit strings of fixed size. This means that certain total functions such as integer addition and multiplication are not implemented exactly. According to the AID convention they should be represented by approximations in the above strict sense, i.e. by *partial* functions. One must hope that the hardware does have built-in checks for arithmetic overflow, otherwise it may sometimes be difficult to combine good efficiency with high program reliability.

In summary: if it is impossible or impractical to implement a given function f, then, according to the AID convention, it should be represented by an approximating function, $f' \sqsubseteq f$. As a side issue the AID convention also implies that explicit abortion is preferable to entering an infinite computation.

Hoare sentences

Hoare Logic is expressed in terms of Hoare sentence schemas, $\vdash \{P\}S\{Q\}$, where P or Q, or both, sometimes stand for arbitrary formulas, not necessarily well-defined. It turns out, however, that there are ways of interpreting the pre- and postconditions so that *the meaning of the Hoare sentence as a whole is always well-defined.* We first refine the model (4.1) of Hoare sentences so that it is never ill-defined:

$$(\forall \sigma_1, \sigma_2 \bullet P_{\sigma_1}^x \wedge \sigma_1 S \sigma_2 \Rightarrow Q_{\sigma_2}^x) == \mathbf{t}$$

Fortunately, the binary relation on states corresponding to a program statement S can always be taken as well-defined. For instance, if an execution of S from the initial state σ_1 leads to the evaluation of an ill-defined expression, then, as we have seen, the execution does not terminate normally, which means that $\sigma_1 S \sigma_2$ is false (i.e. well-defined) for all states σ_2. Therefore, in order to determine the well-definedness of the left hand side of the model, we only have to consider the definedness of P and Q.

Consider first the case where the precondition is ill-defined: $\{\bot\}S\{Q\}$, Q well-defined. The left hand side of the model, $\forall \sigma_1, \sigma_2 \bullet \bot \wedge \sigma_1 S \sigma_2 \Rightarrow Q_{\sigma_1}^x$, is well-defined if and only if $\forall \sigma_1, \sigma_2 \bullet \sigma_1 S \sigma_2 \Rightarrow Q_{\sigma_1}^x$, which is the same as: $(\forall \sigma_1, \sigma_2 \bullet \mathbf{t} \wedge \sigma_1 S \sigma_2 \Rightarrow Q_{\sigma_1}^x) == \mathbf{t}$. The latter is equivalent to the given model, and is also the model of the sentence $\{\mathbf{t}\}S\{Q\}$. Thus, the two sentences are equivalent, which shows that the precondition of a Hoare sentence must be regarded as true if ill-defined. This is called *weak interpretation*.

Consider next the sentence $\{P\}S\{\bot\}$, where P is well-defined. Now the left hand side of the model is well-defined if and only if $\forall \sigma_1, \sigma_2 \bullet \neg(P_{\sigma_1}^x \wedge \sigma_1 S \sigma_2)$, which is the same as: $(\forall \sigma_1, \sigma_2 \bullet P_{\sigma_1}^x \wedge \sigma_1 S \sigma_2 \Rightarrow \mathbf{f}) == \mathbf{t}$. The latter is the model of $\{P\}S\{\mathbf{f}\}$, and again the two models are equivalent, which shows that postconditions must be subjected to *strong interpretation*, i.e. be taken as false if ill-defined.

These interpretations of the pre- and postconditions are expressed by the following general, program independent proof rule:

$$\text{INTPR}: \quad \frac{\vdash \{P\}S\{Q\}}{\vdash \{d_P \Rightarrow P\}\, S\, \{d_Q \wedge Q\}}$$

Notice that $d_P \Rightarrow P$ is $\mathbf{t}$ whenever P is ill-defined, and that $d_Q \wedge Q$ is $\mathbf{f}$ whenever Q is ill-defined. Thus, any Hoare sentence may be strengthened by weakening the precondition and strengthening the postcondition by the corresponding definedness conditions.

The rule actually works both ways, cf. exercise 4.11 below:

$$\text{RPTNI}: \quad \frac{\vdash \{d_P \Rightarrow P\}\, S\, \{d_Q \wedge Q\}}{\vdash \{P\}S\{Q\}}$$

The different interpretations of pre- and postconditions explain why the axioms CONS (section 4.2.1) and SKIP (section 4.3.1) require the assertion P to be well-defined. Notice that $\{\bot\}\mathbf{skip}\{\bot\}$ would imply $\{\mathbf{t}\}\mathbf{skip}\{\mathbf{f}\}$ by INTPR, which is incorrect since **skip** terminates normally.

The above results pertain to the underlying logic explained in section 2.2 and may be applied to arbitrary implications. Thus, an implication $P \Rightarrow Q$ is implicitly interpreted as $(d_P \Rightarrow P) \Rightarrow (d_Q \wedge Q)$. Thus, for instance $P \Rightarrow P$ should be provable only if the weak and strong interpretations of P are equivalent, which is the case if and only if P is well-defined.

Exercises

4.10 It is desired that $\vdash P \Rightarrow Q$ should be formally provable if and only if the formula $P \Rightarrow Q$ is well-defined and true, i.e. if and only if $P \Rightarrow Q == \mathbf{t}$. Show that this strong equality is equivalent to $(d_P \Rightarrow P) \Rightarrow (d_Q \wedge Q)$ (which is a well-defined expression).

4.11 Show that the premise and the conclusion of INTPR have the same refined models.

4.3.3   Assignment

Consider the statement $x := e$, where x is a simple program variable and e is an expression of the same type as that of x. We define

$$\mathcal{V}[x := e] \triangleq \mathcal{V}[e] \cup \{x\}, \qquad \mathcal{W}[x := e] \triangleq \{x\}$$

It follows from CONS that predicates not containing x free are insensitive to any assignment to x:

$$\vdash \{P\}x := e\{P\} \qquad \text{for } x \notin \mathcal{V}[P] \text{ and } P \text{ well-defined} \tag{4.2}$$

Let P be an arbitrary well-defined state predicate and α a new variable. From (4.2) we may then conclude

$$\vdash \{P_\alpha^x\}x := e\{P_\alpha^x\} \tag{4.3}$$

since x is clearly not free in P_α^x, whatever formula P may be. Now let α denote the value assigned to x. Then $\alpha = x$ holds after the assignment, so that the postcondition P_α^x means the same as P. But the assigned value is obtained by evaluating the expression e *prior to* the assignment, thus $\alpha = e$ holds in the precondition. The resulting conclusion is a general axiom schema for assignment to a simple variable:

$$\text{AS}: \quad \vdash \{P_e^x\}x := e\{P\} \quad \text{for } P \text{ well-defined}$$

Notice that this axiom schema is sound even for ill-defined expression e. This is because the assignment statement does not in that case terminate normally, which means that the Hoare sentence holds trivially.

An axiom schema of Hoare logic is conducive to mechanical proof if it specifies how either the precondition or the postcondition may be constructed, given the other condition and the program statement. In particular, it is said to be *left constructive* if:

- the postcondition is arbitrary, i.e. a single meta-variable subject to no side condition (other than, possibly, well-definedness), and the precondition is specified as a syntactic function of the postcondition and constituents of the program statement.

Thus, the axiom schema AS is left constructive: the postcondition is arbitrary and the precondition is obtained from it by performing a specified textual substitution. We may notice that the expression occurring as the right hand side of an assignment statement will in general appear in the precondition also. This shows that the set of evaluatable expressions EE of the programming language should also be part of the formula language FL, and with similar semantics.

If the right hand side e of the assignment statement is an expression well-defined in all states, we may assume that an ideal computer will perform the evaluation and the subsequent assignment in a finite time, always terminating normally. In that case the schema (4.3) is obviously left maximal, and so is AS, the precondition thus being necessary as well as sufficient.

The following specialized assignment axioms, with one exception (RCAS), are all left constructive, and the postcondition is tacitly assumed to be well-defined.

EXAMPLE 4.6
The following are axioms which are instances of the schema AS,

$\vdash \{0=0 \wedge y<z\}x := 0\{x=0 \wedge y<z\}$

$\vdash \{y-(x+1) < z\}x := x + 1\{y-x < z\}$

where the preconditions simplify to $y<z$ and $y-x \leq z$, respectively.

□

Exercises

4.12 Prove $\{x = a\} \; q := 0 \; \{q*y+x = a\}$

4.13 Prove $\{q*y+x = a\} \; x := x - y \; \{q*y+x+y = a\}$

4.14 Prove $\{q*y+x+y = a\} \; q := q+1 \; \{q*y+x = a\}$

The simplicity of AS is appealing but it is based on the assumption that any (simple) assignment statement can only affect the variable of the left hand side, or in other words that it is semantically correct to define $\mathcal{W}[x:=e]$ as the singleton set $\{x\}$. With traditional programming languages this does not always hold, and it is necessary in general to require that:

1. expressions are *free of side effects*, and
2. variables are *alias free* or, more generally, syntactically distinct simple variables represent *disjoint data structures*.

These requirements are not usually enforced by the programming language, and it will be up to the user to program in such a way that they are satisfied. This is normally *good programming practice* because any violation is likely to lead to programs which are difficult to reason about. Restriction 1 is an instance of the NSE convention already introduced in section 4.3.2. Aliasing may occur through the use of pointer variables and, in procedures, as a result of the parameter mechanism. We generally assume that restriction 2 is respected; however, in section 6.4 we briefly consider consequences for the program logic of violating it by unrestricted use of pointers. (It is sometimes necessary to accept resulting aliasing for reasons of program efficiency.)

If the right hand side of an assignment statement is not always well-defined, the same may be true for the precondition of the corresponding axiom AS. Fortunately this will not affect the soundness of the formal logic, but remember that nothing can be proved within our logic about any expression when it is not well-defined (not even the fact that it is ill-defined!). This means that only program properties independent of the results of evaluating ill-defined expressions, if any, can be proved.

Since an assignment statement will not terminate normally if the right hand side is ill-defined, the axiom (4.3) is not left maximal, and then neither is AS. Indeed, it ought to be possible in that case to disprove normal termination. Assuming that the assignment of a well-defined value to a simple variable cannot go wrong, we may define

$$t_{x:=e} \quad \triangleq \quad d_e \tag{4.4}$$

(with respect to an idealized computer). Then we can use the TERM axiom schema and rule DDJ in order to provide a stronger axiom schema for assignment:

$$\text{LMAS}: \quad \vdash \{d_e \Rightarrow P_e^x\}x := e\{P\} \quad \text{for } P \text{ well-defined}$$

The schema is left maximal (again with respect to an idealized machine). It is also left constructive, provided that the condition d_e can be derived from e.

We are now able to prove, for instance, $\{y = 0\}z := x/y\{\mathbf{f}\}$ by left construction. LMAS gives the precondition $d_{x/y} \Rightarrow \mathbf{f}$, which simplifies to $\neg d_{x/y}$, which is known to stand for $y = 0$. Notice that left construction with AS only gives the trivial precondition $\mathbf{f}$.

We may if we wish *strengthen* the precondition of AS by conjoining the normal termination condition:

$$\text{TCAS}: \quad \vdash \{d_e \wedge P_e^x\}x := e\{P\} \quad \text{for } P \text{ well-defined}$$

The resulting precondition corresponds to the requirement of *total correctness*, since it includes a guarantee that the statement will terminate normally if executed by an idealized machine. Even if executed by a real machine there is a guarantee that the right hand side is well-defined as it stands, i.e. at the current level of abstraction, so any abnormal behaviour would have to be for other reasons.

Notice that the occurrences of the expression e in the preconditions of LMAS and TCAS need only be considered in the context of being well-defined.

Right construction

By letting α of (4.3) denote the value of x prior to the assignment, the precondition becomes P, i.e. an arbitrary well-defined formula. But then we have in general no explicit expression for α in the postcondition, in terms of the current program variables, because the old value of x was lost as a result of the assignment operation. We may, however, claim that x had a value α such that P was true and e was well-defined and evaluated to the current value of x:

$$\text{RCAS}: \quad \{P\}x := e\{\exists \alpha \bullet P_\alpha^x \wedge d_{e_\alpha^x} \wedge x = e_\alpha^x\}$$
$$\text{for } \alpha \notin \mathcal{V}[P, e, x] \text{ and } P \text{ well-defined}$$

RCAS is right constructive provided that the predicate d_e is known (any weaker condition may be used instead, including the empty one). It is quite clumsy, however, compared to AS and LMAS. This accounts for the fact that left construction is generally a more practical strategy for analysis than right construction. Another important advantage of analysis by left construction is that it offers an opportunity to introduce local guards against specific kinds of erroneous behaviour, as in TCAS.

However, right construction is useful sometimes, and in order to demonstrate that our formalisms hang together we show the equivalence of RCAS and LMAS. We assume for the proofs that $\alpha \notin \mathcal{V}[P] \cup \mathcal{V}[e] \cup \{x\}$.

Proof of RCAS given LMAS

1. $\vdash \{d_e \Rightarrow \exists\alpha \bullet P_\alpha^x \wedge d_{e_\alpha^x} \wedge e = e_\alpha^x\} \; x := e \; \{\exists\alpha \bullet P_\alpha^x \wedge d_{e_\alpha^x} \wedge x = e_\alpha^x\}$
   $\qquad\qquad\qquad\qquad\qquad\qquad\qquad\qquad\qquad\qquad$ (LMAS, $\alpha \notin \mathcal{V}[e] \cup \{x\}$)
2. $\vdash P \Rightarrow (d_e \Rightarrow \exists\alpha \bullet P_\alpha^x \wedge d_{e_\alpha^x} \wedge e = e_\alpha^x)$ $\qquad$ (math.)
3. $\vdash \{P\} \; x := e \; \{\exists\alpha \bullet P_\alpha^x \wedge d_{e_\alpha^x} \wedge x = e_\alpha^x\}$ $\qquad$ (2, 1, CQL)

Since α is not the same variable as x there is exactly one free occurrence of x in the postcondition of 1. And since $\alpha \notin \mathcal{V}[e]$ no name conflict with α occurs in the substitution of e for x. To prove line 2 take x for α (using rule $\exists$I backwards).

∎

Proof of LMAS given RCAS

1. $\vdash \{d_e \Rightarrow P_e^x\} \; x := e \; \{\exists\alpha \bullet (d_e \Rightarrow P_e^x)_\alpha^x \wedge d_{e_\alpha^x} \wedge x = e_\alpha^x\}$ (RCAS, $\alpha \notin \mathcal{V}[P]$)
2. $\vdash (\exists\alpha \bullet (d_e \Rightarrow P_e^x)_\alpha^x \wedge d_{e_\alpha^x} \wedge x = e_\alpha^x) \Rightarrow P$ $\qquad$ (math.)
3. $\vdash \{d_e \Rightarrow P_e^x\} \; x := e \; \{P\}$ $\qquad$ (1, 2, CQR)

Rules T$\Rightarrow$, A$\exists$ ($\alpha \notin \mathcal{V}[P]$!), and A$\wedge$ applied to line 2 show that we have to prove P assuming $(d_e \Rightarrow P_e^x)_\alpha^x$, $x = e_\alpha^x$, and $d_{e_\alpha^x}$. But lemma (2.5) p. 14 implies that $(d_e \Rightarrow P_e^x)_\alpha^x$ is the same as $d_{e_\alpha^x} \Rightarrow P_{e_\alpha^x}^x$, which gives P by the other two assumptions.

∎

Exercise

4.15 Prove the following Hoare sentences using AS:
   1. $\{x = \alpha\}x := e\{x = e_\alpha^x\}$, where α is a variable other than x.
   2. $\{P\}x := f(x)\{P_{f^{-1}(x)}^x\}$, where f is a one-to-one function.

Assignment to subscripted variable

Consider an assignment statement of the form $A[i] := e$, where A is an array. As before, the notation $A.ix$ denotes the index set of A. Let i and j be expressions whose values are legal indices, $i, j \in A.ix$.

Unfortunately, subscripted variables are not alias free: $A[i]$ and $A[j]$ denote the same variable if i and j have the same value. It follows that none of the assignment axiom schemas above can be applied. In fact we have to reinterpret any assignment to a subscripted variable as an assignment to the whole array as such. Fortunately, an array A can be considered a "simple variable" for our purpose; it has a single value which is a *sequence* of element type values. It is therefore reasonable to define

$$\mathcal{V}[A[i]] \triangleq \{A\} \cup \mathcal{V}[i]$$
$$\mathcal{V}[A[i] := e] \triangleq \{A\} \cup \mathcal{V}[i] \cup \mathcal{V}[e]$$
$$\mathcal{W}[A[i] := e] \triangleq \{A\}$$

We introduce the following notation for the value of A (i.e. the sequence) after the above assignment:

$A[i \mapsto e]$ (read: A, but at i take e)
  where $\mathcal{V}[A[i \mapsto e]] \triangleq \{A\} \cup \mathcal{V}[i] \cup \mathcal{V}[e]$

The index set of $A[i \mapsto e]$ is that of A, and for the notation to be well-defined the constituent expressions i and e must be well-defined and the former must evaluate to an index legal for A:

$$d_{A[i \mapsto e]} \triangleq d_i \wedge d_e \wedge i \in A.ix$$

This notation will be part of our formula language, but not of the programming language. It has the following property (see also lemma S9 of section 5.8.8):

AMOD : $\vdash A[x \mapsto y][z] \;=\; \textbf{if } z = x \textbf{ then } y \textbf{ else } A[z] \textbf{ fi}, \quad$ for $x, z \in A.ix$

Reinterpretation of $A[i] := e$ as $A := A[i \mapsto e]$ gives the following axiom schema analogous to AS:

SSAS : $\vdash \{P^A_{A[i \mapsto e]}\} A[i] := e \{P\}$

On the strength of the AID convention we may define

$$t_{A[i] := e} \triangleq d_{A[i \mapsto e]}$$

which may be used to formulate a left maximal version of SSAS by weakening the precondition accordingly. If dynamic subscript checking is omitted the validity of the subscript i should be proved, and thus the weakest precondition for postcondition P will be $d_i \wedge d_e \Rightarrow i \in A.ix \wedge P^A_{A[i \mapsto e]}$, assuming that no subscripting occurs in either i or e.

EXAMPLE 4.7

The following axiom is an instance of SSAS:

$$\vdash \{j \in A.ix \wedge A[i \to 0][j] \neq 0\} \ A[i] := 0 \ \{j \in A.ix \wedge A[j] \neq 0\}$$

(We assume that the shape of an array is fixed at declaration time. Therefore the A of $A.ix$ should be ignored by the substitution algorithm.) The second conjunct of the precondition reduces to

$$\textbf{if } j = i \textbf{ then } 0 \textbf{ else } A[j] \textbf{ fi } \neq 0$$

which is equivalent to $j \neq i \wedge A[j] \neq 0$.

Notice that we may reason as if i were known to be a legal subscript for A; otherwise the assignment statement would by definition abort, in which case any Hoare sentence will do.

$\square$

Exercise

4.16 Prove $\{j = A[j] \neq 1 \Rightarrow A[1] = 1\} \ A[A[j]] := 1 \ \{A[A[j]] = 1\}$, assuming that j and $A[j]$ are legal indices for A. Hints: The precondition specified by SSAS is $A'[A'[j]] = 1$, where $A' = A[A[j] \mapsto 1]$. It helps to consider the cases $A[j] = j$ and $A[j] \neq j$ separately.

Simultaneous assignments

We assume that our programming language can perform simultaneous assignments. The following axiom schema is a natural generalization of AS:

$$\text{STAS}: \quad \vdash \{P^{x_1, x_2, \ldots, x_n}_{e_1, e_2, \ldots, e_k}\} \ x_1, x_2, \ldots, x_n := e_1, e_2, \ldots, e_n \ \{P\}$$

$$\text{for distinct simple variables } x_1, x_2, \ldots, x_n$$

If a left hand variable is subscripted, that particular assignment must be reinterpreted as above, and if there are several variables belonging to the same array, all these assignments must be regarded as a single assignment to the array. So, for instance, assignment to two variables in the same array has the following axiom schema:

$$\text{S2AS}: \quad \vdash \{i_1 \neq i_2 \wedge P^A_{A[i_1 \mapsto e_1][i_2 \mapsto e_2]}\} \ A[i_1], A[i_2] := e_1, e_2 \ \{P\}$$

We insist here also that the left hand variables should be distinct, and since there may be no run time check on distinctness we have to prove it by strengthening the precondition correspondingly.

The notation of simultaneous assignments is useful for expressing the net effect of programs, ignoring all intermediate internal states, cf. section 4.7. Notice that the identity of variables subject to change in a procedure may be (re-)defined through parameter substitution. If aliasing occurs the consequences for the net result are in general non-trivial, so we had better insist that the left hand variables of a multiple assignment be distinct (syntactically as well as semantically).

We introduce a notation for swapping the values of two variables, although it may be defined as a special case of simultaneous assignments:

$$x :=: y \quad \triangleq \quad x, y := y, x$$

In this particular case we do not have to insist on variable distinctness, so the rule for subscripted variable swap can be simplified compared to S2AS:

$$\text{SSW}: \quad \vdash \{P^A_{A[i \to A[j]][j \to A[i]]}\}\ A[i] :=: A[j]\ \{P\}$$

The swap operation terminates normally if both subscripts are well-defined and legal:

$$t_{A[i]:=:A[j]} \quad \triangleq \quad d_i \wedge i \in A.ix \wedge d_j \wedge j \in A.ix$$

If they are also equal, we may conclude that the operation is equivalent to **skip**.

Symbolic execution

The left and right constructive Hoare axiom schemas for assignment represent symbolic computation on predicates. As an alternative it may sometimes be useful to carry out symbolic computation (forwards) on the values of program variables. The following specialized axiom schema explains how. The meta-variable α represents the current symbolic value of the left hand variable. It stands for an expression not containing x (possibly variable-free):

$$\text{ASVC}: \quad \vdash \{x = \alpha\}\ x := e\ \{(d_e)^x_\alpha \wedge x = e^x_\alpha\} \quad \text{for}\ x \notin \mathcal{V}[\alpha]$$

If x represents the entire state space, the postcondition of ASVC is clearly the strongest possible for the given precondition. If not, we may strengthen the sentence by conjoining assertions about the values of other program variables, using the rules CONST and CCJ.

EXAMPLE 4.8
The Hoare sentence $\{x = a \wedge y = b\}\ x := x + y\ \{x = a + b \wedge y = b\}$ follows from ASVC, CONST, and CCJ (or directly from AS after simplification of the constructed precondition!).
□

The principle of symbolic value computation may be generalized to *symbolic execution* of deterministic programs, where the state predicate at each program point identifies the values of program variables as well as a condition for arriving at that point. The latter results from definedness conditions and explicit tests encountered so far. It is sufficient to track the values of the output variables, say $x_1, x_2, \ldots, x_n$, of the program or program section under analysis. A general assignment axiom schema for symbolic program execution would therefore be as follows:

$$\text{ASPX}: \quad \vdash \{P \wedge x = \alpha\} \ x_k := e \ \{P \wedge (d_e)^x_\alpha \wedge x_k = e^x_\alpha \wedge \bigwedge_{i \neq k} x_i = \alpha_i\}$$

$$\text{for} \ \ 1 \leq k \leq n \ \ \text{and} \ \ \mathcal{V}[\alpha, P] \cap \{x\} = \emptyset,$$

$$\text{where } x \text{ stands for } x_1, \ldots, x_n \text{ and } \alpha \text{ stands for } \alpha_1, \ldots, \alpha_n$$

The symbolic values α_i as well as the condition P are either variable free, or are expressed in terms of variables which are unchanged by the program considered, possibly including auxiliary ones naming initial values of x_i's. Notice that none of $x_1, \ldots, x_n$ occur in the new symbolic value, e^x_α, nor in the definedness condition.

The technique of symbolic program execution may be useful if explicit definition of output variables is called for at the end of the program; however, Hoare logic as such is clearly more general since it caters for pre- and postconditions of arbitrary form. It is also better suited for partial correctness analysis.

4.4   Compound Statements

Under this heading we consider control structures for sequencing, branching, repetition, and exits, as well as a somewhat restricted form of **go to**. Rules for reasoning about the introduction and scoping of local variables are also discussed.

For each kind of compound, inference rules are introduced for deducing partial correctness properties of the compound, given partial correctness properties of the constituent statements. Necessary additional criteria for normal termination will be identified in each case. A typical inference rule will have the general form

$$\frac{\vdash \{P_1\}S_1\{Q_1\}; \ \ \vdash \{P_2\}S_2\{Q_2\}; \ \ldots; \ \ \vdash \{P_n\}S_n\{Q_n\}}{\vdash \{P\} \ \textbf{compound}[E, S_1, S_2, \ldots, S_n] \ \{Q\}} \quad n \geq 0$$

where **compound**$[E, S_1, S_2, \ldots, S_n]$ is a syntactic expression denoting some compound statement in which E is a list of zero or more constituent expressions, and the S's are the constituent statements. This implies that there will be a very close correspondence between the proof tree of a program verification, and the program itself seen as a tree of nested statements. Thus, the root of the proof is a sequent of the form $\vdash \{P\}S\{Q\}$, where S is the whole program, whereas proofs for constituent statements occur as subtrees. Here and there are subtrees in ordinary first order logic, typically proofs of verification conditions connected through the use of consequence rules (CQL, CQR of section 4.2).

As with predicate logic it is useful to provide rules for backward as well as forward proof construction. In the present context we prefer to use the terms "top down" (TD) and "bottom up" (BU) instead, since the words backward and forward are counter-intuitive in relation to the program text. It is rather the case where TD in the proof corresponds to "outside in" in the program and BU to "inside out". Notice that the word "top" refers to the *root* of a tree, because of the widespread tradition in computer science of drawing trees upside down.

In a TD rule the pre- and postconditions P, Q of the conclusion should be arbitrary, represented as simple meta-variables, and the rule should indicate by meta-expressions how the pre- and postconditions of the premises may be constructed from P, Q, and E. Thus a TD rule may be used to determine what must be proved for the constituent statements in order to conclude a desired result for the whole compound. A BU rule, on the other hand, must show what can be concluded about the compound from arbitrary Hoare sentences for the constituent statements. Thus, the P_i's and Q_i's of the premises should be simple meta-variables and the precondition and postcondition of the conclusion should be meta-expressions.

Left construction, LC, is a third important proof strategy: Starting with a given postcondition of a compound statement, one constructs the precondition by using left construction over the constituent statements. (This is easy, e.g. if the latter are assignment statements.) Thus, a left constructive inference rule should accept an arbitrary postcondition of the conclusion, represented by a simple meta-variable, and it should indicate by meta-expressions how the postconditions Q_i of the premises may be constructed. Assuming that each corresponding precondition, P_i, can somehow be found, perhaps by left construction over S_i using whatever rules are appropriate for that statement, the rule names the resulting precondition by a simple meta-variable, and finally a meta-expression indicates how the precondition of the conclusion can be constructed from all the formulas now given. It happens that the premises must be proved in a certain order, because the postcondition of one premise depends on the precondition found for another one.

An LC rule is said to be *left maximal* if it permits the construction of the weakest possible precondition of the compound for arbitrary postcondition and arbitrary constituents, assuming that P_i is weakest for Q_i in each premise.

Right construction is not in general a recommended proof strategy, cf. section 4.3.3. We therefore do not identify special RC rules.

If more than one strategy is used in the analysis of a program, the left and right consequence rules are often sufficient to bridge the gaps (but not always, cf. section 4.5). For instance, if we wish to prove $\{P\}S\{Q\}$, and $\{P'\}S\{Q\}$ can be shown by left construction, then CQL (backwards) shows that the implication $P \Rightarrow P'$ remains to be proved.

4.4.1   Sequencing

We use a semicolon or a state predicate enclosed in braces, called a *state assertion*, to separate statements which are to be executed in sequence:

$$\mathcal{V}[S_1; S_2] \triangleq \mathcal{V}[S_1] \cup \mathcal{V}[S_2] \qquad \text{and} \quad \mathcal{W}[S_1; S_2] \triangleq \mathcal{W}[S_1] \cup \mathcal{W}[S_2]$$
$$\mathcal{V}[S_1\{P\}S_2] \triangleq \mathcal{V}[S_1] \cup \mathcal{V}[P] \cup \mathcal{V}[S_2] \quad \text{and} \quad \mathcal{W}[S_1\{P\}S_2] \triangleq \mathcal{W}[S_1] \cup \mathcal{W}[S_2]$$

$$\text{SEQ}: \quad \frac{\vdash \{P\}S_1\{Q\}; \;\; \vdash \{Q\}S_2\{R\}}{\vdash \{P\}\; S_1; S_2 \; \{R\}}$$

The rule is both left and right constructive. Notice that the predicate Q occurs both as the postcondition of S_1 and as the precondition of S_2. Thereby SEQ expresses that S_1 will be executed before S_2 and that no change of state will take place in between; Q thus describes the intermediate state.

SEQ is left maximal for well-defined Q. Otherwise the two occurrences of Q in the premises are interpreted differently. However, since the actual postcondition of S_1, $d_Q \wedge Q$, implies the actual precondition of S_2, $d_Q \Rightarrow Q$, the rule is sound for arbitrary Q which satisfies both premises. In order to obtain left maximality by left construction it is sufficient to apply the interpretation rule INTPR to the second premise before using SEQ. This amounts to replacing Q in the first premise by $d_Q \Rightarrow Q$, which is well-defined.

If SEQ is used for left construction over a sequence of assignments, it would seem that the intermediate state predicate must be well-defined in order to prove the first premise by legally applying an assignment axiom. Fortunately, however, the following theorem shows that we need not worry about the definedness of the intermediate state assertions (if left maximality is not essential):

$$\text{SQAS}: \quad \vdash \{(R_e^y)_d^x\} \; x := d; \; y := e \; \{R\} \quad \text{for } R \text{ well-defined}$$

Proof
Using LMAS we obtain the intermediate result $d_e \Rightarrow R_e^y$, which is well-defined because R is. A second application of LMAS gives the precondition $d_d \Rightarrow (d_e \Rightarrow R_e^y)_d^x$, or $d_d \Rightarrow ((d_e)_d^x \Rightarrow R_{e_d^x,d}^{y,\,x})$, provided that x and y stand for distinct variables. (If the assignments are to the same variable, the substitution of d for x in R should be omitted in the last formula.) Since d is a well-defined expression, $(d_e)_d^x$ is the same as $d_{e_d^x}$ (otherwise the former might not have been well-defined, whereas the latter is). So the constructed precondition is the same as $d_d \wedge d_{e_d^x} \Rightarrow R_{e_d^x,d}^{y,\,x}$. According to the left consequence rule CQL it remains to prove that the precondition of SQAS implies our result, and easy rearrangement shows that we have to prove

$$d_d \wedge d_{e_d^x} \Rightarrow (R_{e_d^x,d}^{y,\,x} \Rightarrow R_{e_d^x,d}^{y,\,x})$$

which is possible if $R_{e_d^x,d}^{y,\,x}$ is a well-defined formula. But that is obvious by the antecedent, since R itself is well-defined. ∎

The following corollary is useful. It expresses the condition that two assignments in sequence can be performed simultaneously:

$$\text{SQAS}': \quad \vdash \{(R_{e,d}^{y,x}\} \; x := d; \; y := e \; \{R\} \quad \text{for } x \notin \mathcal{V}[e] \text{ and } x, y \text{ distinct}$$

If in addition $y \notin \mathcal{V}[d]$ then the two assignments are said to be *disjoint*. In general two statements S_1 and S_2 are said to be disjoint if $\mathcal{W}[S_1] \cap \mathcal{V}[S_2] = \mathcal{W}[S_2] \cap \mathcal{V}[S_1] = \emptyset$. Disjoint statements may be sequenced in any order, as well as being "simultaneous", i.e. concurrent. Notice that $\mathcal{V}[S_1]$ and $\mathcal{V}[S_2]$ do not have to be disjoint sets, provided that S_1 and S_2 only read the variables common to both.

It is fairly obvious that sequencing is associative, in the sense that S_1 and S_2 of SEQ may themselves be statement sequences. Indeed, assume

$$\vdash \{P\}S_1\{Q_1\}, \quad \vdash \{Q_1\}S_2\{Q_2\}, \text{ and } \vdash \{Q_2\}S_3\{R\}$$

Then $\vdash \{P\}S_1; S_2\{Q_2\}$ as well as $\vdash \{Q_1\}S_2; S_3\{R\}$ follow, and both lead to the same result: $\vdash \{P\}S_1; S_2; S_3\{R\}$.

It turns out that many kinds of statements may be analysed by left construction, i.e. *by mechanical means*. Therefore, the use of SEQ for continued left construction is an attractive technique. There is one important drawback, however: the preconditions tend to explode textually. Therefore, and as an aid to readers and verifiers, it is *good programming practice* to include intermediate state predicates at judiciously chosen points, especially whenever formula simplification would otherwise require non-trivial mathematical insight.

If a well-defined intermediate predicate Q is included as a state assertion in the conclusion, we can get a kind of TD rule for the sequencing of statements:

$$\text{TDSEQ}: \quad \frac{\vdash \{P\}S_1\{Q\}; \quad \vdash \{Q\}S_2\{R\}}{\vdash \{P\} \ S_1\{Q\}S_2 \ \{R\}} \quad \text{for } Q \text{ well-defined}$$

State assertions occurring in a program text are intended as internal documentation. For reasons discussed in section 4.8 they are required to be well-defined.

EXAMPLE 4.9
For variables $x_1, x_2 : Int$ the following is a way of interchanging their values, a_1, a_2, using only simple assignments and no additional variable. This can be shown by left construction. In this case textual explosion is easily counteracted by formula simplification:

$$\{P_0\} \ x_1 := x_1 - x_2 \ \{P_1\} \ x_2 := x_1 + x_2 \ \{P_2\} \ x_1 := x_2 - x_1 \ \{x_2 = a_1 \wedge x_1 = a_2\}$$

Left construction gives

P_2 equal to $x_2 = a_1 \wedge x_2 - x_1 = a_2$
P_1 equal to $x_1 + x_2 = a_1 \wedge (x_1 + x_2) - x_1 = a_2$ equal to $x_1 + x_2 = a_1 \wedge x_2 = a_2$
P_0 equal to $(x_1 - x_2) + x_2 = a_1 \wedge x_2 = a_2$ equal to $x_1 = a_1 \wedge x_2 = a_2$

□

Exercises

4.17 Prove the Hoare sentence $\{q*y+x = a\}\ x := x-y;\ q := q+1\ \{q*y+x = a\}$.

4.18 Construct and prove a program for performing a cyclic left shift on the simple integer variables x_1, x_2, x_3 with the initial values a_1, a_2, a_3, using only simple assignments and no auxiliary program variable. Hint: See the above example.

4.19 Generalize the result of problem 2 to an arbitrary number, n, of variables, $n \geq 2$.

4.20 Consider the statements $A[i] :=: A[j]$; $A[j] :=: A[k]$, where $i, j, k \in A.ix$, but not necessarily distinct. Construct the weakest preconditions for the postassertions $A[i] = a$, $A[j] = b$, and $A[k] = c$, respectively. Hint: Try to avoid textual explosion by introducing suitable abbreviations.

4.4.2 Branching

We adopt the traditional imperative **if-then-else-fi** construct, where the terminating **fi** acts as a closing parenthesis allowing both branches to be statement lists:

$$\mathcal{V}[\text{if } B \text{ then } S_1 \text{ else } S_2 \text{ fi}] \quad \triangleq \quad \mathcal{V}[B] \cup \mathcal{V}[S_1] \cup \mathcal{V}[S_2]$$
$$\mathcal{W}[\text{if } B \text{ then } S_1 \text{ else } S_2 \text{ fi}] \quad \triangleq \quad \mathcal{W}[S_1] \cup \mathcal{W}[S_2]$$

In a TD rule for an if-construct the pre- and postconditions, P, Q, are given for the compound. In order to find the preconditions of the premises we must reason forwards through the test, as shown in figure 4.1.

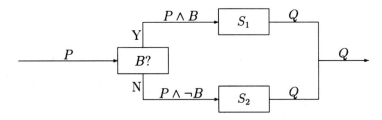

Figure 4.1: Top down reasoning

In a LC rule the postcondition Q is given, and we assume that corresponding preconditions, P_1, P_2, may be found for the premises. Then, reasoning backwards through the **if**-test, as shown in figure 4.2, the precondition of the compound may be constructed.

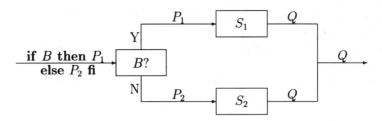

Figure 4.2: Left constructive reasoning

The corresponding rules follow from figures 4.1 and 4.2:

$$\text{TDIF}: \quad \frac{\vdash \{P \wedge B\}S_1\{Q\}; \;\; \vdash \{P \wedge \neg B\}S_2\{Q\}}{\vdash \{P\} \text{ if } B \text{ then } S_1 \text{ else } S_2 \text{ fi } \{Q\}}$$

$$\text{LCIF}: \quad \frac{\vdash \{P_1\}S_1\{Q\}; \;\; \vdash \{P_2\}S_2\{Q\}}{\vdash \{\text{if } B \text{ then } P_1 \text{ else } P_2 \text{ fi}\} \text{ if } B \text{ then } S_1 \text{ else } S_2 \text{ fi } \{Q\}}$$

LCIF is left maximal provided the expression B is well-defined in all states. Otherwise we obtain a left maximal rule by weakening the precondition by d_B. The precondition of either premise of TDIF may be strengthened by d_B. This weakens both premises, and the rule itself is thereby strengthened.

We introduce a shorthand version of the imperative **if**-construct **if** B **then** S **fi** with a default **else**-branch equal to **skip**. Inference rules for the shorthand version follow easily from TDIF, LCIF, and SKIP. We have also simplified the second premise of the TD rule by means of CQL (used backwards):

$$\text{TDSHIF}: \quad \frac{\vdash \{P \wedge B\}S\{Q\}; \;\; \vdash P \wedge \neg B \Rightarrow Q}{\vdash \{P\} \text{ if } B \text{ then } S \text{ fi } \{Q\}}$$

$$\text{LCSHIF}: \quad \frac{\vdash \{P\}S\{Q\}}{\vdash \{\text{if } B \text{ then } P \text{ else } Q \text{ fi}\} \text{ if } B \text{ then } S \text{ fi } \{Q\}}$$

Notice that the textual size of preconditions typically more than doubles as the result of left construction through an **if**-construct.

Exercises

4.21   Prove the equivalence of rules TDIF and LCIF. Hint: Use TDIF backwards (top down!) when constructing the proof of LCIF.

4.22 Construct a BU rule for the **if**-construct, and prove it equivalent to TDIF.

4.23 The following program sorts 5 numbers, given by the variables $x_1, \ldots, x_5$, with a worst case minimum of tests and a near-minimum of swaps. Prove it correct with respect to the given specification. (The specification does not say all there is to say; what is missing?)

$\{\mathbf{t}\}$
if $x_1 > x_4$ **then** $x_1 :=: x_4$ **fi**;
if $x_2 > x_5$ **then** $x_2 :=: x_5$ **fi**;
if $x_1 > x_2$ **then** $x_1 :=: x_2$; $x_4 :=: x_5$ **fi**;
if $x_2 > x_3$ **then** $x_2 :=: x_3$; **if** $x_1 > x_2$ **then** $x_1 :=: x_2$ **fi**
       else if $x_3 > x_5$ **then** $x_3 :=: x_5$ **fi fi**;
if $x_3 > x_4$ **then** $x_3 :=: x_4$; **if** $x_2 > x_3$ **then** $x_2 :=: x_3$ **fi**
       else if $x_4 > x_5$ **then** $x_4 :=: x_5$ **fi fi**
$\{x_1 \leq x_2 \leq x_3 \leq x_4 \leq x_5\}$

Hint: If you try to use left construction the whole way, you may drown yourself with nested **if**'s. So try to figure out some intermediate state predicates. (Use forward reasoning in order to find them; it is easy in this case because swap operations are reversible.)

4.4.3   Free loops

We add a terminating **od** to the traditional **while** construct in order to save additional statement brackets in the case where the loop body is a compound:

$$\mathcal{V}[\textbf{while } B \textbf{ do } S \textbf{ od}] \triangleq \mathcal{V}[B] \cup \mathcal{V}[S], \quad \mathcal{W}[\textbf{while } B \textbf{ do } S \textbf{ od}] \triangleq \mathcal{W}[S]$$

There is no general inference rule for loops based on the undecorated program text alone; it is necessary to specify a state predicate, called a *loop invariant*, at some point in the loop which cannot be bypassed at any execution. The standard loop rule given by Hoare uses an invariant, I, positioned in front of the loop test:

$$\text{WDO}: \quad \frac{\vdash \{I \wedge B\} S \{I\}}{\vdash \{I\} \textbf{ while } B \textbf{ do } S \textbf{ od } \{I \wedge \neg B\}}$$

Notice that the loop invariant determines all the predicates that occur in the rule, so the rule does not fit in directly with any of the proof strategies identified earlier. However, using consequence rules in addition it may be adjusted to any desired strategy, provided that a suitable loop invariant is given in advance, preferably as part of the program text. For instance, a "TD version" of WDO would be as follows:

$$\text{TDWDO}: \frac{\vdash P \Rightarrow I; \;\; \vdash \{I \land B\}S\{I\}; \;\; \vdash I \land \neg B \Rightarrow Q}{\vdash \{P\} \; \{I\}\textbf{while } B \textbf{ do } S \textbf{ od } \{Q\}}$$

for I well-defined

The additional premises are verification conditions associated with the entry into and exit out of the loop. The proof of invariance of I typically results in a third verification condition. For instance, if the loop body S can be analysed by left construction, resulting in a precondition I', this verification condition is $I \land B \Rightarrow I'$. Unfortunately the traditional **while** construct does not provide a good place for a loop invariant in front of the loop test.

A "left constructive" rule for the **while**-construct can be obtained by specifying a loop invariant J after the loop test. In this case the only verification condition is concerned with the invariance of J. The rule follows by reasoning backwards through the loop test (cf. left construction over an **if**-construct):

$$\text{LCWDO}: \frac{\vdash \{J\}S\{\textbf{if } B \textbf{ then } J \textbf{ else } Q \textbf{ fi}\}}{\vdash \{\textbf{if } B \textbf{ then } J \textbf{ else } Q \textbf{ fi}\} \textbf{ while } B \textbf{ do } \{J\} S \textbf{ od } \{Q\}}$$

for J well-defined.

Notice that many predicates can function as invariants in the sense of WDO for a given loop. **t** and **f** are two trivial examples. But not all choices lead to useful pre- and postconditions, and not all are provable even if valid for a suitable precondition. The rule shows that the postcondition is a strengthening of the invariant positioned in front of the loop test. Conversely, if a sufficiently strong postcondition is given for the loop, a suitable loop invariant at this point can be obtained by weakening the postcondition in some way; but the ways are many and often non-trivial, and no specific strategy is uniformly applicable. This is one place where programmer's intuition and ingenuity is often called for.

As we have seen earlier, a good programming strategy is to let the design of the invariant and the loop itself go hand in hand, perhaps after some initial trial and error. Certainly, loop invariants, formalized or not, are very important parts of the internal program documentation as an aid to understanding the program and reasoning about it, even if full formal verification is not intended. (There do exist loops, however, whose invariants are so obvious that including them in the program text would cause more irritation than enlightenment.)

In order to give some additional insight into the role of loop invariants we show how an invariant may (sometimes) be constructed from a given pre- or postcondition of the loop as a whole. The methods consist of constructing a sequence of predicates relating to successive (or predecessive) passages of control. Let the loop be **while** B **do** S **od**, assuming for simplicity that the loop test B is well-defined (in all states).

1. Let P_0 be a given well-defined precondition. Find predicates $P_1, P_2, \ldots$ satisfying

$$\{P_i \wedge B\}S\{P_{i+1}\} \quad \text{for } i \geq 0, \ i \text{ fresh}$$

Then, clearly, one of the P_i's must hold every time control enters the loop test. Thus, $I : \exists i \bullet i \geq 0 \wedge P_i$ is a valid invariant before the loop test, and the final postcondition $I \wedge \neg B$ follows from WDO. If each of $P_1, P_2, \ldots$ is the strongest possible for the given precondition, the same is true for the invariant and the final postcondition.

2. Let Q be a given well-defined postcondition. Find predicates $Q_1, Q_2, \ldots$ satisfying

$$\{Q_1\}S\{\neg B \Rightarrow Q\}, \quad \text{and} \quad \{Q_{i+1}\}S\{B \Rightarrow Q_i\} \quad \text{for } i > 0, \ i \text{ fresh}$$

Then $J : \forall i \bullet i > 0 \Rightarrow Q_i$ is a valid invariant after the loop test (cf. exercise 4.24 below) and therefore, according to LCWDO, **if** B **then** J **else** Q **fi** is a sufficiently strong initial condition. In order to see this we may argue as follows. If the loop terminates immediately, then B is false initially and $\neg B \wedge Q$ is a sufficient precondition. If it terminates after $i > 0$ iterations, then B was true i times in succession and then false. In this case the properties of the Q_i's show that $B \wedge Q_i$ is a sufficient precondition. But the precondition has to cater for all possible $i > 0$; hence the quantifier. Notice that there is no assumption that loop termination will actually occur, therefore the invariant and the initial precondition only provide the usual partial correctness guarantee. If each Q_i is the weakest possible for the given postcondition, the resulting Hoare sentence for the loop construct is left maximal.

3. The following construction, analogous to the preceding one, gives an invariant and initial precondition which are strong enough to guarantee loop termination with a given postcondition, Q, provided that each execution of the loop body terminates normally. Find $R_1, R_2, \ldots$ satisfying

$$\{R_1\}S\{\neg B \wedge Q\}, \quad \text{and} \quad \{R_{i+1}\}S\{B \wedge R_i\} \quad \text{for } i > 0, \ i \text{ fresh}$$

Then $K : \exists i \bullet i > 0 \wedge R_i$ is invariant after the loop test, and the corresponding loop precondition is **if** B **then** K **else** Q **fi**. That it guarantees termination with Q (for terminating loop body) is shown by the following intuitive argument. If B is false initially, then Q holds and the loop terminates immediately with Q. Assume that B holds initially. Then K asserts that there is a positive i such that R_i holds. Let k_0 be the smallest such number. The properties of the R's then show that the loop will be executed k_0 times with $\neg B \wedge Q$ holding after the last one. Termination with Q follows.

It turns out that this construction can only provide the weakest possible precondition in the case where the loop body is a deterministic program. Otherwise the number of remaining loop body executions may not be uniquely determined by the current state. We may compensate for that by using a slightly more complicated expression, **if** B **then** R_i **else** Q **fi**, as the postcondition for defining R_{i+1}. A similar construction was first given by Dijkstra[9].

Notice that these constructions can only succeed, in the sense of leading to a concrete invariant, if the general form of P_i, respectively Q_i and R_i, satisfying the given criteria can be found. This is generally a non-trivial task. It may be noted that strategy 3 is not applicable to non-terminating loops, whereas strategy 2 may be used to find invariants which are valid in all cases.

EXAMPLE 4.10

We consider the following specified program for computing the quotient and remainder in dividing x by y, for $x, y : Int$:

$$\{x \geq 0 \wedge y > 0\}$$
$$\textbf{var } q, r := 0, x;$$
$$\{I\}\textbf{while } B : y \leq r \textbf{ do } \{J\} \ S : q, r := q+1, r-y \textbf{ od}$$
$$\{Q : x = q * y + r \wedge 0 \leq r < y\}$$

Reasoning forwards it is easy to see that $P_k : q = k \wedge r = x - k*y \geq 0$ describes the state after $k \geq 0$ executions of the loop body. In particular P_0 holds initially, and $\{P_k \wedge B\}S\{P_{k+1}\}$ is provable. Consequently, an invariant at the top of the loop is

$$
\begin{aligned}
I &\Longleftrightarrow \exists k \bullet k \geq 0 \wedge q = k \wedge r = x - k*y \geq 0 \\
&\Longleftrightarrow (\exists k \bullet q = k) \wedge q \geq 0 \wedge r = x - q*y \geq 0 \\
&\Longleftrightarrow q \geq 0 \wedge x = q*y + r \wedge 0 \leq r
\end{aligned}
$$

Clearly $I \wedge \neg B$ implies the postcondition Q.

Using left construction from the given postcondition Q we find

$$
\begin{array}{lll}
\neg B \Rightarrow Q &\Longleftrightarrow r < y \Rightarrow x = q*y+r \wedge 0 \leq r & \text{(slightly simplified)} \\
Q_1 &\Longleftrightarrow r < 2*y \Rightarrow x = q*y+r \wedge y \leq r & \text{(by left construction)} \\
B \Rightarrow Q_1 &\Longleftrightarrow y \leq r < 2*y \Rightarrow x = q*y+r & \text{(slightly simplified)} \\
Q_2 &\Longleftrightarrow 2*y \leq r < 3*y \Rightarrow x = q*y+r & \text{(by left construction)}
\end{array}
$$

At this point we guess that Q_k has the general form $k*y \leq r < (k+1)*y \Rightarrow x = q*y+r$, for $k \geq 2$, which is verified by proving $\{Q_{k+1}\}S\{B \Rightarrow Q_k\}$. Although the general formula for $k=1$ is weaker than Q_1 as constructed, they are equivalent under the assumption of $y \leq r$ which holds after the loop test. Consequently, a sufficiently strong invariant at that position is

$$J \iff \forall k \bullet k > 0 \wedge k * y \leq r < (k+1) * y \Rightarrow x = q * y + r$$
$$\iff (\exists k \bullet k > 0 \wedge k * y \leq r < (k+1) * y) \Rightarrow x = q * y + r$$
$$\iff 0 < y \leq r \Rightarrow x = q * y + r$$

where the implication antecedent is an assumption that the loop will terminate. As all left constructions have been left maximal we can now construct the precondition P for the program which is weakest in the partial correctness sense. (Notice that J occurs in the context of $y \leq r$.)

$$P \iff \text{if } y \leq r \text{ then } J \text{ else } Q \text{ fi } {}^{q,r}_{0,x}$$
$$\iff \text{if } y \leq x \text{ then } J^{q,r}_{0,x} \text{ else } Q^{q,r}_{0,x} \text{ fi}$$
$$\iff \text{if } y < x \text{ then t else } 0 \leq x < y \text{ fi}$$
$$\iff y \leq x \vee 0 \leq x$$

This is thus the weakest precondition for not terminating with a wrong result. It is implied by the given program precondition (which also guarantees loop termination).

Using left construction according to strategy 3 we find

$$R_k \iff k * y \leq r < (k+1) * y \wedge x = q * y + r, \quad \text{for } k > 0$$

$$J \iff \exists k \bullet k > 0 \wedge R_k$$
$$\iff 0 < y \leq r \wedge x = q * y + r$$

$$I \iff \text{if } y \leq r \text{ then } J \text{ else } x = q * y + r \wedge 0 \leq r < y \text{ fi}$$
$$\iff x = q * y + r \wedge 0 < y \wedge (y \leq r \vee 0 \leq r)$$
$$\iff x = q * y + r \wedge 0 < y \wedge 0 \leq r$$

The corresponding program precondition, $I^{q,r}_{0,x}$, is identical to the one given.

□

Exercises

4.24 Prove the three general invariants described above. Hints: The rules EEXST and UUNIV of exercise 4.4 are useful, as well as DDJ and CCJ of exercise 4.2 of section 4.2. It is also useful to know that **if** B **then** C **else** D **fi** is equivalent to $B \wedge C \vee \neg B \wedge D$, as well as to $(B \Rightarrow C) \wedge (\neg B \Rightarrow D)$.

4.25 Prove the partial correctness of the following program for computing the integer square root of a given non-negative integer, n. (All program variables are of type *Int*.)

$$\{n \geq 0\} \ x := 0; \ y := n; \ q := 1;$$
$$\textbf{while } q \leq n \textbf{ do } q := 4 * q \textbf{ od};$$
$$\textbf{while } q \neq 1 \textbf{ do } q := q/4;$$

$$\textbf{if } y < x + q \textbf{ then } x := x/2$$
$$\textbf{else } y := y - (x + q); \; x := x/2 + q \textbf{ fi}$$
$$\textbf{od}$$
$$\{x^2 \le n < (x+1)^2 \wedge y = n - x^2\}$$

A good invariant of the second loop is

$$0 \le y = n - x^2/q < 2x + q \; \wedge \; x \bmod q = 0 \; \wedge \; \exists k \bullet k \ge 0 \wedge q = 4^k$$

Loop termination

It is important to realize that proof rules such as WDO and LCWDO only express arguments about *invariance*. In order to prove loop termination we have to provide an additional argument showing that some kind of *progress* will take place. Since no Hoare sentence can assert normal termination of its constituent program section, there is no way to assert loop termination within our formal framework. Thus any proof of normal termination must be at least partly informal.

Remark

> As we have seen, invariants may well be so strong as to guarantee loop termination, as for instance those constructed using strategy 3 given above on p. 85. The informal part of our termination argument in that case essentially consisted in linking the existentially quantified variable of the resulting invariant, $\exists i \bullet i > 0 \wedge R_i$, to the number of remaining loop body executions.

The usual way of capturing the idea of progress is to introduce the concept of a *progress function* also-called a *variant*. It is an expression in program variables whose value (e.g. at the position chosen for the invariant) is a non-negative integer which can be shown to decrease with each execution of the loop body. Since the decrementation cannot go on for ever, it is then intuitively obvious that the loop must terminate. (It may happen that the concept of non-negative integers ordered arithmetically is not quite good enough for a termination argument to go through. If so, a progress function producing tuples of non-negative integers, ordered lexicographically, can usually do the trick.)

The formalizable parts of the termination argument consist of formulating a progress function f and proving the following assertions. (The ultimate inference step, concluding that the loop will actually terminate, must remain outside the formal Hoare logic.)

For WDO: $I \wedge B \Rightarrow f \ge 0$ and
$\{I \wedge B \wedge f = \alpha\} \, S \, \{f < \alpha\}$ for $\alpha \notin W[S]$

For LCWDO: $J \Rightarrow f \ge 0$ and
$\{J \wedge f = \alpha\} \, S \, \{B \Rightarrow f < \alpha\}$ for $\alpha \notin W[S]$

If d_B, the well-definedness condition for the while-test, is known, and we also prove

$$I \Rightarrow d_B, \quad \text{respectively} \ \ J \vee Q \Rightarrow d_B$$

we may conclude that the whole loop construct *terminates normally*, provided that any execution of the loop body does (for the precondition which follows from the analysis).

A loop invariant I and a progress function f for a given loop can, in a metaphorical sense, be seen as "projections" of the given algorithm on "axes" of invariance and progress, respectively, as far as operations on variables in $\mathcal{V}[I, f]$ are concerned. Conversely, I together with a strategy for reducing the value of f, essentially define an iterative algorithm on these variables. In [9] Dijkstra shows how a correctly terminating iterative algorithm may be "derived" from a given postcondition Q by choosing a loop invariant which is a suitable weakening of Q, as well as suitable progress mechanisms. This programming strategy may be useful (at least in retrospect!) whenever desired final states can be precisely specified. It happens, however, that good invariants and progress schemes are hard to find except by trial and error.

Exercises

4.26 Prove termination of the loops of exercise 4.25, as well as that of example 4.10.

4.27 Construct and prove a program satisfying the same specification as the one of example 4.10, using program variables which satisfy the following invariant of the main loop:

$$x = q * z + r \wedge 0 \leq r < z \wedge \exists k \bullet k \geq 0 \wedge z = 2^k * y$$

Progress by halving z in each step. Hint: Establish the invariant by computing a sufficiently large z in an initial loop.

4.28 Let A be an array of integers, indexed from 1 to n $(n \geq 0)$ and sorted in ascending order. Use "binary search" to determine where a given integer x occurs in the array, if at all. The algorithm must satisfy the loop invariant

$$0 \leq i < j \leq n+1 \ \wedge \ A[i] \leq x < A[j]$$

where i and j are program variables, and $A[0] = -\infty$ and $A[n+1] = \infty$ are hypothetical boundary elements (never to be accessed by the algorithm). Upon termination, $1 \leq i \leq n \wedge A[i] = x$ must hold if and only if x occurs in A. Progress by halving the interval $[i..j]$ in each step. Prove correctness including normal termination.

A generalized loop construct

It happens that loops do not naturally conform to the structure of the while loop, but need to have the loop test in a different position. For the sake of programming flexibility we introduce a construct where the while-test counts as a separate statement, which can be any one of the list of statements which form the loop body:

> **loop** ...; **while** B; ... **repeat**

(The fact that the cue word **while** is used in both loop constructs should cause no confusion.) Another advantage of this syntactic construct is that it provides a good place for an invariant anywhere in the loop. There is, however, a price to pay in the form of a slightly more complicated inference rule in the general case:

$$\text{LWR1}: \quad \frac{\vdash \{P\}S_1\{I\}; \ \vdash \{I \wedge B\}S_2\{P\}}{\vdash \{P\} \textbf{ loop } \{P\} \ S_1 \ \{I\} \textbf{ while } B; \ S_2 \textbf{ repeat } \{I \wedge \neg B\}}$$

> for P and I well-defined

The rule corresponds to WDO in the sense that a loop invariant is required immediately in front of the while-test. In the case where S_1 is empty (or **skip**) we may choose I for P, whereby the rule essentially reduces to WDO.

The following rule is more left constructive, in permitting an arbitrary postcondition. It requires a loop invariant either at the top of the loop or immediately after the loop test (cf. the rule LCWDO above):

$$\text{LWR2}: \quad \frac{\vdash \{P\} \ S_1 \ \{\textbf{if } B \textbf{ then } J \textbf{ else } Q \textbf{ fi}\}; \ \vdash \{J\}S_2\{P\}}{\vdash \{P\} \textbf{ loop } \{P\} \ S_1; \textbf{ while } B \ \{J\} \ S_2 \textbf{ repeat } \{Q\}}$$

> for P and J well-defined

If only one of P and J is given, the other may possibly be computed by left construction. In that case there is only one verification condition implicit in the rule, concerned with the invariance of the given invariant.

The formalizable part of a termination argument depends on where in the loop the progress function is identified:

At the top:	prove	$P \Rightarrow f \geq 0$
	and	$\{P \wedge f = \alpha\} \ S_1; \textbf{ if } B \textbf{ then } S_2 \textbf{ else abort fi } \{f < \alpha\}.$
Before the test:	prove	$I \wedge B \Rightarrow f \geq 0$
	and	$\{I \wedge B \wedge f = \alpha\} \ S_2; S_1 \ \{f < \alpha\}.$
After the test:	prove	$J \Rightarrow f = \alpha$
	and	$\{J \wedge f = \alpha\} \ S_2; S_1 \ \{B \Rightarrow f < \alpha\}.$

Exercises

4.29 Prove that the program schema S_1; **while** B **do** S_2; S_1 **od** satisfies LWR1.

4.30 Prove that LWR1 and LWR2 are equivalent.

4.31 Verify the following annotated program. (All variables are of type *Int.*)

$\{b \geq 0\}\ x := 1;\ y := a;\ d := b;$
  loop $\{x * y^d = a^b \wedge d \geq 0\}$
    if $(d\ \textbf{mod}\ 2) \neq 0$ **then** $x := x * y$ **fi**;
    $d := d/2;$
   while $d \neq 0;$
    $y := y^2$
  repeat
$\{x = a^b\}$

Prove also that $y \leq a^b$ everywhere if $a, b \geq 1$ initially. (The last result ensures that arithmetic overflow will only occur if the value a^b is out of range.) Hint: The loop invariant must be strengthened.

4.4.4 Local variables

We consider a *scope construct* as follows for the introduction of local program variables. It is a syntactic compound consisting of a list of statements, S, preceded by a *variable declaration* and followed by a *scope terminator*:

 var $v : T = e;\ S;$ **endvar** v

The declaration introduces a new program variable, v, and defines its type and its initial value. The type indication may be omitted; if so, the type of the variable is defined to be that of the initializing expression e. The syntactic scope of v is the statement list S; the variable is said to be *local to* the scope construct. Notice that the syntactic scope of v does not include the initializing expression; thereby circular definition of the initial value is prevented. (Occurrences of v in e would refer to a non-local variable of that same name.) For notational convenience we consider the scope terminator as optional if the scope construct is the last member of a (maximal) statement list. It is practical to generalize the declaration construct to cater for the simultaneous introduction of several variables, using some suitable syntax.

 Variable declarations are syntactically analogous to quantifiers in expressions, in the sense that a variable declared local to a statement list S is not considered to be a (free) variable of the scope construct as a whole. The free variables of the scope construct are said to be *non-local* to the construct:

$$\mathcal{V}[\textbf{var}\ v : T = e;\ S;\ \textbf{endvar}\ v] \quad \triangleq \quad \mathcal{V}[e] \cup (\mathcal{V}[S] - \{v\})$$
$$\mathcal{W}[\textbf{var}\ v : T = e;\ S;\ \textbf{endvar}\ v] \quad \triangleq \quad \mathcal{W}[S] - \{v\}$$

An important motivation for introducing local program variables, rather than using a fixed set of global ones, is to limit as much as possible the set of variables which may occur free at any point of a program. Thereby one can establish better checks against incorrect variable occurrences, as well as a syntactic guarantee against certain kinds of irrelevant information in state assertions (about program variables currently not in use). A concept of locality is an essential part of structures such as procedures and classes, cf. section 4.6 and chapter 6.

With respect to inference rules we choose to treat variable declarations and scope terminators as separate statements, rather than being the head and tail of a single syntactic construct. This provides some additional flexibility which is useful in connection with "mythical" program sections, cf. section 4.8, and there is no harm in permitting scopes to overlap arbitrarily, as long as each scope can only be entered going through the declaration. It is sufficient to require that any scope termination, explicit or not, occurs to the right of the corresponding declaration and in the same statement list (provided that explicit jumps into scopes are forbidden, cf. section 4.4.6).

We provide left and right constructive rules for the declaration of initialized variables as well as explicit scope terminators.

$$
\begin{array}{lll}
\text{LCIV}: & \vdash \{P_e^v\} \ \textbf{var} \ v : T = e \ \{P\} & \\
\text{RCST}: & \vdash \{Q\} \ \textbf{endvar} \ v \ \{\exists v : T \bullet Q\} & \\
\text{RCIV}: & \vdash \{P\} \ \textbf{var} \ v : T = e \ \{P \wedge v = e\} & \text{for } v \notin \mathcal{V}[P] \\
\text{LCST}: & \vdash \{Q\} \ \textbf{endvar} \ v \ \{Q\} & \text{for } v \notin \mathcal{V}[Q]
\end{array}
$$

LCIV and RCST may be combined to a bottom up rule for scope constructs, and RCIV and LCST together provide a top down rule:

$$
\text{BUIV}: \quad \frac{\vdash \{P\}S\{Q\}}{\vdash \{P_e^v\} \ \textbf{var} \ v : T = e; \ S; \ \textbf{endvar} \ v \ \{\exists v : T \bullet Q\}}
$$

$$
\text{TDIV}: \quad \frac{\vdash \{P \wedge v = e\}S\{Q\}}{\vdash \{P\} \ \textbf{var} \ v := e; \ S; \ \textbf{endvar} \ v \ \{Q\}} \qquad \text{for } v \notin \mathcal{V}[P, Q, e]
$$

The side condition of TDIV indicates that the rule is not directly usable if there is a non-local variable v occurring within P, Q. However, the rule may be generalized to cater for that situation, simply by replacing P, Q, and e in the premise by $P_{v'}^v$, $Q_{v'}^v$, and $e_{v'}^v$, respectively, where v' is a fresh variable. (For the purpose of program documentation it would be appropriate to introduce v' as a "mythical" program constant, cf. section 4.8.) Since the non-local variable has to be renamed anyway in local state assertions, the reusage of variable names in textually nested scopes is not very useful when programming in a style suitable for verification. Notice that BUIV is as general as can be in the context of such reusage: all free occurrences of v in P and Q refer to the local variable, and they are removed by substitution and quantification respectively. Any free v's introduced into the precondition through copies of the initializing expression e by definition refer to the non-local variable.

There are cases where immediate initialization of variables is inappropriate and therefore superfluous. For instance, the individual variables of an array containing a growing table may be initialized to new table entries as need arises. In order not to introduce unnecessary overhead a majority of standard imperative programming languages only provide for the declaration of uninitialized variables. We therefore introduce the option of omitting the initialization as part of a declaration (but not in that case the type indication). The following rules would appear to cater for this case:

LCUV : $\vdash \{\forall v : T \bullet P\}$ **var** $v : T \{P\}$

RCUV : $\vdash \{P\}$ **var** $v : T \{P\}$ for $v \notin \mathcal{V}[P]$

The universal quantifier introduced in LCUV reflects the fact that the postcondition must hold for arbitrary initial value of v. Unfortunately the initial contents of the storage cells representing v in a computer may be the results of previous usage of these cells for other purposes, and may not be meaningful representations of any value at all of type T, cf. sections 5.6 and 5.9. The rule RCUV appears to avoid this problem by the requirement that there be no free v in P, but the rule BUTINV of section 4.2.3 permits the postcondition to be strengthened by v **in** T, which is an instance of the permanent type invariant for T. The fact that type invariants may not hold for uninitialized variables implies that our formal system as it now stands is not sound for all programs. In fact a program declaring and accessing uninitialized variables may behave unpredictably, even if verified formally using the above rules.

Several alternative remedies are possible:

1. Default initialization if none is specified in a declaration. This is our preferred solution for practical programming, whether formal verification is intended or not, even though it may entail some superfluous overhead. After all, forgetting to initialize is one of the most common sources of programming error; and if there is no default initialization, debugging is made difficult by the fact that program behaviour is unpredictable in terms of the program text, and that it may even depend on the previous contents of the computer memory. Uninitialized pointer variables are especially troublesome.

2. Regarding an uninitialized variable as ill-defined initially, i.e. as *having no value*. This is an intuitively attractive solution, but it may lead to quite expensive overhead since, according to the AID convention, any access to a variable prior to its first value assignment must then lead to program abortion. The requirement is certainly infeasible for traditional programming language implementations. Also, the logic would become more complicated, since the definedness of program variables would become context dependent.

3. Redefining the syntactic scope of program variables so as to be restricted to areas following (alternative) initializing assignments, as proposed by Dijkstra

in [9]. This, however, requires fairly complicated syntactic rules which sometimes lead to unnatural programs. Also, arrays must be treated in a very
different way from that of traditional programming.

4. Removing rule LCUV and exercising caution not to apply type invariants
to uninitialized variables. Although this will not render the logic formally
sound it is probably the optimum strategy for applying the techniques of
this book to programming in traditional languages. If the compiler offers
syntactic checks producing warnings against access to possibly uninitialized
variables, the logic will be sound for programs passing those checks. Notice
that the type invariant is likely to hold anyway for uninitialized variables of
certain basic types such as the type *Int* of integers, which means that LCUV
is in fact sound for these types.

It is useful to introduce a distinction between program variables and program
constants, the latter being an initialized variable not subject to change:

$$\mathcal{V}[\textbf{const } c := e;\ S;\ \textbf{endconst } c] \quad \triangleq \quad \mathcal{V}[e] \cup (\mathcal{V}[S] - \{c\})$$
$$\mathcal{W}[\textbf{const } c := e;\ S;\ \textbf{endconst } c] \quad \triangleq \quad \mathcal{W}[S] \qquad \text{for } c \notin \mathcal{W}[S]$$

Notice that the statement list S would be illegal if $c \in \mathcal{W}[S]$. The construct satisfies
proof rules analogous to those for initialized local variables. The advantage of the
construct is mainly to make possible a kind of simple syntactic consistency check,
viz. that $c \notin \mathcal{W}[S]$ holds for any c declared as constant.

Exercises

4.32 Prove the equivalence of rules TDIV and BUIV for the assumptions stated,
as well as the equivalence of analogous scope construct rules for uninitialized local
variables.

4.33 Give and prove LC scope construct rules for initialized and uninitialized
local variables.

4.4.5 Controlled loops

We consider a variant of the traditional **for**-statement, of the form

> **for** $k := a$ **to** b **do** S **od**

where k is a simple variable and a and b expressions, all of integer type (or any
other type with successor and predecessor functions as well as ordering relations,
e.g. an enumeration type as in Pascal). The meaning is standard: the loop body
S is to executed $(b - a + 1)$ times for $k = a,\ a + 1,\ \ldots,\ b$ if $a \leq b$, and not

at all if $a > b$. Since the final value of k may depend on the implementation, we choose to define the controlling variable k as local to the **for**-statement, and with the scope S:

$$\mathcal{V}[\textbf{for } k := a \textbf{ to } b \textbf{ do } S \textbf{ od}] \quad \triangleq \quad \mathcal{V}[a] \cup \mathcal{V}[b] \cup (\mathcal{V}[S] - \{k\})$$
$$\mathcal{W}[\textbf{for } k := a \textbf{ to } b \textbf{ do } S \textbf{ od}] \quad \triangleq \quad \mathcal{W}[S]$$

In order to simplify reasoning we also insist that S does not change the values of k, a, or b:

$$\mathcal{W}[S] \cap (\{k\} \cup \mathcal{V}[a] \cup \mathcal{V}[b]) = \emptyset$$

The following annotated schematic implementation of the **for**-statement can be used to construct an inference rule. The implementation is such that no value outside the range $[a..b]$ has to occur at execution time, nor is there a need for the annotation to refer to such values. This is important if a and b are the first and last values of an enumeration type.

$$\{P_a^k\} \textbf{ if } a \leq b \textbf{ then}$$
$$\{a \leq b \wedge P_a^k\} \textbf{ var } k := a;$$
$$\textbf{loop } \{a \leq k \leq b \wedge P\} \ S \ \{a \leq k \leq b \wedge Q\}$$
$$\textbf{while } k < b$$
$$\{a \leq k < b \wedge Q\} \ k := k + 1 \ \{a \leq k \leq b \wedge P\}$$
$$\textbf{repeat } \{a \leq k \leq b \wedge Q \wedge k \geq b\}$$
$$\textbf{fi } \{Q_b^k\}$$

In order to verify the program schema we must prove the following sentences and formulas.

$$a \leq b \wedge P_a^k \Rightarrow (a \leq k \leq b \wedge P)_a^k \tag{4.5}$$
$$\{a \leq k \leq b \wedge P\} \ S \ \{a \leq k \leq b \wedge Q\} \tag{4.6}$$
$$\{a \leq k < b \wedge Q\} \ k := k + 1 \ \{a \leq k \leq b \wedge P\} \tag{4.7}$$
$$a \leq k \leq b \wedge Q \wedge k \geq b \Rightarrow Q_b^k \tag{4.8}$$
$$P_a^k \wedge a > b \Rightarrow Q_b^k \tag{4.9}$$

The verification conditions (4.5) and (4.8) together validate the first premise of the TDSHIF rule (using BUIV), and (4.9) is the second premise. (4.5) and (4.8), as well as parts of (4.6) and (4.7) can be proved once and for all, whereas the remainder of (4.6) and (4.7) as well as the whole of (4.9) must be proved for each individual instance. This is stated by the following inference rule:

$$\text{FOR:} \quad \frac{\vdash \{a \leq k \leq b \wedge P\} S \{Q\}; \ \vdash a \leq k < b \wedge Q \Rightarrow P_{k+1}^k; \ \vdash a > b \wedge P_a^k \Rightarrow Q_b^k}{\vdash \{P_a^k\} \textbf{ for } k := a \textbf{ to } b \textbf{ do } S \textbf{ od } \{Q_b^k\}}$$

In view of the fact that S does not change the value of either k or b, loop termination can be proved once and for all using the progress function $b - k$.

The rule is surprisingly complicated, but given a suitable "pre-invariant" P and "post-invariant" Q of slightly different forms, it does protect one from having to reason about values outside the range $[a..b]$. This may be important if the range is an enumeration type (cf. section 5.8.1).

EXAMPLE 4.11
$\{t\}$ **for** $k := 1$ **to** N **do**
    $\{\forall i \bullet 1 \leq i < k \Rightarrow A[i] = 0\}$ $A[k] := 0$ $\{\forall i \bullet 1 \leq i \leq k \Rightarrow A[i] = 0\}$**od**
$\{\forall i \bullet 1 \leq i \leq N \Rightarrow A[i] = 0\}$

(This is a case where the invariants are too obvious to be helpful to any programmer, and it would be better if a verification system could construct them automatically. However, the example did provide the material for the very first exercise in formal reasoning of chapter 2.)
$\square$

We may simplify the FOR rule by taking Q to be P_{k+1}^k; then the second premise is trivially satisfied. In practical programming it usually the case that the value of a does not exceed $b+1$. If so, the last premise is also redundant. It is sufficient to require $a \leq b+1$ to hold in the initial state (it need not be a universally valid assumption):

$$\text{SFOR}: \quad \frac{\vdash \{a \leq k \leq b \land P\}\ S\ \{P_{k+1}^k\}}{\vdash \{a \leq b+1 \land P_a^k\}\ \textbf{for}\ k := a\ \textbf{to}\ b\ \textbf{do}\ S\ \textbf{od}\ \{P_{b+1}^k\}}$$

We indicate downward counting by writing **dto** instead of **to**. Rules corresponding to FOR and SFOR are obtained by reversing inequalities and replacing the successor function by the predecessor function:

$$\text{FORD}: \quad \frac{\vdash \{a \geq k \geq b \land P\}S\{Q\};\quad \vdash a \geq k > b \land Q \Rightarrow P_{k-1}^k;\quad \vdash a < b \land P_a^k \Rightarrow Q_b^k}{\vdash \{P_a^k\}\ \textbf{for}\ k := a\ \textbf{dto}\ b\ \textbf{do}\ S\ \textbf{od}\ \{Q_b^k\}}$$

$$\text{SFORD}: \quad \frac{\vdash \{a \geq k \geq b \land P\}\ S\ \{P_{k-1}^k\}}{\vdash \{a \geq b-1 \land P_a^k\}\ \textbf{for}\ k := a\ \textbf{dto}\ b\ \textbf{do}\ S\ \textbf{od}\ \{P_{b-1}^k\}}$$

Exercises

4.34 Show that the following schematic implementation of the **for**-statement satisfies the SFOR rule:

   var $k := a$; **while** $k \leq b$ **do** S; $k := k + 1$ **od endvar** k

Hint: Consider first the case $a \leq b+1$.

4.35 Verify the following program for sorting an array A of integers indexed from 1 to n:

$\{N \geq 1\}$ **for** $i := N$ **dto** 2 **do**
    $\{I\}$ **for** $j := 1$ **to** $i - 1$ **do**
        $\{I \wedge J\}$ **if** $A[j] > A[j+1]$ **then** $A[j] :=: A[j+1]$ **fi od od**
$\{\forall r, s \bullet 1 \leq r < s \leq N \Rightarrow A[r] \leq A[s]\}$

where

$\quad I$ is $\forall r, s \bullet 1 \leq r < s \leq N \wedge s > i \Rightarrow A[r] \leq A[s]$, and
$\quad J$ is $\forall t \bullet 1 \leq t < j \leq N \Rightarrow A[t] \leq A[j]$

The invariant I expresses that the array segment $A[(i \mid 1)..N]$ is sorted and contains the $N - i$ largest elements.

4.4.6 Jumps

The use of jump statements is strongly discouraged by the proponents of "structured programming", for several reasons:

- Jumps do not contribute to program structure, such as program modularization, and may be used as a substitute for structure; they may even interfere with program structure.
- Jumps have no place in an orderly program development, but facilitate bad solutions to unforeseen problems.
- The use of jumps is error prone. It is easy to forget about assumptions implicit at remote program locations, and there is a corresponding danger that states possible at the location of a jump may be incompatible with assumptions made at the destination.

However, each of these points is arguable. It may, for instance, be possible to formulate an easy and well structured solution to a problem, provided certain conditions are fulfilled which arise as natural by-products of the solution algorithm itself. Then it may be useful to make an *exit* out of the appropriate part of the program in the case where the assumed condition turns out to be invalid, in order to enter a different mode of behaviour. A compiler might be organized like this, the assumed condition being that the user program is syntactically correct.

It has even been argued [2] that some algorithms are best formulated as "spaghetti programs", which oscillate between classes of states identified and described during program development, and where each such state class is made to correspond to a program label. The clarity gained by bending the algorithm into a more well structured shape may not be worth the additional mental effort required. Furthermore, the introduction of new variables and/or duplication of program text may be necessary in order to get rid of the explicit jumps. If a sufficiently accurate and explicit state assertion is provided for each label, this mode of programming will not be especially error prone.

Jump statements are harmless axiomatically, provided that jumps *into* compound statements are forbidden. Then, at least, they will not destroy program structure.

It is impossible, however, to specify a general axiom schema for jump statements. The postcondition **f** can certainly be postulated, because control will not proceed normally, but the precondition must imply the state assertion associated with the jump destination, and the latter depends on the context of the jump statement. What we must do is to provide inference rules for constructs defining one or more jump destinations, and whose constituents *contain all occurrences of jumps to these destinations*. In the proofs about the constituents, i.e. in the premises of the rule, we are then entitled to introduce *assumptions* about the jump statements that may occur, of the form

$$\{P\} \ \langle \text{jump to} \dots \rangle \ \{\mathbf{f}\}$$

where the precondition P becomes associated with the jump destination through occurrences elsewhere in the proof rule.

Exits

The simplest form of jump is a forward one exiting from a named compound statement.

$$L : \langle \text{beginning of compound} \rangle \dots; \ \textbf{exit } L; \ \dots \ \langle \text{end of compound} \rangle$$

The associated inference rule is

$$\text{EXIT} : \quad \frac{\{Q\} \ \textbf{exit } L \ \{\mathbf{f}\} \ \vdash \ \{P\} \, CS \{Q\}}{\vdash \{P\} L : CS \{Q\}} \quad \text{for } Q \text{ well-defined}$$

where CS stands for a compound statement and L is an identifier labelling the compound. (If CS is a statement list, then L should be understood as labelling the whole list.) If the proof of the premise succeeds, we may conclude that Q holds upon normal termination of CS. If an occurrence of **exit** L within CS is executed, then CS does not terminate normally, but $L : CS$ does, and, according to the assumption, Q holds in this case as well.

It is necessary to forbid syntactically nested occurrences of the same label L, otherwise ambiguities would arise. Notice that the assumption must be discarded in the conclusion of this particular step of a complete proof (if we shall get rid of it at all), therefore nothing can be proved about any occurrence of **exit** L occurring outside CS. The inference rule is TD as well as LC. It is because Q occurs as a precondition in the premise and as the postcondition of the conclusion that it must be well-defined. Otherwise the rule would not be sound.

EXAMPLE 4.12

Let the construct **loop** S **repeat** be defined as an infinite repetition if S contains no **while**-clause:

$$\text{INFREP}: \quad \frac{\vdash \{I\}S\{I\}}{\vdash \{I\} \textbf{ loop } S \textbf{ repeat } \{\mathbf{f}\}}$$

We then derive the following inference rule:

$$\frac{\vdash \{I \wedge B\}S\{I\}}{\vdash \{I\} \; L: \textbf{loop if } B \textbf{ then } S \textbf{ else exit } L \textbf{ fi repeat } \{I \wedge \neg B\}}$$

1. $\vdash \{I \wedge B\}S\{I\}$	(premise)
2. $\{I \wedge B\}\textbf{exit } L\{\mathbf{f}\} \vdash \{I \wedge B\}\textbf{exit } L\{\mathbf{f}\}$	(trivial)
3. $\vdash \mathbf{f} \Rightarrow I$	(tautology)
4. $\{I \wedge B\}\textbf{exit } L\{\mathbf{f}\} \vdash \{I \wedge B\}\textbf{exit } L\{I\}$	(2,3, CQR)
5. $\{I \wedge B\}\textbf{exit } L\{\mathbf{f}\} \vdash \{I\}\textbf{if } B \textbf{ then } S \textbf{ else exit } L \textbf{ fi}\{I\}$	(1,4, TDIF)
6. $\{I \wedge B\}\textbf{exit } L\{\mathbf{f}\} \vdash \{I\}\textbf{loop if } B \textbf{ then } S \textbf{ else exit } L \textbf{ fi repeat}\{\mathbf{f}\}$	
	(5, INFREP)
7. $\vdash \mathbf{f} \Rightarrow I \wedge \neg B$	(tautology)
8. $\{I \wedge B\}\textbf{exit } L\{\mathbf{f}\} \vdash \{I\}\textbf{loop if } B \textbf{ then } S \textbf{ else exit } L \textbf{ fi repeat}\{I \wedge \neg B\}$	
	(6,7, CQR)
9. $\vdash \{I\}L: \textbf{loop if } B \textbf{ then } S \textbf{ else exit } L \textbf{ fi repeat}\{I \wedge \neg B\}$	(8, EXIT)

The proof is easy to construct top down, i.e. backwards. It shows that the labelled construct in the conclusion behaves as the loop **while** B **do** S **od** in terms of partial correctness. But the same termination proof would work, so they must be equivalent.

In a similar way it may be proved that the **while**-clause of a **loop-while-repeat** construct behaves such as a conditional **exit** out of a labelled loop. The latter mechanism is stronger since exits may occur at arbitrarily deep levels of nesting, e.g. within inner loops; this is at the cost, however, of a more complicated syntactic and semantic machinery.

◻

Exercise

4.36 As exercise 4.28 in all respects, except that the loop invariant is slightly different: $0 \leq i < j \leq n+1 \; \wedge \; A[i] < x < A[j]$.

Go-to statements

We provide an inference rule for dealing with labels occurring on members of a single statement list, given that all corresponding **go-to** statements occur within the same list, possibly at deeper levels of syntactic nesting:

GOTO :
$$\frac{\{P_j\} \text{ go to } L_j \ \{\mathbf{f}\}, \ j = 1..n \ \vdash \{P_i\}S_i\{P_{i+1}\}; \ \text{ for } i = 0..n}{\vdash \{P_0\} \ S_0; \ L_1 : S_1; \ \ldots; \ L_n : S_n \ \{P_{n+1}\}}$$

The given statement sequence has been partitioned into $n+1$ consecutive segments $S_0; \ L_1 : S_1; \ L_2 : S_2; \ \ldots; \ L_n : S_n$ by the insertion of n labels. To each label L_i is associated a predicate P_i, which characterizes the state at the position of the label, i.e. between the subsequences S_{i-1} and S_i, $i = 1, 2, \ldots, n$. So, in order to conclude the specification (P_0, P_{n+1}) for the whole sequence, it is necessary to require proofs of $\{P_i\}S_i\{P_{i+1}\}$ for $i = 0, 1, \ldots, n$. (This corresponds to the premises needed for n applications of the sequencing rule SEQ.) In our case, however, S_i is allowed to contain jumps, say **go to** L_j, and since it leads to a program point where P_j is expected to hold, P_j must hold at the jump as well. This is enforced by including the assumption $\{P_j\}$**go to** $L_j\{\mathbf{f}\}$, and since each statement subsequence may contain jumps to all labels, appropriate assumptions for all jumps are allowed for each of the $n+1$ premises.

If all jumps are in the forward direction, the rule is LC, each P_i being constructed prior to its use as the precondition of **go-to** statements. If there are backward jumps it is necessary to provide in advance at least one assertion at some cut point of every loop, i.e. a loop invariant. However, as mentioned above it is advisable to formulate the assertion associated with every label in advance, as part of the program design.

Notice that the labels considered in the GOTO rule must occur at the outermost syntactic level of a statement list, which means that corresponding **go to**'s occurring at deeper levels can cause jumps out of, but not into compounds such as loops and branchings. For a **go to** L_j occurring outside the list no assumption is available, so nothing at all is provable for jumps into the list. (Again, nested use of the same label must be disallowed.) In order to prevent jumps into the scope of local variables, any such scope should be seen as a separate syntactic unit in the present context.

EXAMPLE 4.13

We may implement the loop **while** B **do** S **od** as follows by means of explicit jumps:

$L_1 :$ **if** $\neg B$ **then go to** L_2 **fi**; S; **go to** L_1; $L_2 :$ **skip**

or $L_1 : S_1; \ L_2 :$ **skip**, where S_1 stands for the subsequence of the first three statements. We may now derive an inference rule for the implementation which corresponds to the rule WDO for **while**-loops:

$$\frac{\vdash \{I \wedge B\}S\{I\}}{\vdash \{I\} \ L_1 : S_1; \ L_2 : \textbf{skip} \ \{I \wedge B\}}$$

choosing $P_0 \Leftrightarrow P_1 \Leftrightarrow I$ and $P_2 \Leftrightarrow P_3 \Leftrightarrow I \wedge \neg B$ (cheating a little in the use of GOTO by taking the subsequence S_0 to be empty). For the proof given below it is assumed that both I and B are well-defined. A few obvious proof steps have been omitted. (The proof may be generalized to arbitrary I and B by replacing the predicates P_1 and P_2 by their strong interpretations, and the postcondition of the **if**-construct by its weak interpretation.)

1. $\{I \wedge \neg B\}$**go to** $L_2\{\mathbf{f}\} \vdash \{I \wedge \neg B\}$**go to** $L_2\{I \wedge B\}$ (CQR)
2. $\vdash I \wedge B \Rightarrow I \wedge B$ (well-def.)
3. $\{I \wedge \neg B\}$**go to** $L_2\{\mathbf{f}\} \vdash \{I\}$**if** $\neg B$ **then go to** L_2 **fi**$\{I \wedge B\}$ (1,2, TDIF)
4. $\vdash \{I \wedge B\}S\{I\}$ (premise)
5. $\{I\}$**go to** $L_1\{\mathbf{f}\} \vdash \{I\}$**go to** $L_1\{I \wedge \neg B\}$ (CQR)
6. $\{I\}$**go to** $L_1\{\mathbf{f}\}, \{I \wedge \neg B\}$**go to** $L_2\{\mathbf{f}\} \vdash \{I\}S_1\{I \wedge \neg B\}$ (3,4,5, SEQ)
7. $\vdash \{I \wedge \neg B\}$**skip**$\{I \wedge \neg B\}$ (SKIP, well def.)
8. $\vdash \{I\}\ L_1\colon S_1;\ L_2\colon$ **skip** $\{I \wedge \neg B\}$ (6,7, GOTO)

□

Exercises

4.37 Formulate and prove an inference rule for a multi-exit construct

$$CS \text{ on } L_1 \to S_1 \;[]\; L2 \to S_2 \;[]\; \cdots \;[]\; L_n \to S_n \text{ no}$$

where CS is a single compound statement containing occurrences of exit statements, **exit** L_i, i=1,2,...,n, leading out of CS and into the appropriate alternative branch S_i. Any branch may contain exits leading to textually following ones. The construct may be implemented as follows in terms of **go-to** statements and labels:

$$CS;\ \textbf{go to } L;\ L_1\colon S_1;\ \textbf{go to } L;\ \ldots;\ L_n\colon S_n;\ L\colon \textbf{skip}$$

where L is an unused label and **exit** statements are replaced by corresponding **go-to** statements.

4.5   Adaptation

When combining different proof strategies in the verification of a program, we need proof rules for smoothing the seams. For instance, we may wish to utilize an established result $\{P\}S\{Q\}$ (bottom up fashion) in order to reason about an occurrence of S in a program context where the precondition or postcondition of S, or both, must be different, say P', Q' respectively. Typically, S could be an invocation of a procedure for which an external specification has been given and proved, away from the context in which the procedure is used (cf. section 4.6). As we have seen, the consequence rules, CQL and CQR, may be used to bridge such gaps provided that the implications $P' \Rightarrow P$ and $Q \Rightarrow Q'$ are provable. Also the rule AUX of section 4.2.2 is sometimes useful, instantiating auxiliary variables in P, Q to suitable expressions. However, these three rules are not always sufficient; something stronger is needed in general.

To be specific, we wish to construct a precondition of a program segment S for arbitrary given postcondition R, using a given external specification $\{P\}S\{Q\}$ but not the internal details of S. We shall, however, make use of the sets $\mathcal{V}[S]$ and $\mathcal{W}[S]$, which presumably may be constructed mechanically from the program text S.

An inference rule for "adapting" the given specification to the new postcondition R was formulated by Hoare in [18], based on the following reasoning: If P is required in the precondition, then Q must hold upon normal termination of S. If the precondition also requires that Q implies R for all values of the out-variables, $\{x\} = \mathcal{W}[S]$, then that implication must hold upon normal termination, and therefore also R (by modus ponens). Any auxiliary variables in $\{P\}S\{Q\}$, $\{y\} = \mathcal{V}[P, Q] - \mathcal{V}[R]$, now only occur in the new precondition (assuming no name conflicts with variables of R), and may thus be existentially quantified according to the rule EXST of section 4.2, giving: $\{\exists y \bullet P \wedge \forall x \bullet Q \Rightarrow R\}\ S\ \{R\}$ (which holds for well-defined R).

The following rule is a slight generalization of that of [18] in that it allows for the renaming of auxiliaries in the premise, in order to permit an arbitrary new postcondition:

$$\text{ADAP}: \quad \frac{\vdash \{P\}S\{Q\}}{\vdash \{\exists z \bullet (P_z^y \wedge \forall x \bullet (Q_z^y \Rightarrow R))\}S\{R\}}$$

$$\text{for } \{x\} = \mathcal{W}[S], \quad \{y\} = \mathcal{V}[P, Q] - \mathcal{V}[S],$$
$$\{z\} \cap (\mathcal{V}[R] \cup \mathcal{V}[S]) = \emptyset, \text{ and } R \text{ well-defined}$$

Notice that $\{z\}$, the set of renamed auxiliaries, need not all be different from the original ones, but they must be distinct from the variables of R and S.

ADAP is left constructive, but the constructed precondition is not in general the weakest possible. Thus, putting **f** for P in ADAP we get the precondition **f** for any R, whereas $\forall x \bullet R$ would be sufficiently strong. Also, putting **t** for R gives the precondition $\exists y \bullet P$, whereas **t** is good enough. Notice, however, that if the precondition of the premise implies normal termination of S, then so does that of the conclusion.

EXAMPLE 4.14

Given $\vdash \{v = v_0\}\ v := f(v, w)\ \{v = f(v_0, w)\}$ where f is a total function. We use ADAP to construct a precondition (-schema) sufficient for arbitrary postcondition R. Assume for simplicity that v_0 does not occur free in R.

Here $\{x\} = \mathcal{W}[S] = \{v\}$, $\mathcal{V}[P] = \{v, v_0\}$, $\mathcal{V}[Q] = \{v, v_0, w\}$, $\mathcal{V}[S] = \{v, w\}$, and $\{y\} = \{v_0\}$. We may choose $\{z\} = \{y\}$ since $\{v_0\} \notin \mathcal{V}[R] \cup \mathcal{V}[S]$.

According to ADAP the precondition is:

$$\exists v_0 \bullet (v = v_0 \land \forall v \bullet (v = f(v_0, w) \Rightarrow R))$$

$$\Leftrightarrow \quad \exists v_0 \bullet (v = v_0 \land \forall v \bullet (v = f(v_0, w) \Rightarrow R^v_{f(v_0,w)}))$$

$$\Leftrightarrow \quad \exists v_0 \bullet (v = v_0 \land (\exists v \bullet (v = f(v_0, w)) \Rightarrow R^v_{f(v_0,w)}))$$

$$\Leftrightarrow \quad \exists v_0 \bullet (v = v_0 \land R^v_{f(v_0,w)}) \qquad\qquad\qquad (f(v_0, w) \text{ is well-def.})$$

$$\Leftrightarrow \quad \exists v_0 \bullet (v = v_0 \land R^v_{f(v,w)})$$

$$\Leftrightarrow \quad (\exists v_0 \bullet v = v_0) \land R^v_{f(v,w)} \qquad\qquad\qquad (v_0 \notin \mathcal{V}[R])$$

$$\Leftrightarrow \quad R^v_{f(v,w)}$$

In this case the resulting Hoare schema, $\{R^v_{f(v,w)}\}\ x := f(v, w)\ \{R\}$, is left maximal.
□

The following proof shows a formal derivation of ADAP for the case where Q and R are both well-defined, using rules of section 4.2. The proof corresponds closely to the informal reasoning given above. The side conditions add up to those of ADAP. (A closer analysis shows that Q need not be well-defined.)

1. $\vdash \{P\}S\{Q\}$ (premise)
2. $\vdash \{P^y_z\}S\{Q^y_z\}$ for $\{y\} = \mathcal{V}[P, Q] - \mathcal{V}[S]$ and $\{z\} \cap \mathcal{V}[S] = \emptyset$ (1, AUX)
3. $\vdash \{\forall x \bullet (Q^y_z \Rightarrow R)\}S\{\forall x \bullet (Q^y_z \Rightarrow R)\}$ for $\{x\} = \mathcal{W}[S]$ (CONS,w-def.)
4. $\vdash \{P^y_z \land \forall x \bullet (Q^y_z \Rightarrow R)\}S\{Q^y_z \land \forall x \bullet (Q^y_z \Rightarrow R)\}$ (2,3, CCJ)
5. $\vdash (Q^y_z \land \forall x \bullet (Q^y_z \Rightarrow R)) \Rightarrow R$ (tautology)
6. $\vdash \{P^y_z \land \forall x \bullet (Q^y_z \Rightarrow R)\}S\{R\}$ (4,5, CQR)
7. $\vdash \{\exists z \bullet (P^y_z \land \forall x \bullet (Q^y_z \Rightarrow R))\}S\{R\}$ for $\{z\} \cap \mathcal{V}[S, R] = \emptyset$ (6, EXST)

Notice that the sets $\mathcal{V}[S]$ and $\mathcal{W}[S]$, as well as the variable sets of P, Q, R, play a crucial role in constructing the precondition of the ADAP conclusion. In particular, if the former two do not contain all relevant variables the soundness of our formal logic will be lost. If $\mathcal{W}[S]$ is too small we may prove constancy of variables which actually change, and if $\mathcal{V}[S]$ is too small we are allowed to existentially quantify variables whose values prior to S may affect the result of S. On the other hand, unless these sets are minimal the constructed precondition will not be as weak as it might have been.

This discussion once more shows the importance of computing variable sets $\mathcal{V}[S]$ and $\mathcal{W}[S]$ which are correct in the semantic sense, i.e. large enough and as small as possible. As mentioned in section 4.3.3 the phenomenon of aliasing, which can occur in many programming languages, causes problems in this connection. Also the use of procedures referring directly to non-local variables complicates the $\mathcal{V}[S]$ and $\mathcal{W}[S]$ functions, and if the language in addition provides for recursion, nested procedure declarations, and the transmission of procedures as parameters, the problem of computing the minimal (in a certain syntactic sense) $\mathcal{V}$ may actually be unsolvable. The function $\mathcal{V}$, as defined for expressions, computes sets which are large enough, provided functions have no hidden arguments.

Exercises

4.38 Derive the rules CONS and EXST from ADAP and standard rules.

4.39 Derive the rule AUX from ADAP and standard rules.

4.6 Procedures

In this section we assume the existence of a procedure declaration of the following form:

> **proc** $p(\textbf{val } a, \textbf{ var } x) == S$

where a is a list of typed formal "value parameters" and x is a typed list of formal "variable parameters". The scope of each parameter is the procedure body S. The procedure p is invoked by a **call**-statement of the form

> **call** $p(e, v)$

where e is a list of expressions, the actual value parameters, and v is a list of variables, the actual variable parameters. For a given invocation the formal value parameters are interpreted as local program variables whose initial values are the values of the actual parameter expressions, and the formal variable parameters may be considered aliases for the corresponding actual parameter variables.

It is good programming practice to indicate explicitly the variables which may be affected by a procedure call. We therefore assume that the procedure body does not refer directly to non-local variables: $\mathcal{V}[S] \subseteq \{a, x\}$. (Otherwise these non-local variables would have to be treated as additional, implicit parameters.) The variable sets of a call for the procedure p then are:

$$\mathcal{V}[\textbf{call } p(e, v)] \triangleq \mathcal{V}[e, v], \text{ and } \mathcal{W}[\textbf{call } p(e, v)] \triangleq \mathcal{W}[v := v]$$

assuming that all variable parameters may be changed as the result of the call. Notice that the occurrence of a subscripted variable parameter implies that the whole array is an output variable of the call.

In order that aliasing should cause no problems for the reasoning about the details of the procedure body, it is necessary to assume that *the actual variable parameters are mutually distinct*. It is good programming practice to observe that restriction as far as all kinds of "variable" or "output" parameters are concerned. In that case the manner in which such parameters are implemented is of no concern, be it transmission by "location" as in FORTRAN, or "copy-in/copy-out" (or even "call by name" as in Algol/Simula, provided that subscripts of actual variable parameters do no themselves depend on variable parameters).

For our own purposes we may then use the following model for the statement **call** $p(e, v)$, which corresponds to parameter transmission by copying:

var $a, x := e, v;\ S;\ v := x;$ **endvar** a, x

in which the occurrence of e and both occurrences of v should be considered outside the scope of a, x. (The traditional assignment operator works the wrong way textually!) Assume for the moment that all actual variable parameters are simple variables. Then left construction over the model gives, for well-defined Q,

$$\{P_{e,v}^{a,x}\}\ \textbf{var}\ a, x := e, v\ \{P\}\ S\ \{Q_x^v\}\ v := x;\ \textbf{endvar}\ a, x\ \{Q\}$$

assuming no name conflicts between free variables of Q and the formal parameters $\{a, x\}$. More precisely, it is sufficient to require $\mathcal{V}[Q] \cap \{a, x\} - \{v\} = \emptyset$, since all occurrences of actual parameters v in Q are removed by substitution. (Notice that these substitutions are meaningless unless the latter are mutually distinct.) The resulting proof rule is left constructive except for the restriction on Q:

$$\text{LCPC}: \quad \frac{\vdash \{P\}S\{Q_x^v\}}{\vdash \{P_{e,v}^{a,x}\}\ \textbf{call}\ p(e, v)\ \{Q\}} \quad \text{for } \mathcal{V}[Q] \cap \{a, x\} - \{v\} = \emptyset$$

The rule is sound even if Q is not well-defined. It is easily generalized to take an arbitrary postcondition by performing additional variable substitutions on Q in the premise and on P in the conclusion, respectively $Q_{x,y'}^{v,y}$ and $P_{e,v,y}^{a,x,y'}$, where y is the list of conflicting variables in Q, $\{y\} = \mathcal{V}[Q] \cap \{a, x\} - \{v\}$, and y' is a list of fresh variables. The precondition may be weakened by the condition d_e that the actual value parameter expressions be well-defined.

LCPC may also be adjusted to cater for subscripted actual variable parameters. For instance, if $A[i]$ is an actual parameter corresponding to the formal variable parameter $x1$, then our model contains the copying operation $A[i] := x1$, which must be regarded as an assignment to A as a whole. Thus A must be replaced by $A[i \mapsto x1]$ in the postcondition of the premise (and in general $\mathcal{V}[A[i]] \cap \{a, x\} = \emptyset$ must be required). Furthermore, if several subscripted variables from the same array occur as actual variable parameters, the subscript values must be proved unequal in order to prevent alias problems within the procedure body. For instance, assuming **proc** $p'(\textbf{var}\ x1, x2) == S'$ we may formulate the following specialized version of LCPC:

$$\text{LCPC}': \quad \frac{\vdash \{P\}S'\{Q_{A[i \mapsto x1][j \mapsto x2]}^A\}}{\vdash \{i \neq j \wedge P_{A[i],A[j]}^{x1,\ x2}\}\ \textbf{call}\ p'(A[i], A[j])\ \{Q\}}$$
$$\text{for } \mathcal{V}[Q, i, j] \cap \{x1, x2\} = \emptyset.$$

Notice the postcondition of the premise. The modification to Q corresponds to left construction over the final assignments to the actual **var** parameters, $A[i], A[j] := x_1, x_2$ in the model of the call.

A BU rule for procedure call is as follows:

$$\text{BUPC}: \quad \frac{\vdash \{P\}S\{Q\}}{\vdash \{P_{e,v}^{a,x}\} \textbf{ call } p(e,v) \; \{(\exists a \bullet Q)_v^x\}}$$

$$\text{for } (\mathcal{V}[P,Q] - \mathcal{V}[S]) \cap \mathcal{V}[e,v] = \emptyset$$

where the restriction requires that auxiliary variables in the premise must be re-named if necessary, so as not to clash with variables occurring in the call statement.

BUPC follows from LCPC, in the case of simple actual variable parameters, by proving $Q \Rightarrow ((\exists a \bullet Q)_v^x)_x^v$. But we can show that no variable in the list v is free in $\exists a \bullet Q$, unless it is also a member of the list x:

$$
\begin{aligned}
(\mathcal{V}[\exists a \bullet Q] - \{x\}) \cap \{v\} \; &= \; (\mathcal{V}[Q] - \{a\} - \{x\}) \cap \{v\} \quad &&\text{(by definition)} \\
&\subseteq \; (\mathcal{V}[Q] - \mathcal{V}[S]) \cap \{v\} &&\text{(since } \mathcal{V}[S] \subseteq \{a,x\}) \\
&\subseteq \; (\mathcal{V}[P,Q] - \mathcal{V}[S]) \cap \mathcal{V}[e,v] \\
&= \; \emptyset &&\text{(by assumption)}
\end{aligned}
$$

Thus, by lemma (2.6) p. 14 $((\exists a \bullet Q)_v^x)_x^v$ is the same as $\exists a \bullet Q$, which is implied by Q.

The rule holds for subscripted actual variable parameters as well, provided that the precondition of the conclusion is strengthened by any necessary subscript in-equality, and that no subscript depends on variable parameters. If the formal and actual value parameters also remain constant over the procedure invocation,

$$\{a\} \cap \mathcal{W}[S] = \mathcal{V}[e] \cap \mathcal{W}[\textbf{call } p(e,v)] = \emptyset$$

then a somewhat stronger postcondition $Q_{e,v}^{a,x}$ may be specified for the conclusion.

When using LCPC one usually has to apply adaptation to a given procedure specification in order to prove the premise, whereas the use of BUPC generally involves adaptation of the conclusion.

Exercise

4.40 Show that the following adapted version of BUPC holds, analogous to LCPC$'$ above, in spite of the fact that $A \in \mathcal{W}[\textbf{call } p'(A[i], A[j])]$:

$$\frac{\vdash \{P\}S'\{Q\}}{\vdash \{i \neq j \wedge P_{A[i],A[j]}^{x1,\; x2} \wedge \forall x1, x2 \bullet Q \Rightarrow R_{A[i \mapsto x_1][j \mapsto x_2]}^{A}\} \textbf{ call } p'(A[i], A[j]) \; \{R\}}$$

for $\mathcal{V}[P,Q] \cap \mathcal{V}[A,i,j,R] = \emptyset$, $\;A \notin \mathcal{V}[i,j]$, and R well-defined

Hint: Take advantage of the fact that A can be modified only at the two specified indices.

Recursion

In order to prove a specification $\{P\}S\{Q\}$ for the body S of a recursive procedure p we have to reason about the outcome of each call for p inside S. But for that purpose we need a result about the body S, and so on indefinitely. Fortunately, it is appropriate to break this circle of reasoning by introducing *assumptions* about the recursive calls which correspond to the result $\{P\}S\{Q\}$ we are trying to prove. The assumptions correspond to induction hypotheses in an induction proof with respect to depth of recursion. Clearly, for any given terminating invocation of the procedure, each textually contained recursive call necessarily has a maximum recursion depth less than the maximum depth of the given invocation. That justifies the use of induction hypotheses for the recursive calls. In the following rule of direct recursion the assumptions are derived using BUPC, auxiliaries of $\{P\}S\{Q\}$ renamed as necessary:

$$\text{DREC}: \quad \frac{\{P^{a,\,x}_{e_i,v_i}\} \text{ call } p(e_i, v_i)\ \{(\exists a \bullet Q)^x_{v_i}\}\ i = 1..n\ \vdash \{P\}S\{Q\}}{\vdash \{P\}S\{Q\}}$$

It is assumed that S textually contains n recursive calls for p, and there is one assumption for each of them. If the formal value parameters remain constant over S and the actual value parameters e_i remain constant over the i'th recursive call, the postcondition of the corresponding assumption may be strengthened to $Q^{a,\,x}_{e_i,v_i}$.

For mutual recursion in a set of procedures a more elaborate rule (or, rather, set of rules) is needed. For each conclusion there will be one premise for each procedure in the cluster, and for each premise there may be assumptions about all the procedures called recursively.

For recursive procedures there is an *a priori* possibility of non-termination due to infinite recursion. The DREC rule only expresses the invariant fact that P, Q, suitably modified, are valid pre- and postconditions for each invocation of the procedure body in a recursion, provided that P holds at entry to the initial invocation.

A proof of termination may be based on an integer valued *progress function* f, $\mathcal{V}[f] \subseteq \mathcal{V}[S]$, such that $\vdash P \Rightarrow f \geq 0$, and such that its value decreases with increasing level of recursion. (It happens that more highly structured function values are needed in order to prove termination, cf. section 4.4.3.) The additional reasoning is included in the following embellished version of DREC:

$$\frac{\vdash P \Rightarrow f \geq 0;}{\{f^{a,\,x}_{e_i,v_i} < \alpha \wedge P^{a,\,x}_{e_i,v_i}\} \text{ call } p(e_i, v_i)\ \{(\exists a \bullet Q)^x_{v_i}\},\ i = 1..n\ \vdash \{P \wedge f = \alpha\}S\{Q\}}{\vdash \{P\}S\{Q\}}$$

The conclusion that the recursion involved in a given invocation of p will actually terminate is informal as usual.

EXAMPLE 4.15

We prove $\{a \geq 0\}S\{x = a!\}$, where S is the body of the procedure *Fac*:

proc *Fac*(**val** $a : Int$, **var** $x : Int$) ==
if $a = 0$ **then** $x := 1$ **else**   **call** $Fac(a-1, x)$; $x := a * x$ **fi**

and where the factorial function satisfies the following axioms:

A1: $\vdash 0! = 1$
A2: $\vdash x \geq 0 \Rightarrow (x+1)! = (x+1) * x!$

Since $\mathcal{W}[S] = \mathcal{W}[\textbf{call } Fac(a-1, x)] = \{x\}$, the formal parameter a is constant over S and the actual value parameter $a-1$ remains unchanged over the recursive call. We may therefore introduce a fairly strong assumption:

$$\{a-1 \geq 0\} \textbf{ call } Fac(a-1, x) \ \{x = (a-1)!\} \tag{4.10}$$

By TDIF we now have to prove

$$\{a \geq 0 \wedge a = 0\} \ x := 1 \ \{x = a!\}$$

which follows from A1. We also have to prove

$$\{a \geq 0 \wedge a \neq 0\} \textbf{ call } Fac(a-1, x); \ x := a * x \ \{x = a!\}$$

Using AS this amounts to proving

$$\{a > 0\} \textbf{ call } Fac(a-1, x) \ \{a * x = a!\}$$

But the precondition is equivalent to that of (4.10), and since the condition does not depend on x we may use the proof rules CONST and CJ of section 4.2 to strengthen the postcondition of (4.10). By CQR the resulting verification condition is $a > 0 \wedge x = (a-1)! \Rightarrow a * x = a!$, which follows from A2. An alternative proof strategy is to adapt (4.10) with respect to the postcondition $a * x = a!$, obtaining the precondition $a > 0 \wedge (\forall x \bullet x = (a-1)! \Rightarrow a * x = a!)$, which reduces to $a > 0$.

Normal termination is proved by considering the progress function a (meaning the function $\lambda a, x \bullet a$), since the precondition of the procedure body is $a \geq 0$, and the first actual parameter of the recursive call is $a-1$.

$\square$

Exercises

4.41   Assume that

$$\{P\} \textbf{ loop while } B(x); \ x := f(x) \textbf{ repeat } \{Q\}$$

may be proved. Use this fact to prove $\{P\} \textbf{ call } p \ \{Q\}$, where

proc p == **if** $B(x)$ **then** $x := f(x)$; **call** p **fi**

Show also that a proof of termination of the loop may be used to prove termination of the recursion. Hint: Identify the verification conditions involved in proving the loop.

4.42   Define

> **proc** $div(\textbf{val}\ x,y : Nat,\ \textbf{var}\ z : Nat)\ ==$
>   **if** $x<y$ **then** $z := 0$ **else call** $div(x-y,z);\ z:+z+1$ **fi**

Prove $\{t\}$ **call** $div(a,b,v)\ \{0 \le a-v*b < b\}$, and that the recursion terminates for $b \neq 0$. Compare the proofs with those of example 4.3.

4.43   Let *BinTree* be a type of data structure representing binary trees, and let the following functions be given:

$emp :$	$\rightarrow BinTree$	(empty tree)
$lsub : BinTree \rightarrow BinTree$		(left subtree)
$rsub : BinTree \rightarrow BinTree$		(right subtree)
$D : BinTree \rightarrow Int$		(maximum depth)

where the maximum depth function satisfies the following axioms:

A1: $\vdash D(emp) = 0$
A2: $\vdash t \neq emp \Rightarrow D(t) = max(D(lsub(t)), D(rsub(t))) + 1$

Prove $\{t\}\ d := 0;\ \textbf{call}\ plumb(T,0)\ \{d = D(T)\}$

where   **proc** $plumb(\textbf{val}\ t : BinTree,\ k : Int)\ ==$
           if $t = emp$ **then** $d := max(d,k)$
           else call $plumb(lsub(t), k+1);$ **call** $plumb(rsub(t), k+1)$ **fi end**

for a given binary tree T and *Int* variable d. Hint: The non-trivial part of the exercise consists of formulating a sufficiently strong Hoare sentence for the procedure body which holds at all levels of recursion.

4.7   Effect Functions

In this section only *deterministic* programs are considered, unless otherwise explicitly stated. Let S be a program section where x is the list of out-variables of S, $\{x\} = \mathcal{W}[S]$. Since S is deterministic, the effect of executing S is completely determined by the initial state together with S itself. This means that there exists a program of the form

> **if** t_S **then** $x := e_S$ **else abort fi**   (4.11)

which *models* S in the sense that it has the same net overall effect whenever S terminates normally, and it behaves abnormally whenever S does. Here t_S, as usual, stands for the condition that S will terminate normally, and e_S stands for an expression defining the so-called *effect function* of S. It is a tuple expressing the final values of the out-variables of S. These values can depend on the initial state, but clearly, only through variables occurring in S, i.e. $\mathcal{V}[e_S] \subseteq \mathcal{V}[S]$. Strictly speaking, the effect function of S is $\lambda w \bullet e_S$, where the list of arguments, w, corresponds to the program variables, thus $\mathcal{V}[S] \subseteq \{w\}$. Obviously, e_S is well-defined whenever S terminates normally.

e_S is in general an expression *tuple* corresponding to the list of variables in $\mathcal{W}[S]$, and $x := e_S$ thus stands for simultaneous assignments to these variables, $x_1, x_2, \ldots := e_S.\mathbf{1}, e_S.\mathbf{2}, \ldots$, where the right hand sides denote the components of e_S (cf. section 5.8.4). We may, however, simplify the notation a little by seeing the effect as an assignment to a *tuple of variables*: $(x_1, x_2, \ldots) := e_S$. Correspondingly, the notations $P^x_{e_S}$ and $P^{(x_1, x_2, \ldots)}_{e_S}$ both stand for $P^{x_1,\ x_2,\ \ldots}_{e_S.\mathbf{1}, e_S.\mathbf{2}, \ldots}$.

4.7.1   Effect function theorems

Assume that the Hoare sentence $\{P\}S\{Q\}$ is proven, Q well-defined. Left construction over the model (4.11) shows that $t_S \Rightarrow Q^x_{e_S}$ is the weakest precondition which guarantees Q upon normal termination of S. Since P also guarantees Q upon normal termination, we may conclude that

$$P \Rightarrow (t_S \Rightarrow Q^x_{e_S}) \tag{4.12}$$

is a valid formula. (Notice that P may not be the *weakest* possible precondition for the postcondition Q; therefore the implication is one-way.) This reasoning justifies the introduction of the following *effect function rule*, in which the well-definedness assumption for Q may be dropped:

$$\text{EFR}: \quad \frac{\vdash \{P\}S\{Q\}}{\vdash t_S \Rightarrow (P \Rightarrow Q^x_{e_S})} \quad \text{for } \{x\} = \mathcal{W}[S]$$

The conclusion of EFR, which is a simple rearrangement of (4.12), is called an *effect function theorem*, EFT. It can be understood as an axiom for t_S and e_S, seen as functions of the program variables.

If the Hoare sentence of the premise is sufficiently strong the EFT will imply a complete definition of the effect function over the domain defined by t_S: $t_S \Rightarrow e_S = E$, where E is an explicit expression. Substituting E for e_S in the EFT gives $t_S \Rightarrow (P \Rightarrow Q^x_E)$, where the formula enclosed in parentheses is another explicit expression, say G. Thus, for a sufficiently strong premise of EFR the resulting EFT can be expressed in the form:

$$t_S \Rightarrow G \wedge e_S = E, \quad \text{where} \quad G \Leftrightarrow P \Rightarrow Q^x_E \tag{4.13}$$

Whereas e_S can be determined completely by an EFT (over some domain t_S), the same is not the case for the normal termination condition itself. However, since

$t_S \Rightarrow G$, the formula G is a *necessary* condition for the normal termination of S, which we call a *partial termination guard*. (Notice that the precondition $\neg G$ does imply abnormal behaviour of S.) Our inability to conclude a sufficient condition for normal termination is in accord with the fact that Hoare Logic only deals with partial correctness. However, the weaker the precondition P of the EFR premise, the stronger the partial termination guard in general. If P is somehow known to be the truly weakest precondition for a sufficiently strong postcondition Q then we may conclude, outside the formal logic, that the corresponding G is in fact equivalent to t_S.

We shall assume that a constructed termination guard G is well-defined (if not, $d_G \wedge G$ must be used instead because the guard is interpreted strongly in the EFT). We also assume that it is a sufficient condition for the well-definedness of the actual effect function expression: $d_G \wedge (G \Rightarrow d_E)$. Then the expression

$$GE_S \triangleq \text{if } G \text{ then } E \text{ else } \bot \text{ fi} \tag{4.14}$$

defines what we call a *guarded effect function* of S. It represents an explicit partial specification of S in the sense that S, whenever it terminates normally, has exactly the same net effect as the assignment $x := GE_S$, where $\{x\} = \mathcal{W}[S]$, and it behaves abnormally at least when explicitly required by the specification. If $G = t_S$ then GE_S is a total specification of S, and it is sufficient that E is well-defined whenever S terminates normally (on an idealized computer). If G is weaker than t_S then E should be well-defined on a correspondingly larger domain.

EXAMPLE 4.16

Let S be some statement which always behaves abnormally, such as **loop while t repeat** or **abort**. Then we can prove $\{\mathbf{t}\}S\{\mathbf{f}\}$, which gives the EFT $t_S \Rightarrow (\mathbf{t} \Rightarrow \mathbf{f})$. Hence t_S is exactly the constant $\mathbf{f}$. This is the only case when complete determination of a termination predicate is possible in Hoare Logic. □

EXAMPLE 4.17

Let S be

if $m < 100$ **then** $m := m + 1$ **else abort fi**

in which case $\mathcal{V}[S] = \mathcal{W}[S] = \{m\}$. In order to get a strong Hoare sentence for S a good postcondition is $m = m_0$, where m_0 is an auxiliary variable. Left construction gives $\vdash \{m < 100 \Rightarrow m + 1 = m_0\}S\{m = m_0\}$.

Use of EFR and $\forall$I proves

$$\forall m_0 \bullet t_S \Rightarrow ((m < 100 \Rightarrow m + 1 = m_0) \Rightarrow e_S = m_0), \quad \text{equivalent to}$$
$$\forall m_0 \bullet t_S \Rightarrow ((\neg m < 100 \vee m + 1 = m_0) \Rightarrow e_S = m_0), \quad \text{equivalent to}$$
$$\forall m_0 \bullet t_S \Rightarrow (\neg m < 100 \Rightarrow e_S = m_0) \wedge (m + 1 = m_0 \Rightarrow e_S = m_0)$$

Since none of t_S or e_S contains free m_0, the EFT is further equivalent to

$$t_S \Rightarrow (\forall m_0 \bullet \neg m < 100 \Rightarrow e_S = m_0) \wedge (\forall m_0 \bullet m+1 = m_0 \Rightarrow e_S = m_0), \quad \text{and to}$$
$$t_S \Rightarrow (\neg m < 100 \Rightarrow \forall m_0 \bullet e_S = m_0) \wedge ((\exists m_0 \bullet m+1 = m_0) \Rightarrow e_S = m+1)$$

But the value of e_S is determined by m alone, so $\forall m_0 \bullet e_S = m_0$ is false. Furthermore $\exists m_0 \bullet m + 1 = m_0$ is true since $m + 1$ is well-defined. Hence the EFT is equivalent to

$$t_S \Rightarrow (m < 100 \wedge e_S = m + 1)$$

which is of the form (4.13). Notice that we have arrived at an expression for the effect function which is always well-defined, even though S is known to behave abnormally for $m \geq 100$. Thus, **if** $m < 100$ **then** $m+1$ **else** $\bot$ **fi**, as well as $m+1$ are valid guarded effect functions. The Hoare Logic shows that the partial termination guard, $m < 100$, is a necessary condition for normal termination; in this case, however, it is (likely to be) sufficient as well.

□

4.7.2   Effect function validation

Let G be a formula and E an expression whose value is a tuple corresponding to the list of out-variables of program S. Assume that both are well-defined whenever S terminates normally, and that $\mathcal{V}[E, G] \subseteq \mathcal{V}[S]$. In order to show that E expresses an effect function for S and G a partial termination guard, the following formulas must be proved:

$$\text{EF:} \quad t_S \Rightarrow e_S = E \qquad \text{and} \qquad \text{TG:} \quad t_S \Rightarrow G$$

which together constitute (4.13). They follow by proving the Hoare sentences

$$\text{EFS:} \quad \{E = x_0\} S \{x = x_0\} \qquad \text{and} \qquad \text{TGS:} \quad \{\neg G\} S \{\mathbf{f}\}$$

where $\{x\} = \mathcal{V}[S]$ and x_0 is an auxiliary variable list, $\{x_0\} \cap \mathcal{V}[S] = \emptyset$.

Proof
The sentence EFS implies the EFT $\forall x_0 \bullet t_S \Rightarrow (E = x_0 \Rightarrow e_S = x_0)$ (after $\forall$I). Since none of t_S, e_S, and E contains free x_0, and since the last occurrence of x_0 may be replaced by E, the EFT is equivalent to $t_S \Rightarrow (\exists x_0 \bullet E = x_0) \Rightarrow e_S = E$, which reduces to EF. TGS implies the EFT $t_S \Rightarrow (\neg G \Rightarrow \mathbf{f})$, which immediately reduces to TG. ∎

Validation of EFS and TGS can be carried out by the top down strategy for given E and G. However, TGS can also be used to construct G (by left construction and negation of the result).

Exercise

4.44 Show that the middle loop of the program of exercise 4.35

> **for** $j := 1$ **to** $i - 1$ **do**
> **if** $A[j] > A[j + 1]$ **then** $A[j] :=: A[j + 1]$ **fi od**

has the effect function expression $f(A, i)$ whose value is a sequence of length N, and where the function f can be defined inductively as follows:

$$f(A, i)[k] \triangleq \begin{cases} A[k] & \text{if } i < k \leq N \\ A[t] & \text{if } k = i \\ A[k + 1] & \text{if } t \leq k < i \\ f(A, t - 1)[k] & \text{if } 1 \leq k < t \end{cases}$$

$$\text{where } t \text{ is uniquely defined by} \quad \forall r \bullet \ 1 \leq r < t \Rightarrow A[r] \leq A[t]$$
$$\text{and} \quad \forall r \bullet \ t < r \leq N \Rightarrow A[r] < A[t]$$

Notice that the unique definition of t would matter if the array components were data objects with a sorting key and the inequalities only considered the key. (For such objects x, y the relation $x \leq y \wedge y \leq x$ would only imply equal key values, and not $x = y$.)

4.7.3 Adaptation by effect function

Suppose an EFT for S of the form (4.13) is known. We make use of that for the purpose of adaptation as follows. Left construction over the model (4.11) gives

$$\vdash \{(t_S \Rightarrow R^x_{e_S})\} S \{R\} \qquad \text{for } R \text{ well-defined} \tag{4.15}$$

From this we may conclude the following rule of adaptation, valid for deterministic statement S:

$$\text{ADAP}' : \quad \frac{\vdash t_S \Rightarrow G \wedge e_S = E}{\vdash \{G \Rightarrow R^x_E\} S \{R\}} \quad \text{for } \{x\} = \mathcal{W}[S] \text{ and } R \text{ well-defined}$$

Proof

The left consequence rule shows that we must prove $\vdash (G \Rightarrow R^x_E) \Rightarrow (t_S \Rightarrow R^x_{e_S})$. That is: assuming $G \Rightarrow R^x_E$ and t_S, prove $R^x_{e_S}$. But t_S and the premise of ADAP' imply G, which gives R^x_E by the first assumption. $e_S = E$ is also implied, which gives $R^x_{e_S}$ by substitution. ∎

ADAP' is a simpler rule than the standard rule of adaptation, ADAP, because the constructed precondition is quantifier free. The left consequence rule permits the precondition of any Hoare sentence to be strengthened. We may therefore, if we so wish, use the precondition R_E^x (if E is well-defined in the context provided by R), thereby obtaining an even simpler rule. If we strengthen the precondition even more, writing $G \wedge R_E^x$, it will protect against some specific cases of abnormal behaviour.

Notice that ADAP′ is only sound for deterministic program S. The reason for the difficulty is the fact that two executions of a non-deterministic program may give different results even if the initial states are the same, which means that the premise of ADAP′ could only hold for "non-deterministic expressions" E which do not satisfy the reflexive law of equality, $E = E$.

It is possible to use an EFT directly to obtain a left constructive rule of adaptation, not knowing an explicit effect function. The EFT and (4.15) give

$$\vdash \{(P \Rightarrow Q_{e_S}^x) \Rightarrow R_{e_S}^x\} \; S \; \{R\} \qquad \text{for } R \text{ well-defined} \qquad (4.16)$$

by CQL. (Informal proof: $P \Rightarrow Q_{e_S}^x$ is weaker than t_S by the EFT. So, the precondition of (4.16) is stronger than that of (4.15).) Let y be the list of auxiliary variables, $\{y\} = \mathcal{V}[P, Q] - \mathcal{V}[S]$. Assuming for the moment that these variables do not occur in R, the precondition of (4.16) may be existentially quantified with respect to y (rule EXST). Since the auxiliaries do not occur in $R_{e_S}^x$ (remember that $\mathcal{V}[e_S] \subseteq \mathcal{V}[S]$) the quantifier may be localized to the precedent of the implication:

$$\vdash \{(\forall y \bullet P \Rightarrow Q_{e_S}^x) \Rightarrow R_{e_S}^x\} \; S \; \{R\} \qquad \text{for } R \text{ well-defined} \qquad (4.17)$$

It is now clear that the quantified variables can be named freely as long as they do not clash with the other variables of $P \Rightarrow Q_{e_S}^x$, at most $\mathcal{V}[S]$. Name conflicts between the auxiliaries and variables of R not in S are therefore harmless. If the expression denoted by e_S is unknown, the best we can do is to introduce a variable, or tuple of variables, to stand for its value. In order to guarantee the postcondition R the precondition must hold for all values of these new variables:

$$\text{ADAP″}: \quad \frac{\vdash \{P\}S\{Q\}}{\vdash \{\forall x' \bullet (\forall y \bullet P \Rightarrow Q_{x'}^x) \Rightarrow R_{x'}^x\}S\{R\}}$$

$$\text{for } \{x\} = \mathcal{W}[S], \quad \{y\} = \mathcal{V}[P, Q] - \mathcal{V}[S],$$
$$\{x'\} \cap \mathcal{V}[P, S, Q] = \emptyset, \text{ and } R \text{ well-defined}$$

ADAP″ is sound for arbitrary P, Q, not necessarily well-defined, and for arbitrary S, not necessarily deterministic. The conclusion of ADAP″ is the strongest possible one for given $\mathcal{V}[S]$ and $\mathcal{W}[S]$.

Exercise

4.45 Derive ADAP, given ADAP″ and standard rules.

4.7.4 Procedure call by effect function

Let $GE_p ==$ **if** G **then** E **else** $\perp$ **fi** be a guarded effect function for the procedure p, **proc** $p(\textbf{val }a, \textbf{ var }x) == S$ **end**:

$$\vdash t_S \Rightarrow G \wedge e_p = E$$

where e_p is a tuple consisting of the x-components of e_S. (Any a-components assigned to in S may be ignored because value parameters are variables local to the procedure.) We consider the statement **call** $p(e, v)$, where the actual parameters v are simple variables, and wish to construct the weakest possible precondition for the call, given the postcondition and the guarded effect function GE_p. It is fairly obvious that the corresponding guarded effect function of the call is:

$$GE_{\textbf{call }p(e,v)} == \textbf{if } d_e \wedge G_{e,v}^{a,x} \textbf{ then } E_{e,v}^{a,x} \textbf{ else } \perp \textbf{ fi}$$

where the termination guard may be strengthened by d_e because these actual parameters are evaluated prior to the execution of the procedure body, and the expression tuple $E_{e,v}^{a,x}$ corresponds to the actual parameters v. Thus, using the rule ADAP' we may derive the following rule for left construction over the procedure call:

$$\text{PCEF}: \quad \frac{\vdash t_S \Rightarrow G \wedge e_p = E}{\vdash \{d_e \wedge G_{e,v}^{a,x} \Rightarrow Q_{E_{e,v}^{a,x}}^v\}\textbf{call }p(e,v)\{Q\}} \quad \text{for } Q \text{ well-defined}$$

For the sake of completeness we derive PCEF more formally. According to the generalized version of rule LCPC we shall use $Q_{y',x}^{y,\,v}$ as the postcondition for left construction over the procedure body, where y is the list of variables in Q, other than v's, which have name conflicts with formal parameters, $\{y\} = \mathcal{V}[Q] \cap \{a,x\} - \{v\}$, and y' is a corresponding list of fresh variables. ADAP' gives

$$\vdash \{G \Rightarrow (Q_{y',x}^{y,\,v})_E^x\} \; S \; \{Q_{y',x}^{y,\,v}\}$$

where the precondition meta-expression simplifies to $G \Rightarrow Q_{y',E}^{y,\,v}$ since $Q_{y',x}^{y,\,v}$ contains no other x's than those which have replaced the v's. Now the generalized LCPC specifies the following precondition of the procedure call:

$$d_e \Rightarrow (G \Rightarrow Q_{y',E}^{y,\,v})_{e,v,y}^{a,x,y'}$$

Since the conflicting formal parameters (other than v's) are replaced by fresh variables, the only occurrences of formal parameters in the modified Q are those contained in the copies of the expression E. Therefore this meta-expression simplifies to $d_e \wedge G' \Rightarrow Q_{E'}^v$, where the primes indicate substitution of e for a and v for x. This concludes the derivation.

4.7.5   Function procedures

A function procedure is a procedure which returns a function value, and which is used as a function syntactically. Thus, an activation of a function procedure is an expression whose value is the function value returned. There should be no side effects. We assume that the procedure identifier is used as an out-variable receiving the function value. The declaration of a function procedure *fp* might be as follows:

$$\textbf{func } fp(x : T_x) : T == S \qquad \text{for } \mathcal{V}[S] \subseteq \{x, fp\} \text{ and } fp \in \mathcal{W}[S]$$

where x is a list of formal parameters, T_x is the list of their types, and T is the type of the function value. (Any parameter not transmitted by value should remain unchanged by S in order to avoid side effects.) Thus, the procedure represents a function $fp : T_x \longrightarrow T$.

Let GE_{fp} be a guarded effect function of the function procedure:

$$GE_{fp} == \textbf{if } G \textbf{ then } E \textbf{ else } \bot \textbf{ fi}$$

where E and G are validated as explained in section 4.7.2, taking *fp* as the only output variable of the procedure body.

GE_{fp} provides a mathematical characterization of the function *fp*, in the sense that the latter is known to *approximate* the function $\lambda x : T_x \bullet GE_{fp}$. If $G = t_S$ then the correspondence is exact (possibly except for strictness properties, and for execution on an ideal computer); however, in general the function procedure may behave abnormally for an argument list a such that the guarded effect function is well-defined. Thus, $fp(a) \sqsubseteq (GE_{fp})_a^x$. If the parameters x are transmitted by value then *fp* represents a strict function.

For a recursive function procedure the recursive applications may be interpreted as applications of the postulated guarded effect function during the validation proofs.

EXAMPLE 4.18
We declare a function procedure for the factorial function:

$$\textbf{func } fac(x : Int) : Int ==$$
$$fac := \textbf{if } x{=}0 \textbf{ then } 1 \textbf{ else } fac(x{-}1) * x \textbf{ fi}$$

and postulate the guarded effect function: $GE_{fac} == \textbf{if } x \geq 0 \textbf{ then } x! \textbf{ else } \bot \textbf{ fi}$. The validation of GE_{fac} follows almost immediately from the standard axioms $\vdash 0! = 1$ and $\vdash x > 0 \Rightarrow x! = (x{-}1)! * x$ by replacing the recursive application of *fac* in the procedure body by $\textbf{if } x{-}1 \geq 0 \textbf{ then } (x{-}1)! \textbf{ else } \bot \textbf{ fi}$.

□

4.8   Mythical Program Sections

In this section we tie together a couple of loose ends by introducing the concept of mythical program text. The idea provides a general technique of program documentation.

We consider program texts in general as consisting of *mythical, non-mythical,* and *mixed* sections. Mythical sections are statements or lists of statements included in curly brackets; they are intended as program documentation, facilitating understanding and reasoning, and are to be ignored during program execution. Mythical sections cannot be nested. The syntax of the mythical program text is an extension of the ordinary one, allowing certain new constructs (see below). The whole formula language (FL) is also available in mythical expressions, including logical quantifiers as well as "abstract" types and functions not implemented as part of the programming language.

Let S be a statement (or list of statements) not textually inside any pair of curly brackets. If S contains no curly brackets it is defined as a non-mythical program section, otherwise it is said to be mixed. A program variable or constant is said to be mythical if (and only if) declared in a mythical program section, and in that case the scope termination, if explicit, must occur in a mythical section too. Notice that the role of declarations and scope terminators as separate statements makes it possible for the scope of a mythical variable or constant to include non-mythical and mixed program sections.

The concept of mythical sections may be generalized to include mythical formal and actual parameters (arguments) to procedures and functions.

Two program texts are associated with any mixed program text PT; both must be syntactically correct:

- PT_{eff} — the *effective* program — obtained by deleting (or replacing by a semicolon or comma if required by the syntactic context) each mythical section, and

- PT_{log} — the *logical* program— obtained by deleting (or replacing by a semicolon or comma if required by the syntactic context) each left or right curly bracket separately.

Clearly, PT_{log} should be considered in relation to a suitably extended, hypothetical programming language, somehow implemented so that any well-defined expression evaluates to its mathematically defined value.

The syntactic functions $\mathcal{V}$ and $\mathcal{W}$ do not distinguish between mythical and non-mythical sections:

$$\mathcal{V}[PT] = \mathcal{V}[PT_{log}] \quad \text{and} \quad \mathcal{W}[PT] = \mathcal{W}[PT_{log}]$$

Let $\mathcal{M}_S$ and $\mathcal{N}_S$ be the sets of mythical and non-mythical variables, respectively, whose scopes contain S, where S is a statement in PT_{log} or PT_{eff}. Then standard variable binding rules imply that PT must satisfy the following requirements:

1. $\mathcal{V}[S] \subseteq \mathcal{M}_S \cup \mathcal{N}_S$, for any statement S contained in PT_{log}, and
2. $\mathcal{V}[S] \subseteq \mathcal{N}_S$, for any statement S contained in PT_{eff}.

We intend to reason about PT_{log} and would like the results to be applicable to the behaviour of PT_{eff}:

$$\text{MYTH} : \quad \frac{\vdash \{P\}PT_{log}\{Q\}}{\vdash \{\exists myth \bullet P\}PT_{eff}\{\exists myth \bullet Q\}}$$

where *myth* is the list of mythical variables non-local to PT, $\{myth\} = \mathcal{M}_{PT}$. Then the (hypothetical) behaviour of PT_{log} must be identical to that of PT_{eff} as far as operations on non-mythical variables are concerned. In particular, MYTH implies that PT_{eff} behaves abnormally whenever PT_{log} would. We may actually conclude the converse too: PT_{eff} must terminate normally whenever PT_{log} would, because the former is obtained form the latter by *deleting* program text.

In order for the rule MYTH to be sound, every mythical statement S contained in PT must satisfy the following additional requirements:

3. $\mathcal{W}[S] \subseteq \mathcal{M}_S$, and
4. S terminates normally whenever executed, for the given precondition P of PT.

Requirement 3 ensures that no mythical state component can influence any value assigned to any non-mythical state component, or the path of the program control outside mythical sections. This is because all expressions, including if-tests and loop-tests, containing mythical variables (except possibly in argument positions identified as mythical) must belong to an entirely mythical statement, in view of 2 and the syntactic correctness of PT_{eff}.

In order to simplify the validation of restriction 4 as much as possible, we forbid the use of aborting statements (with one exception, see below), as well as free loops and **call**-statements. There remains, however, the non-trivial restriction that expressions occurring in mythical statements should be well-defined.

4.8.1   State assertions

In order to make state predicates, which are added as internal documentation to a program, acceptable as mythical program text we have to extend our programming language. Thus, single Boolean expressions are allowed to occur as a new kind of basic statements, called *state assertions*. The operational meaning of a state assertion B shall be to check that B holds, and to cause abortion otherwise:

if $\neg B$ then abort fi

If a state assertion is ill-defined, its execution does not terminate normally, as if it had been false. This shows that state assertions will be interpreted *strongly*. Since state assertions do not contribute to the progress of an algorithm, they are primarily intended to occur in mythical sections. But there is no reason to also forbid their use as non-mythical consistency checks, if expressed in non-mythical and executable terms.

Considering restriction 4 above we have to compensate for the introduction of implicit aborts in mythical sections by proving that these aborts will not be encountered during any hypothetical execution of PT_{log}, provided that a stated precondition to PT is satisfied initially. We therefore adopt a left constructive axiom schema for mythical state assertions in which the precondition implies normal termination:

$$\text{MYSA}: \quad \vdash \{d_B \wedge B \wedge Q\} \{B\} \{Q\} \quad \text{for } Q \text{ well-defined}$$

For a non-mythical state assertion, however, we may use a left maximal axiom schema for ordinary partial correctness reasoning:

$$\text{NMSA}: \quad \vdash \{d_B \wedge B \Rightarrow Q\} \, B \, \{Q\} \quad \text{for } Q \text{ well-defined}$$

Our notation for mythical program sections implies that any valid Hoare sentence $\{P\}S\{Q\}$ may alternatively be seen as a mixed statement sequence beginning and ending with a mythical state assertion, which might be embedded in a larger program text, provided P and Q are well-defined. Fortunately, MYSA implies $\vdash \{R\}\{R\}\{R\}$ for well-defined R; so the mixed statement sequence $\{P\}S\{Q\}$ satisfies the same Hoare sentence as S itself. It also terminates normally if and only if S does, provided that the initial state satisfies P.

NMSA implies $\vdash \{R\}R\{R\}$ for arbitrary R, well-defined or not. Thus, for arbitrary P, Q we conclude that $\{P\}P; S; Q\{Q\}$ is valid if and only if $\{P\}S\{Q\}$ is.

Notice that the state assertion **t** is equivalent to **skip**, whether mythical or not, whereas **f** and $\perp$ are equivalent to **abort** if non-mythical. A mythical state assertion **f**, or $\perp$, asserts that control does not reach this point in a verified program. (Notice that any formula, not necessarily well-defined in all states, may occur as a mythical state assertion, provided it can be proved that it will not be executed whenever ill-defined.)

4.8.2 Mythical program constants

The idea that a Hoare sentence $\{P\}S\{Q\}$ can be seen as a mixed program text does not quite work if P, Q contain auxiliary variables, unless embedded in a larger program within the scope of such program variables or constants. It is sometimes useful to declare such constants *within the precondition* of a Hoare sentence. For this purpose we introduce declarations of the form **const** $c : T \bullet R$, where T is a type and R is an arbitrary formula possibly restricting the value of c. If R is identically true it may be omitted together with the dot. In programming terms

c is called a "non-deterministic constant" since the restricting predicate may not determine its value uniquely. Declarations of this form are only allowed as mythical program text, but they are also acceptable as preconditions of Hoare sentences, with the logical meaning $\exists c : T \bullet R$. The scope of the constant c, however, includes the whole sentence. Such a Hoare sentence cannot be embedded within the scope of another quantity named c.

The new construct satisfies the following left and right constructive rules for well-defined P, Q:

$$\text{LCMC}: \quad \vdash \{(\exists c : T \bullet R) \wedge \forall c : T \bullet R \Rightarrow Q\} \; \{\mathbf{const}\; c : T \bullet R\} \; \{Q\}$$

$$\text{RCMC}: \quad \vdash \{P\} \; \{\mathbf{const}\; c : T \bullet R\} \; \{P \wedge R\} \quad \text{for } c \notin \mathcal{V}[P]$$

The construct may be generalized to cater for a list of constants. Notice that the declaration $\mathbf{const}\; c : T \bullet c = e$ is equivalent to $\mathbf{const}\; c : T = e$ for $c \notin \mathcal{V}[e]$. As a precondition it would have the logical value $\mathbf{t}$.

The following rule for "constant instantiation" is sometimes necessary, for instance in connection with adaptation:

$$\text{CINST}: \quad \frac{\vdash \{\mathbf{const}\; c : T \bullet P\} \; S \; \{Q\}}{\vdash \{P_e^c\} \; S_e^c \; \{Q_e^c\}} \quad \text{for } \mathcal{V}[e] \cap \mathcal{W}[S] = \emptyset$$

Notice that the constant c may well occur (as a non-local) in mythical sections of S. Such occurrences must also be replaced.

EXAMPLE 4.19

Given $\{\mathbf{const}\; c : T \bullet P\} S \{Q\}$ we may use CINST to obtain $\{P\}S\{Q\}$, in which the constant c is "instantiated" to a free (auxiliary) variable c, provided that $c \notin \mathcal{V}[S]$. The result may in turn be adapted using ADAP or ADAP''.
□

Exercise

4.46 "Towers of Hanoi". The following recursive procedure moves a pile of n discs from one place, a, to another, c, using a third pile, b, for temporary storage. In each step the top disc from one pile is moved to the top of another in such a way that the disc order is unchanged in the final result. The piles are represented as objects of type "sequence of discs", where discs are objects of an unspecified type:

$$\mathbf{type}\; Pile == \mathbf{seq}\; Disc, \quad \mathbf{type}\; Disc == \cdots$$

In this exercise the concept of sequences is used informally, juxtaposing piles and discs to get new piles in intuitively obvious ways. The prefix operator # gives the length of a sequence, and ε stands for an empty sequence. The right end of a sequence corresponds to the top of the pile. (Sequences and sequence operators are formalized in section 5.8.8.)

Verify the annotated procedure body, given that the statement ˙**call** *move-top(a, c)* satisfies the specification corresponding to the adjacent state assertions, and that $\mathcal{W}[\textbf{call } movetop(a,c)] = \{a,c\}$. Strengthen the internal state assertions as necessary, and take as given all intuitively obvious lemmas about sequences needed in order to prove the verification conditions:

proc *move*(**val** $n : Int$, **var** $a, b, c : Pile$) ==
$\quad\quad$ {**const** $\alpha, \beta, \gamma, \delta : Pile \bullet 0 \leq n \leq \#a \wedge \#\delta = n \wedge a = \alpha\delta \wedge b = \beta \wedge c = \gamma$}
$\quad\quad$ **if** $n \neq 0$ **then** {**const** $d : Disc$, $\delta' : Pile \bullet \delta = d\delta'$}
$\quad\quad\quad\quad$ **call** *move*$(n - 1, a, c, b)$
$\quad\quad\quad\quad$ {$a = \alpha d \wedge c = \gamma$}
$\quad\quad\quad\quad$ **call** *movetop*(a, c)
$\quad\quad\quad\quad$ {$a = \alpha \wedge c = \gamma d$}
$\quad\quad\quad\quad$ **call** *move*$(n - 1, b, a, c)$
$\quad\quad$ **fi** {$a = \alpha \wedge b = \beta \wedge c = \gamma\delta$}

Hint: It is sufficient to adapt the allowable assumptions about the two recursive calls by means of the rules CINT, CONST, and CCJ.

Prove also that

$$\{\textbf{const } \pi : Pile \bullet p = \pi \wedge q = r = \varepsilon\} \textbf{ call } move(\#p, p, q, r) \{p = q = \varepsilon \wedge r = \pi\}$$

for **var** $p, q, r : Pile$, and that all piles at each step of the algorithm are sorted according to decreasing disc size if that is true for pile p initially. The letter ε stands for an empty sequence.

4.8.3 Mythical variables

Consider a state assertion of the form $\exists x \bullet P$ occurring in a program S, and suppose we can prove its validity by pointing out an expression e such that P holds for e. If the construction of e is non-trivial the proof of P_e^x is easier than that of $\exists x \bullet P$, and therefore S might be better documented if we include this more explicit state assertion. It can happen that the expression e is a complicated one when it has to be expressed in terms of existing program variables, but that it would be easy to express if we were to enrich the program with suitable new variables. Since these variables, as well as the operations on them, would contribute nothing to the actual results of the program, they should be *mythical*. Sometimes a good solution is to introduce a single variable, say v, to be updated in such a way that its value is that of e at all times, and to use the state assertion P_v^x.

EXAMPLE 4.20
The following algorithm for computing the integer square root of a given integer n was the subject of exercise 4.25:

$\{n \geq 0\}$ $x := 0;\ y := n;\ q := 1;$
    $\textbf{while}\ q \leq n\ \textbf{do}\ q := 4 * q\ \textbf{od};$
    $\textbf{loop}\ \{0 \leq y = n - x^2/q < 2x + q\ \wedge\ x \bmod q = 0\ \wedge\ \exists k \bullet k \geq 0 \wedge q = 4^k\}$
    $\textbf{while}\ q \neq 1;$
        $q := q/4;$
        $\textbf{if}\ y < x + q\ \textbf{then}\ x := x/2$
        $\textbf{else}\ y := y - (x + q);\ x := x/2 + q\ \textbf{fi}$
    $\textbf{repeat}$
$\{x^2 \leq n < (x+1)^2 \wedge y = n - x^2\}$

The existentially quantified conjunct of the invariant of the second loop expresses the fact that the value of the variable q is a non-negative power of 4. Introducing the concept of logarithm to the base 4 we can manage without the quantifier: $q > 0 \wedge q = 4^{log_4 q}$. A better idea perhaps is to express the exponent in terms of the number of times the two loop bodies have been executed, using a mythical counter k:

$\{n \geq 0\}$ $x := 0;\ y := n;\ q := 1\ \{\textbf{var}\ k := 0\}$
    $\textbf{while}\ q \leq n\ \textbf{do}\ q := 4 * q\ \{k := k+1\}\ \textbf{od};$
    $\textbf{loop}\ \{0 \leq y = n - x^2/q < 2x + q\ \wedge\ x \bmod q = 0\ \wedge\ k \geq 0 \wedge q = 4^k\}$
    $\textbf{while}\ q \neq 1;$
        $q := q/4\ \{k := k-1\}$
        $\textbf{if}\ y < x + q\ \textbf{then}\ x := x/2$
        $\textbf{else}\ y := y - (x + q);\ x := x/2 + q\ \textbf{fi}$
    $\textbf{repeat}$
$\{x^2 \leq n < (x+1)^2 \wedge y = n - x^2\}$

A more substantial example of the technique of trading existential quantifiers for mythical variables is shown below (example 4.21).
□

Sometimes a good way to document an algorithm is to include a simple "abstract" version of it in terms of mythical operations on mythical variables, as well as state assertions which explain the relation between the mythical variables and the non-mythical ones. See example 4.22 below.

Another important application of mythical program variables is to accumulate information about past states and past actions, not available, directly or at all, through the current values of non-mythical variables. In particular, it may be necessary to record information about interactions between the program and its environment or about interactions between concurrent processes. See section 4.9 on input/output.

We include a notation for non-deterministic initialization of mythical variables analogous to that of mythical constants: **var** $v : T \bullet P$, satisfying rules similar to LCMC and RCMC (and admissible as the precondition of Hoare sentences, although this is probably less useful). Non-deterministic update of mythical variables, however, is useful. We therefore admit constructs of the form **some** $x : T \bullet P$ as the right hand sides of mythical assignments. The construct evaluates to a value of type T, which satisfies the predicate P but is otherwise unspecified. x is a bound variable with the scope P. If P is identically true the construct may be simplified to **some** T. Non-deterministic assignment is characterized as follows syntactically and semantically:

$$\mathcal{V}[\textbf{some } x{:}T \bullet P] \triangleq \mathcal{V}[P] - \{x\}, \qquad \mathcal{W}[\textbf{some } x{:}T \bullet P] \triangleq \emptyset$$

$$d_{\textbf{some } x{:}T \bullet P} \triangleq d_{\exists x{:}T \bullet P} \wedge \exists x{:}T \bullet P$$

$$\text{NDAS}: \quad \vdash \{(\exists x{:}T \bullet P) \wedge (\forall x{:}T \bullet P \Rightarrow Q_x^v)\} \; \{v := \textbf{some } x{:}T \bullet P\} \; \{Q\}$$

In the special case where the predicate P is identically true, the non-deterministic assignment axiom is much simpler:

$$\text{SNDAS}: \quad \vdash \{\forall v{:}T \bullet Q\} \; \{v := \textbf{some } T\} \; \{Q\}, \quad \text{for } \textbf{var } v{:}T$$

Notice that **some**-constructs are only allowed as right hand sides of (mythical) assignment statements, not as expressions in general; the latter would lead to logical difficulties such as the reflexivity property of equality breaking down. For the same reason the concept of effect function is not very useful for non-deterministic assignments.

EXAMPLE 4.21
The following is an annotated version of Hoare's algorithm *FIND* [19], which locates the element number f according to size in an array A indexed from 1 to n, for $1 \leq f \leq N$, with logarithmic average efficiency. The invariants needed for the partial correctness proof (I_m, I_n, I_i, I_j) are as in [19]:

$\{1 \leq f \leq N\}$
FIND : **var** $m, n := 1, N$;
$\qquad$ **loop** $\{I_m \wedge I_n\}$ **while** $m < n$;
$\qquad\qquad$ **var** $i, j, r := m, n, A[f]$ $\{$**var** $i', j' := r, r\}$

loop $\{I\}$ **while** $i \le j$;
   loop $\{I\}$**while** $A[i] < r$; $i := i + 1$ **repeat**
   loop $\{I \wedge r \le A[i]\}$ **while** $r < A[j]$; $j := j - 1$ **repeat**
   $\{I \wedge A[j] \le r \le A[i]\}$
   if $i \le j$ **then** $A[i] :=: A[j]$ $\{i', j' := j, i\}$ $i, j := i + 1, j - 1$ **fi**
  repeat $\{I \wedge j < i\}$
  if $i \le f$ **then** $m := i$ **else if** $f \le j$ **then** $n := j$ **else exit** *FIND* **fi fi**
 repeat $\{I_m \wedge I_n \wedge n \le m\}$ **endvar** m, n
$\{\forall p, q \bullet\ 1 \le p \le f \le q \le N \Rightarrow A[p] \le A[f] \le A[q]\}$

where I_m is $1 \le m \le f \wedge \forall p, q \bullet\ 1 \le p < m \le q \le N \Rightarrow A[p] \le A[q]$,
     I_n is $f \le n \le N \wedge \forall p, q \bullet\ 1 \le p \le n < q \le N \Rightarrow A[p] \le A[q]$,
     I_i is $m \le i \wedge \forall p \bullet\ 1 \le p < i \Rightarrow A[p] \le r$,
     I_j is $j \le n \wedge \forall q \bullet\ j < q \le N \Rightarrow r \le A[q]$, and
     I is $I_m \wedge I_n \wedge I_i \wedge I_j$.

The main idea of the algorithm is to *partition* an array by permutation into a left part and a right part such that all members of the former are less than or equal to those of the latter. The invariants I_m and I_n state that the array is partitioned immediately to the left of m and immediately to the right of n, and that $1 \le m \le f \le n \le N$. This implies that the array segment $A[m..n]$ contains the element we are looking for. A variable i scans the array from index m towards the right, passing over "small" elements only (I_i), compared to a discriminating value r; and j scans from index n towards the left, passing over "large" elements only (I_j). When both scans have stopped at elements of the wrong size, and have not yet crossed over, these elements are swapped and both scans are advanced. When they do cross over, a partitioning of $A[m..n]$ has been obtained, and the part containing index f is taken as the new middle segment.

   In his discussion Hoare shows the termination of the inner loops by postulating the existence of an element of the wrong size ahead of either scan:

$$(\exists i' \bullet i \le i' \le n \wedge r \le A[i']) \ \wedge\ \exists j' \bullet m \le j' \le j \wedge A[j'] \le r$$

(which holds at the top of the middle loop provided $i \le j$). The above program is embellished by mythical variables i', j' pointing to such elements. Initially the chosen discriminating element will terminate both scans, and in later rounds elements of the wrong size encountered in either scan have been pushed ahead. Thus, strengthening the middle loop invariant by

$$i \le j \Rightarrow i \le i' \le n \wedge r \le A[i'] \wedge m \le j' \le j \wedge A[j'] \le r$$

is sufficient to prove the termination of either scan. The expressions $i'-i$ and $j-j'$ may serve as progress functions for these loops. Proving the termination of the middle loop follows easily, and that of the outermost one becomes possible as well, see exercise 4.47.

□

EXAMPLE 4.22

The following algorithm selects a repetition-free sequence from a given finite set of elements, say choosing a bridge hand from a deck of cards. The array A is initialized to $[1..N]$, the sequence of integers $1, 2, \ldots, N$. The final contents of $A[1..n]$, where $n \leq N$, is the selected sequence. It is chosen "at random", provided that the function $random(a, b)$, where $a \leq b$, chooses randomly from the numbers $a, a+1, \ldots, b$:

> **var** A : **array** $\{1..N\} = [1..N]$;
> **for** $i := 1$ **to** n **do const** $j := random(i, N)$; $A[i] :=: A[j]$ **od**

If N is large and n is not, it is better to simulate the array A by two short ones, a and b of length n, where $a = A[1..n]$ and b records those elements of $A[n+1..N]$ that have been altered. Since these elements necessarily have values in the range $\{1..n\}$, we may represent each altered element $A[j] = k$, $n < j \leq N$, by putting $b[k] = j$, and letting unused elements of b have some harmless value, such as the initial one. The resulting algorithm, however, is not immediately understandable; therefore it is useful to include the easy one as mythical program text and to explain the purpose of a and b in terms of A:

> $\{$**var** A : **array** $:= [1..N]\}$
> **var** a : **array** $\{1..n\} = [1..n]$, b : **array** $\{1..n\} = [1..n]$;
> **for** $i := 1$ **to** n **do const** $j := random(i, N)$ $\{A[i] :=: A[j]\}$
>   **if** $j \leq n$ **then** $a[i] :=: a[j]$ **else**
> $b[i] := j$; $k := 1$; **loop while** $b[k] \neq j$; $k := k+1$ **repeat**; $b[i] := i$;
> $b[k] := k$; $b[a[i]] := j$; $a[i] :=$ **if** $k = i$ **then** j **else** k **fi fi**
> $\{A[1..n] = a \ \wedge \ A[n+1..N] = [1..N][b[1..i] \mapsto [1..i]][n+1..N]\}$
> **od** $\{a = A[1..n]\}$

The postcondition is probably more informative than an attempt to express formally the notion of repetition-free random sequence. The indicated role of b is expressed using notations defined in section 5.8.8. In particular, the notation $[b[1..i] \mapsto [1..i]]$ indicates updating of the preceding sequence at a list of indices: $[b[1] \mapsto 1][b[2] \mapsto 2] \ldots [b[i] \mapsto i]$. Notice that updates at indices less than or equal to n are irrelevant for the $[n+1..N]$ segment of the result.

□

Exercises

4.47 Prove the claims of example 4.21 above. Prove also the termination of the outermost loop, as well as the well-definedness of all subscripted variables. Hint: It is necessary to strengthen the postcondition of the middle loop by $m < i \wedge j < n$. For that purpose the invariant of that loop must also be strengthened.

4.48   Prove the second algorithm of example 4.22. Hint: In order to be provable the post-invariant of the loop must be strengthened by conjuncts expressing that A and b are repetition-free, and that all $a[i+1..n]$ are less than or equal to n.

4.9   Input/Output

Input and output operations are interactions between a program execution and its environment, during which data objects are transmitted into or out of the program. The kind of objects transmitted will depend on the level of abstraction at which the program is viewed, be it bits, characters, numbers, or more complicated objects such as tables or pictures. In any case the interactions may be summed up as a *time-ordered sequence of individual data transmissions*.

Consider the simple case of a program with a single input channel IC and a single output channel OC, which is supposed to read some data from IC, write some results on OC, and then terminate. In this case the external specification of the program can probably be expressed as a relation between two separate sequences of data: the input sequence and the output sequence, the mutual temporal order of input and output transmissions during program execution being irrelevant.

Let OC be a channel for outputting data objects of type T, introduced by the declaration **chan** OC : **out** T. Output operations on OC have the form $OC.write(e)$, where e is an expression of type T. The correspondence between the time sequence of output operations and the total sequence of output data, seen externally, may be formalized by introducing a mythical program variable, $OC.h$ associated with OC, whose value at any time is the sequence of output data produced so far, the "output history". That invariant is established by initializing $OC.h$ to an empty sequence, and is maintained by associating with each output operation on OC a mythical update of $OC.h$, extending it by the data object written out.

We might thus add mythical statements as follows, where ε stands for an empty sequence, and the operator $\vdash$ extends a given sequence by a new element at the right end (for more details about sequence types and operations on sequences see section 5.8.8):

> To   **chan** OC : **out** T associate $\{\textbf{var}\ OC.h : \textbf{seq}\ T = \varepsilon\}$,
> to $OC.write(e)$ associate $\{OC.h := OC.h \vdash e\}$.

It would be possible to treat input axiomatically by providing a mythical sequence valued variable representing the complete sequence of input data to come. This might be a natural way of thinking in the case where the input is in fact a file on some mass storage. However, mass storage files are better represented as non-mythical program variables, global to the program in the case of long term data storage.

We prefer to treat input in a manner analogous to output, introducing for any input channel *IC* a mythical variable *IC.h* accumulating the *input history*:

To	**chan** $IC : \textbf{in } T$	associate	$\{\textbf{var } IC.h : \textbf{seq } T = \varepsilon\},$
to	$IC.read(v)$	associate	$\{IC.h := IC.h \vdash v\}.$

Not specifying in advance the input to come, the *read* statement itself must be understood as a *non-deterministic* assignment to its variable parameter, $v :=$ **some** T (in this special case performed on a non-mythical variable!).

There are several advantages in treating input in this manner, philosophical and mathematical, as well as practical:

- For an interactive program the input provided by the user will depend on the output given so far, so invariants relating input and output histories may be useful, and it may even be desirable to specify explicitly how these histories are merged in time.

- When dealing with concurrent processes interacting through communication channels, then, for a given channel, the output history of one process is in a simple relation to the input history of another.

- The complete future input to programs not intended to terminate, such as operating systems, nodes in a communication network, or process control programs, would require the specification of infinite sequences, whereas finite sequences are sufficient in order to express invariants on the I/O histories of any non-terminating loop.

We simplify the notation indicated above by letting the channel itself denote its own input or output history, mythically updated by *read* or *write* statements. This leads to the following left constructive axiom schemas, where ⟨kind⟩ stands for **in**, **out**, or **in/out**:

CHAN :	$\vdash \{Q_\varepsilon^C\}$ **chan** $C : \langle kind \rangle\ T\ \{Q\}$		
INP :	$\vdash \{\forall v : T \bullet Q_{C \vdash v}^C\}\ C.read(v)\ \{Q\},$	for	**chan** $C : \textbf{in } T$
			and **var** $v : T$
OUTP :	$\vdash \{Q_{C \vdash e}^C\}\ C.write(e)\ \{Q\},$	for	**chan** $C : \textbf{out } T$

For an **in/out** channel the associated history consists of inputs as well as outputs and could be of the type **seq** $(\{\textbf{in}, \textbf{out}\} \times T)$, each term specifying the direction of transmission: $(\textbf{in}, t)$ or $(\textbf{out}, t)$, where $t : T$ is the value transmitted. The axioms for input and output on **in/out** channels must be corresponding modifications of those above.

For programs with several input and/or output channels a more complete external specification is possible if the individual channel histories are replaced by a single total I/O history, where each term in addition identifies the channel on which the corresponding I/O event occurred.

EXAMPLE 4.23
Consider the following simple non-terminating program.

> **chan** X : **in** *Int*, Y : **out** *Int* $\{X = Y = \varepsilon\}$
> **loop** $\{Y = dbl(X)\}$ **var** v : *Int*; $X.read(v)$; $Y.write(2 * v)$ **repeat**

The loop invariant obviously holds, provided that the function

> dbl : **seq** *Int* $\rightarrow$ **seq** *Int*

computes the result sequence by doubling the terms of the argument sequence. In fact, we may mimic the algorithm of the program exactly by providing the following pair of axioms defining the function inductively (cf. section 5.2), where the operator $\dashv$ appends a new element at the left end of a sequence:

> A1: $\vdash dbl(\varepsilon) = \varepsilon$
> A2: $\vdash dbl(x \dashv X) = (2 * x) \dashv dbl(X)$

The verification conditions of the loop are

> entry: $X = Y = \varepsilon \Rightarrow Y = dbl(X)$
> invariance: $Y = dbl(X) \Rightarrow \forall \alpha \bullet Y \vdash (2 * \alpha) = dbl(X \vdash \alpha)$

The truth of both formulas is fairly obvious, but the latter can only be formally proved by induction. If, however, we define the *dbl* function inductively with respect to the right append operator rather than left append:

> A2′: $\vdash dbl(X \vdash x) = dbl(X) \vdash (2 * x)$

then both verification conditions may be proved directly.

From this example we draw the conclusion that sequence functions intended to be used for the documentation and verification of iterative programs may best be defined in terms of the right append operator. Notice, however, that the evaluation of sequence expressions on the basis of such function definitions is likely to correspond to algorithms working the "wrong" way. This may be demonstrated by evaluating an application of the function *dbl* to a sequence of length 2, using the axioms A2′ and A1:

> $dbl(\varepsilon \vdash 1 \vdash 2) \stackrel{A2'}{=} dbl(\varepsilon \vdash 1) \vdash 4 \stackrel{A2'}{=} dbl(\varepsilon) \vdash 2 \vdash 4 \stackrel{A1}{=} \varepsilon \vdash 2 \vdash 4$

□

Exercise

4.49 Verify the following externally specified program:

$\{t\}$ **chan** X, Y : **in** *Int*, Z : **out** *Int*;
    var x, y : *Int*; $X.read(x)$; $Y.read(y)$;
L : **loop if** $y < x$ **then** $Z.write(y)$; $Y.read(y)$
         else if $x < M$ **then** $Z.write(x)$; $X.read(x)$
         else exit L **fi fi**
    repeat
$\{X \neq \varepsilon \ \wedge\ Y \neq \varepsilon \ \wedge\ rt(Y) \geq rt(X) \geq M \ \wedge$
    $(ndec(X) \wedge ndec(Y) \Rightarrow Z = merge(lr(X), lr(Y)))\}$

Here *ndec* is a predicate stating that the terms of the argument sequence are in non-decreasing order, M is a large integer assumed to signal the end of input on channels X and Y, the functions rt and lr take the right term and "left remainder" of a non-empty sequence, and the merge function is defined as follows:

MRG1: $\vdash merge(X, \varepsilon) = X$
MRG2: $\vdash merge(\varepsilon, Y) = Y$
MRG3: $\vdash merge(X \vdash x, Y \vdash y) = $ **if** $y < x$ **then** $merge(X, Y \vdash y) \vdash x$
                          else $merge(X \vdash x, Y) \vdash y$ **fi**

Notice the need to assume that the input sequences are sorted. Otherwise the program and the *merge* function give different results. (Try examples!)
   Hint: A reasonable loop invariant to try first would be

$X \neq \varepsilon \ \wedge\ Y \neq \varepsilon \ \wedge\ x = rt(X) \ \wedge\ y = rt(Y) \ \wedge$
    $(ndec(X) \wedge ndec(Y) \Rightarrow Z = merge(lr(X), lr(Y)))$

At least, this invariant leads to the desired program postcondition. However, in trying to prove its invariance you will discover a need to strengthen the antecedent of the verification condition. Strengthen the loop invariant accordingly and try again.

Chapter 5

Data Types

For a programmer working with a strongly typed language, a "type" can be seen as a set of data objects which may occur as values of program variables of that type, and be given as input to or be the output from procedures and functions according to the rules of strong typing.

Take for instance the type *integer* (in the sequel called *Int*) of signed whole numbers. When programming in terms of integers we do not want to think of the actual representation of them as bit strings on some computer; we only consider properties that are in some sense independent of particular implementations, so-called "abstract" properties, thinking of *Int* as a corresponding "abstract type". So, it does not matter whether integer values are represented as strings of binary digits or decimal digits, or even as signed roman numbers, provided that the associated arithmetic operations are tailored to fit the representation (except for the obvious inefficiencies in space and time that would be associated with roman representation).

This means that we prefer to think of the integers provided by an implementation as mathematical objects, and in particular to reason about the operations on them in terms of familiar arithmetic laws. Although we sometimes do have to be conscious of the fact that only integers in a certain range are provided for, we usually do not have to care about number size because the range will be large enough for most practical purposes, and the computer should tell if the bounds happen to be violated in some particular computation. Notice that the properties of the arithmetic operations are probably more important to us than what numbers "are".

In our view a type T is a *pair*:

$$T \triangleq (V_T, F_T)$$

where V_T is the value set of the type T, and F_T a set of functions syntactically associated to T. We shall, however, from time to time disregard this definition, writing e.g. $x \, \epsilon \, T$, meaning $x \, \epsilon \, V_T$. The idea of associating a set of functions with a type is important for several reasons:

- In designing an abstract type T a useful starting point is to list a set of functions that will be required for operating on T-values, including their profiles. We want to keep the concept of T-values as representation independent as possible, and concentrate instead on the functions and their properties.
- As we shall see, the value set V_T can be defined indirectly (and more or less completely) in terms of a certain subset of F_T. Thereby these functions will be very strongly associated with the type semantically.
- Associating functions with particular types is a generally useful way of grouping and classifying functions. Normally, the type T occurs in the profile of every function in F_T.
- Simple rules for function overloading can be devised based on type association. For instance, we shall associate an equality relation with every type, each represented by the operator $\hat{} = \hat{}$. For each occurrence of the operator the relation is the one associated with the type of the operands.
- When programming in an object oriented style, data objects can have associated procedures and functions whose names have an entirely local significance. "Dot notation", say $X.P$, is traditionally used to denote the procedure P owned by an object X. For a strongly typed language, however, the set of associated procedures is the same for all objects of the same type (or class). Thus X of $X.P(\ldots)$ can be seen as a distinguished parameter of P identifying P as one of the procedures associated with its type.

As indicated above we commence the design of an abstract data type T by identifying a set of $n > 0$ functions that will be needed for generating and operating on T values. For each function we specify its profile:

$$\textbf{func } f_i : \ D_{i,1} \times D_{i,2} \times \cdots \times D_{i,n_i} \longrightarrow C_i, \quad n_i \geq 0, \quad i = 1, 2, \ldots, n$$

(We often prefix the profile by the key word **func** in order to indicate clearly that a function is being introduced.) Types other than T occurring in a profile are assumed to be previously defined. Since these types (if any) are needed in order to describe the T-functions, they are said to be types *underlying* T.

The following classification of the functions in F_T is useful:

- *producers*, $PRD_T \triangleq \{f_i \, \epsilon \, F_T \bullet C_i = T\}$, are functions producing T values,
- *relative constants*, $CST_T \triangleq \{f_i \, \epsilon \, PRD_T \bullet D_{i,1}, \ldots, D_{i,n_i} \neq T\}$, are producers with no T argument (possibly no argument at all), and
- *observers*, $OBS_T \triangleq \{f_i \, \epsilon \, F_T \bullet C_i \neq T\}$, are functions having one or more T objects among their arguments and producing values of types other than T, thereby "observing" properties of the T objects.

Clearly, $PRD_T \cup OBS_T = F_T$, $PRD_T \cap OBS_T = \emptyset$, and $CST_T \subseteq PRD_T$.

Notice that we think of the operations as functions in the mathematical sense, not as modifications of stored structures, even if the "values" we are talking about are the contents of large data bases. It is our intention to use abstract types primarily to *reason about programs*, and reasoning is simpler in terms of spaceless and timeless values than in terms of stored data structures subject to change. In order to simplify the reasoning about stored structures we may use variables of abstract types subjected to assignments of abstract values.

EXAMPLE 5.1

Let S be a program variable, i.e. a stored data object, of type *Intstack*, "stack of integers". In an object oriented setting the operation of pushing an integer n onto S might be expressed as $S.PUSH(n)$. Abstractly we may look at this operation as an assignment to S of a new *Intstack* value:

$$S := push(S, n), \quad \text{where} \quad \textbf{func } push : Intstack \times Int \longrightarrow Intstack$$

Let the effect of a *POP* operation $S.POP(x)$, be to remove the top element of S and assign it to the variable x of type *Int*. It would be regarded as a simultaneous assignment to x and S:

$$x, S := top(S), pop(S), \quad \text{where} \quad \textbf{func } top : Intstack \longrightarrow Int$$
$$\textbf{func } pop : Intstack \longrightarrow Intstack$$

It is reasonable to initialize any *Intstack* variable to an empty stack:

$$\textbf{var } S : Intstack = estack, \quad \text{where} \quad \textbf{func } estack : \longrightarrow Intstack$$

Thus, a minimal set of associated functions to consider could be

$$F_{Intstack} = \{estack, \ push, \ top, \ pop\}$$

The function *top* is an observer, the others are producers. *estack* is a constant.

□

Having identified the names and profiles of a set F_T of functions, the next task is to give meanings to T values and to the functions. The general approach of algebraic specification of "abstract types" is to introduce axioms in the form of equations, expressing laws such as $pop(push(S, x)) = S$ and $x+y = y+x$ for operators on stacks and numbers, respectively. The value sets are generally implicit, if defined at all, and are thus very abstract indeed. In this style the user has great freedom in choosing his axioms, but on the whole the tools of algebra are quite demanding mathematically: there is little guidance as to which laws to write down, there are difficult logical questions concerning consistency and completeness, and an axiom set for one type may permit different value sets depending on axioms for other types.

We avoid most of these mathematical difficulties by being a little less abstract: by giving a (more) explicit definition of every value set, and by using a style of axiomatization which amounts to explicit function definition. In this style consistency and completeness can in most cases be controlled syntactically. The specifications will lend themselves to semi-mechanical reasoning through term rewriting. Actually, the specification style can be seen as a kind of applicative programming language which can be directly implemented on computers. But, as already stated, our intention is primarily to specify concepts useful for program documentation and formal reasoning.

The specification tools will be explained in a way which does not require knowledge of algebra. The notations used could form part of a formal specification language.

5.1   Generators

In programming languages such as Pascal or Ada new basic data types may be defined through explicit enumeration of the value set, say,

$$\textbf{type } Suit = \{clubs, diamonds, hearts, spades\}$$

where a predefined set of functions, such as *successor*, *predecessor*, as well as equality and ordering relations go along with the type, in addition to the constants listed. Notice that the latter may be regarded as functions of arity zero.

The constants listed in an enumeration of T-values will be called *generator functions*, and the list itself will be called a *generator basis* for T, denoted G_T. We now extend these ideas in a non-trivial way by permitting *arbitrary* producer functions as members of a generator basis (provided that the basis contains at least one relative constant), writing e.g.

$$G_T = \{g_1, g_2, \ldots, g_n\}, \qquad \text{for } n \geq 1, \;\; \forall i \bullet g_i \, \epsilon \, PRD_T, \;\; \exists i \bullet g_i \, \epsilon \, CST_T$$

The effect of specifying a generator basis for the type T is to express the fact or intention that

- *all values of type T may be finitely expressed by T-generators alone (possibly applied to values of other types).*

Variable free expressions in generators are called *basic expressions*. Generator functions are by definition *total and strict*. Thus, all basic expressions are well-defined. We say that a type is *generated* by the functions contained in its generator basis.

The set of all basic expressions of type T is called the *generator universe* of T, GU_T. If the generator basis contains producers other than relative constants then, since generators are total, the generator universe is necessarily infinite (although every element of GU_T is a finite expression). Clearly, the generator basis must contain relative constants to serve as starting points in creating the generator universe. It is usually advantageous to choose generator bases as small as possible.

EXAMPLE 5.2
The values of type Boolean are expressed as **t** and **f**.

> **func t, f** : $\longrightarrow Bool$
> $G_{Bool} = \{\mathbf{t}, \mathbf{f}\}$ gives $GU_{Bool} = \{\mathbf{t}, \mathbf{f}\}$

In the same way we may define the generator universe of any enumeration type in the sense of Pascal.

□

EXAMPLE 5.3
According to the Italian mathematician Peano, all natural numbers (i.e. non-negative integers) may be expressed using only two functions, the constant zero and the successor function:

> **func** 0 : $\longrightarrow Nat$, $\mathbf{S\hat{\ }}$: $Nat \longrightarrow Nat$
> $G_{Nat} = \{0, \mathbf{S\hat{\ }}\}$ gives $GU_{Nat} = \{0, \mathbf{S}0, \mathbf{SS}0, \mathbf{SSS}0, \ldots\}$

A few comments are in order:
- The syntax by which the elements of the generator universe are expressed textually is not important. The idea behind the syntax is the notion of a nest of successor function applications, the argument of the innermost one being the constant zero.
- This way of expressing natural numbers is analogous to roman representation in its extreme, also called "unary" representation.

□

EXAMPLE 5.4
The concept of *sequences* is of fundamental importance to programming and program specification. Strings, arrays, files, lists, and for that matter most hardware memory units, are essentially spatial sequences, and in some form or another sequences in time are essential for reasoning about the interactions of a data process with its environment, be it other data processes running concurrently or the outside world.

We consider finite sequences over an arbitrary and unspecified base type T, denoted **seq** T. Let the value space of T be $\{a, b, \ldots\}$, and let the following functions be among those associated with **seq** T:

func ε :		$\longrightarrow$ **seq** T	(empty sequence)
func $\hat{\ }\vdash\hat{\ }$:	**seq** $T \times T$	$\longrightarrow$ **seq** T	(append right)
func $\hat{\ }\dashv\hat{\ }$:	$T \times$ **seq** T	$\longrightarrow$ **seq** T	(append left)
func $\hat{\ }\dashv\vdash\hat{\ }$:	**seq** $T \times$ **seq** T	$\longrightarrow$ **seq** T	(concatenate)
func $\langle\hat{\ }\rangle$:	T	$\longrightarrow$ **seq** T	(singleton)
func $\langle\hat{\ }, \hat{\ }\rangle$:	$T \times T$	$\longrightarrow$ **seq** T	(doubleton)
func $\langle\hat{\ }, \hat{\ }, \hat{\ }\rangle$:	$T \times T \times T$	$\longrightarrow$ **seq** T	(trebleton)
$\vdots$	$\vdots$	$\vdots$	$\vdots$

Several useful alternative generator bases may be defined by means of these functions:

Right appending: $G^1_{\mathbf{seq}\,T} = \{\varepsilon, \,\hat{}\vdash\hat{}\,\}$
gives $GU^1_{\mathbf{seq}\,T} = \{\varepsilon, \;\varepsilon\vdash a, \;\varepsilon\vdash b, \;\ldots, \;\varepsilon\vdash a\vdash a, \;\varepsilon\vdash a\vdash b, \;\ldots\}.$

Left appending: $G^2_{\mathbf{seq}\,T} = \{\varepsilon, \,\hat{}\dashv\hat{}\,\}$
gives $GU^2_{\mathbf{seq}\,T} = \{e, \;a\dashv\varepsilon, \;b\dashv\varepsilon, \;\ldots, \;a\dashv a\dashv\varepsilon, \;b\dashv a\dashv\varepsilon, \;\ldots\}.$

Concatenation: $G^3_{\mathbf{seq}\,T} = \{\varepsilon, \langle\hat{}\rangle, \,\hat{}\vdash\!\!\vdash\hat{}\,\}$
gives

$$GU^3_{\mathbf{seq}\,T} = \{\; \begin{array}{llll} \varepsilon, & \langle a\rangle, & \langle b\rangle, & \cdots \\[4pt] \varepsilon \vdash\!\!\vdash \varepsilon, & \varepsilon \vdash\!\!\vdash \langle a\rangle, & \varepsilon \vdash\!\!\vdash \langle b\rangle, & \cdots \\[4pt] \langle a\rangle \vdash\!\!\vdash \varepsilon, & \langle a\rangle \vdash\!\!\vdash \langle a\rangle, & \langle a\rangle \vdash\!\!\vdash \langle b\rangle, & \cdots \\[4pt] \vdots & \vdots & \vdots & \ddots \;\}. \end{array}$$

Explicit notation: $G^4_{\mathbf{seq}\,T} = \{\varepsilon, \langle\hat{}\rangle, \langle\hat{},\hat{}\rangle, \langle\hat{},\hat{},\hat{}\rangle, \ldots\}$
gives $GU^4_{\mathbf{seq}\,T} = \{\varepsilon, \langle a\rangle, \langle b\rangle, \ldots, \langle a, a\rangle, \langle a, b\rangle, \ldots\}.$

Notice that the last generator basis contains an infinite set of functions. For that reason it may fall outside the framework of a simple formal specification language. □

EXAMPLE 5.5

The type *Intstack* of example 5.1 would have the set $\{empty, push\}$ as its minimal generator basis. The corresponding generator universe is structurally similar to that of **seq** *Int*, say, according to the generator basis $\{\varepsilon, \,\hat{}\vdash\hat{}\,\}$. Still, it may be practical to distinguish between a specialized stack concept with a few associated stack operators on the one hand, and on the other a general purpose sequence type with a much larger set of associated functions, cf. section 5.8.8. □

EXAMPLE 5.6

As a last example consider the type of finite sets over some given base type T, denoted **set** T. Its value space consists of subsets of $V_T = \{a, b, \ldots\}$, and one possible generator basis is

$$G_{\mathbf{set}\,T} = \{\emptyset, add\}, \quad \text{where}$$

func $\emptyset : \longrightarrow \mathbf{set}\,T$ \hfill (empty set)
func $add : \mathbf{set}\,T \times T \longrightarrow \mathbf{set}\,T$ \hfill (add one element)

which gives $GU_{\textbf{set } T} = \{$ $\emptyset,$

$$
\begin{array}{lll}
add(\emptyset, a), & add(\emptyset, b), & \dots \\
add(add(\emptyset, a), a), & add(add(\emptyset, a), b), & \dots \\
add(add(\emptyset, b), a), & add(add(\emptyset, b), b), & \dots \\
\quad\vdots & \quad\vdots & \ddots\}.
\end{array}
$$

□

Some, but not all, of the generator bases in the above examples have the very important property that the elements of the corresponding generator universe all *have different values* of the type under definition, according to the intended meaning of the generator functions. This so-called *one-to-one property* simplifies the mathematics of abstract types considerably for the following reason:

- *We may simply define the value space to be identical to (or represented by) the corresponding generator universe.*

The important fact is that for a one-to-one generator basis each abstract value corresponds to exactly one basic expression (given that unique representations are used for arguments of underlying types, if any). Thus, it is merely a matter of words whether that expression is said to be, or to represent the abstract value.

Only two of the generator bases shown above do not have the one-to-one property: the concatenation basis for sequences and the one for sets. Obviously concatenating ε left or right should make no difference to an abstract sequence value, and we want the concatenation operator to be associative, so that e.g. the basic expressions $((\langle a\rangle \dashv \langle b\rangle)\dashv\langle c\rangle)$ and $\langle a\rangle\dashv(\langle b\rangle\dashv\langle c\rangle)$ should represent the same sequence value, although they are syntactically different. In the case of sets the order of element inclusions should be disregarded, as well as multiple inclusions of the same element.

Fortunately, both of the first two alternatives of example 5.4 are (finite) one-to-one bases for sequences. The set concept is more difficult in the sense that no finite one-to-one generator basis seems to exist for infinite base type T. We return to the question of many-to-one generator bases in section 5.5.

In the following we require that any type is defined in terms of a single, uniquely specified generator basis. We identify the generator basis of a type by a specification statement of the form: **genbas** $g_1, \dots, g_n$, where the type is identified by the context.

5.2 Function Definition

As explained already, certain syntactic aspects of functions are defined through function profiles; in addition there is a need to define the semantic aspects, or *meaning*, of the functions. The generators of a type T are essentially taken as

given functions with no other semantic information than the fact that they span
the set of abstract T values. However, T functions outside the generator basis must
be given meaning through axioms, which in our specification style serve to specify
these functions *completely and constructively* in terms of generators, possibly as
partial functions.

A constructive function definition in principle provides an algorithm for obtaining the function value, if it exists, for given argument values. Let f be a
non-generator function

func $f: D_1 \times D_2 \times \cdots \times D_n \longrightarrow C$

It may be specified semantically by writing

def $f(x_1, x_2, \ldots, x_n)$ == RHS

where $x_1, x_2, \ldots, x_n$ are mutually distinct variables called *formal arguments*. The
type of each x_i is D_i, as required by the function profile, and their scope is the right
hand side of the definition. The right hand side must be a quantifier-free expression
of type C, such that $\mathcal{V}[\text{RHS}] \subseteq \{x_1, \ldots, x_n\}$. The result of this specification is to
incorporate the formula

$\forall x_1 : D_1, \ldots, x_n : D_n \bullet f(x_1, \ldots, x_n)$ == RHS

as an axiom of the underlying logical system.

If all functions occurring in the RHS are semantically defined already, the axiom
is said to be a *direct definition*. If partial functions occur in the RHS it may
not always be well-defined. The strong equality operator in the definition is used
in order to indicate that the well-definedness of the left hand expression shall be
exactly that of the right hand side (for arguments well-defined or not).

We need the expressive power provided by recursion, so the function being specified must be allowed to occur in its own RHS. Also the specification of groups
of functions by mutual recursion may be needed. A recursive definition for which
the recursion does not always terminate, specifies a partial function, ill-defined for
those argument values that lead to non-termination. This understanding agrees
with the mathematical notion of "least fixed point semantics". (In this approach
a recursive function definition is regarded as an equation in an unknown function.
Any function satisfying it is called a fixed point of the equation; in particular the
least fixed point is the least defined function which solves the equation.)

EXAMPLE 5.7
A function f taking an argument (list) x, semantically defined by

def $f(x)$ == $f(x)$

is ill-defined everywhere. (Any function strongly satisfies this equation, and the least defined of all functions is the one which is ill-defined everywhere.) Operationally this definition would correspond to an infinite computation; therefore, in accordance with the AID convention (cf. section 4.3.2) an operationally better right hand side, also always ill-defined, would be the constant $\perp$ which leads to immediate abortion on evaluation.

□

EXAMPLE 5.8

The divide function on natural numbers (with generators 0 and $\mathbf{S}\hat{}$)

> **func** $\hat{}/\hat{}$: $Nat \times Nat \longrightarrow Nat$
> **def** $x/y ==$ **if** $x < y$ **then** 0 **else** $\mathbf{S}((x-y)/y)$ **fi**

is partial. It is ill-defined for y equal to zero and well-defined otherwise, given that the operators $\hat{}<\hat{}$ and $\hat{}-\hat{}$ have their usual meaning.

□

To determine the domain of well-definedness for a recursively defined function is in general non-trivial mathematically. We return to the question of well-definedness in section 5.2.1. Recall also section 4.3.2.

Consider the situation where an abstract type T is being defined, a generator basis $\{g_1, \ldots, g_n\}$ has been specified, and now a non-basic T-function is to be specified semantically. We are then faced with the difficulty that the set of available T-functions is severely limited. To be specific the set is limited to

- the basic generators,
- an **if** construct for T values (definable, given the type *Bool*), and
- possibly equality over T (at least if the generator basis is specified to be one-to-one, cf. section 5.5).

For instance, the definition of example 5.8 above makes use of functions $-$ and $<$, and it is hard to see how they could be defined only in terms of equality, **if**, and the generators 0 and $\mathbf{S}$ without the use of quantifiers, even permitting recursion.

To help out we introduce a new mechanism into our expression language, a **case** construct as in Pascal, but generalized to a pattern matching mechanism able to discriminate according to a generator basis with non-constant generator functions. The general format is

> **case** <discriminant> **of** <discriminator$_1$ >→<alternative$_1$ >
> | <discriminator$_2$ >→<alternative$_2$ >
> $$\vdots$$
> | <discriminator$_n$ >→<alternative$_n$ >
>   **fo**

where the discriminant is an expression, say of type T, whose value (a basic expression!) determines which branch to take. There is one branch for each function in the generator basis for T, say $g_1, \ldots, g_n$. The discriminator number i is of the form $g_i(\bar{x}_i)$. It introduces a list $\bar{x}_i$ (possibly empty) of distinct variables matching the domain of g_i, whose scope is the i'th alternative. If the discriminant value is of the form $g_i(\bar{e}_i)$, then the branch headed by $g_i(\bar{x})$ is taken, with the formal arguments $\bar{x}$ set equal to the actual arguments $\bar{e}_i$ of the g_i application. This is formalized as follows for arbitrary n-ary generator g:

$$\text{CASE}: \quad \vdash \textbf{case } g(e_1, \ldots, e_n) \textbf{ of } g(x_1, \ldots, x_n) \to e \mid \ldots \textbf{ fo} = e^{x_1, \ldots, x_n}_{e_1, \ldots, e_n}$$

As a shortcut any number of alternatives may be collected together in one final branch headed by the cue word **others**.

EXAMPLE 5.9
The semantics of an **if** construct choosing between values of arbitrary type T may be defined by a **case** construct discriminating on the Boolean argument.

> **func** if ˆ then ˆ else ˆ **fi** : $Bool \times T \times T \longrightarrow T$
> **def**   if b then x else y **fi** $==$ **case** b **of** $\text{t} \to x \mid \text{f} \to y$ **fo**

□

A defining **case** construct discriminating on a variable v is said to express definition by *generator induction* on v. If the type of v is generated by constants, the generator induction is trivial in the sense that it degenerates to the choice between alternative direct definitions, one for each possible value of v. Example 5.9 is like this. If, however, there are generators which are not relative constants the corresponding discriminators correspond to an infinite set of possible values. The corresponding alternatives typically are recursive, e.g. by containing applications of the function being defined.

EXAMPLE 5.10
We define the semantics of the operators $+$ and $<$ applied to natural numbers, using the **case**-construct

> **func** ˆ$+$ˆ : $Nat \times Nat \longrightarrow Nat$
> **func** ˆ$<$ˆ : $Nat \times Nat \longrightarrow Bool$
> **def** $x + y ==$ **case** y **of** $0 \to x \mid \text{S}z \to \text{S}(x + z)$ **fo**
> **def** $x < y ==$ **case** y **of** $0 \to \text{f} \mid \text{S}y \to$
>   **case** x **of** $0 \to \text{t} \mid \text{S}x \to x < y$ **fo fo**

(An outer argument name may be reused in an inner discriminator; this implies, however, that the outer argument will be inaccessible in the inner alternative.)
□

An alternative syntax for expressing definition by generator induction is to write one defining equation for each **case** branch, using left hand sides containing the corresponding discriminators. Thus, the definition of the $<$ operator corresponds to the following set of **case**-free axioms:

$$\vdash x < 0 \quad == \quad \mathbf{f}$$
$$\vdash 0 < \mathbf{S}y \quad == \quad \mathbf{t}$$
$$\vdash \mathbf{S}x < \mathbf{S}y \quad == \quad x < y$$

The idea of generator induction expressed by axiom sets of this form was pioneered by John Guttag [14] (among others), and they are for that reason sometimes called "Guttag axioms". We often prefer the **case**-construct, because its structure is more explicit, especially when nested inductions are used. It is also more general if we allow discriminants to be arbitrary expressions, not only variables.

EXAMPLE 5.11

We provide semantic definitions of the sequence type and the functions defined syntactically in example 5.4, taking the right append operator as a generator:

genbas ε, $\hat{\ }\vdash\hat{\ }$
def $x \dashv q \quad == \quad$ **case** q **of** $\varepsilon \to \varepsilon \vdash x \mid q' \vdash y \to (x \dashv q') \vdash y$ **fo**
def $q \vdash r \quad == \quad$ **case** r **of** $\varepsilon \to q \mid r' \vdash x \to (q \vdash r') \vdash x$ **fo**
def $\langle x \rangle \quad == \quad \varepsilon \vdash x$
def $\langle x, y \rangle \quad == \quad \varepsilon \vdash x \vdash y$
def $\langle x, y, z \rangle \quad == \quad \varepsilon \vdash x \vdash y \vdash z$
$$\vdots \qquad\qquad \vdots$$

□

It is fairly easy to see that the functions defined in the last two examples are total. Remember that well-defined arguments are abstract values of the right type, i.e. variable-free generator expressions. Then, for instance, the recursive occurrence of the function $\hat{\ } < \hat{\ }$ is applied to arguments *less deeply nested* than those of the left hand side. Thus, the recursion cannot go on for ever, and this fact may be verified by simple syntactic checking. (In the **case**-free recursive axiom the syntactic arguments of the recursive application are proper subexpressions of those in the left hand side.) The same is true for the second argument of each recursive application of the functions $\hat{\ }+\hat{\ }$, $\hat{\ }\dashv\hat{\ }$, and $\hat{\ }\vdash\hat{\ }$, and that is also sufficient to ensure termination.

Thus, when using generator inductive function definitions, recursion may be "tamed" by the following syntactic check which provides a sufficient condition for termination. The check requires that every recursive function application is in a certain sense "guarded" by generator induction in some argument:

- In defining a function f there should be an argument position of f, say number i, such that for every recursive application of f the i'th syntactic argument is:
    - a proper subexpression of the i'th argument of the left hand side, if the function definition has the form of a **case**-free axiom set, or
    - an argument of a discriminator on the i'th argument of f, if f is defined by a single equation containing a **case**-construct.

exists (this is the unsolvable halting problem again, cf. p. 64), so any sufficient syntactic condition must necessarily restrict our power to define total functions. Still, the technique of generator induction makes it possible to formulate quite powerful termination criteria in fairly simple ways.

The check proposed above is not particularly good from this point of view; it may be improved in several ways. For instance, if nested induction is applied to an argument of f, it is sufficient to apply the proper subexpression condition to a subexpression of the left hand side argument (as in example 5.14 below). And if generator induction is applied to more than one argument, these arguments may be considered in some chosen sequence, checking the subexpression property lexicographically, i.e. first comparing the first pair of arguments in the sequence and if they are equal the next pair, and so forth (see example 5.15). Syntactic checking can also be generalized to provide sufficient termination criteria for indirect recursion in sets of interdependent function definitions.

We characterize function definitions which pass a syntactic termination check such as the one given above, or some suitably generalized version, as belonging to the set of *terminating generator inductive*, TGI, definitions, which also includes non-recursive function definitions. Right hand sides of TGI definitions may only contain generators and TGI-defined functions, in addition to case constructs discriminating on variables. Clearly, all functions definable in this way are total.

We extend the set of TGI-definable functions to include certain partial ones by allowing the ill-defined constant $\perp$ to occur in right hand sides. The TGI-definable partial functions have the important property that definedness is effectively decidable. Simply redefine $\perp$ as an abstract value, i.e. a kind of generator included in every generator basis. Then any variable-free expression in TGI-defined functions is well-defined in the usual sense if and only if its "value" in the redefined sense is not $\perp$ (remembering that generators are by definition strict functions, so that $g(\dots, \perp, \dots)$ has the "value" $\perp$ for any generator g).

In mathematical terms a TGI function definition is an equation with *a single solution*. In other words it defines a function uniquely with no need to appeal to the "least fixed point" principle.

EXAMPLE 5.12
Subtraction on natural numbers, $\hat{\ } \stackrel{.}{-} \hat{\ } : Nat \times Nat \longrightarrow Nat$, may be taken to be a partial function, ill-defined if the result seen as a signed integer were negative.

The function may be TGI defined as follows:

   def $x \doteq y$ == **case** y **of** $0 \to x \mid \mathbf{S}y \to$
                           case x **of** $0 \to \bot \mid \mathbf{S}x \to x \doteq y$ **fo fo**

□

EXAMPLE 5.13

The definition of natural number division of example 5.8 is not TGI, nor is that of example 4.4. The following definition, however, is TGI. It uses an auxiliary function

    func ˆ**mod**ˆ : $Nat \times Nat \longrightarrow Nat$

computing the division remainder, also TGI-defined:

    def x **mod** y == **case** y **of** $0 \to \bot \mid \mathbf{S}y' \to$
                    case x **of** $0 \to 0 \mid \mathbf{S}x' \to$
                    if x' **mod** $y = y'$ **then** 0 **else** $\mathbf{S}(x' \bmod y)$ **fi fo fo**
    def x/y == **case** y **of** $0 \to \bot \mid \mathbf{S}y' \to$
                    case x **of** $0 \to 0 \mid \mathbf{S}x' \to$
                    if x' **mod** $y = y'$ **then** $\mathbf{S}(x'/y)$ **else** x'/y **fi fo fo**

□

EXAMPLE 5.14

    func norepˆ : **seq** $T \longrightarrow Bool$
    def   **norep** q == **case** q **of** $\varepsilon \to \mathbf{t} \mid q \vdash x \to$
                    case q **of** $\varepsilon \to \mathbf{t} \mid q \vdash y \to$
                    $y \neq x \wedge$ **norep** $q \vdash y \wedge$ **norep** $q \vdash x$ **fo fo**

The **norep** predicate holds for a given sequence iff no T-value occurs more than once. The last alternative corresponds to the **case**-free axiom

    $\vdash$ **norep** $q \vdash y \vdash x$ == $y \neq x \wedge$ **norep** $q \vdash y \wedge$ **norep** $q \vdash x$

where the rightmost recursive function application does not satisfy the simple subexpression requirement. However, the definition is, none the less, TGI since the subterm $q \vdash y$ of the left hand side argument has been replaced by its proper subterm q.

□

EXAMPLE 5.15

The "Ackermann function" is of interest in certain mathematical contexts because it does not belong to the class of so-called "primitive recursive" functions. Its definition is included here as an example where the termination check must be applied lexicographically:

> **func** $Ack : Nat \times Nat \longrightarrow Nat$

> **def** $Ack(x, y)$ ==   **case** x **of** $0 \rightarrow \mathbf{S}y \mid \mathbf{S}x' \rightarrow$
> $\qquad\qquad$ **case** y **of** $0 \rightarrow Ack(x', \mathbf{S}0) \mid \mathbf{S}y' \rightarrow$
> $\qquad\qquad$ $Ack(x', Ack(x, y'))$ **fo fo**

There are three recursive applications to consider: $Ack(x', \mathbf{S}0)$, $Ack(x', Ack(x, y'))$, and $Ack(x, y')$, where the last one is a subterm of the second. We check the arguments from left to right: In the two first cases the left argument x' is smaller than that of the left hand side, x. In the third case the left argument is identical to the left hand one, but the second argument y' is smaller than that of the left hand side, y. This shows that the definition is TGI.
◻

Exercises

5.1   Define the natural number operators $=$, $\leq$, and $*$ by generator induction with respect to the basis $0, \mathbf{S}\hat{}\,$.

5.2   Define the sequence predicate $\hat{}\,\mathbf{in}\hat{}\, : T \times \mathbf{seq}\,T \longrightarrow Bool$, where x **in** q means "x occurs in q".

Function definition by multiple induction can be avoided by introducing suitable auxiliary functions. Define the predicate **norep**$\hat{}\,$ of example 5.14 by single induction using the auxiliary predicate $\hat{}\,\mathbf{in}\hat{}\,$.

5.3   For type T with generator basis $g_1, g_2, \ldots, g_n$, where

> **func** $g_i : D_{i1} \times \cdots \times D_{i,n_i} \rightarrow T$ for $i = 1, 2, \ldots, n$

define the functions

> **func** $isg_i :$ $T \rightarrow Bool$ for $i = 1, 2, \ldots, n$
> **func** $arg_{ij} :$ $T \rightarrow D_{ij}$ for $j = 1, 2, \ldots, n_i, \ i = 1, 2, \ldots, n$

where $isg_i(t)$ means "the value of t is of the form $g_i(\ldots)$", and the value of $arg_{ij}(t)$, for t such that $isg_i(t)$ holds, is the j'th argument of that g_i application. Indicate how **case**-constructs over T may be mimicked by **if**'s using these functions.

5.4 Define the function *sort* : **seq** $T \longrightarrow$ **seq** T which sorts a given sequence by putting its elements in non-decreasing order, assuming a total order defined on T. Hint: Define an auxiliary function which inserts a given T-value in the (rightmost) correct position of a sorted sequence, preserving sortedness.

5.2.1 Definedness conditions

In the context of TGI function definitions we make an exception to the rule that variables are considered well-defined: those introduced in the left hand side of a TGI definition will be allowed to take the "value" $\bot$ in addition to ordinary values.

The use of strong equality in function definitions is intended to indicate that the left and right hand sides are *equally defined*. It follows that defined functions are not in general strict.

EXAMPLE 5.16

>   **func** *arg1* : $T \times U \longrightarrow T$
>   **def**   *arg1* $(x, y) == x$

The function *arg1* is strict in its first argument, but not in its second argument, $d_{arg1(e_1,e_2)} = d_{e_1}$.
□

It is reasonable to insist on strictness in inductive arguments. We therefore define

$$d_{\textbf{case } e \textbf{ of } |_i \, g_i(...)\to e_i \textbf{ fo}} \triangleq d_e \wedge \textbf{case } e \textbf{ of } |_i \, g_i(...) \to d_{e_i} \textbf{ fo}$$

This corresponds to having an additional implied branch in every case construct with the discriminator $\bot$ and the result $\bot$. Strictness in inductive arguments implies that TGI defined functions are necessarily *monotonic* (with respect to well-definedness). In view of the strictness of generator functions it also implies that variables introduced in discriminators are necessarily well-defined.

For any TGI function definition, say **def** $f(...) ==$ RHS, a TGI definition of the general definedness condition for f-applications may be mechanically derived by applying the syntactic definedness operator to both sides of the defining equation: **def** $d_{f(...)} == d_{\text{RHS}}$.

The definedness operator on any TGI right hand side is completely defined by the following rules (cf. also section 4.3.2). It is assumed that generator induction is expressed in terms of **case**-constructs:

- Generators are total and strict (in particular, constant generators are well-defined).
- $\bot$ is ill-defined.

- The definedness of any compound Boolean expression is as specified in section 4.3.2.
- The definedness of **case** constructs is as given above.
- d_x is **t**, unless x is a variable explicitly introduced in the left hand side of the defining equation. If so, this meta-expression can be taken to represent a new variable of type *Bool*, always well-defined.

It can be shown that any definedness definition derived from a TGI-definition is itself TGI. Furthermore, the definedness condition thus defined is itself well-defined for arbitrary TGI expression e, i.e. d_{d_e} is true.

EXAMPLE 5.17
We derive the definedness conditions for applications of some of the functions defined in the above examples.

def $d_{\textbf{if } b \textbf{ then } x \textbf{ else } y \textbf{ fi}} == d_b \wedge \textbf{case } b \textbf{ of t} \rightarrow d_x \mid \textbf{f} \rightarrow d_y \textbf{ fo}$

$$\textbf{def } d_{x+y} \quad == d_y \wedge \textbf{case } y \textbf{ of } 0 \rightarrow d_x \mid \textbf{S}y' \rightarrow d_{x+y'} \textbf{ fo}$$
$$== d_x \wedge d_y$$

$$\textbf{def } d_{x<y} \quad == d_y \wedge \textbf{case } y \textbf{ of } 0 \rightarrow \textbf{t} \mid \textbf{S}y' \rightarrow$$
$$d_x \wedge \textbf{case } x \textbf{ of } 0 \rightarrow \textbf{t} \mid \textbf{S}x' \rightarrow d_{x'<y'} \textbf{ fo fo}$$
$$== d_y \wedge (y = 0 \vee d_x)$$

$$\textbf{def } d_{x \dot- y} \quad == d_y \wedge \textbf{case } y \textbf{ of } 0 \rightarrow d_x \mid \textbf{S}y' \rightarrow$$
$$d_x \wedge \textbf{case } x \textbf{ of } 0 \rightarrow \textbf{f} \mid \textbf{S}x' \rightarrow d_{x' \dot- y'} \textbf{ fo fo}$$
$$== d_x \wedge d_y \wedge y \le x$$

$$\textbf{def } d_{x \bmod y} == d_y \wedge \textbf{case } y \textbf{ of } 0 \rightarrow \textbf{f} \mid \textbf{S}y' \rightarrow$$
$$d_x \wedge \textbf{case } x \textbf{ of } 0 \rightarrow \textbf{t} \mid \textbf{S}x' \rightarrow$$
$$d_{x' \bmod y} \wedge \textbf{if } x' \bmod y = y' \textbf{ then t else } d_{x' \bmod y}$$
$$\textbf{fi fo fo}$$
$$== d_x \wedge d_y \wedge y \ne 0$$

$$\textbf{def } d_{x/y} \quad == d_y \wedge \textbf{case } y \textbf{ of } 0 \rightarrow \textbf{f} \mid \textbf{S}y' \rightarrow$$
$$d_x \wedge \textbf{case } x \textbf{ of } 0 \rightarrow \textbf{t} \mid \textbf{S}x' \rightarrow d_{x'/y} \textbf{ fo fo}$$
$$== d_x \wedge d_y \wedge y \ne 0$$

Since an inductive definition derived from a TGI function definition is itself TGI, the derived equation is satisfied by exactly one function. Therefore each simplified, non-recursive right hand side may be validated simply by checking that it satisfies the inductive defining equation. (Notice that variables introduced in any discriminator are well-defined, because the discriminand is well-defined and generators are strict functions.)

The **if**-operator is taken as strict in its first argument when applied to non-Boolean values, in accordance with the general rule for **case**-constructs. The other functions turn out to be strict in all arguments, except $<$ which is non-strict in its first argument (when defined as in example 5.10).

☐

The definedness predicate D_f of a function f may be derived from the general definedness condition of f-applications by requiring the arguments of the application to be well-defined:

$$d_{e_1} \wedge \cdots \wedge d_{e_n} \Rightarrow D_f(e_1, \ldots, e_n) = d_{f(e_1, \ldots, e_n)}$$

It follows that the first three functions of example 5.17 are total, whereas the last three are partial. The definedness predicates of the latter are

$$D_{\char`\^{}\_\char`\^}(x,y) = (y \leq x) \quad \text{and} \quad D_{\char`\^{}\mathbf{mod}\char`\^}(x,y) = D_{\char`\^/\char`\^}(x,y) = (y \neq 0)$$

The Boolean operators, as defined in section 4.3.2, are non-strict in all arguments (except the negation operator $\neg\char`\^$ which is strict). The reason for this choice is to have as many logical tautologies as possible strongly equal to **t**, in order to facilitate reasoning about partial functions. As we have seen, this goal cannot be achieved completely; in particular, tautologies such as $P \vee \neg P$ and $P \Rightarrow P$, which depend on the fact that **t** and **f** are the only truth values, are not strongly true ($\bot$ behaves as a third one!).

If we relaxed the strictness requirement on inductive arguments, allowing the "generator" $\bot$ to select well-defined results, the non-strict Boolean operators could be defined as follows:

def $x \wedge y ==$ **case** x **of** $\mathbf{t} \to y \mid \mathbf{f} \to \mathbf{f} \mid \bot \to$
      case y **of** $\mathbf{f} \to \mathbf{f} \mid$ **others** $\to \bot$ **fo fo**

def $x \vee y ==$ **case** x **of** $\mathbf{t} \to \mathbf{t} \mid \mathbf{f} \to y \mid \bot \to$
      case y **of** $\mathbf{t} \to \mathbf{t} \mid$ **others** $\to \bot$ **fo fo**

def $x \Rightarrow y ==$ **case** x **of** $\mathbf{t} \to y \mid \mathbf{f} \to \mathbf{t} \mid \bot \to$
      case y **of** $\mathbf{t} \to \mathbf{t} \mid$ **others** $\to \bot$ **fo fo**

def if x **then** y **else** z **fi** $==$
     case x **of** $\mathbf{t} \to y \mid \mathbf{f} \to z \mid \bot \to$
     case (y,z) **of** $(\mathbf{t},\mathbf{t}) \to \mathbf{t} \mid (\mathbf{f},\mathbf{f}) \to \mathbf{f} \mid$ **others** $\to \bot$ **fo fo**

Treating $\bot$ as an ordinary additional generator is unproblematical for types whose generators are constants. In general, however, this would lead to ambiguity in discrimination. A discriminand of the form $g(\bot)$, where g is a generator, would be a basic expression since the argument is also a generator. Thus the g-branch must be the right choice. But if we insist that $\perp$ is ill-defined and that generators are strict functions, the $\perp$-branch must be chosen. We return to this problem in section 5.3.1.

Exercise

5.5   Show that these Boolean operator definitions lead to definedness conditions as specified in section 4.3.2. In this context the definedness requirement of discriminands should be dropped.

5.3   Abstract Evaluation and Simplification

As we have seen, standard bottom up (i.e. arguments first) expression evaluation implements strict functions. In order to implement non-strict functions one generally needs fairly complicated parameter passing schemes, such as "call by name" as in Algol/Simula or "lazy evaluation" as in some LISP dialects.

In the context of TGI-defined functions, however, there exists a powerful technique of expression processing which can be used for the purpose of simplifying expressions containing free, unassigned variables, as well as for evaluating variable-free ones. The technique consists of regarding TGI axiom sets, **case**-free versions, as sets of textual left-to-right *rewrite rules*, which can be applied to expressions without changing their meaning. To apply an axiom $L == R$ as a rewrite rule to an expression E means to instantiate variables in L so that the L-instance matches a subexpression in E (or E itself) and then to replace this subexpression by the corresponding instance of R. We say that the result, E', is *derived* from E by an application of the rule, and use the following notation in order to express that fact:

$$E \xrightarrow{L==R} E'$$

An expression such that no rewrite rule can be applied is said to be *irreducible* with respect to the given rewrite rule set.

For a Boolean expression E this idea of textual rewriting corresponds exactly to the backward usage of the inference rule TEQ of section 2.2.5 in order to construct a proof tree for E by equational reasoning. The proof succeeds if E can be rewritten to $\mathbf{t}$ (using a rule $P == \mathbf{t}$ for any axiom P, including $x = x$, for the final rewrite step), in which case we also say that E *evaluates to* $\mathbf{t}$.

Any set $\mathcal{R}$ of **case**-free TGI axioms has the following very important properties:

- *Termination:* When applied as rewrite rules to any expression, rewriting necessarily terminates with an irreducible expression after a finite number of steps. The termination property of $\mathcal{R}$ is a result of the textual restriction on the use of recursion in TGI axioms.

- *Confluence:* All terminating sequences of rewrite steps starting with a given expression lead to the same final result. The fact that the final result is independent of the order in which rules of $\mathcal{R}$ are applied follows from the fact that at most one TGI axiom is applicable at any given point in an expression. In this sense the left hand sides of the rules in $\mathcal{R}$ are "non-overlapping".

- *Ground completeness:* For any variable-free (also called *ground*) expression E in generators and functions TGI-defined in $\mathcal{R}$, the irreducible final result is a basic expression, i.e. the *abstract value* of E.

A set of rewrite rules which is both terminating and confluent is said to be *convergent*.

EXAMPLE 5.18

Using the following **case**-free axiom set for natural number addition we prove that $2+2=4$, where 2 is defined as **SS0** and 4 is defined as **SSSS0**. We assume that the operator **S^** binds more strongly than ^+^ :

A1. $x + 0 == x$
A2. $x + Sy == S(x + y)$

$$\mathbf{SS0} + \mathbf{SS0} \xrightarrow{A2} \mathbf{S(SS0 + S0)} \xrightarrow{A2} \mathbf{SS(SS0 + 0)} \xrightarrow{A1} \mathbf{SSSS0}$$

It is clear that the rewriting process had to terminate, since one **S** application is removed from the second addend in each A2-step.

□

EXAMPLE 5.19

The confluence property of an axiom set ensures that the final result is independent of the rewrite strategy. The following derivations prove that $x+1+1$ is equal to $x+2$ for arbitrary natural number x, using top down and bottom up strategy respectively:

$$(x + \mathbf{S0}) + \mathbf{S0} \xrightarrow{A2} \mathbf{S}((x + \mathbf{S0}) + 0) \xrightarrow{A1} \mathbf{S}(x + \mathbf{S0}) \xrightarrow{A2} \mathbf{SS}(x + 0) \xrightarrow{A1} \mathbf{SS}x$$
$$(x + \mathbf{S0}) + \mathbf{S0} \xrightarrow{A2} \mathbf{S}(x + 0) + \mathbf{S0} \xrightarrow{A1} \mathbf{S}x + \mathbf{S0} \xrightarrow{A2} \mathbf{S}(\mathbf{S}x + 0) \xrightarrow{A1} \mathbf{SS}x$$

where the common final result is also the one obtained by rewriting $x+2 = x+\mathbf{SS0}$.

□

EXAMPLE 5.20

Although the final result is strategy independent for a convergent system, the number of steps needed in a derivation is not. Using the definition of example 5.14 we may simplify as follows:

$$\textbf{norep } q \vdash x \vdash y \vdash x \longrightarrow x \neq y \wedge \textbf{norep } q \vdash x \vdash y \wedge \textbf{norep } q \vdash x \vdash x \longrightarrow$$
$$x \neq y \wedge \textbf{norep } q \vdash x \vdash y \wedge x \neq x \wedge \textbf{norep } q \vdash x \wedge \textbf{norep } q \vdash x$$

Given rules $(x \neq x) == \textbf{f}$, $(x \wedge \textbf{f}) == \textbf{f}$, and $(\textbf{f} \wedge x) == \textbf{f}$, the whole formula may be reduced to $\textbf{f}$ in 4 more steps for, say, left associative $\hat{\wedge}$ operator and optimum strategy. Clearly, much longer derivations are possible.
□

EXAMPLE 5.21

Let $\textbf{P}^\hat{} : Nat \longrightarrow Nat$ be the predecessor function. Then the following is a meaningful definition of addition on natural numbers, although not TGI:

$$\textbf{def } x + y == \textbf{if } y = 0 \textbf{ then } x \textbf{ else } \textbf{S}x + \textbf{P}y \textbf{ fi}$$

It is clear that the definition is useful for bottom up evaluation of variable-free sums, but used as a rewrite rule it leads to non-termination since the recursion is not guarded by generator induction:

$$u + v \longrightarrow \textbf{if } u = 0 \textbf{ then } v \textbf{ else } \textbf{S}u + \textbf{P}v \textbf{ fi}$$
$$\longrightarrow \textbf{if } u = 0 \textbf{ then } v \textbf{ else if } \textbf{P}v = 0 \textbf{ then } \textbf{S}u \textbf{ else } \textbf{SS}u + \textbf{PP}v \textbf{ fi fi}$$
$$\longrightarrow \cdots$$

□

Sometimes equational theorems may be added to the TGI set as new rewrite rules without losing convergence. Thereby the automatic reasoning power may be improved. There is a body of theory on the subject of rewrite rule convergence. The first paper on the subject, by D. E. Knuth and P. Bendix [24], describes sufficient criteria for convergence, and even provides an algorithm which may succeed in achieving convergence by adding rules constructed automatically and possibly deleting or simplifying others. See e.g. [8] for more information on this subject.

EXAMPLE 5.22

Let addition on natural numbers be defined as in example 5.18. Then

T1: $0 + y = y$

is a theorem (provable by generator induction, see section 5.4). Accepting T1 as a new rewrite rule implies an overlap with rule A1 since the expression $0 + 0$ matches both left hand sides. However, both rules give the same result, 0, so confluence is not lost. Adding the associative law as a rewrite rule of the form

T2: $(x+y)+z = x+(y+z)$

does, however, lead to the loss of confluence. This is demonstrated by overlaps between T2 and A2 of the form $(u+\mathbf{S}v)+w$. We have

$$\mathbf{S}(u+v)+w \xleftarrow{\text{A2}} (u+\mathbf{S}v)+w \xrightarrow{\text{T2}} u+(\mathbf{S}v+w)$$

where both results are irreducible with respect to {A1,A2,T1,T2}. It turns out that confluence is regained by adding the rule

T3: $\mathbf{S}x+y = \mathbf{S}(x+y)$

In particular, the two results given above are now reducible to the same expression:

$$\mathbf{S}(u+v)+w \xrightarrow{\text{T3}} \mathbf{S}((u+v)+w) \xrightarrow{\text{T2}} \mathbf{S}(u+(v+w))$$
$$u+(\mathbf{S}v+w) \xrightarrow{\text{T3}} u+\mathbf{S}(v+w) \xrightarrow{\text{A2}} \mathbf{S}(u+(v+w))$$

Rewrite systems are very sensitive to the orientation of the rules; it is necessary that any rule application leads to a result which is simpler in some sense. So, in most cases reversing a rule in a terminating set leads to non-termination. It turns out that reversal of T2 does not harm termination in our case. In fact, adding the reverse to {A1,A2} retains confluence as well.

□

An equational theorem used as a rewrite rule should preferably be a strong equality. (If not, one should insist that the right hand side be better defined than the left hand side, cf. the next section.) The theorems considered in example 5.22 are all strong equalities, which follows from the fact that all occurring operators are total and strict functions.

Exercise

5.6 Try to show that the following axiom set is terminating, confluent, and ground complete for conjunctions. There is a sense in which the set is stronger than the TGI-definition of the $\wedge$ operator of the last section. Which sense?

One of the rules listed below is such that the implementation of rewriting with respect to it is somewhat more difficult than the implementation of rewriting with respect to TGI axioms. Which one, and why?

A1. $\mathbf{t} \wedge x == x$
A2. $x \wedge \mathbf{t} == x$
A3. $\mathbf{f} \wedge x == \mathbf{f}$
A4. $x \wedge \mathbf{f} == \mathbf{f}$
A5. $x \wedge x == x$

5.3.1   Term rewriting and definedness

In this section we compare the semantics of TGI function definitions (in terms of **case** constructs) and that of term rewriting based on the corresponding **case**-free axioms. It turns out that there is a discrepancy with respect to definedness of expressions. The difficulties are caused by certain strictness requirements inherent in TGI definitions, whereas (unrestricted) term rewriting permits extreme forms of "lazy evaluation".

Recall that **case** constructs are strict in the discriminand. Thus, any TGI defined function, f, is by definition strict with respect to inductive arguments. We compensate for that by an implied additional branch for the ill-defined case, selecting the result $\bot$. A corresponding axiom $f(\ldots,\bot,\ldots) == \bot$ is implicitly added to the **case**-free set. Now, if all discriminands are of types generated by constants we may simply regard $\bot$ as another generator, and the only ill-defined "value" will be $\bot$. It follows that term rewriting will be strongly correct in this case.

As we have seen already, the situation is different if there are non-constant generators. Then a discriminand of the form $g(\ldots,\bot,\ldots)$, where g is a generator, will match the axiom corresponding to the g-branch, say

$$A_{fg}: \quad f(\ldots,g(\ldots,z,\ldots),\ldots) == \text{RHS}$$

which is wrong in view of the strictness of generators and inductive arguments, unless $\text{RHS}_\bot^z$ is strongly equal to $\bot$. The trouble is that axioms such as A_{fg} are only meant to be strong equalities for well-defined $g(\ldots,z,\ldots)$. In general, if the left hand side of an axiom has an argument which is a generator expression containing variables, that left hand side is by definition strict with respect to these variables. The right hand side is then *better defined* unless it is strict in the same variables. If an axiom does not hold strongly for an ill-defined generator expression in the left hand side, we say that this expression is a "dangerous" argument.

EXAMPLE 5.23
The TGI definition of the predicate $\hat{}<\hat{}$ given in example 5.10 corresponds to the following complete **case**-free axiom set:

A1. $x < 0$ $==$ $\mathbf{f}$
A2.1. $0 < \mathbf{S}y$ $==$ $\mathbf{t}$
A2.2. $\mathbf{S}x < \mathbf{S}y$ $==$ $x < y$
A2.3. $\bot < \mathbf{S}y$ $==$ $\bot$
A3. $x < \bot$ $==$ $\bot$

The axioms A2.3 and A3 correctly express the strictness requirements on the $\hat{}<\hat{}$ arguments, cf. the definedness condition given in example 5.17.

Consider now the expression $0 < \mathbf{S}\bot$. Since the operator $\hat{}<\hat{}$ is strict in its second argument and the generator $\mathbf{S}\hat{}$ is strict by definition, the expression is ill-defined. Nevertheless it may be rewritten to $\mathbf{t}$ in one step using the axiom A2.1.

Clearly, the correct action would be to apply rule A3, in view of the fact that the subterm $\mathbf{S}\bot$ is strongly equal to $\bot$.

Notice that the right hand side of axiom A2.1 is not strict in the left hand variable y, since y does not occur there and the RHS is not $\bot$. For that reason the inductive argument $\mathbf{S}y$ in the left hand side of A2.1 is dangerous.

□

Thus, term rewriting does not in general respect strong equality; whenever an axiom with dangerous arguments is applied, a term may be replaced by a better defined one. However, this does not necessarily imply that the definedness of the expression as a whole will change. Remember that TGI defined functions are monotonic with respect to definedness:

$$e \sqsubseteq e' \Rightarrow f(\ldots, e, \ldots) \sqsubseteq f(\ldots, e', \ldots)$$

This fact implies that derived results are either equally or *better* defined than the original expression. In particular, the definedness of a provably well-defined TGI expression will not change at all. It follows that:

- *Unrestricted TGI term rewriting applied to well-defined expressions is strongly correct (as well as convergent).*

We may try to achieve strong correctness in the general case by adding strictness axioms for the non-constant generators:

$$g(\ldots, \bot, \ldots) == \bot$$

They will not affect the termination property of TGI axioms, but there is overlap between them and axioms such as A_{fg}, which in general leads to the loss of confluence.

EXAMPLE 5.23 (CONTINUED)
We try to add the generator strictness axiom

$$\mathbf{S_S} : \mathbf{S}\bot == \bot$$

But now the expression $0 < \mathbf{S}\bot$ may rewrite to either $\mathbf{t}$ or $\bot$, depending on whether A2.1 or $\mathbf{S_S}$ is applied in the first step.

□

We would regain confluence by restricting rewriting to work bottom up (inside-out). However, since overlap can only occur in inductive arguments of a TGI rule, it is sufficient to require that the corresponding actual arguments are *irreducible* whenever the rule is used in a rewrite step. Still, in order to respect strong equality we must restrict the application of axioms with dangerous arguments by the requirement that the corresponding actual arguments are also *well-defined.*

In the special case of variable-free expressions it turns out that the requirement that *dangerous arguments be irreducible* is sufficient for strong correctness as well as confluence. The former follows from the fact that irreducible variable-free expressions are now either basic or identical to $\perp$. Thus, if an irreducible argument matches a generator expression, it is necessarily well-defined. Confluence then follows by the fact that if an inductive argument is not dangerous and the actual argument is ill-defined, then the right hand side is strongly equal to $\perp$.

- *Term rewriting with respect to TGI axioms, enriched with strictness axioms for all non-constant generators and applied to variable-free expressions, is convergent and strongly correct, provided that dangerous rule arguments are irreducible in each rewrite step.*

Variables in a given expression usually represent well-defined values; it is only in function definitions, and therefore in the TGI rewrite rules themselves, that variables may legally be ill-defined. Even so, tests for well-definedness of dangerous arguments, necessary in order to achieve strongly correct rewriting, are difficult in general (although mechanizable for TGI defined functions). Furthermore, the associated restrictions imposed on rule application would significantly reduce the power of reasoning on well-defined expressions with variables. For that reason unrestricted TGI term rewriting is likely to be a more useful tool in practice, possibly enriched with generator strictness axioms in order to improve the simplification capability. (In order to prevent the loss of confluence one might apply either axiom set to termination, alternately. It is easy to see that any set of generator strictness axioms is convergent separately.)

Exercises

5.7   Show that the expression $S\perp < S0$ has two different irreducible derivatives with respect to the (unrestricted) axioms of the above example. Show that one of them is excluded if dangerous arguments are required to be irreducible.

5.8   Prove the claim that variable-free expressions, irreducible for TGI axioms enriched with strictness axioms of the form indicated above for all non-constant generators, are either basic or $\perp$.

5.3.2   Simplification of Boolean expressions

Proofs of propositional tautologies, i.e. of theorems within the propositional calculus, may be mechanized using the technique of truth tables, or by algorithms based on some constructive formal system such as (part of) the BPC system of chapter 2. Alternatively, using equational axioms for the Boolean operators and term rewriting techniques, the proof of a propositional tautology would be a special case of formula simplification where the final result is **t**.

Unfortunately no set of rewrite rules exists which is convergent in the usual sense, and also complete in the sense that all propositional tautologies can be rewritten to **t**. This is related to the fact that $\wedge$ and $\vee$ are symmetrical (commutative) operators and that rules such as $x \text{ op } y == y \text{ op } x$ lead to non-termination. However, mechanization of the propositional calculus is still possible by adding suitable *ad hoc* features to the term rewriting mechanism. For instance one may construct a complete system by rewriting the Boolean operators in terms of $\neq$ and $\wedge$ (alternatively $=$ and $\vee$) provided that the rewriting mechanism has a way of dealing convergently with associative-commutative operators, see e.g. [8].

Another approach is to rewrite the Boolean operators in terms of Boolean **if**-constructs and add rewrite capabilities corresponding to the following axiom schemas:

IF0: **if** x **then** y **else** z **fi** $==$ **case** x **of t** $\rightarrow y \mid$ **f** $\rightarrow z$ **fo**

IF1: $f(\ldots, \text{if } x \text{ then } y \text{ else } z \text{ fi}, \ldots) ==$
    if x **then** $f(\ldots, y, \ldots)$ **else** $f(\ldots, z, \ldots)$ **fi**

    where f is an arbitrary function, possibly **if–fi**

IF2: **if** A **then** B **else** C **fi** $==$ **if** A **then** $B_{\mathbf{t}}^{A}$ **else** $C_{\mathbf{f}}^{A}$ **fi**

    where A is a Boolean expression and B, C are expressions

IF3: **if** x **then** y **else** y **fi** $== y$

A convergent system complete for the propositional calculus (only well-defined formulas!) is obtained, provided that termination is ensured by suitable restriction of the application of IF1 in the case where f is **if–fi** (e.g. by requiring the inner **if**-construct to be the leftmost argument of the outer one).

It turns out that in general both techniques lead to combinatorial explosion in the amount of work. (In fact it is likely that no "efficient" algorithm exists for Boolean simplification complete for the propositional calculus, although no proof of this has been given.) Both techniques also suffer from the fact that the final irreducible result, for formulas other than tautologies, is likely to be far less readable than the given expression, and thus hardly a "simplified" version at all. However, reasonably successful pattern matching techniques exist for the transformation back to more readable form for the latter method. This method is also useful for simplifying expressions of arbitrary type, containing **if**-constructs.

Notice, however, that IF2 as it stands is far beyond the capability of an ordinary rewriting mechanism. A convergent system that is complete for the propositional calculus may also be obtained as follows, using less expensive *ad hoc* mechanisms:

1. Definition in terms of **if–fi**, **t**, and **f** of all other Boolean operators (including equality).
2. IF0-1: **if t then** x **else** y **fi** $==x$
   IF0-2: **if f then** x **else** y **fi** $==y$.
3. All axioms included in schema IF1, when f ranges over Boolean operators, including **if-fi**. In the latter case application is inhibited if the inner **if-fi** occurs as the second or third argument, unless the leftmost arguments of both constructs are variables, and the inner one is "less than" the outer one according to an arbitrary fixed total order on Boolean variables.
4. IF2-1: **if** x **then if** x **then** y **else** z **fi else** w **fi** $==$ **if** x **then** y **else** w **fi**
   IF2-2: **if** x **then** w **else if** x **then** y **else** z **fi fi** $==$ **if** x **then** w **else** z **fi**.
5. IF3: **if** x **then** y **else** y **fi** $==y$.
6. Any occurrence of a Boolean variable, say v, which is not the first argument of an **if**-construct, is replaced by the expression **if** v **then t else f fi**.

Any irreducible expression is characterized as follows, viewing an **if**-construct as an "if-tree" with the first argument as the root and the second and third arguments as the two subtrees: It is either **t** or **f**, or it is an if-tree where each leaf node is either **t** or **f** and each internal node is a variable. The variables of any leaf directed path occur in strictly "increasing" order. The two subtrees of any internal node are different.

Exercises

5.9 Discuss ways to improve the efficiency of the second system above, e.g. by sequencing axioms or groups of axioms in time.

5.10 A more efficient system results if the axiom IF3 is replaced by

$$\textbf{if } x \textbf{ then t else t fi} == \textbf{t} \quad \text{and} \quad \textbf{if } x \textbf{ then f else f fi} == \textbf{f}$$

Is the modified system complete? Characterize the irreducible expressions.

5.3.3 Quantifiers

No general algorithm exists for evaluating quantified expressions. (The best one can do mechanically is to construct proofs for Boolean expressions which happen to be theorems, see section 2.2.) In particular, quantifiers are not easily handled by rewriting techniques. As an alternative to semiautomatic reasoning about quantifiers we mention another, rather different way of dealing with them: trading them for auxiliary functions. We have already seen how existentially quantified variables of state assertions may be replaced by defined functions, see section 4.8.3. It turns out that one can get rid of universally quantified variables as well, at the expense of defining suitable auxiliary functions.

Predicate calculus is a wonderfully concise and powerful means of expression, but most people find that it takes considerable mental gymnastics to understand heavily quantified formulas. There is a good chance that quantifier-free formulas based on suitable auxiliary functions will be easier to understand, especially if the functions are known in advance, perhaps contained in a specifier's tool kit. They may also be more tractable by term rewriting techniques.

EXAMPLE 5.24

Define the following predicates:

func	$\hat{\ } * \le \hat{\ }$:	**seq** $T \times T$	$\longrightarrow$	*Bool*	(all less than or equal to)
func	$\hat{\ } \le * \hat{\ }$:	$T \times$ **seq** T	$\longrightarrow$	*Bool*	(less than or equal to all)
func	$\hat{\ } * \le * \hat{\ }$:	**seq** $T \times$ **seq** T	$\longrightarrow$	*Bool*	(all less than or equal to all)

def $q * \le x$ == **case** q **of** $\varepsilon \to t \mid q \vdash y \; \to \; q * \le x \wedge y \le x$ **fo**
def $x \le * q$ == **case** q **of** $\varepsilon \to t \mid q \vdash y \; \to \; x \le * q \wedge x \le y$ **fo**
def $q * \le * r$ == **case** r **of** $\varepsilon \to t \mid r \vdash x \; \to \; q * \le * r \wedge q * \le x$ **fo**

These functions, using the notation $A[i..j]$ for the sequence $\langle A[i], A[i+1], \dots, A[j] \rangle$, make it possible to simplify some of the invariants of example 4.19 considerably:

I_m is $1 \le m \le f \wedge A[1..m-1] * \le * A[m..N]$
I_n is $f \le n \le N \wedge A[1..n] * \le * A[n+1..N]$
I_i is $m \le i \wedge A[1..i-1] * \le r$
I_j is $j \le n \wedge r \le * A[j+1..N]$

as well as the final postcondition: $A[1..f] * \le A[f] \le * A[f..N]$.

□

Exercises

5.11 Identify the lemmas needed in order to carry out a formalized proof of the program of example 4.19 based on the above predicates.

5.12 Annotate and prove the program of exercise 4.35 using the above predicates.

5.4 Proof by Generator Induction

The truth value of any variable-free formula may be determined by evaluation, provided that all non-basic functions are constructively defined. If, however, the task is to prove the validity of a formula P with free (or universally quantified) variables, we often have to resort to some form of *proof by induction*.

Let the variable $x : T$ occur free in P, where the type T has the generator basis G_T and the generator universe GU_T. Since GU_T spans the whole value set V_T, we may prove P by proving P_u^x for all expressions $u \in GU_T$. If GU_T is finite, we can prove each case separately; if it is infinite we can make use of the fact that GU_T is partially ordered by the subterm relation

- u is "simpler" than $g(\ldots, u, \ldots)$, for all $u \in GU_T$ and $g \in G_T$.

(Cf. the syntactic termination criterion of section 5.3.) Since the elements of GU_T are expressions of finite size, the order is *well-founded*. This means that there exists no infinite sequence of decreasing elements. The minimal elements are of the form $g(\ldots)$, g being a relative constant (there is at least one in any generator basis!); the order is not concerned with the structure of arguments of other types, if any, i.e. we consider the subterm order as being restricted to basic expressions of type T.

Since G_T is finite it is possible to formulate an induction principle based on this inclusion order. Let the T-generators have the following profiles:

$$ g : \ T_{g,1} \times \cdots \times T_{g,n_g} \longrightarrow T \qquad \text{for } g \in G_T $$

Then an inference rule for proof by induction over T may be expressed as follows:

$$ \text{GIND}_T : \quad \frac{P_{x_i}^x, \text{ for } i \in S_g \ \vdash \ P_{g(x_1,\ldots,x_{n_g})}^x; \text{ for } g \in G_T}{\vdash \forall x : T \bullet P} $$

$$ \text{where } x_1 : T_{g,1}, \ \ldots, \ x_{n_g} : T_{g,n_g} \text{ are fresh variables} $$
$$ \text{and } S_g = \{i \bullet T_{g,i} = T\} $$

There is one premise for each generator, and P may be assumed to hold for each T-argument, if any, of the generator. The assumptions are called *induction hypotheses*. In order that they be as strong as possible it is useful to make the "induction variable" x the only free variable of P (by first quantifying universally all other free variables, not free in assumptions if any).

Generator induction can be seen as an application of ordinary mathematical induction with respect to the level of nesting of basic T-expressions, ignoring arguments of other types. The premises for the relatively constant generators have no assumptions; they correspond collectively to the induction basis. The remaining premises correspond collectively to the induction step. In the case where all basic generators are relative constants, generator induction degenerates to a kind of case analysis.

The premises of GIND_T allow us to conclude inductively that P_e^x holds for arbitrary basic T-expression e. Since the conclusion of GIND_T is $\forall x : T \bullet P$, the rule is a way of formally expressing the fact that GU_T *spans the whole of* V_T, which is the intention of specifying the generator basis G_T. Indeed, the meaning of the corresponding **genbas** statement may be formally defined as the inclusion of the proof rule GIND_T into the underlying logical system.

As the following examples show, proofs by generator induction are mechanizable to a quite large extent by term rewriting, provided that functions occurring in the theorem are TGI defined. They are easiest to carry out if any function applied to the chosen induction variable is also defined by generator induction in the same argument.

EXAMPLE 5.25
Generator induction over natural numbers, with generator basis $\{0, \mathbf{S}\hat{}\}$, is a way of expressing the principle of ordinary mathematical induction:

$$\text{GIND}_{Nat} : \quad \frac{\vdash P_0^x; \; P \vdash P_{\mathbf{S}x}^x}{\vdash \forall x : Nat \bullet P}$$

(provided x is fresh as a free variable, i.e. does not occur free in additional assumptions). We prove the associative law for addition on natural numbers, defined as in example 5.18:

Prove: $\forall x, y, z : Nat \bullet x + (y + z) = (x + y) + z$.
Proof: by induction on z.
0 for z: **Prove:** $\forall x, y : Nat \bullet x + (y + 0) = (x + y) + 0$
$\qquad$ LHS $= x + (y + 0) \xrightarrow{\text{A1}} x + y$, RHS $= (x + y) + 0 \xrightarrow{\text{A1}} x + y$.
$\mathbf{S}z$ for z: **Assuming** $\forall x, y : Nat \bullet x + (y + z) = (x + y) + z$,
$\qquad$ **prove** $\forall x, y : Nat \bullet x + (y + \mathbf{S}z) = (x + y) + \mathbf{S}z$.
$\qquad$ LHS $\xrightarrow{\text{A2}} x + \mathbf{S}(y + z) \xrightarrow{\text{A2}} \mathbf{S}(x + (y + z))$, RHS $\xrightarrow{\text{A2}} \mathbf{S}((x + y) + z)$,
$\qquad$ which are equal by the induction hypothesis.

Notice that most of the reasoning can be automated by a simple system of term rewriting. The proof came out as simple as this because we chose to do induction on the rightmost variable of the left and right hand sides. Proof by induction on x or y will not go through without using either nested induction or a suitable lemma which needs induction for its proof. (Try it!) The reason for this is that addition was defined using induction on the second argument.

$\square$

EXAMPLE 5.26
In order to prove the commutative law of addition, nested inductions are needed. The indentations show the scopes of the various induction hypotheses:

Prove: $\forall x, y : Nat \bullet x + y = y + x$.
Proof: by induction on x.
0 for x: $\quad$ **Prove:** $\forall y : Nat \bullet 0 + y = y + 0$.
$\qquad$ **Proof:** by induction on y.
$\qquad$ 0 for y: trivial.
$\qquad$ $\mathbf{S}y$ for y: **Assuming** $0 + y = y + 0$, $\hspace{3cm}$ (IH1)
$\qquad\qquad$ **prove:** $0 + \mathbf{S}y = \mathbf{S}y + 0$.
$\qquad\qquad$ LHS $\xrightarrow{\text{A2}} \mathbf{S}(0 + y) \overset{\text{IH1}}{=} \mathbf{S}(y + 0) \xrightarrow{\text{A1}} \mathbf{S}y$, RHS $\xrightarrow{\text{A1}} \mathbf{S}y$.

Sx for x: **Assuming** $\forall y : Nat \bullet \ x + y = y + x$,   (IH2)
        prove $\forall y : Nat \bullet \mathbf{S}x + y = y + \mathbf{S}x$.
        Proof: by induction on y.

0 for y: **Prove:** $\mathbf{S}x + 0 = 0 + \mathbf{S}x$.
        LHS $\xrightarrow{\text{A1}}$ $\mathbf{S}x$, RHS $\xrightarrow{\text{A2}}$ $\mathbf{S}(0 + x)$ $\overset{\text{IH2}}{=}$ $\mathbf{S}(x + 0)$ $\xrightarrow{\text{A1}}$ $\mathbf{S}x$.

Sy for y: **Assuming** $\mathbf{S}x + y = y + \mathbf{S}x$,   (IH3)
        prove: $\mathbf{S}x + \mathbf{S}y = \mathbf{S}y + \mathbf{S}x$.
        LHS $\xrightarrow{\text{A2}}$ $\mathbf{S}(\mathbf{S}x + y)$ $\overset{\text{IH3}}{=}$ $\mathbf{S}(y + \mathbf{S}x)$ $\xrightarrow{\text{A2}}$ $\mathbf{SS}(y + x)$,
        RHS $\xrightarrow{\text{A2}}$ $\mathbf{S}(\mathbf{S}y + x)$ $\overset{\text{IH2}}{=}$ $\mathbf{S}(x + \mathbf{S}y)$ $\xrightarrow{\text{A2}}$ $\mathbf{SS}(x + y)$
        $\overset{\text{IH2}}{=}$ $\mathbf{SS}(y + x)$.

This proof is not particularly smart, but it does demonstrate the use of the quantifier of IH2. Three different instances of IH2 occur, the bound variable instantiated to 0, **S**y, and y, respectively. A shorter proof can be obtained by simplifying the formula $\mathbf{S}x + y = y + \mathbf{S}x$ before doing the induction on y.
□

EXAMPLE 5.27

Generator induction over sequences, given the generator basis $\{\varepsilon, \hat{\ } \vdash \hat{\ }\}$, proceeds as follows:

$$\text{GIND}_{\mathbf{seq}\,T} : \quad \frac{\vdash P_\varepsilon^q; \ P \vdash P_{q \vdash x}^q}{\vdash \forall q : \mathbf{seq}\,T \bullet P} \quad \text{for } x : T \text{ a fresh variable}$$

We define the length function for sequences:

    func $\#\hat{\ } : \mathbf{seq}\,T \longrightarrow Nat$
    def $\#q == \mathbf{case}\ q\ \mathbf{of}\ \varepsilon \to 0 \mid q \vdash x \ \to\ \mathbf{S}\#q\ \mathbf{fo}$

and prove that the length of a concatenated sequence is the sum of the lengths of the parts. Sequence concatenation is as defined in example 5.11.

Prove: $\forall q, r : \mathbf{seq}\,T \bullet \#(q \dashv r) = \#q + \#r$.
Proof: by induction on r.
ε for r: LHS $= \#(q \dashv \varepsilon) \longrightarrow \#q$, RHS $= \#q + \#\varepsilon \longrightarrow \#q + 0 \longrightarrow \#q$.
$r \vdash x$ for r: **Assuming** $\forall q : \mathbf{seq}\,T \bullet \#(q \dashv r) = \#q + \#r$,
              prove: $\#(q \dashv (r \vdash x)) = \#q + \#(r \vdash x)$.
              LHS $\longrightarrow \#((q \dashv r) \vdash x) \longrightarrow \mathbf{S}\#(q \dashv r)$ $\overset{\text{IH}}{=}$ $\mathbf{S}(\#q + \#r)$,
              RHS $\longrightarrow \#q + \mathbf{S}\#r \longrightarrow \mathbf{S}(\#q + \#r)$.

□

Not all theorems about TGI defined functions can be proved as easily and mechanistically as examples 5.25–5.27 suggest. It happens that non-trivial lemmas are needed in order to carry out a proof whose formulation requires some degree of mathematical insight. The following is a simple example.

EXAMPLE 5.28
Define a function for reversing a sequence:

> **func** $rev :$ **seq** $T \longrightarrow$ **seq** T
> **def** $rev(q) ==$ **case** q **of** $\varepsilon \rightarrow \varepsilon \mid q \vdash x \rightarrow x \dashv rev(q)$ **fo**

We try to prove the following obvious theorem: $\forall q :$ **seq** $T \bullet rev(rev(q)) = q$ by induction on q:

> ε for q: LHS $= rev(rev(\varepsilon)) \longrightarrow rev(\varepsilon) \longrightarrow \varepsilon =$ RHS.
> $q \vdash x$ for q: **Assuming** $rev(rev(q)) = q$,   (IH)
>   **prove:** $rev(rev(q \vdash x)) = q \vdash x$.
>   LHS $\longrightarrow rev(x \dashv rev(q))$, which is irreducible.
>   RHS is irreducible.

So the formula   F: $rev(x \dashv rev(q)) = q \vdash x$ remains to be proved, for which the induction hypothesis appears to offer no help. The only obvious thing we can try now is to take the induction hypothesis explicitly into account and try to prove $\forall q :$ **seq** $T \bullet$ IH $\Rightarrow$ F by induction on q. However, this attempt also fails.

□

The examples given above demonstrate that much of the formula processing involved in generator inductive proofs about TGI defined functions may be mechanized by term rewriting. The main difficulties are concerned with the formulation and application of lemmas, if necessary, and with the application of induction hypotheses. Assume that lemmas and hypotheses are quantifier free, except for global universal quantifiers. Then, in general, one has to prove a sequent of the form $\forall x \bullet Q \mid P$, where P and Q are quantifier free, x is a list of variables, and Q is a conjunction of lemmas and induction hypotheses.

Using a term rewriting system one general approach is to replace the sequent by an implication, $(\forall x \bullet Q) \Rightarrow P$; however, since the system is unable to deal with the local quantifier (an existential one globally), suitable instances, $Q_1, \ldots, Q_n$ must be chosen manually and the formula $\bigwedge_i Q_i \Rightarrow P$ be processed by term rewriting. Even so, if any conjuncts of Q are equations these will not be available to the system for necessary substitutions of equals for equals in the proof.

If the quantified assumption Q consists of equations our problem may be solved by adding these equations to the set of TGI axioms as new rewrite rules, provided that the rewrite convergence is retained. Then the necessary instances will be found automatically and the complete proof may go through by term rewriting. (Notice that induction variables of induction hypotheses are not quantified and should therefore be regarded as constants by the system.) As mentioned already, the test for convergence can be automated, as shown by Knuth and Bendix in [24]. Furthermore, their so-called "completion procedure" is sometimes able to find an equivalent convergent set of rewrite rules, e.g. by adding more rules, see example 5.22. (It turns out that completion procedures such as that of Knuth and Bendix can be used to carry out actual proofs about TGI defined functions, by adding the theorem itself, or its negation, as an additional rewrite rule, see e.g. [8].)

Exercises

5.13   Prove the lemma $\forall q : \mathbf{seq}\,T \bullet rev(x \dashv q) = rev(q) \vdash x$ by generator induction on q (using the definition of left append given in example 5.11).

5.14   Prove the theorem of example 5.28 using this lemma.

5.15   Define the predicate *ndec* of exercise 4.49, and prove the formula

$$\forall q : \mathbf{seq}\,T \bullet ndec(sort(q))$$

where there is a total order on T and the function *sort* is as defined in exercise 5.4.

5.5   The Equality Relation

Any type T has an associated equality relation $=^T$ with the profile

   func $\hat{\ } =^T \hat{\ } : \quad T \times T \longrightarrow Bool$

(We usually omit the superscript, since the intended relation may be inferred from the type of its arguments.) If the value space V_T of type T had been specified as a set of identified elements, then the equality relation could have been taken for granted. But as we have seen, V_T is specified indirectly and incompletely through the set GU_T of variable-free generator expressions, whose elements are not necessarily in a one-to-one correspondence with abstract T-values. However, regardless of how this correspondence is intended to be, the equality relation $=^T$ must satisfy the axioms and inference rules mentioned in section 2.2, i.e. axioms of reflexivity and rules for the substitution of equals for equals. This means that each equality relation will in fact be an *equivalence relation*, satisfying the standard equivalence axioms:

E1:	$\vdash x = x$	(reflexivity)
E2:	$\vdash x = y \Rightarrow y = x$	(symmetry)
E3:	$\vdash x = y \wedge y = z \Rightarrow x = z$	(transitivity)

In addition the substitution property may be expressed as a set of axioms, one for each argument of each syntactically defined function f.

E4: $\vdash x = y \Rightarrow f(\ldots, x, \ldots) = f(\ldots, y, \ldots)$ (substitution)

Relations satisfying all the axioms E1–4 are called *congruence relations*. (Notice that the two occurrences of the equality operator in a given E4 axiom may be associated with different types.)

The fact that $=^T$ is an equivalence relation implies that it partitions the generator universe GU_T into disjoint subsets called *equivalence classes*. Each equivalence class contains all those basic T-expressions which have equal values according to $=^T$.

EXAMPLE 5.29

Consider the type **set** T, where T is an arbitrary given type, with generator basis $\{\emptyset, add\}$, as defined in example 5.6. We indicate a few of the equivalence classes that we would like to see in $GU_{\textbf{set } T}$:

$\{\emptyset\}$
$\{add(\emptyset, a),\ add(add(\emptyset, a), a),\ \ldots\}$
$\{add(\emptyset, b),\ add(add(\emptyset, b), b),\ \ldots\}$

$\vdots$

$\{add(add(\emptyset, a), b),\ add(add(\emptyset, b), a),\ add(add(add(\emptyset, a), a), b),\ \ldots\}$

$\vdots$

□

Since all expressions in one equivalence class denote the same abstract value, and any two expressions belonging to different equivalence classes denote different values, *we may take the equivalence classes as representing the abstract values*. Let S be some set partitioned by an equivalence relation E. The set of equivalence classes is called the *quotient* set of S with respect to E, denoted S/E. We thus arrive at the following explicit definition of the value set of a type from a given generator universe and a given equality relation:

$$V_T \triangleq GU_T / =^T$$

As we have seen, one defines the generator universe by specifying the generator basis. We now consider various means of defining the equality relation semantically as an equivalence (congruence) relation on the generator universe. The strongest such relation sees any two elements of GU_T as different (assuming that arguments of underlying types are uniquely represented). This corresponds to the notion of a one-to-one generator basis; the resulting equivalence classes are singleton sets, $V_T = \{\{u\} \bullet u \in GU_T\}$. The weakest possible relation holds for all pairs and groups together the elements of GU_T into a single equivalence class. This would correspond to a degenerate type with only one value, $V_T = \{GU_T\}$.

Let the generator basis for T be $\{g_1, g_2, \ldots, g_n\}$, g_i of arity n_i. If it is one-to-one the equality relation for T may be TGI defined as follows, in terms of **case**-free axioms:

$$\vdash g_i(\ldots) = g_j(\ldots) == \mathbf{f}, \qquad \text{for } i, j \in \{1..n\},\ i \neq j$$
$$\vdash g_i(x_1, \ldots, x_{n_i}) = g_i(y_1, \ldots, y_{n_i}) == x_1 = y_1 \wedge \ldots \wedge x_{n_i} = y_{n_i}, \qquad \text{for } i \in \{1..n\}$$

(where the right hand side of the second schema is $\mathbf{t}$ for $n_i = 0$). Since these axioms may be constructed mechanically, given the generator basis, we choose a syntactically simpler way of indicating the one-to-one property:

1-1 genbas $g_1, g_2, \ldots, g_n$

This case is also mathematically simple in the following very important sense:

- The required additional axioms E1–4 are necessarily satisfied and thus cannot lead to logical inconsistency.

This follows from the fact that equality on T-values, defined as above, corresponds to syntactic equality on basic T-expressions (up to semantic equality on subexpressions of underlying types).

EXAMPLE 5.30

The type *Bool* has a one-to-one generator basis; **1-1 genbas f,t**.

□

Before considering techniques for defining the equality relation on type T in the case of a many-to-one generator basis, we point out the fact that merely defining new functions by induction over T generally contributes to the semantics of $=^T$. This is a result of the E-axioms. In particular, E4 applied to a new T-observer may result in new provable *inequalities*. We may think of the function as a new observation tool which makes it possible to distinguish semantically between previously indistinguishable elements of GU_T.

EXAMPLE 5.31

Define a type AB as follows:

> **func** $\quad a, b: \longrightarrow AB,\ eqa : AB \longrightarrow Bool$
> **genbas** a, b
> **def** $\quad eqa(x) == \mathbf{case}\ x\ \mathbf{of}\ a \to \mathbf{t} \mid b \to \mathbf{f}\ \mathbf{fo}$

Clearly, $GU_{AB} = \{a, b\}$. Now, $\mathbf{t}$ and $\mathbf{f}$ are different Boolean values, and so, by the above definition, are $eqa(a)$ and $eqa(b)$. Thus $a \neq b$ follows from E4 applied to the predicate eqa, $\vdash x = y \Rightarrow eqa(x) = eqa(y)$, which shows that the generator basis is one-to-one. So explicit specification of the one-to-one property in this case would have no consequence for the structure of the value set, but would introduce an explicit definition of the equality relation over AB. Consistency would be preserved.

□

Also the definition of producer functions may contribute to the semantics of equality, as shown in the following example.

EXAMPLE 5.32

Redefine the type *Nat* with the following functions.

> **func** $0: \longrightarrow Nat,$ **S**$\hat{\ }$ $: Nat \longrightarrow Nat,$ $is0: Nat \longrightarrow Bool$
> **genbas** $0, \mathbf{S}\hat{\ }$
> **def** $is0(x) ==$ **case** x **of** $0 \to \mathbf{t} \mid$ **others** $\to \mathbf{f}$ **fo**

Applying E4 to *is0* we may prove $0 \neq \mathbf{S}x$ for arbitrary natural number x, but the predicate does not distinguish between different non-zero numbers. We add a predecessor function (a producer !) to the system:

> **func** $\mathbf{P}\hat{\ } : Nat \to Nat$
> **def** $\mathbf{P}x ==$ **case** x **of** $0 \to \perp \mid \mathbf{S}x \to x$ **fo**

Now we can prove that the generator basis is one-to-one. Let u_1 and u_2 be two syntactically different elements of GU_{Nat}, say u_1 is $\mathbf{S}^m 0$ and u_2 is $\mathbf{S}^n 0$, where $0 \leq m < n$. Then the expressions $is0(\mathbf{P}^m u_1)$ and $is0(\mathbf{P}^m u_2)$ are both well-defined and evaluate to $\mathbf{t}$ and $\mathbf{f}$, respectively. E4 applied to *is0* and repeated use of E4 applied to $\mathbf{P}\hat{\ }$ prove that u_1 and u_2 are different semantically.

□

It will be seen that E1–4 can only provide *negative* information about equality over a type T, except for instances of $x = x$. When seen as an equivalence relation over GU_T, these axioms, together with inductive function definitions, provide a "lower bound" on the strength of the predicate. In order to define equality completely for a many-to-one generator basis, positive information is needed. We present four techniques for specifying equality in the many-to-one case.

5.5.1 Equational axioms

Axioms of the form $e = e'$, where e and e' are generator expressions of type T, not necessarily variable-free, may be used to provide an "upper bound" on the strength of the GU_T equivalence relation. It will be possible to choose axioms such that they define equality completely in conjunction with the E-axioms and inductive function definitions. However, it is in general a non-trivial task to decide whether the definition is complete and whether consistency is retained.

This mode of specification is therefore not considered an easy tool for non-specialists, but it happens that the axioms can be given the form of convergent rewrite rules which will reduce any variable-free generator expression to a unique representative of its equivalence class, a "canonical form". In that case variable-free T-equalities could be evaluated by term rewriting if the defining axioms for equality over a one-to-one basis were included. The latter would, however, have to be restricted by *ad hoc* means to apply to irreducible variable-free equations only.

Otherwise convergence, as well as logical consistency, would be lost. (Why?) See also section 5.5.4.

EXAMPLE 5.33

Let the type **set** T be as in example 5.29. We would like the equivalence classes of $GU_{\textbf{set } T}$ to be as indicated in that example. Define a membership predicate:

> **func** $\hat{}\ \epsilon\ \hat{}$: T × **set** T ⟶ *Bool*
> **def** $x \epsilon s ==$ **case** s **of** $\emptyset \to$ **f** $\mid add(s', y) \to x = y \lor x \epsilon s'$ **fo**

The predicate is able to distinguish between elements belonging to different intended equivalence classes, and not between elements belonging to the same equivalence class. The following equational axioms

> S1: $add(add(s, x), y) = add(add(s, y), x)$ (commutativity)
> S2: $add(add(s, x), x) = add(s, x)$ (idempotency)

express that elements of $GU_{\textbf{set } T}$ which are indistinguishable by the $\hat{}\ \epsilon\ \hat{}$ predicate, do in fact belong to the same equivalence class. S1 and S2 preserve convergence of a TGI system if logically consistent, provided that the former is restricted to apply only to cases such that the actual argument for x is, say, "greater" than that for y, according to some fixed total order on expressions. Then the canonical elements of $GU_{\textbf{set } T}$ are of the form $add(\ldots add(\emptyset, a_1), \ldots, a_k)$, where the T-values $a_1, \ldots, a_k$ are distinct and in "increasing" order.

□

EXAMPLE 5.34

Given the same generator basis as in example 5.33 an entirely different type would result if we specified an equality relation of maximal strength, i.e. the one-to-one property. The value space would in that case be structurally similar to that of **seq** T with the one-to-one generator basis $\{\varepsilon, \vdash\}$.

□

EXAMPLE 5.35

By requiring commutativity as in example 5.33 axiom S1, but not idempotency, we restrict the equivalence over $GU_{\textbf{set } T}$ to be of at most an intermediate strength, corresponding to the concept **bag** T. A "bag", also called a multiset, over T is a collection of T-values where values may occur more than once but are not ordered as in a sequence. The equivalence relation becomes completely defined if we introduce a function observing the multiplicity of a T-value in a bag:

> **func** mpc : **set** T × T ⟶ *Nat*   (semantically **bag**, not **set** !)
> **def** $mpc(s, x) ==$ **case** s **of** $\emptyset \to 0 \mid add(s, y) \to$
> $\qquad\qquad\qquad$ **if** $x = y$ **then** $mpc(s, x) + 1$ **else** $mpc(s, x)$ **fi fo**

□

As mentioned already, there is in general no syntactic guarantee for consistency when equality is defined in the context of a many-to-one generator basis. For instance, consistency is lost if the *mpc* definition is added to the specifications of example 5.33. That is because E4 applied to *mpc* contradicts the idempotency axiom S2. Whenever a function f is defined by generator induction over a many-to-one generator basis, consistency may become lost through violation of the schema E4 applied to f. Intuitively, the reason for this danger is that generator induction over T reveals the whole structure of GU_T, including those aspects that ought to be hidden away within the equivalence classes. In order to show that consistency is retained it is sufficient to prove the substitution axiom

$$t_1 = t_2 \Rightarrow f(\overline{x}, t_1, \overline{y}) = f(\overline{x}, t_2, \overline{y})$$

for each inductive argument of f, such that a **case**-construct over a type with a many-to-one generator basis occurs at some textual level of the induction.

If the left equality of the substitution axiom is indirectly defined through equational axioms, $e_i = e_i'$, $i \in \{1..n\}$, it is sufficient to prove the relevant instances of $f(\overline{x}, e_i, \overline{y}) = f(\overline{x}, e_i', \overline{y})$ for every i.

5.5.2 Observation basis

A more direct and easy to use way of defining the equivalence relation over GU_T is to specify a set of functions which may be used to observe "all there is to see" in abstract T-values, or, more precisely, to decide whether any two elements of GU_T represent the same abstract value or not. Such a list of functions is called an *observation basis* for T. Let the observation basis for T be defined by a specification statement of the form

obsbas $h_1, h_2, \ldots, h_m$

where $m > 0$, $\forall i \bullet h_i \in (F_T - G_T) - CST_T$, and $\exists i \bullet h_i \in OBS_T$. Usually all h_i are observers, but producer functions may be meaningful too, provided that the function value is an element of GU_T which is "simpler" in the sense of section 5.4 than each of its argument values of type T. (Generators are thereby excluded.) The specification defines equality as a total and strict function over $T \times T$:

$$t_1 =^T t_2 \quad \triangleq \quad \textbf{if } d_{t_1} \wedge d_{t_2} \quad \textbf{then } \bigwedge_{i=1}^m \forall \overline{x_i}, \overline{y_i} \bullet \ h_i(\overline{x_i}, t_1, \overline{y_i}) == h_i(\overline{x_i}, t_2, \overline{y_i})$$
$$\textbf{else } \perp \textbf{ fi}$$

where $\overline{x_i}, \overline{y_i}$ are suitable variable lists, possibly empty. (It is assumed in this definition that exactly one argument of each h_i is of type T; in general there must be one conjunct for each T argument.) The strong equalities in the right hand side are necessary for those basic observers which are partial functions. Notice that the definition is recursive if the observation basis includes producer functions.

The recursion necessarily terminates, as a consequence of the restriction stated for these producers.

An observation basis clearly provides a complete definition of the equality relation, but does not in general provide a constructive one. Still, if a simple observation basis can be defined for a type, it will provide a useful tool for reasoning about equality. There is another very important advantage in defining equality over T in this way:

- Consistency is guaranteed if no function outside the observation basis is defined by generator induction over T.

That $=^T$ satisfies E1–3 follows from the fact that the equalities occurring in the right hand side of the defining axiom are equivalence relations. (This is provable by induction if $=^T$ itself occurs in the right hand sides, see above.) The defining axiom clearly implies that E4 applied to each of the basic observers holds. Also, the validity of E4 applied to each of the non-constant generators follows easily.

The above observation indicates a way of specifying a type T and associated functions, with syntactic guarantees for completeness and consistency, even if no one-to-one generator basis can be found. It is necessary that all producer functions are total and strict, and that an observation basis can be found as required below (it may be necessary to extend F_T by auxiliary observer functions for this purpose):

1. Specify a generator basis consisting of *all producers*.
2. Specify an observation basis consisting of *total unary observer functions*, $h_i :$ $T \longrightarrow U_i$, $i \in \{1..m\}$, TGI defined by generator induction. (Thus, the corresponding **case**-free axioms will be of the form $h_i(f(\ldots)) == RHS$ for $f \in PRD_T$.)
3. Define any additional observer function directly in terms of basic observer values on the arguments of type T.

Now all non-generator functions in F_T are TGI defined, including T-equality. The latter follows from the fact that the basic observers are unary and total; thus, no quantifier occurs in the definition, and the observers are necessarily strict. The value space V_T can in this case be seen as (a subset of) the Cartesian product $V_{U_1} \times \cdots \times V_{U_m}$. See section 5.8.9 for a construct of this kind.

EXAMPLE 5.36

The type **set** T has an observation basis consisting of the function $\hat{\epsilon}\hat{\ }$, defined in example 5.33: **obsbas** $\hat{\ }\epsilon\hat{\ }$. For the sake of demonstration we attempt a construction such as the one above. It cannot succeed in all respects, however, since the chosen observer is a binary function. Thus, the **obsbas** specification implies the following non-constructive definition of equality over **set** T:

> **def** $s_1 =^{\textbf{set } T} s_2 == \forall x : T \bullet x \in s_1 = x \in s_2$

Extending the generator basis $\{\emptyset, add\}$ by the **set** union operator:

> **func** $\hat{\ }\cup\hat{\ } : \textbf{set } T \times \textbf{set } T \longrightarrow \textbf{set } T$

would require another axiom in the inductive definition of our basic observer:

$$\vdash x \,\epsilon\, (s \cup t) == x \,\epsilon\, s \lor x \,\epsilon\, t$$

which can be seen as an indirect definition of the union operator. There would
be no way, however, to define constructively the observer $\#\hat{} : \mathbf{set}\, T \longrightarrow Nat$,
which counts the number of elements in a set, in terms of $\hat{}\,\epsilon\,\hat{}$ applications (for
an unspecified element type T).

The value space $V_{\mathbf{set}\, T}$ can in this case be seen as the space $T \longrightarrow Bool$ of
total functions, or rather, since the sets are finite, as the space of initialized maps
from T to $Bool$, $Imap\{T, Bool\}$, initialized to $\mathbf{f}$ everywhere. (The concept $Imap$ is
defined formally in section 5.8.10.)

□

EXAMPLE 5.37
The type $\mathbf{bag}\, T$ has an observation basis consisting of the multiplicity function
$mpc : \mathbf{bag}\, T \times T \longrightarrow Nat$, defined semantically as in example 5.35. Consequently,
the value space $V_{\mathbf{bag}\, T}$ can be seen as the space of maps of type $Imap\{T, Nat\}$
initialized to 0 everywhere.

□

EXAMPLE 5.38
Consider the type Nat with the functions $is0$ and $\mathbf{P}\hat{}$, defined in example 5.32. The
specification $\mathbf{obsbas}\; is0, \mathbf{P}\hat{}$ is semantically correct, but it has no consequence for
the structure of the value space. As shown in example 5.31 the function definitions
already imply the one-to-one property of the generator basis. It would, however,
introduce the following explicit definition of the equality relation over Nat:

$$\mathbf{def}\; x =^{Nat} y == is0(x) = is0(y) \land (\neg is0(x) \Rightarrow \mathbf{P}x =^{Nat} \mathbf{P}y)$$

where the last conjunct is an interpretation of the strong equality $\mathbf{P}x ==^{Nat} \mathbf{P}y$.
The definition is constructive, but not TGI (because the recursion is not "guarded"
by generator induction). It may be compared with the definition corresponding to
an explicit **1-1** specification, which is TGI:

$$\mathbf{def}\; x =^{Nat} y == \mathbf{case}\; x \;\mathbf{of}\; 0 \to \mathbf{case}\; y \;\mathbf{of}\; 0 \to \mathbf{t} \mid \mathbf{S}y \to \mathbf{f}\;\mathbf{fo}$$
$$\mid \mathbf{S}x \to \mathbf{case}\; y \;\mathbf{of}\; 0 \to \mathbf{f} \mid \mathbf{S}y \to x = y \;\mathbf{fo}\;\mathbf{fo}$$

The former definition is useless for term rewriting purposes, since it is not a terminating rewrite rule.

□

5.5.3   Explicit definition

It is possible to treat the equality relation as an ordinary observer function and provide an explicit TGI definition. The advantage of this technique is that any variable-free equation can then be evaluated by term rewriting, provided that the same is true for the left and right hand sides. However, there is a fairly heavy proof obligation in validating all of E1–4. Also, the definition is sometimes quite complicated and leads to a term rewriting system of low efficiency and low capability for general purpose reasoning.

EXAMPLE 5.39
Equality over **set** T may be defined using the subset predicate as an auxiliary function:

$$\textbf{func}\ \hat{}\ \subseteq\ \hat{}\ :\ \textbf{set}\,T\ \times\ \textbf{set}\,T\ \longrightarrow\ Bool$$
$$\textbf{def}\ s \subseteq t \quad == \textbf{case}\ s\ \textbf{of}\ \emptyset \to \textbf{t}\ |\ add(s,x) \to x \,\epsilon\, t \wedge s \subseteq t\ \textbf{fo}$$
$$\textbf{def}\ s =^{\textbf{set}\,T} t\ == s \subseteq t \wedge t \subseteq s$$

In order to prove that E1–4 are satisfied by this definition it would be useful to establish the definition of example 5.36 as a lemma. Notice that E1–4 for $=^{\textbf{set}\,T}$ cannot be assumed in these proofs. Fortunately, however, we may still use standard proof techniques, such as term rewriting, in carrying them out, relying on an equality relation over **set** T which satisfies E1–4 by definition and is otherwise ill-defined. It is only after we have shown that the function $=^{\textbf{set}\,T}$ is a congruence relation that we may accept it as the equality relation over **set** T.
□

5.5.4   Canonic representations

Assume that we are able to identify a set of canonical forms, as explained in section 5.5.1. So, for each equivalence class of the generator universe there is exactly one canonic element which could be a unique representative of that class. Assume also that we can give a TGI definition of a total function $crep : T \longrightarrow T$ computing the canonical form of any basic T-expression. We may then use the $crep$ function to define equality on T explicitly and constructively as syntactic equality on canonical representations (up to semantic equality on subterms of underlying types):

$$\textbf{def}\ t = t'\ == \textbf{case}\ (crep(t), crep(t'))\ \textbf{of}$$
$$|\ \underset{i\,\epsilon\,\{1..n\}}{\quad} (g_i(\bar{w}_i), g_i(\bar{w}'_i)) \to \bar{w}_i = \bar{w}'_i\ |\ \textbf{others}\ \to \textbf{f}\ \textbf{fo}$$

So far this is just a special case of the technique described in the last subsection. But if in addition every **case**-construct discriminating on an expression of type T is modified by applying the *crep* function to the discriminant (except possibly if occurring in the definition of *crep* itself) then generator induction over T considers canonic representatives only, which means that *logical consistency will be preserved.*

Unfortunately, **case**-constructs discriminating on expressions other than variables cannot in general be replaced by **case**-free axioms that are directly suitable for term rewriting. It is easy, however, to extend a rewriting algorithm to cater for such constructs. Still, there will be a substantial loss of computational efficiency and reasoning power.

A better idea is to augment any application of a T-generator by a subsequent application of *crep*. This ensures that *all legal* expressions of type T represent canonic elements of GU_T, provided that *crep* has the "subterm property": *any type T subterm of a canonic representative is itself canonic.* The subterm property is needed in order to ensure that T-variables introduced in **case**-discriminators of type T are canonic if the discriminant is. As a result we can reason as if the generator basis is one-to-one, because the only basic expressions we can talk about are the canonic representatives. In particular, equality is the usual syntactic equality, and consistency cannot be violated by TGI function definitions.

Another useful (and reasonable) property for a *crep* function is that of idempotency: $crep(crep(e)) = crep(e)$, for arbitrary element e of GU_T. Now, in the above framework idempotency of *crep* implies $crep(e) = e$ (syntactically), since the T-expression e stands for a canonic representative. As a result superfluous applications of *crep* are harmless and, more importantly, we may omit applications which are provably superfluous.

When specifying functions in terms of canonic representations in a many-to-one T universe it is thus possible to improve evaluation efficiency by taking advantage of the properties of the chosen canonic forms. Sometimes the efficiency gain may be very substantial, as exemplified below. The disadvantage is that one has to focus on the properties of a particular data representation rather than on the concept as such. Consequently, the definitions tend to have a flavour of algorithmic implementation rather than abstract specification. This is not always an advantage for the purpose of easy reasoning.

A comparable technique for obtaining unique representations of T values is to regard the subset $\{t : T \bullet t \text{ is canonical}\}$ as a *subtype* of T, see example 5.48, or even as an entirely separate type T', and "simulate" T by T' as in section 5.9.

EXAMPLE 5.40
Assume that the type T is totally ordered by the predicate $\char94 < \char94 : T \times T \longrightarrow Bool$. Then a set of canonical forms of the type **set** T of example 5.29 can be the set of nested *add* applications whose list of T-arguments is repetition-free and sorted, say, in ascending sequence. The *crep* function can be defined as follows by nested

induction. It may be shown to have the subterm and idempotency properties:

$$\textbf{def } crep(s) == \textbf{case } s \textbf{ of } \emptyset \to \emptyset \mid add(t, x) \to$$
$$\textbf{case } t \textbf{ of } \emptyset \to s \mid add(u, y) \to$$
$$\textbf{if } x = y \textbf{ then } t \textbf{ else}$$
$$\textbf{if } y < x \textbf{ then } s \textbf{ else}$$
$$add(crep(add(u, x)), y) \textbf{ fi fi fo fo}$$

In view of the above usage strategy we may assume that *crep* is applied to a generator application and, if the generator is *add*, that its argument, t, is canonical because it is expressible in legal terms. Then, due to the subterm property, the value of u is also canonical. Thus, in the case where $s = add(add(u, y), x)$ s is already canonic if $y < x$. If $x < y$, *crep* must be applied to the inner *add* in order that x be inserted in the right position of u, but the result of the outer *add* is necessarily canonic.

We may now define the subset relation exactly as in example 5.39 of the last subsection. However, better evaluation efficiency can be obtained as follows (why?), if that is important:

$$\textbf{def } s \subseteq t == \textbf{case } s \textbf{ of } \emptyset \to \textbf{t} \mid add(s', x) \to$$
$$\textbf{case } t \textbf{ of } \emptyset \to \textbf{f} \mid add(t', y) \to$$
$$x = y \wedge s' \subseteq t' \ \vee \ x < y \wedge s \subseteq t' \textbf{ fo fo}$$

Set union, $\widehat{\ } \cup \widehat{\ } : \textbf{set } T \times \textbf{set } T \longrightarrow \textbf{set } T$, may be explained as the result of adding the elements of one operand to the other, one by one. In order to produce canonic results *crep* applications are necessary.

$$\textbf{def } s \cup t == \textbf{case } t \textbf{ of } \emptyset \to s \mid add(t', y) \to crep(add(s \cup t', y)) \textbf{ fo}$$

By exploiting the fact that s and t are canonic it is possible to get rid of the *crep* applications, but at the price of making the function definition rather less obvious:

$$\textbf{def } s \cup t == \textbf{case } s \textbf{ of } \emptyset \to t \mid add(s', x) \to$$
$$\textbf{case } t \textbf{ of } \emptyset \to s \mid add(t', y) \to$$
$$\textbf{if } x < y \textbf{ then } add(s \cup t', y) \textbf{ else}$$
$$\textbf{if } y < x \textbf{ then } add(s' \cup t, x) \textbf{ else}$$
$$add(s' \cup t', x) \textbf{ fi fi fo fo}$$

(In order to establish the TGI property of this definition we would have to consider the combined complexity of the two **set** arguments.)

□

Exercises

5.16   Formalize the property *canonic* : **set** $T \longrightarrow Bool$ common to canonic sets and prove that any **set** subterm of a canonic set is itself canonic.

5.17 Prove that the defined *crep* function produces canonic sets for the given usage strategy. Hint: It is necessary to prove the formulas:

$$canonic(crep(\emptyset)) \quad \text{and} \quad canonic(s) \Rightarrow canonic(crep(add(s,x))).$$

5.18 Prove the correctness of the latter definition of set union, i.e. that it is equivalent to the former definition.

5.6 Subtypes

We introduce the notion of *subtypes*. If T is defined as a subtype of (or is identical to) U we write $T \preceq U$. U is said to be a *supertype* of T. The value space of a subtype is included in that of its supertype, and the set of associated functions contains that of its supertype:

$$T \preceq U \Rightarrow V_T \subseteq V_U \wedge F_U \subseteq F_T$$

The subtype relation is a *partial order* on types, i.e. the following general criteria are satisfied:

$$\begin{array}{ll} T \preceq T & \text{(reflexivity)} \\ T \preceq U \wedge U \preceq V \Rightarrow T \preceq V & \text{(transitivity)} \\ T \preceq U \wedge U \preceq T \Rightarrow T = U & \text{(asymmetry)} \end{array}$$

The operator $\prec$ stands for the corresponding "strong" relation

$$T \prec U \Leftrightarrow T \preceq U \wedge T \neq U$$

Let $\oslash$ denote the "empty" type, defined as the type of the expression $\perp$. $\oslash$ is the universally minimal subtype, i.e. $\oslash \preceq T$ holds for all types T. Consequently, $V_\oslash = \emptyset$ and $F_\oslash = \{\text{all declared functions}\}$. The latter models the fact that any function can be legally applied to $\perp$.

It follows from the way subtypes are defined in the sequel that any non-empty type T has a *unique* maximal supertype, possibly T itself. Types with the same maximal supertype are said to be *related*. Any two related types, T_1, T_2, have a unique minimal common supertype, denoted $T_1 \sqcup T_2$, where $V_{T_1 \sqcup T_2} = V_{T_1} \cup V_{T_2}$.

Types which are *disjoint*, $\leftrightsquigarrow$, are known to have no values in common:

$$T \leftrightsquigarrow U \Rightarrow V_T \cap V_U = \emptyset$$

Unrelated types are disjoint by definition, and $\oslash \leftrightsquigarrow T$ holds for any type T.

The relational operators $=$, $\preceq$, $\prec$, $\leftrightsquigarrow$ for types are intended to convey "syntactic" information, i.e. information available for the textual type checking of expressions. They are established by syntactic conventions for the definition of types and subtypes, which imply the validity of the corresponding semantic relationships. The reverse implications do not hold in general. For instance, types T_1 and T_2 may be unequal and unrelated syntactically even if they are identical in all semantic respects. Still, a given language implementation may permit syntactic relationships to be established through semantic proofs.

The concept of subtypes has several purposes:

- To provide a mechanism for specializing a given type by restricting its value set and/or extending its set of associated non-basic functions.

- To obtain more flexibility within the framework of strong typing. Since a value of a type T belongs to V_U if $T \preceq U$, it is an acceptable U argument. For instance a natural number, i.e. a value of type *Nat*, is at the same time an integer of type *Int*, provided that *Nat* is defined as a subtype of *Int*.

- To provide a convenient way of treating partial functions. A function partial on some given domain will be total on a suitable subdomain. For instance the division operator on natural numbers is partial on the domain $Nat \times Nat$, but total on $Nat \times Nat1$, where *Nat1* is a subtype of *Nat* consisting of the strictly positive integers. Thus the expression x/y is well-defined for $x\!:\!Nat$ and $y\!:\!Nat1$.

- To obtain stronger typing through "syntactic theorems" in the form of additional function profiles. For instance, addition on natural numbers, $\hat{\ }+\hat{\ }$: $Nat \times Nat \longrightarrow Nat$ satisfies the following stronger profile $\hat{\ }+\hat{\ }$: $Nat \times Nat1 \longrightarrow Nat1$. Thus, a suitably adjusted typing algorithm can see that the expression $x+1$ is of type *Nat1*, for $x\!:\!Nat$, and that $x/(x+1)$ is therefore well-defined.

- Syntactic theorems of the form $\cdots \longrightarrow \oslash$ may enable the typing algorithm to identify ill-defined expressions. In particular $\cdots \times \oslash \times \cdots \longrightarrow \oslash$ holds for any function strict with respect to the argument in question. Furthermore functions are by definition ill-defined for argument values *outside the explicitly declared domain*. Thus, if two non-empty types T and T' are known to be disjoint, then a function with a declared domain $\cdots \times T \times \cdots$ is known to satisfy the profile $\cdots \times T' \times \cdots \longrightarrow \oslash$. Notice that additional function profiles should be considered weaker than explicitly given ones, in the sense that they do *not* specify ill-definedness outside their domains.

The concept of well-formed formulas of section 2.1 may be generalized as follows in order to cater for subtypes and additional function profiles:

- An expression $f(e_1, \ldots, e_n)$, where each e_i is an expression of type T_i, is well-formed if there is an f-profile with domain part $U_1 \times \cdots \times U_n$ such that $T_i \preceq U_i$ for all $i \in \{1..n\}$. Its type is the smallest type occurring as the codomain of such profiles, if any. (The set of profiles should be such that this smallest type is always unique.) If no such profiles exist the expression is ill-formed. A **case**-expression is well-formed if and only if the types of the alternatives are related, and its type is the minimal common supertype of the alternative types.

With this typing algorithm well-formed expressions of type other than $\oslash$ are well-defined provided every occurring function is total on the user defined domain. And it has a value whose type is included in that of the expression. Notice that a profile for a function f provides an *upper bound* for the type of the function value for argument types included in the domain. In general an application to such arguments may result in a value of a proper subtype, or may be ill-defined if partial functions occur. Any well-formed expression of type $\oslash$ is ill-defined.

Consider an expression $f(e)$ where e is of type U and f has the domain T. If $U \preceq T$ then e is an acceptable argument; otherwise, if T and U are related but $U \preceq T$ does not hold, then the function application may be meaningful, but only if the value of e happens to belong to V_T. In this case a so-called *coercion* must be applied to e, checking that its value does belong to V_T, and formally converting its type to T. Clearly, this coercion should be a strict partial function, giving an ill-defined result if the argument value does not pass the check.

For any type T the following postfix operators are implicitly introduced, associated with the maximal supertype U of T:

func ˆ **isa** $T :\ U \longrightarrow Bool$
func ˆ **as** $T :\ U \longrightarrow T$

x **isa** T stands for $x \in V_T$ and is formally defined in the sequel. x **as** T is an explicit coercion test, strongly equal to **if** x **isa** T **then** x **else** $\bot$ **fi**. Notice that both operators are *unary*; the type name is considered a syntactic part of the operator symbol.

It is practical to permit implicit coercion to subtypes. So, for e and f as above, where $T \prec U$, $f(e)$ means $f(e$ **as** $T)$. The typing algorithm must be suitably adjusted, inserting the ("cheapest" possible) coercions necessary in order to make a function application well-formed according to the given set of profiles for the function. The coercion e **as** T is syntactically legal if and only if the type of e is included in the maximal supertype U of T. Thus (built-in) coercion is possible only between related types. The type of e **as** T is T unless the type of e is known to be disjoint with T. In the latter case the resulting type is $\oslash$.

A syntactic device for preventing redundant implicit coercion tests is useful. We write e **qua** T in order to change the type of e to a related type T. It is assumed that e **isa** T can be proved in the given context. Notice that this device is now essential for providing a non-circular formal definition of coercion:

def $\quad x$ **as** $T\ ==\ $ **if** x **isa** T **then** x **qua** T **else** $\bot$ **fi**

EXAMPLE 5.41
Let $x, y : Nat$, and take ˆ$/$ˆ to be a total function on the domain $\quad Nat \times Nat1$, where $Nat1 \prec Nat$ as indicated above. Then the expression x/y is well-defined if

$y \neq 0$, and ill-defined for $y = 0$ because the implied coercion of y to *Nat1* fails in that case.

∎

The requirement that the value set of a subtype of T should be contained in that of T implies that the subtype mechanism considered here is somewhat different from the "subclass" mechanism of some programming languages. (For instance, in Simula the value space of a class is essentially a Cartesian product, and a subclass may be formed by adding new components to it.) One important advantage of the subtype concept considered here is the fact that a large class of theorems for T values *remain valid for the subtype.* More precisely: a theorem (in the form of a first order formula, a Hoare sentence, or a sequent) with a free variable $x : T$ remains valid if x is restricted to range over a subtype of T.

The following proof rules show how to reason about quantification over subtypes. The rules are useful for top down (backward) proof construction. (Choosing U to be the maximal supertype of T makes the premise uniquely specified in terms of the conclusion.) Notice that $\forall x : U \bullet P$ is sufficient to conclude $\forall x : T \bullet P$ for $T \preceq U$, whereas $\exists x : T \bullet P$ does not in general follow from $\exists x : U \bullet P$. For example, $\exists x : Nat \bullet x = 0$ is true whereas $\exists x : Nat1 \bullet x = 0$ is not:

$$\text{\textsf{∀SUBTY}} : \quad \frac{\vdash \forall x : U \bullet x \operatorname{\textbf{isa}} T \Rightarrow P}{\vdash \forall x : T \bullet P} \quad \text{for } T \preceq U$$

$$\text{\textsf{∃SUBTY}} : \quad \frac{\vdash \exists x : U \bullet x \operatorname{\textbf{isa}} T \wedge P}{\vdash \exists x : T \bullet P} \quad \text{for } T \preceq U$$

Generator induction

The proof rule GIND_T for generator induction over type T, given in section 5.4, may be generalized in a natural way to cater for the existence of subtypes:

$$\text{GGIND}_T : \quad \frac{P_{x_i}^x, \text{ for } i \in S_g \vdash P_{g(x_1, \ldots, x_{n_g})}^x; \text{ for } g \in G_T}{\vdash \forall x : T \bullet P}$$
$$\text{where } x_1 : T_{g,k}, \ldots, x_{n_g} : T_{g,n_g} \text{ are fresh variables}$$
$$\text{and } S_g = \{i \bullet T_{g,i} \preceq T\}$$

Thus the rule permits an induction hypothesis for each inductive argument x_i whose type is included in T, which is reasonable since $x_i \in V_T$ is then ensured. It means that GGIND_T is a full-strength induction rule for any maximal type T, in admitting induction hypotheses for all inductive arguments ranging over V_T or any subset of V_T.

If T is a subtype a possible proof strategy is to rewrite the proof goal according to ∀SUBTY and prove the resulting formula $\forall x : U \bullet x \operatorname{\textbf{isa}} T \Rightarrow P$ using GGIND_U, where U is the maximal supertype of T. This can be seen as a special case of a more general strategy: find a formula $\forall x : U \bullet P'$, provable by induction over U, such that $P' \wedge x \operatorname{isa} T \Rightarrow P$. The more general approach is necessary if non-empty induction hypotheses on inductive argument values outside T are needed in order to carry out the proofs of the premises.

Convexity

A (sub-)type T is said to be *convex* if:

* For arbitrary basic expression $g(e_1, \ldots, e_{n_g})$ of type T, each subterm e_i is of a type T_i which is either unrelated to T or is included in T. Formally: $T_i \preceq U \Rightarrow T_i \preceq T$, where U is the maximal supertype of T.

EXAMPLE 5.42

A subtype of **seq** T consisting of sequences of length less than or equal to 10 is convex, since any subterm of a basic expression of that type either denotes a shorter sequence or is of the unrelated type T. The subtype of sequences of length equal to 10 is not convex.

□

EXAMPLE 5.43

Let T be a type with a many-to-one generator basis, and let a function *crep* be defined for computing canonical forms, as in section 5.5.4. The set of canonical forms, seen as a subtype of T, is convex if and only if the *crep* function has the "subterm property".

□

It is a consequence of the language mechanisms for type and subtype definition explained in the sequel that no basic expression of a type unrelated to T can contain any subterm of a type related to T. Therefore any value of a convex type T with maximal supertype U can be constructed (by U-generators!) without "stepping outside" T. It follows that any maximal type is convex.

Notice that induction over a convex type T will not be concerned at all with inductive argument values outside T. Consequently GGIND$_T$, combined with the use of $\forall$SUBTY if necessary, provides a maximally strong induction strategy.

For a convex subtype T the concepts of observer functions and relative constants carry over in natural ways: they are functions whose codomain or argument types, respectively, are *unrelated to* T. The producer set, in addition to functions with codomain included in T, may contain restrictions of supertype producers, in particular generators. (Notice that generators viewed as producers of a subtype may not be total functions.)

We consider two kinds of subtypes: *syntactic* subtypes and *semantic* subtypes.

5.6.1   Syntactic subtypes

A family of syntactic subtypes is introduced by defining a type T as the union of a set of *basic subtypes* that are mutually disjoint, writing e.g.

$$\textbf{type } T \textbf{ by } T_1, T_2, \ldots, T_n, \qquad \text{where } T_i \not\leftrightarrow T_j \text{ for } i \neq j$$

All the types are to be semantically defined simultaneously, including all intermediate subtypes, $T_{i_1} \sqcup \ldots \sqcup T_{i_k}$, whether explicitly named or not. T is called the main type of the family. It is the maximal supertype of all types in the family, $T = T_1 \sqcup T_2 \sqcup \ldots \sqcup T_n$.

The generator basis for the whole family consists of functions whose codomains are basic types, such that each basic type occurs as the codomain of at least one generator. T, as well as any of its syntactic subtypes may occur in the domains of the generators. For a one-to-one generator basis the basic types are necessarily disjoint; however, for a many-to-one basis disjointness requires an additional proof. Since the basic subtypes are disjoint, disjointness of any pair of types in the family is decidable textually. All members of the family have the same set of associated functions.

The generator basis $G_{T'}$ for any syntactic subtype T' of T by definition consists of those generators whose codomains are included in T'. Let x be a variable of type T. The type membership test $x \, \textbf{isa} \, T'$ is formalized as follows:

$$\textbf{def } x \, \textbf{isa} \, T' \;\; == \;\; \textbf{case } x \textbf{ of } \underset{g \, \epsilon \, G_{T'}}{\big|} \; g(\ldots) \rightarrow \textbf{t} \mid \textbf{others} \; \rightarrow \textbf{f fo}$$

The convexity criterion is decidable syntactically for any syntactic subtype T'. It follows from the general definition that T' is convex if and only if it is the main type of a self-contained subfamily.

For TGI defined functions on types with syntactic subtypes a maximally strong signature (set of profiles) may be constructed mechanically as follows:

1. (Initialize.) For any set of mutually recursive functions construct a set $\mathcal{P}$ containing profiles for each function, whose domain parts are all possible combinations of types (including $\oslash$) contained in the prescribed function domain, and whose codomain parts are $\oslash$. Construct for each profile in $\mathcal{P}$ an instance of the corresponding defining equation with arguments of the indicated types.

2. (Iterate.) Determine the type of the right hand side of each definition instance, using the current set $\mathcal{P}$ of profiles (as well as maximally strong signatures for other functions). Replace the codomain parts of the current profiles by the types obtained from the analysis of the corresponding right hand sides. Continue iterating as long as changes occur.

3. (Minimize.) Remove all redundant profiles from $\mathcal{P}$. A profile $D \longrightarrow T$, where D is a type product, is redundant if there is a stronger profile $D' \longrightarrow T'$ in $\mathcal{P}$

for the same function. "Stronger" means that the domain is larger or equal and the codomain is smaller or equal: $D \preceq D' \wedge T' \preceq T$. $D \preceq D'$ is true if the $\preceq$ relation holds for each pair of type components. Now $\mathcal{P}$ is maximally strong for the given functions, and also minimal.

EXAMPLE 5.44

In order to improve the strength of typing it is useful to define the type *Bool* in terms of two singleton syntactic subtypes:

> **type** *Bool* **by** *False, True*
> **func f** : $\longrightarrow$ *False*
>   **t** : $\longrightarrow$ *True*
> **1-1 genbas f, t**

Now the standard Boolean operators defined in earlier sections have the maximally strong (minimal) signatures shown in figure 5.1.

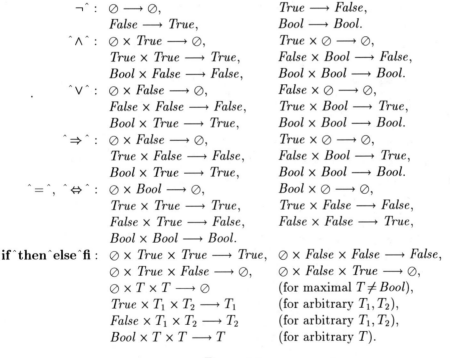

$$
\begin{aligned}
\neg\hat{}\; : \quad & \oslash \longrightarrow \oslash, & & True \longrightarrow False, \\
& False \longrightarrow True, & & Bool \longrightarrow Bool. \\
\hat{}\wedge\hat{}\; : \quad & \oslash \times True \longrightarrow \oslash, & & True \times \oslash \longrightarrow \oslash, \\
& True \times True \longrightarrow True, & & False \times Bool \longrightarrow False, \\
& Bool \times False \longrightarrow False, & & Bool \times Bool \longrightarrow Bool. \\
\hat{}\vee\hat{}\; : \quad & \oslash \times False \longrightarrow \oslash, & & False \times \oslash \longrightarrow \oslash, \\
& False \times False \longrightarrow False, & & True \times Bool \longrightarrow True, \\
& Bool \times True \longrightarrow True, & & Bool \times Bool \longrightarrow Bool. \\
\hat{}\Rightarrow\hat{}\; : \quad & \oslash \times False \longrightarrow \oslash, & & True \times \oslash \longrightarrow \oslash, \\
& True \times False \longrightarrow False, & & False \times Bool \longrightarrow True, \\
& Bool \times True \longrightarrow True, & & Bool \times Bool \longrightarrow Bool. \\
\hat{}=\hat{},\;\hat{}\Leftrightarrow\hat{}\; : \quad & \oslash \times Bool \longrightarrow \oslash, & & Bool \times \oslash \longrightarrow \oslash, \\
& True \times True \longrightarrow True, & & True \times False \longrightarrow False, \\
& False \times True \longrightarrow False, & & False \times False \longrightarrow True, \\
& Bool \times Bool \longrightarrow Bool. \\
\end{aligned}
$$

$$
\begin{aligned}
\textbf{if}\hat{}\,\textbf{then}\hat{}\,\textbf{else}\hat{}\,\textbf{fi}\; : \quad & \oslash \times True \times True \longrightarrow True, & & \oslash \times False \times False \longrightarrow False, \\
& \oslash \times True \times False \longrightarrow \oslash, & & \oslash \times False \times True \longrightarrow \oslash, \\
& \oslash \times T \times T \longrightarrow \oslash & & (\text{for maximal } T \neq Bool), \\
& True \times T_1 \times T_2 \longrightarrow T_1 & & (\text{for arbitrary } T_1, T_2), \\
& False \times T_1 \times T_2 \longrightarrow T_2 & & (\text{for arbitrary } T_1, T_2), \\
& Bool \times T \times T \longrightarrow T & & (\text{for arbitrary } T).
\end{aligned}
$$

Figure 5.1

Notice that the additional profiles provide strictness information. Since the Boolean basic types are singletons the typing algorithm is essentially able to evaluate variable-free purely Boolean expressions.

□

When doing proof by induction over a syntactic subtype, say proving $\forall x : T \cdot P$, the range of the induction variable will be correctly restricted simply by reducing the generator set appropriately. Thus, rewriting the proof goal using $\forall$SUBTY, as explained in the last section is not required in this case. And if the subtype is convex the proof rule GGIND$_T$ as it stands is maximally strong.

For a non-convex syntactic subtype T, however, there will occur inductive arguments ranging over related types not included in T. Let x_i be such an inductive argument of type T' not disjoint from T. Then there should be a semantically guarded induction hypothesis for x_i, as indicated by the following strengthened rule for induction over a (non-convex) syntactic subtype:

$$\text{SGIND}_T : \quad \frac{x_i \, \textbf{isa} \, T \Rightarrow P^x_{x_i}, \ \text{for} \ i \, \epsilon \, S_g \ \vdash P^x_{g(x_1,\ldots,x_{n_g})}; \ \text{for} \ g \, \epsilon \, G_T}{\vdash \forall x : T \cdot P}$$

$$\text{where} \ x_1 : T_{g,1}, \ \ldots, \ x_{n_g} : T_{g,n_g} \ \text{are fresh variables}$$
$$\text{and} \ \ S_g = \{i \cdot \neg T_{g,i} \diamondsuit T\}$$

Clearly, the membership test is redundant whenever $T_{g,i} \preceq T$, since it is identically true in that case. Consider a premise of the form

$$y \, \textbf{isa} \, T \Rightarrow P^x_y \ \vdash \ P^x_{g(\ldots,y,\ldots)}$$

with a non-trivially guarded induction hypothesis. If the type T' of y is convex, an alternative is to prove $P^x_{g(\ldots,y,\ldots)}$, assumption omitted, by induction on y using GGIND$_{T'}$. Cf. the following example.

EXAMPLE 5.45

We partition the type of natural numbers into the singleton type $Zero$, $V_{Zero} = \{0\}$, and $Nat1$, $V_{Nat1} = \{1, 2, \ldots\}$:

> **type** *Nat* **by** *Zero*, *Nat1* :
> **func** 0 : $\longrightarrow$ *Zero*
> **func** S^ :   *Nat* $\longrightarrow$ *Nat1*
> **1-1 genbas** 0, S^
>
> **func** ^+^ : *Nat* $\times$ *Nat* $\longrightarrow$ *Nat*
> **def** $x+y ==$ **case** y **of** $0 \to x \mid \text{S}y' \to \text{S}(x+y')$ **fo**

The function ^+^ satisfies the following set of profiles:

$$
\begin{aligned}
\oslash \times Nat \ &\longrightarrow \ \oslash \\
Nat \times \oslash \ &\longrightarrow \ \oslash \\
Zero \times Zero \ &\longrightarrow \ Zero \\
Nat1 \times Nat \ &\longrightarrow \ Nat1 \\
Nat \times Nat1 \ &\longrightarrow \ Nat1 \\
Nat \times Nat \ &\longrightarrow \ Nat
\end{aligned}
$$

It follows as a byproduct that $\hat{} + \hat{}$ is a strict function. Notice that the typing algorithm is capable of seeing that $0+0=0$, but not that $1+0=1$. This is because *Zero* is a singleton type, whereas *Nat1* is not.

Clearly, *Nat* is convex, being a maximal type, and *Zero* is convex too in a trivial way. But *Nat1* is not, because its generator $\mathbf{S}\hat{}$ has a domain related to but not included in *Nat1*. We may give two alternative rules for proof by induction over the subtype *Nat1*:

$$\text{SGIND}_{Nat1} : \quad \frac{y \neq 0 \Rightarrow P_y^x \vdash P_{\mathbf{S}y}^x}{\vdash \forall x : Nat1 \bullet P} \quad \text{(for } y : Nat)$$

$$\text{GSIND}_{Nat1} : \quad \frac{\vdash P_{\mathbf{S}0}^x; \quad P_{\mathbf{S}z}^x \vdash P_{\mathbf{S}\mathbf{S}z}^x}{\vdash \forall x : Nat1 \bullet P} \quad \text{(for } z : Nat)$$

Notice that the induction hypothesis in SGIND_{Nat1} is void unless y is of the form $\mathbf{S}z$. In GSIND_{Nat1} this is made more explicit. The latter rule follows from the former after using GGIND_{Nat} to deduce $\vdash \forall y : Nat \bullet P_{\mathbf{S}y}^x$ from the premises. $\square$

Exercises

5.19 Show that the relational operator $\hat{} < \hat{}$, defined as in example 5.10, has the following minimal, maximally strong signature:

$$
\begin{aligned}
\oslash \times Nat1 &\longrightarrow \oslash \\
\oslash \times Nat &\longrightarrow False \\
Nat \times \oslash &\longrightarrow \oslash \\
Zero \times Nat1 &\longrightarrow True \\
Nat \times Zero &\longrightarrow False \\
Nat \times Nat &\longrightarrow Bool
\end{aligned}
$$

5.20 Try to make the iteration part of the signature construction algorithm more efficient.

5.6.2 Semantic subtypes

A semantic subtype may be obtained by restricting the value space of a given type by some predicate, writing e.g.

type $T == \{x : U \bullet P\}$

where the right hand side is called a *subtype expression*, by definition identifying a (semantic) subtype of U. The restricting predicate P is assumed to be *well-defined*.

The corresponding subtype membership test is an application of the restricting predicate. Notice that the operator will be associated with the *maximal* supertype of T, which need not be U:

def $x \, \mathbf{isa} \, T \; == \; x \, \mathbf{isa} \, U \wedge P$

Semantic subtyping is a much stronger mechanism than the classification of generators which leads to syntactic subtypes. However, there is less syntactic control of semantic subtypes. In particular, semantic proofs are needed in general in order to verify functions with semantically restricted codomains, if explicit membership tests are to be avoided.

Semantic subtypes of given types may be introduced "incrementally" as need arises. This represents an important administrative advantage over syntactic subtypes, which have to be introduced and defined simultaneously. A semantic subtype "inherits" the functions associated with its supertype and may be specialized further by additional associated functions. In the next section we show how function association and inheritance may be specified formally.

EXAMPLE 5.46
We may specify the set of even natural numbers as a semantic subset of *Nat*:

type $EvNat \; == \; \{x : Nat \bullet x \bmod 2 = 0\}$

where the function $\hat{} \, \mathbf{mod} \, \hat{} : Nat \times Nat \longrightarrow Bool$ is as defined in example 5.13. The syntactic theorem $\hat{} + \hat{} : EvNat \times EvNat \longrightarrow EvNat$ is valid, but requires a semantic proof that the sum of two even numbers is even.
□

EXAMPLE 5.47
On a given computer natural numbers may have to be less than or equal to a given number n in order to be efficiently represented. We therefore define a semantic subtype of naturals bounded by n:

type $BdNatn \; == \; \{x : Nat \bullet x \leq n\}$

func $plus : BdNatn \times BdNatn \longrightarrow BdNatn$
def $plus(x, y) \; == \; (x + y) \, \mathbf{as} \, BdNatn$

The coercion is necessary in order to check that the function value is within the bound. There are ways of "overloading" the $+$-operator by redefining it for *BdNatn* arguments, rather than using another function name, but we do not want to get lost in such detail at this point.
□

EXAMPLE 5.48
Sorted sequences of natural numbers are structures of the subtype $\{q : \mathbf{seq}\ Nat \bullet /\leq q\}$. Repetition-free sorted sequences of positive natural numbers belong to the subtype $\{q : \mathbf{seq}\ Nat1 \bullet /< q\}$.
□

The types occurring in the two last examples are all convex with respect to the standard generator bases; that of example 5.46 is not.
Semantic subtypes have the following properties:

$$\text{SEMSUB1}: \quad T' \prec T \Rightarrow \{x : T' \bullet P\} \prec \{x : T \bullet P\}$$
$$\text{SEMSUB2}: \quad T \diamond\!\!\!\rightarrow T' \Rightarrow \{x . T \bullet P\} \diamond\!\!\!\rightarrow \{x : T' \bullet P'\}$$
$$\text{SEMSUB3}: \quad \{x : \{x : T \bullet P\} \bullet Q\} = \{x : T \bullet P \wedge Q\}$$
$$\text{SEMSUB4}: \quad (\forall x : T \bullet P' \Rightarrow P) \Rightarrow \{x : T \bullet P'\} \preceq \{x : T \bullet P\}$$
$$\text{SEMSUB5}: \quad (\forall x : T \bullet \neg(P \wedge P')) \Rightarrow \{x : T \bullet P\} \diamond\!\!\!\rightarrow \{x : T \bullet P'\}$$

Let T' and T'' be the two semantic subtypes occurring in SEMSUB3, $T'' \preceq T' \preceq T$, and let e be an expression of type T. SEMSUB3 shows that e **as** T'' is strongly equal to $(e$ **as** $T')$ **as** T''. This is consistent with the above definition of coercion operators. SEMSUB4 and SEMSUB5 suggest ways to establish syntactic type relationships through semantic proofs.

EXAMPLE 5.49
The following are consequences of SEMSUB4 and SEMSUB5, respectively:

$$m \leq n \;\Rightarrow\; \{x : Nat \bullet x \leq m\} \preceq \{x : Nat \bullet x \leq n\}$$
$$m \neq n \;\Rightarrow\; \{q : \mathbf{seq}\ T \bullet \#q = m\} \diamond\!\!\!\rightarrow \{q : \mathbf{seq}\ T \bullet \#q = n\}$$

The second subtype of example 5.48 is a proper subtype of the first one. This follows from SEMSUB1 by MONOTY of section 5.7 and $Nat1 \prec Nat$, and SEMSUB4 by proving $/< q \Rightarrow /\leq q$ for $q : \mathbf{seq}\ Nat1$.
□

5.7   Parameterized Types and Modules

There is a need for "type schemas" which, when given a list of types, produce a new type according to a specified pattern. The pattern is a type definition formulated in terms of unspecified types, so-called "formal type parameters". We have already seen examples of such patterns treated very informally, such as sequences and sets of elements of unspecified type. A type schema thus represents a whole class of types. It may be *instantiated* to a specific type by substituting actual types for the formal ones.

Now we shall have to be more formal in our attitude toward types, recognizing that a type definition consists of a left hand side introducing a type (schema) name and possibly a list of formal parameters, and a right hand side, according to the following general syntax:

type Name{formal type parameters} == right hand side

The type name is of global significance as a defined type and is referred to locally, i.e. within the right hand side, as the *type under definition*. The formal parameters have only local significance. In the case where a family of syntactic subtypes is defined, the left hand side must be more elaborate, introducing the basic and intermediate subtypes as well, defined globally and under definition locally. The right hand side is either a *type expression* or a *type module*, or a type expression followed by a *module increment*.

- A *type expression* is either:
  - a single name which may denote a parameterless defined type, a formal type parameter, or a type under definition (in which case parameters, if any, are omitted in order to prevent certain kinds of meaningless type definitions), or
  - a semantic subtype expression (cf. the last section), where the indicated supertype is a type expression, and whose associated function set is that of the supertype, where the latter is extended by a coercion function from the supertype to the subtype, or
  - a compound expression obtained from the left hand side of a type definition, in which the formal type parameters are replaced by actual type expressions. The compound expression denotes the type obtained by instantiating the corresponding right hand side type schema with these actual parameters (or possibly a member of a syntactic subtype family so defined). Example: *Bintree*{*Nat*} denotes the type of binary trees of natural numbers, cf. example 5.52. Some more or less traditional *ad hoc* and mixfix notations are used in addition to the standard one, such as {$a..b$}, **seq** T, and a few others.
- A *type module* is a structure of the form

  module list of module items **endmodule**

where a module item is either a function profile (one for each new function), a **genbas**-statement (exactly one), a function definition (one for each non-basic function), an **obsbas**-statement (at most one), or a *lemma*-item containing a proven closed formula. A type module should uniquely define the value space(s) of the type(s) under definition and possibly define additional functions. We regard the functions introduced in a type module as formally associated with the type(s) under definition. This implies that the members of a syntactic subtype family have the *same* set of associated functions. It also implies that different instances of a type schema have *similar* sets of associated functions.

Let T be the (main) type under definition for a given type module. Then the module is understood to contain the following predefined items:

func $\hat{\ } = \hat{\ } : T \times T \longrightarrow Bool$
func $\hat{\ } \neq \hat{\ } : T \times T \longrightarrow Bool$
def $x \neq y == \neg x = y$
func **if**$\hat{\ }$**then**$\hat{\ }$**else**$\hat{\ }$**fi** : $Bool \times T \times T \longrightarrow T$
def **if** b **then** x **else** y **fi** == **case** b **of** **t** $\rightarrow x$ | **f** $\rightarrow y$ **fo**
func $\hat{\ }$ **isa** $T : T \longrightarrow True$
def x **isa** $T ==$ **t**
func $\hat{\ }$ **as** $T : T \longrightarrow T$
def x **as** $T == x$

The $\hat{\ } = \hat{\ }$ relation will be defined explicitly or implicitly as explained in sections 5.5.2–4. Since the five functions are defined for all types, they may be assumed to apply to arguments of formal types as well.

If the module defines a syntactic subtype family, additional membership test and coercion operators are introduced and defined for the subtypes. Furthermore, whenever a semantic subtype is introduced and named, the function set of the maximal supertype is augmented with corresponding test and coercion operators.

- A *module increment* is of the same form as a type module, but may only contain profiles and definitions of functions, as well as lemmas. It serves to define a subtype of the type identified by the preceding type expression, by extending the set of associated functions by those defined in the module increment.

In addition to type modules, other kinds of modules may be useful, for instance for the introduction of groups of interrelated functions, not to be associated with a specific type (see below). See also chapter 6, where a somewhat more machine oriented kind of module, *class* modules, is discussed.

It is sometimes necessary in a parameterized module to introduce *assumptions* about formal type parameters: that the corresponding actual types should have certain associated functions in addition to the standard ones mentioned above, satisfying certain minimal requirements. The assumptions could consist of *profiles* syntactically characterizing these functions in terms of formal and defined types, as well as *axioms* expressing semantic requirements. For instance, in a module *Sorting*$\{T\}$ dealing with sequences of type T elements, it must be assumed that there are functions such as $\hat{\ } < \hat{\ }$, $\hat{\ } \leq \hat{\ } : T \times T \longrightarrow Bool$, having the properties expected of ordering relations, such as $\vdash x < y < z \Rightarrow x < z$ and $\vdash x \leq y \Leftrightarrow x < y \vee x = y$, for $x, y, z : T$.

It would be convenient to collect lists of such profiles and axioms into modules of yet another kind, which could be used to express such concepts as $PartialOrder\{T\}$ and $TotalOrder\{T\}$. Then assumptions about formal types could be succinctly expressed by referring to such "property modules". Thus, the module $Sorting\{T\}$ would need to assume the property $TotalOrder\{T\}$. When instantiating the former with a defined actual type, say $Sorting\{Nat\}$ or $Sorting\{Text\}$, there would be an obligation to validate that the actual type provided had the required property. In standard types the corresponding proofs might have been carried out in advance, if so the validation would reduce to syntactic checking.

It is outside the scope of this book to discuss in detail how these briefly sketched ideas, or similar ones, could be formalized. In the few cases where assumptions about formal types are needed in subsequent specifications, they will be expressed informally.

Parameterized types may be seen as higher order functions which, when applied to given types, produce new types. As such they are *monotonic* with respect to the subtype relation

$$\text{MONOTY}: \quad \vdash T' \preceq T \Rightarrow U\{\ldots,T',\ldots\} \preceq U\{\ldots,T,\ldots\}$$

MONOTY is easy to justify in the case where U is defined by a type module specifying a one-to-one generator basis. Assume $T' \preceq T$. If the corresponding formal type parameter of U does *not* occur in the generator domains (if U is a syntactic subtype, those of the whole family), the value spaces of the two U instances are identical. If it *does* occur, the generator universe of $U(\ldots,T',\ldots)$ is contained in that of $U(\ldots,T,\ldots)$ because $V_{T'} \subseteq V_T$.

If the generator basis of U is many-to-one, or if U is a semantic subtype, similar arguments apply, provided that neither the equality relation nor a restricting predicate depends on properties of actual type parameters. The only way for this to happen would be where either depended on functions introduced through assumptions in U, say for a function f assumed to exist for the formal type parameter corresponding to T and T'. (For instance, in order to define a general concept of sorted sequences, parameterized by the element type, the restricting predicate must be expressed in terms of an assumed ordering relation for that type.) Then the validity of MONOTY may depend on the two versions of f being sufficiently similar. Now, the subtype T' normally inherits f from T unchanged, and if redefined in T' the new f must be an *approximation* to that of T (according to restrictions stated in the next section), caused by replacing occurrences of T bt T' in the f-profile. It follows that MONOTY is sound if neither equality relations nor semantic subtype restrictions are allowed to depend on assumed producer functions.

A coercion from $U\{\ldots,T,\ldots\}$ to $U\{\ldots,T',\ldots\}$ would have to apply coercion from T to T' for every T value contained in a given data structure of type $U\{\ldots,T,\ldots\}$. Notice that MONOTY is consistent with the axiom SEMSUB1 of the last section.

There may be a need for types with "value parameters". For instance, *BdNatn* of example 5.47 should have the natural number n as a formal parameter. A formal value parameter should be type specified, e.g. *BdNat*$\{n : Nat\}$, and a corresponding actual one should be a well-defined expression of a type contained in that of the formal parameter. The syntax of type definitions and type expressions given above should be extended correspondingly.

In the following example a value parameter is used to determine the equality relation in a type with a many-to-one generator basis.

EXAMPLE 5.50
We may define the type of integers modulo a given $n > 0$ in the following way:

type *Mod*$\{n : Nat1\}$ ==
module
func 0 : $\longrightarrow$ *Mod*
func Cˆ : *Mod* $\longrightarrow$ *Mod*   (successor in cycle)
genbas 0, Cˆ

func *nat* : *Mod* $\longrightarrow$ *Nat*   (integer equivalent)
def $nat(x)$ == **case** x **of** $0 \to 0 \mid Cx' \to$
                    if S $nat(x') = n$ **then** 0 **else S** $nat(x')$ **fi fo**

obsbas *nat*

func ˆ$\oplus$ˆ : *Mod* $\longrightarrow$ *Mod*   (modulo addition)
def $x \oplus y$ == **case** y **of** $0 \to x \mid Cy' \to C(x \oplus y')$ **fo**
endmodule

☐

From now on we require all function profiles and definitions to occur within modules, and that *a type under definition (if any) occurs in every profile*, as an argument type or as the codomain. Most functions will be associated in a natural way with some particular type, but counterexamples do exist. See section 5.8.10 for an example of a function where no argument type, nor the codomain, can be taken as a type under definition. For that reason a kind of module is needed, introducing and defining a group of functions, but defining no type:

funcs Name{formal parameters} == **module** ... **endmodule**

Since a function module defines no type it must not contain basis statements. Function modules are useful structuring mechanisms in their own right.

5.7.1   Function overloading

We assume that type definitions can be so ordered that all types used in a type definition are defined earlier in the sequence. The usage of types defined earlier leads to the concept of a *definition hierarchy*. If a type U, or any of its associated functions, is used in the definition of T (and U is not a type under definition), then T is said to *depend* on U and to be *above* U in the definition hierarchy. (Function modules count as types in this connection.) The type *Bool* is at the bottom of the hierarchy; any other (non-empty) type is above *Bool*. Also, an instance of a type schema is above its actual type parameters. A semantic subtype is above its supertype, whereas the members of a syntactic subtype family are regarded as equivalent with respect to the definition hierarchy. The relation induced by the definition hierarchy is to be transitive by definition.

If two types T and U are mutually dependent through generator functions, i.e. those of T have U arguments and vice versa, the definitions cannot be ordered as assumed above. However, we can still comply with the ordering requirement by the trick of defining them simultaneously as syntactic subtypes of a common main type.

It is reasonable to permit *function overloading* by using the same function name or mixfix operator for functions in different type modules. This has been done already for equality, inequality, and **if**-constructs. There is an obvious advantage in making synonymous functions similar with respect to syntactic and semantic properties. For functions occurring in types related as semantic subtypes it is useful to insist on quite strong similarity.

Let T' be a semantic subtype of T. Although T' normally inherits all T-functions unchanged, redefinition of any function T-function f is allowed, subject to the following restrictions:

1. A new profile may be specified for f in which any occurrence of T (or a semantic supertype of T) is replaced by T'. If f is an observer function, its codomain may be replaced by a subtype, provided all values of f on the restricted domain belong to the subtype.

2. If a new semantic definition is given, it must comply with the old one in the sense that the new function is identical to the old one on the restricted domain, for function values in the restricted codomain, and is otherwise ill-defined. (The new definition may, however, be more efficient by taking advantage of a smaller function domain.) If no semantic definition is given, a default definition is assumed consisting of an application of the old function, whose value is coerced to the subtype, if relevant.

It follows that any redefined function is an *approximation* to the old one. In particular, restricting the codomain of a generator in general redefines it as a partial function in the subtype. A redefined function is said to be a *natural restriction* of that of the supertype if it is identical to the latter on the restricted domain. Thus, it is required that all redefined observers be natural restrictions. It may also happen that a redefined producer function is a natural restriction, even if the codomain is redefined. For example, let $f : \textbf{seq } Nat \longrightarrow \textbf{seq } Nat$ be some function whose value is a subsequence of its argument. Consider its restriction to the subtype of sorted sequences. The restriction is natural since any subsequence of a sorted sequence is itself sorted.

We use the following main rule of overloading. Remember that the typing algorithm works bottom up, so that the type of a function application is determined from given argument types:

- For an application $f(e_1, \ldots, e_n)$ with given argument types, consider the definition hierarchy restricted to these types. Then f denotes a function associated with one of the maximal types of this hierarchy.

This rule is a generalization of the simple rule of "dot notation" often used in object oriented programming. It works well for functions with domains containing occurrences of types under definition. In that case the corresponding actual argument type is usually the only maximal one, and the selected function is the natural choice and nearly always the one desired.

For instance, consider the expression $f(t, u)$, where the argument types are T and U, respectively. If T has an associated function f with domain $T \times U$, then T is above U, and vice versa. Thus, in these cases exactly one of T and U is maximal and has a matching associated function. In the case where T and U are not comparable in the definition hierarchy, neither module can contain occurrences of the other type, which usually means that neither contains an applicable f-profile, and that f is a relative constant associated with some other type. (If, however, U has a semantic supertype U' then T might contain a matching f-profile with domain $T \times U'$. If U also contains a matching profile with domain $T' \times U$, where T' is a semantic supertype of T, then $f(t, u)$ is actually ambiguous.)

If coercion to semantic subtypes is automatic, more possibilities for ambiguities arise in general, since types related to the maximal ones must be searched for matching profiles if the rule, as it stands, gives no match. Even so, no match may be found for relative constants, since they are associated with types not occurring in their domains. If overloading and automatic interpretation of relative constants are desired, the search must be further extended. It can, however, be limited to modules which are above all actual argument types (if any) in the definition hierarchy, possibly in an order determined by distance in some sense. For (absolute) constants the search would have to cover all defined functions in a given environment, which is quite dangerous because new ambiguities are too easily introduced in old specifications by introducing new constants, or even as the result of introducing new instances of type schemas containing constants.

Too liberal and complicated overloading rules are dangerous anyway, especially when combined with rules of automatic coercion, because the resulting function interpretations may be *unexpected* (which is worse than being ambiguous). Some safety is gained, however, by limiting the function search to the current module and those on which it depends, i.e. those *below* it in the definition hierarchy. Such limitation in turn implies that a type T can only become dependent on another type U if the latter, or one dependent on it, occurs *explicitly* in the definition of T.

Otherwise U is not a candidate for search when interpreting function applications in T, which means that no function associated with U is accessible in T, and that the names of these functions do not conflict with any use in T of the same function names. Notice, however, that such conflicts may well arise in a type dependent on both T and U.

Function modules count as types with respect to function overloading. Notice, however, that functions belonging to a function module are such as relative constants since there is no type under definition in their domains.

Some syntactic mechanism is needed for resolving ambiguities and for overriding given overloading rules. We write $T'f$ in order to identify the function f associated with the type (or group) T, or $T'(e)$ to identify the main operator of the expression e if it is infixed or is some other mixfix construct beginning with an operand. Notice that an occurrence of $T'f$ in U makes U dependent on T.

Implicit interpretation of overloaded functions implies that those actually applied in an expression may depend on the types of the variables that occur. In particular, replacing the type U of a variable x in a formula by a semantic subtype T will result in a reinterpretation of $f(x)$, for $f \in F_U$, if f has been redefined in T. Now, if the redefined f is a natural restriction, the reinterpretation does not change the meaning of $f(x)$ on the domain T, but otherwise it becomes *less defined* on T.

Such type replacement occurs in the proof rules ∀SUBTY and ∃SUBTY of section 5.6 and results in the loss of soundness: given a proof of the premise, showing that it is well-defined and true, it can still happen that the conclusion is ill-defined. See example 5.51 below.

In general it is necessary to give an additional well-definedness proof for the conclusion; however, a sufficient condition is that any U-function occurring in the formula P is a natural restriction in T if redefined. Fortunately, both rules are sound for backward proof construction, given a well-defined conclusion.

EXAMPLE 5.51
The semantic subtype definition

> **type** $BdNat\{n : Nat\} == \{x : Nat \bullet x \leq n\}$
> **module func** $\hat{\ }+\hat{\ } : BdNat \times BdNat \longrightarrow BdNat$
> **def** $x + y == Nat'(x + y)$ **as** $BdNat$
> **endmodule**

is a rephrasing of that of example 5.47, which is fully formalized and possibly more useful. The explicit semantic redefinition is identical to the one that would otherwise have been assumed.

As an example of faulty use of the proof rule ∀SUBEQ we may consider the theorem $\forall x : Nat \bullet x \leq 10 \Rightarrow x < x+1$. The rule gives the conclusion $\forall x : BdNat\{10\} \bullet x < x+1$, which is ill-defined (and interpreted as false). A sufficiently guarded conclusion, say $\forall x : BdNat\{10\} \bullet x \neq 10 \Rightarrow x < x+1$, would correspond to the premise $\forall x : Nat \bullet x < 10 \Rightarrow x < x+1$ (after simplification). The corresponding forward deduction is strongly correct, even with the indicated redefinition of the addition operator.

□

EXAMPLE 5.52

As a more substantial example of a subtype hierarchy we first define a concept of binary trees. Since some natural observer functions are ill-defined for an empty tree, we introduce the types of empty and non-empty trees as basic subtypes. The sequence operators used are formally defined in section 5.8.8:

> **type** *Bintree*$\{T\}$ **by** *Nil*, *Bintree1*$\{T\}$ ==
> **module**
> **func** *nil* : $\longrightarrow$ *Nil*   (empty tree)
> **func** *tree* : *Bintree* $\times$ *T* $\times$ *Bintree* $\longrightarrow$ *Bintree1*   (non-empty tree)
> **1-1 genbas** *nil*, *tree*
> **func** $\hat{\ }.lsub$: *Bintree1* $\longrightarrow$ *Bintree*   (left subtree)
> **func** $\hat{\ }.val$: *Bintree1* $\longrightarrow$ *T*   (node value)
> **func** $\hat{\ }.rsub$: *Bintree1* $\longrightarrow$ *Bintree*   (right subtree)
> **def** *tree*$(x,y,z).lsub$ == x
> **def** *tree*$(x,y,z).val$ == y
> **def** *tree*$(x,y,z).rsub$ == z
>
> **func** *has* : *Bintree* $\times$ *T* $\longrightarrow$ *Bool*   (occurrence test)
> **def** *has*(t,v) == **case** t **of** *nil* $\rightarrow$ **f** $\mid$ *tree*$(x,y,z) \rightarrow$
> $\qquad\qquad$ *has*$(x,v) \lor y = v \lor$ *has*(z,v) **fo**
>
> $\vdots$
>
> **func** *infix* : *Bintree* $\longrightarrow$ **seq** *T*   (infix node sequence)
> **def** *infix*(t) == **case** t **of** *nil* $\rightarrow \varepsilon \mid$ *tree*$(x,y,z) \rightarrow$
> $\qquad\qquad$ *infix*$(x) \vdash y \dashv$ *infix*(z) **fo**
>
> $\vdots$
>
> **endmodule**

Assuming that the node type T is totally ordered by the operator $\hat{\ } < \hat{\ }$ we may define the concept of search trees as the subtype of binary trees such that the infix node sequence is strictly ascending (expressed by the operator $/<\hat{\ }$):

> **type** *Stree*$\{T\}$ == $\{t : Bintree\{T\} \bullet /< infix(t)\}$
> **module**
> **func** *has* : *Stree* $\times$ *T* $\longrightarrow$ *Bool*   (revised occurrence test)
> **def** *has*(t,v) == **case** t **of** *nil* $\rightarrow$ **f** $\mid$ *tree*$(x,y,z) \rightarrow$
> $\qquad\qquad$ **if** $v < y$ **then** *has*$(x$ **qua** *Stree*, $v)$ **else**
> $\qquad\qquad\quad$ **if** $y < v$ **then** *has*$(z$ **qua** *Stree*, $v)$ **else** t **fi fi fo**

func *add* : *Stree* × *T* ⟶ *Stree*   (include value not there)
def   *add*(*t*, *v*) == **case** *t* **of** *nil* → *tree*(*nil*, *v*, *nil*) | *tree*(*x*, *y*, *z*) →
                 if $v < y$ **then** *tree*(*add*(*x* **qua** *Stree*, *v*), *y*, *z*) **else**
                   if $y < v$ **then** *tree*(*x*, *y*, *add*(*z* **qua** *Stree*, *v*)) **else**
                   t **fi fi fo qua** *Stree*

    ⋮

endmodule

The search tree property permits the occurrence test to be redefined with better average efficiency. Let *has'* denote the redefined function. We may prove $has(t, v) == has'(t, v)$ by induction on t : *Search Tree*. In the non-trivial case we have to prove $has(tree(x, y, z), v) == has'(tree(x, y, z), v)$. Use of the function definitions and the induction hypotheses for x and z lead to the proof goal

$$has(x, v) \lor y = v \lor has(z, v) == \text{ \textbf{if} } v < y \text{ \textbf{then} } has(x \text{ \textbf{qua} } Stree, \ v) \text{ \textbf{else}}$$
$$\text{\textbf{if} } y < v \text{ \textbf{then} } has(z \text{ \textbf{qua} } Stree, \ v) \text{ \textbf{else} } t \text{ \textbf{fi fi}}$$

Using the definition of the *infix* function and suitable lemmas on sequences it is easy to see that both sides are true if and only if x occurs in $infix(tree(x, y, z))$, given that this sequence is sorted.

    There is no natural way of adding a single node to an arbitrary binary tree, so this operation is an extension to the *Stree* function set. It is up to the specifier to prove that the function value of *add* is in fact a search tree, and that the left and right subtrees of a given one are search trees as well. The latter holds because the subtype *Search Tree* is *convex*.

    It follows that the type conversions of the variables x and z in the definition of *has* and *add* of *Stree* could be omitted if the convexity property was made known to the textual typing algorithm once and for all by some syntactic indication, say by adding the keyword **convex** to the *Stree* module prefix. The associated proof obligation would be to show

$$/ < infix(nil) \quad \text{and} \quad / < infix(tree(x, y, z)) \Rightarrow / < infix(x) \land / < infix(z)$$

The latter follows by a simple lemma on sequences: $/ < (q_1 \vdash q_2 \vdash q_3) \Rightarrow / < q_2$.

☐

EXAMPLE 5.53
Section 5.5.4 explains how the concept of canonic forms may be used to obtain unique representations of abstract values with a many-to-one generator basis. This technique may be formalized in terms of a semantic subtype with redefined generators and equality relation. We first define the type **set** *T* and a few associated

functions as a type module, where the equality relation is defined through an observation basis as in example 5.36. Assuming a total order $\hat{}<\hat{}$ for T, as in example 5.40, the property of canonic sets may be expressed as a unary predicate:

type set T ==
module
    func $\emptyset : \longrightarrow$ **set**
    func $add :$ **set** $\times T \longrightarrow$ **set**
    genbas $\emptyset, add$
    func $\hat{}\;\epsilon\;\hat{} : T \times$ **set** $\longrightarrow Bool$
    def $x \epsilon s ==$ **case** s **of** $\emptyset \to \mathbf{f} \mid add(s', x') \to x = x' \vee x \epsilon s'$ **fo**
    obsbas $\hat{}\;\epsilon\;\hat{}$
    func $\hat{}\cup\hat{} :$ **set** $\times$ **set** $\longrightarrow$ **set**
    def $s \cup t ==$ **case** t **of** $\emptyset \to s \mid add(t', y) \to add(s \cup t', y)$ **fo**
    func $canonic :$ **set** $\longrightarrow Bool$
    def $canonic(s) ==$ **case** s **of** $\emptyset \to \mathbf{t} \mid add(t, x) \to$
                        case t **of** $\emptyset \to \mathbf{t} \mid add(u, y) \to$
                              $y < x \wedge canonic(t)$ **fo fo**
endmodule

We may now define a type of canonic sets as a convex subtype of **set** T, in which the generators are redefined such that only canonic sets are produced. Then it looks as if the generator basis is one-to-one, and consequently the equality relation can be redefined as syntactic equality on basic expressions:

type $CSet\{T\}$ == $\{s :$ **set** $T \bullet canonic(s)\}$ **convex**
 module
    func $\emptyset : \longrightarrow CSet$
    def $\emptyset ==$ **set**'$\emptyset$ **qua** $CSet$
    func $add : CSet \times T \longrightarrow CSet$
    def $add(cs, x) ==$ **case** cs **of** $\emptyset \to$ **set**'$add(\emptyset, x) \mid add(cs', x') \to$
                 if $x' < x$ **then** **set**'$add(cs, x)$ **else**
                     if $x' = x$ **then** cs **else**
                          set'$add(add(cs', x), x')$ **fi fi fo qua** $CSet$
    func $\hat{}=\hat{} : CSet \times CSet \longrightarrow$ **Bool**
    def $cs = ct ==$ **case** (cs, ct) **of** $(\emptyset, \emptyset) \to \mathbf{t}$
                         $\mid (add(cs', x), add(ct', y)) \to cs' = ct' \wedge x = y$
                         $\mid$ **others** $\to \mathbf{f}$ **fo**
    func $crep :$ **set** $\longrightarrow Cset$
    def $crep(s) ==$ **case** s **of** $\emptyset \to \emptyset \mid add(s', x) \to add(crep(s'), x)$ **fo**
endmodule

Notice that $CSet$ values are (canonic) expressions in the **set** generators, which means that the latter occur as discriminators on canonic sets. As a result of the convexity indication, however, the set argument of an *add* discriminator is now of type *CSet*. Consequently, the inner *add* application in the last **else** branch of the *add* redefinition refers to the redefined one. The same is true for the *add* application occurring in the *crep* definition.

The redefinition of equality as well as the definition of the *crep* function (cf. the example 5.40) may be constructed mechanically from the given generator basis, and could have been added automatically if the purpose of the subtype had been indicated syntactically.

The proof obligations associated with the given specifications are as follows, expressed in terms of variables $s, t : \textbf{set } T$ and $x : T$, and decorating redefined functions with primes:

convexity: $\quad canonic(\emptyset) \quad$ and $\quad canonic(add(s, x)) \Rightarrow canonic(s)$

add' : $\qquad canonic(s) \Rightarrow canonic(add'(s, x)) \quad$ and
$\qquad canonic(s) \Rightarrow (x \in add'(s, x)) = (x \in add(s, x))$

$='$: $\qquad canonic(s) \wedge canonic(t) \Rightarrow (s =' t) = (\forall x : T \bullet (x \in s) = (x \in t))$

$\cup$: $\qquad (x \in (s \cup crep(t))) = (x \in (s \cup t))$

The validation of convexity requires a proof of $canonic(\emptyset)$, which also justifies the redefinition of $\emptyset$ (and is obvious). The first proof obligation for add' corresponds to the **qua** *CSet* notation in the right hand side of the definition, and the second one is to prove that add' correctly redefines *add*. (It follows that add' is a natural restriction of *add*.) Notice that the definition of **set** equality has been inserted. The proof of correct redefinition of equality justifies the choice of canonic representations.

Notice that the *crep* function is not needed in constructive function definitions in *CSet*, since canonic forms are constructed by the redefined generators. It is, however, useful for expressing consistency requirements associated with inductive function definitions in the **set** module. This is exemplified by the last proof obligation, where *crep* has been applied to the inductive argument of $\cup$. It is better suited for proof by term rewriting techniques than the corresponding substitution axiom, which has the form of an implication. Notice also that the quantifier inherent in the **obsbas**-defined **set** equality could be made implicit.

If the $\cup$ operator is redefined in *CSet* for better evaluation efficiency (e.g. as in example 5.40), the associated proof of correctness can be expressed as:

$$(x \in (crep(s) \cup' crep(t))) = (x \in (s \cup t))$$

which at the same time proves the consistency of the original definition.

$\square$

Exercises

5.21   Carry out the proof obligations of the last example.

5.22 Redefine the **set** $\,\hat{}\,\epsilon\,\hat{}\,$ operator in *CSet* for optimum evaluation efficiency, and prove its correctness.

5.8   Standard Types

In this section we survey some useful standard types and constructs for type formation. They are directly definable in terms of the general mechanisms introduced earlier in this chapter, excepting a certain amount of *ad hoc* syntax. We assume that the type *Bool* with associated operators is defined as in earlier sections. (The binary Boolean operators are not really definable in terms of the standard mechanisms, as they are non-strict in all arguments.)

5.8.1   Enumerations

As mentioned already at the beginning of section 5.1, any enumeration type, as in Pascal, is easy to define within the general framework. One simply declares the listed value names as constants of that type, and defines a one-to-one generator basis consisting of these constants. Standard functions such as *succ*, *pred*, and ordering relations that go along with enumeration types, are easily defined by "generator induction", which here reduces to direct definition by cases.

It is sometimes useful to specify coercion, possibly automatic, between types which are not mutually related. In the case of enumeration types, coercion to integers, e.g. *Nat1*, is natural.

EXAMPLE 5.54
The type definition **type** *Card_suit* $==$ {*clubs, diamonds, hearts, spades*} can be understood as shorthand for the following specifications:

type *Card_suit* $==$ **module**
func *clubs, diamonds, hearts, spades* : $\longrightarrow$ *Card_suit*
1-1 genbas *clubs, diamonds, hearts, spades*
func *succ, pred* : *Card_suit* $\longrightarrow$ *Card_suit*
def *succ*(x) $==$ **case** x **of** *clubs* $\rightarrow$ *diamonds* | *diamonds* $\rightarrow$ *hearts*
                          | *hearts* $\rightarrow$ *spades* | *spades* $\rightarrow \bot$ **fo**
def *pred*(x) $==$ **case** x **of** *clubs* $\rightarrow \bot$ | *diamonds* $\rightarrow$ *clubs*
                          | *hearts* $\rightarrow$ *diamonds* | *spades* $\rightarrow$ *hearts* **fo**
lma $\forall x : Card\_suit \bullet (x \neq clubs \Rightarrow succ(pred(x)) = x) \wedge$
                          $(x \neq spades \Rightarrow pred(succ(x)) = x)$

func $\hat{}\,<\,\hat{}, \hat{}\,>\,\hat{}, \hat{}\,\leq\,\hat{}, \hat{}\,\geq\,\hat{}$: *Card_suit* $\times$ *Card_suit* $\longrightarrow$ *Bool*

def $x < y ==$ **case** x **of** *clubs* $\to$ **case** y **of** *clubs* $\to$ **f others** $\to$ **t fo**... **fo**

def $x > y == y < x$

def $x \leq y == x < y \vee x = y$

def $x \geq y == y \leq x$

lma $\forall x, y, z : Card\_suit \bullet x < y < z \Rightarrow x < z$ (transitivity)

lma $\forall x, y : Card\_suit \bullet \quad \neg(x < y \wedge y < x)$ (antisymmetry)

lma $\forall x, y : Card\_suit \bullet \quad x < y \vee x = y \vee y < x$ (totality)

lma $\forall x, y, z : Card\_suit \bullet x < succ(x) \wedge$
$$(x \leq y \leq succ(x) \Rightarrow x = y \vee y = succ(x)) \quad \text{(linearity)}$$

func *min, max* : $Card\_suit \times Card\_suit \longrightarrow Card\_suit$

def $min(x, y) ==$ **if** $x < y$ **then** x **else** y **fi**

def $max(x, y) ==$ **if** $x < y$ **then** y **else** x **fi**

lma $\forall x, y : Int \bullet min(x, y) \leq max(x, y)$

def x **as** *Nat1* $==$ **case** x **of** *clubs* $\to 1 \mid$ *diamonds* $\to 2$
$$hearts \to 3 \mid spades \to 4 \text{ \textbf{fo}}$$

endmodule

The four named lemmas express the fact that *Card_suit* is linearly ordered by the relation $<$ (with respect to the successor function *succ*). The other relational operators are in the standard relationship to the former.

$\square$

Notice that the constants introduced in an enumeration type are not easily overloaded. However, the additional overloading rule of section 5.8 does have the following convenient consequence: if a type expression such as $\{a, b, c\}$ occurs in a module, then other occurrences of a, b, or c in the module denote these same constants, provided that the names are not used for other purposes in the module. But if the type expression $\{b, c, d\}$ also occurs, then b and c are ambiguous.

5.8.2   Integers

As we have seen earlier the type *Nat* of natural numbers can conveniently be defined in terms of a one-to-one generator basis consisting of two functions, 0 (zero) and $\mathbf{S}\hat{}$ (successor). It is more difficult to find a good way to define the type *Int* of integers, including negative integers. In order to reach into the negative numbers it is necessary to introduce a third generator, for instance a predecessor function, $\mathbf{P}\hat{}$, or a negation function, $\mathbf{N}\hat{}$. The problem is that neither $\{0, \mathbf{S}\hat{}, \mathbf{P}\hat{}\}$ nor $\{0, \mathbf{S}\hat{}, \mathbf{N}\hat{}\}$ is a one-to-one generator basis if $\mathbf{S}\hat{}$, $\mathbf{P}\hat{}$ and $\mathbf{N}\hat{}$ are *Int* $\longrightarrow$ *Int* functions.

It is possible, however, to construct a one-to-one basis by means of generators *defined on syntactic subtypes*. We define *Int* as the union of three basic subtypes: *Zero*, *Nat1*, and *Neg1*, with corresponding value sets $\{0\}$, $\{1, 2, 3, \ldots\}$, and $\{-1, -2, -3, \ldots\}$. The last two are spanned by $\mathbf{S}\hat{}$ and $\mathbf{N}\hat{}$. The one-to-one property is established by restricting these operators to arguments which are non-negative and positive numbers, respectively. (An alternative is to use a predecessor operator $\mathbf{P}\hat{}$ defined for non-positive numbers instead of $\mathbf{N}\hat{}$.) An arbitrary *ad hoc* syntax is used to define the three syntactic subtypes *Nat*, *Neg*, and *Nzo*, which are between *Int* and the basic ones in the subtype hierarchy:

> **type** *Int* **by** *Zero*, *Nat1*, *Neg1*
> **with** *Nat* **as** *Zero* $\sqcup$ *Nat1*,
>   *Neg* **as** *Zero* $\sqcup$ *Neg1*,
>   *Nzo* **as** *Nat1* $\sqcup$ *Neg1* ==
> **module**
> **func** 0 : $\longrightarrow$ *Zero*
> **func** $\mathbf{S}\hat{}$: *Nat* $\longrightarrow$ *Nat1*
> **func** $\mathbf{N}\hat{}$: *Nat1* $\longrightarrow$ *Neg1*
> **1-1 genbas** $0, \mathbf{S}\hat{}, \mathbf{N}\hat{}$

The corresponding generator universe, $\{0, \mathbf{S}0, \mathbf{SS}0, \ldots, \mathbf{N}0, \mathbf{NSS}0, \ldots\}$, is clearly in a one-to-one correspondence with the set of integers.

We define successor and negation functions total on the entire *Int*:

> **func** *succ* : *Int* $\longrightarrow$ *Int*
> **def** *succ*(x) == **case** x **of** $\mathbf{NS}x' \rightarrow \mathbf{N}x'$ | **others** $\rightarrow \mathbf{S}x$ **fo**
> **func** $-\hat{}$: *Int* $\longrightarrow$ *Int*
> **def** $-x ==$ **case** x **of** $0 \rightarrow 0$ | $\mathbf{N}x' \rightarrow x'$ | **others** $\rightarrow \mathbf{N}x$ **fo**

The discriminator $\mathbf{NS}x'$ in the definition of *succ* is shorthand for a nested **case**-construct on the argument of $\mathbf{N}$. Since the domain of $\mathbf{N}$, *Nat1*, has only one generator, the corresponding discriminator, $\mathbf{S}x'$, is inserted as the argument of the former, and the inner **case**-construct is omitted. Notice that the variable x introduced in the definition of *succ* is of type *Int*. Subtracting *Neg1*, which is the type of the discriminator $\mathbf{NS}x'$, the remainder is *Nat* which is the type of x in the **others** branch, matching the domain of $\mathbf{S}\hat{}$. A similar syntactic calculation applies to the definition of $-\hat{}$.

We then define some of the standard operators on integers, including binary minus and a partial subtraction operator $\hat{}\,\dot{-}\,\hat{}$ on natural numbers:

> **func** *pred* : *Int* $\longrightarrow$ *Int*
> **def** *pred*(x) == **case** x **of** $0 \rightarrow \mathbf{NS}0$ | $\mathbf{S}x' \rightarrow x'$ | $\mathbf{N}x' \rightarrow \mathbf{NS}x'$ **fo**

> **func** $\hat{}+\hat{}$, $\hat{}-\hat{}$: *Int* $\times$ *Int* $\longrightarrow$ *Int*
> **def** $x + y ==$ **case** x **of** $0 \rightarrow y$ | $\mathbf{S}x' \rightarrow$

$$\textbf{case } y \textbf{ of } 0 \to x \mid \textbf{S}y' \to x' + y' \mid \textbf{N}y' \to x' - y' \textbf{ fo}$$
$$\mid \textbf{N}x' \to$$
$$\textbf{case } y \textbf{ of } 0 \to x \mid \textbf{S}y' \to y' - x' \mid \textbf{N}y' \to \textbf{N}(x' + y') \textbf{ fo fo}$$

def $x - y ==$ **case** x **of** $0 \to -y \mid \textbf{S}x' \to$
$$\textbf{case } y \textbf{ of } 0 \to x \mid \textbf{S}y' \to x' - y' \mid \textbf{N}y' \to x' + y' \textbf{ fo}$$
$$\mid \textbf{N}x' \to$$
$$\textbf{case } y \textbf{ of } 0 \to x \mid \textbf{S}y' \to \textbf{N}(x' + y') \mid \textbf{N}y' \to y' - x' \textbf{ fo fo}$$

lma $\forall x, y : Int \bullet x + y = y + x$ $\hfill$ (commutativity)

lma $\forall x, y, z : Int \bullet x + (y+z) = (x+y) + z$ $\hfill$ (associativity)

lma $\forall x, y : Int \bullet x - y = x + (-y)$

func $\hat{\ } \dot{-} \hat{\ } :\ Nat \times Nat \longrightarrow Nat$

def $x \dot{-} y ==$ **case** y **of** $0 \to x \mid \textbf{S}y' \to$
$$\textbf{case } x \textbf{ of } 0 \to \bot \mid \textbf{S}x' \to x' \dot{-} y' \textbf{ fo fo}$$

func $\hat{\ } * \hat{\ } :\ Int \times Int \longrightarrow Int$ $\hfill$ (multiplication)

def $x * y ==$ **case** y **of** $0 \to 0 \mid \textbf{S}y' \to x * y' + x \mid \textbf{N}y' \to -(x * y')$ **fo**

lma $\forall x, y : Int \bullet x * y = y * x$ $\hfill$ (commutativity)

lma $\forall x, y, z : Int \bullet x * (y * z) = (x * y) * z$ $\hfill$ (associativity)

lma $\forall x, y, z : Int \bullet x * (y + z) = x * y + x * z$ $\hfill$ (distributivity)

func $\hat{\ } \textbf{mod} \hat{\ } :\ Int \times Nat1 \longrightarrow Nat$

def $x \textbf{ mod } \textbf{S}y ==$ **case** x **of** $0 \to 0 \mid \textbf{S}x' \to$
$$\textbf{if } x' \textbf{ mod } \textbf{S}y = y \textbf{ then } 0 \textbf{ else } \textbf{S}(x' \textbf{ mod } \textbf{S}y) \textbf{ fi}$$
$$\mid \textbf{N}x' \to$$
$$\textbf{if } x' \textbf{ mod } \textbf{S}y = 0 \textbf{ then } 0 \textbf{ else } \textbf{S}y - (x' \textbf{ mod } \textbf{S}y) \textbf{ fi fo}$$

func $\hat{\ } / \hat{\ } :\ Int \times Nzo \longrightarrow Int$

def $x/y ==$ **case** y **of** $\textbf{S}y' \to$
$$\textbf{case } x \textbf{ of } 0 \to 0 \mid \textbf{S}x' \to$$
$$\textbf{if } x' \textbf{ mod } y = y' \textbf{ then } \textbf{S}(x'/y) \textbf{ else } x'/y \textbf{ fi}$$
$$\mid \textbf{N}x' \to \textbf{N}(x'/y) \textbf{ fo}$$
$$\mid \textbf{N}y' \to -(x/y') \textbf{ fo}$$

lma $\forall x : Int,\ y : Nat1 \bullet (x/y) * y + (x \textbf{ mod } y) = x$

The functions $\hat{\ } + \hat{\ }$ and $\hat{\ } - \hat{\ }$ are mutually recursive. However, since each recursive function application reduces the combined syntactic complexity of the two arguments, it is clear that the definitions are TGI. The left hand side $x \textbf{ mod } \textbf{S}y$ indicates an omitted single branch **case**-construct, whose discriminator has been inserted as a left hand argument. Notice that the domain of well-definedness of partial subtraction on natural numbers cannot be determined syntactically. Therefore an explicit $\bot$ case cannot be avoided.

We also define the standard arithmetic relational operators, as well as the operators *min* and *max*:

func $\; \hat{}<\hat{}, \; \hat{}>\hat{}, \; \hat{}\leq\hat{}, \; \hat{}\geq\hat{} \; : \; Int \times Int \longrightarrow Bool$
def $\quad x < y == $ **case** x **of** $0 \to$ **case** y **of** $Sy' \to$ **t** $\mid$ **others** $\to$ **f fo**
$\qquad\qquad\qquad\qquad \mid Sx' \to$ **case** y **of** $Sy' \to x' < y' \mid$ **others** $\to$ **f fo**
$\qquad\qquad\qquad\qquad \mid Nx' \to$ **case** y **of** $Ny' \to y' < x' \mid$ **others** $\to$ **t fo fo**
def $\quad x > y == y < x$
def $\quad x \leq y == x < y \lor x = y$
def $\quad x \geq y == y \leq x$
lma $\quad \forall x, y, z : Int \bullet x < y < z \Rightarrow x < z$ $\qquad\qquad$ (transitivity)
lma $\quad \forall x, y : Int \bullet \quad \neg(x < y \land y < x)$ $\qquad\qquad$ (antisymmetry)
lma $\quad \forall x, y : Int \bullet \quad x < y \lor x = y \lor y < x$ $\qquad\quad$ (totality)
lma $\quad \forall x, y, z : Int \bullet x < succ(x) \land$
$\qquad\qquad\qquad (x \leq y \leq succ(x) \Rightarrow x = y \lor y = succ(x))$ (linearity)
func $\; min, max : \; Int \times Int \longrightarrow Int$
def $\quad min(x, y) == $ **if** $x < y$ **then** x **else** y **fi**
def $\quad max(x, y) == $ **if** $x < y$ **then** y **else** x **fi**
lma $\quad \forall x, y : Int \bullet min(x, y) \leq max(x, y)$

The named lemmas express the fact that the type *Int* is linearly ordered. Notice that, except for the semantic definition of the $\hat{}<\hat{}$ operator and the identity of the type under definition, these specifications are exact copies of those of enumeration types, according to example 5.54. This indicates that it would be useful in a specification language to have a way of defining parameterized modules forming subspecifications and ways of including them as parts of other modules. In this particular case one can see a whole hierarchy of subspecifications, such as one defining the operators $\hat{}\leq\hat{}, \; \hat{}>\hat{}, \; \hat{}\geq\hat{}$ in terms of $\hat{}<\hat{}$, and others expressing order concepts of increasing strength, e.g. partial, total, and linear order, by successively adding more specifications. Clearly, these concepts may apply to relations with different notations in different types, which shows that function names should be replaceable in the corresponding modules.

The concepts of commutativity, associativity, and distributivity are further examples of general properties which may deserve to be expressed in some kind of module. It is sometimes necessary to *assume* the existence of functions with stated properties to be associated with types represented by formal parameters; see, for example, the next section where a linear ordering relation must be assumed.

For the sake of completeness we finally define integer literals in standard decimal notation by a kind of "syntactic induction" used informally:

$\qquad$ DIG $\;::= 0 \mid 1 \mid 2 \mid 3 \mid 4 \mid 5 \mid 6 \mid 7 \mid 8 \mid 9$
$\qquad$ LIT $\;\;::= $ DIG $\mid$ LIT DIG

$\qquad$ **func** LIT: $\longrightarrow Nat$
$\qquad$ **def** $\quad 1 == S0$
$\qquad$ **def** $\quad 2 == SS0$

$\vdots$

def $9 == \mathrm{SSSSSSSSS}0$
def   LIT DIG $==$ LIT $* \mathbf{S}9 + $ DIG
endmodule

Proof by generator induction over *Int* follows the general proof schema: There is one premise for each generator, and since the domains of $\mathbf{S}\hat{}$ and $\mathbf{N}\hat{}$ are included in *Int*, these premises have unrestricted induction hypotheses:

$$\mathrm{GIND}_{Int} : \quad \frac{\vdash P_0^x; \quad P_y^x \vdash P_{\mathbf{S}y}^x; \quad P_z^x \vdash P_{\mathbf{N}z}^x}{\vdash \forall x : Int \bullet P} \quad \text{for } y : Nat, \; z : Neg$$

Exercises

5.23   Give TGI definitions of the above functions relative to a one-to-one generator basis consisting of 0 and suitably restricted versions of $\mathbf{S}$ and $\mathbf{P}$.

5.24   Prove the lemmas included in the above module.

5.8.3   Interval types

An interval construct $\{x : T \bullet a \leq x \leq b\}$, where a and b are of type T, is a meaningful semantic subtype of T, provided that T is linearly ordered (by the standard operators). Taking T as a formal parameter, the linear order property represents an assumption on T which, if expressed formally, should make available the relevant relational operator used to express the restricting predicate:

$$\textbf{type } \; Interval\{T, \, a : T, \, b : T\} == \{x : T \bullet a \leq x \leq b\}$$

We shall use the *ad hoc* notation $\{e_1..e_2\}$ for interval types, where e_1 and e_2 are expressions of related types T_1 and T_2, and the actual type parameter is implicitly defined as the least common non-interval supertype of T_1 and T_2 which is linearly ordered. It follows e.g. that $\{1..10\} \prec Nat1$, and $\{-1..1\} \prec Int$ (because the smallest common supertype, *Nzo*, is not linearly ordered).

We may conclude from SEMSUB1 and SEMSUB4 that an interval contained in another interval is also a subtype of the latter:

$$a \leq a' \wedge b' \leq b \Rightarrow \{a'..b'\} \preceq \{a..b\}$$

This serves to strengthen the typing algorithm in those cases where interval inclusion can be decided textually.

One might find it useful to associate constant functions *lo* and *hi* with the *Interval* types, equal to the value parameters a and b, respectively. Then, however, the subterm relations given above would no longer hold, since the *lo* and *hi* functions associated with different *Interval* instances would be incompatible.

5.8.4   Cartesian products

A Cartesian product $T_1 \times T_2 \times \cdots \times T_n$, $n > 1$ represents the set of tuples $(t_1, t_2, \ldots, t_n)$, such that t_i is of type T_i, $i \in \{1..n\}$. The concept could be catered for within the general framework by looking at the tuple construct as a mixfix notation for a tuple-generating function, and defining it as a one-to-one generator basis all by itself. A schematic definition follows below of a type *Cprodn* corresponding to a Cartesian product with n components, where the final n of "*Cprodn*" stands for an arbitrary natural number, including 0. In addition, "selector" functions $a_1, a_2, \ldots a_n$ are defined for extracting the individual components of a *Cprodn* value:

> **type** $Cprodn\{T_1, T_2, \ldots, T_n\}$ ==
> **module**
> **func** $(\hat{\ }, \ldots, \hat{\ })$: $T_1 \times T_2 \times \cdots \times T_n \longrightarrow Cprodn$
> **1-1 genbas** $(\hat{\ }, \ldots, \hat{\ })$
> **func** $\hat{\ }.a_i$: $Cprodn \longrightarrow T_i$ (for $i \in \{1..n\}$)
> **def** $(x_1, x_2, \ldots, x_n).a_i == x_i$ (for $i \in \{1..n\}$)
> **endmodule**

The **case** construct has been omitted in the definition of a_i because *Cprodn* has a single generator.

The above specification corresponds to the record class concept of traditional programming languages. In the sequel we shall use the more compact notation of a "labelled Cartesian product", $a_1 : T_1 \times a_2 : T_2 \times \cdots \times a_n : T_n$, as well as an *ad hoc* notation for applications of the corresponding generator function: $(a_1 : e_1, \ldots, a_n : e_n)$, where e_i is an expression of type T_i, for $i \in \{1..n\}$, and the labels are optional. We occasionally use the *ad hoc* notations $t.1$, $t.2$, etc., to denote the components of a tuple belonging to an unlabelled Cartesian product.

Notice that the case $n = 0$ is useful; *Cprod0* is a kind of "null" type whose only abstract value is the empty tuple (). See section 5.8.5 for examples of its use. In a sense the case $n = 1$ has already occurred in notations of the form $\{x : T \bullet P(x)\}$, which now generalizes to $\{x_1 : T_1 \times \cdots \times x_n : T_n \bullet P(x_1, \ldots, x_n)\}$ for $n \geq 1$.

EXAMPLE 5.55

> **type** *Playing_card* == *suit* : *Card_suit* $\times$ *val* : *Card_val*

where the type *Card_val* is defined in the next section. Let C : *Playing_card*. Then the *suit* of C is denoted *C.suit* (or *C.1*), and its *val* component is *C.val* (or *C.2*).

□

5.8.5   Disjoint unions

A disjoint union is a set of values belonging to one of two or more possible types, together with a mechanism for deciding to which of the possible types a given value belongs. Any particular disjoint union may be constructed by defining a one-to-one generator basis consisting of "injector" functions, one for each member type, as in the following schematic type definition, where $n \geq 2$:

> **type** $Disjun\{T_1, T_2, \ldots, T_n\}$ ==
> **module**
> **func** $a_i : T_i \longrightarrow Disjun$ (for $i \in \{1..n\}$)
> **1-1 genbas** $a_1, a_2, \ldots, a_n$
> **endmodule**

A useful shorthand type expression for this construct is a "labelled disjoint union":

$$a_1 : T_1 + a_2 : T_2 + \cdots + a_n : T_n, \qquad \text{for } n \geq 2$$

Notice that the "labels" in this case denote generator functions, not observer functions as in the case of labelled Cartesian products. Notice also that the type members of a disjoint union need not be mutually disjoint, or even different.

   In order to distinguish between the possible alternatives for a given value x of the above disjoint union, ordinary case constructs may be used. For instance, the expression

$$\textbf{case } x \textbf{ of } \quad |_{i \in \{1..n\}} \quad a_i(x) \rightarrow f_i(x) \textbf{ fo}, \qquad \text{where } f_i : T_i \rightarrow T, \ i \in \{1..n\}$$

applies a function with a suitable domain to x, depending on the alternative to which it belongs. Notice that the x occurring inside the i'th branch is a new variable of type T_i.

EXAMPLE 5.56

> **type** $Card\_val$ == $low : \{2..10\} + high : \{knight,\ queen,\ king,\ ace\}$
> **module**
> **func** $succ : Card\_val \longrightarrow Card\_val$
> **def** $succ(c) ==$ **case** c **of** $low(n) \rightarrow$ **if** $n = 10$ **then** $high(knight)$
> $\qquad\qquad\qquad\qquad\qquad\qquad\qquad$ **else** $low(Sn)$ **fi**
> $\qquad\qquad\qquad | \ high(h) \rightarrow high(succ(h))$ **fo**
> **func** $\ ^<{}^\ : Card\_val \times Card\_val \longrightarrow Bool$
> **def** $c < d ==$ **case** (c, d) **of** $(low(m), low(n)) \rightarrow m < n$
> $\qquad\qquad\qquad\qquad\qquad | \ (low(m), high(i)) \rightarrow \textbf{t}$
> $\qquad\qquad\qquad\qquad\qquad | \ (high(h), low(n)) \rightarrow \textbf{f}$
> $\qquad\qquad\qquad\qquad\qquad | \ (high(h), high(i)) \rightarrow h < i$ **fo**
> **endmodule**

□

The concepts of Cartesian products and disjoint unions together provide the same power of value set formation as the mechanism of one-to-one generator bases. For example, the type $a_1 : Cprod0 + \cdots + a_n : Cprod0$ has the same value set as the enumeration type $\{a_1, \ldots, a_n\}$. A generator basis containing functions other than relative constants corresponds to a "recursive" type definition. For instance we could define

type $Nat\ ==\ 0 : Cprod0 + \mathbf{S}\char`^ : Nat$

and a type of binary trees could be defined as follows:

type $BinTree\{T\}\ ==$
$\quad nil : Cprod0 + tree : (lsub : BinTree \times node : T \times rsub : BinTree)$

Notice, however, that syntactic subtypes can at best be mimicked by introducing *ad hoc* coercion rules. Thus, in order to construct a value set such as that of *Int*, section 5.8.2, one would have to do something like the following:

type $Nat1\ ==\ 1 : Cprod0 + \mathbf{S}\char`^ : Nat1$
type $Nat\ \ ==\ 0 : Cprod0 + pos : Nat1$
type $Int\ \ \ ==\ nonneg : Nat + neg : Nat1$

where the integer 1 would have to be written $nonneg(pos(1))$, unless the two injector applications were somehow made to be implicit.

5.8.6 Finite sets

The mixfix notation **set** T denotes the type of finite sets of type T elements, i.e. $V_{\mathbf{set}\ T}$ is the set of finite subsets of V_T. As we have seen already no (finite) one-to-one generator basis exists for the **set** concept. The best we can do is probably to define the type in terms of two basic subtypes: *Eset*, the type of the empty set (a singleton type), generated by the constant $\emptyset$, and **set1** T, the type of non-empty sets, generated by adding one element at a time. The fact that the former subtype is parameterless indicates that there is no need to distinguish between different kinds of empty sets. Thus, the subtype *Eset* is common to all instances of the type schema **set** T.

The **set** T definition is intended to serve as a reusable specification designed for maximum ease of semi-mechanical reasoning. For that reason we choose not to base the definition on particular canonical forms, as in section 5.5.4, in spite of the evaluation efficiency and consistency guarantee which can be obtained using that strategy. Maximum simplicity is more important, and consistency proofs are only needed once for each inductively defined function. By defining the equality relation explicitly we stay completely within the TGI framework. Again the associated proof burden (of showing congruence) is a one-time effort. We add lemmas

corresponding to alternative equality definitions, as well as lemmas corresponding
to indirect definition of several operators with respect to an observation basis:

type set T **by** *Eset*, **set1** T ==
module
func $\emptyset :\longrightarrow Eset$ (empty set)
func *add* : **set** $\times T \longrightarrow$ **set1**   (add element)
genbas $\emptyset, add$

func $\hat{\epsilon}\hat{}$: $T \times$ **set** $\longrightarrow$ *Bool*   (set membership)
def $x \epsilon s ==$ **case** s **of** $\emptyset \to \mathbf{f} \mid add(s', y) \to x = y \lor x \epsilon s$ **fo**
func $\hat{}\subseteq\hat{}$: **set** $\times$ **set** $\longrightarrow$ *Bool*   (set inclusion)
def $s \subseteq t ==$ **case** s **of** $\emptyset \to \mathbf{t} \mid add(s', x) \to x \epsilon t \land s' \subseteq t$ **fo**
lma $\forall s, t :$ **set** $\bullet (s \subseteq t) = \forall x : T \bullet x \epsilon s \Rightarrow x \epsilon t$

def $s =^{\mathbf{set}} t == s \subseteq t \land t \subseteq s$
lma $\forall s :$ **set**, $x, y : T \bullet add(add(s, x), y) = add(add(s, y), x)$ (commutativity)
lma $\forall s :$ **set**, $x : T \bullet add(add(s, x), x) = add(s, x)$ (idempotency)
lma $\forall s, t :$ **set** $\bullet (s = t) = \forall x : T \bullet x \epsilon s = x \epsilon t$ (obsbas $\hat{\epsilon}\hat{}$)

func *sub* : **set** $\times T \longrightarrow$ **set**   (remove element)
def $sub(s, x) ==$ **case** s **of** $\emptyset \to \emptyset \mid add(s, y) \to$
                if $x = y$ **then** $sub(s, x)$ **else**
                    $add(sub(s, x), y)$ **fi fo**

func $\#\hat{}$: **set** $\longrightarrow$ *Nat*   (set cardinality)
def $\# s ==$ **case** s **of** $\emptyset \to 0 \mid add(s, x) \to$
             if $x \epsilon s$ **then** $\# s$ **else** $\mathbf{S}\# s$ **fi fo**

func $\hat{}\cup\hat{}$: **set** $\times$ **set** $\longrightarrow$ **set**   (set union)
def $s \cup t ==$ **case** t **of** $\emptyset \to s \mid add(t', x) \to add(s \cup t', x)$ **fo**
lma $\forall s, t :$ **set**, $x : T \bullet (x \epsilon (s \cup t)) = (x \epsilon s \lor x \epsilon t)$

func $\hat{}\cap\hat{}$: **set** $\times$ **set** $\longrightarrow$ **set**   (set intersection)
def $s \cap t ==$ **case** t **of** $\emptyset \to \emptyset \mid add(t', x) \to$
                if $x \epsilon s$ **then** $add(s \cap t', x)$ **else** $s \cap t'$ **fo**
lma $\forall s, t :$ **set**, $x : T \bullet (x \epsilon (s \cap t)) = (x \epsilon s \land x \epsilon t)$

func $\hat{}-\hat{}$: **set** $\times$ **set** $\longrightarrow$ **set**   (set subtraction)
def $s - t ==$ **case** t **of** $\emptyset \to s \mid add(t', x) \to sub(s - t', x)$ **fo**
lma $\forall s, t :$ **set**, $x : T \bullet (x \epsilon (s - t)) = (x \epsilon s \land x \not\epsilon t)$

func $\{\hat{}\}$: $T \longrightarrow$ **set1**   (singleton set)

def $\{x\} == add(\emptyset, x)$
func $\{\char94, \char94\} : T \times T \longrightarrow \mathbf{set1}$ (doubleton set
def $\{x, y\} == add(add(\emptyset, x), y)$ if $x \neq y$)
  $\vdots$

endmodule

Notice that all functions defined are total.

Exercises

5.25 Prove the lemmas listed in the **set** module.

5.26 Let $s, t : \mathbf{set}\, T$. Prove the following equalities for $s, t : \mathbf{set}\, T$:
   1. $s \cap t = s - (s - t)$
   2. $s \cup t = s \cup (t - s)$

5.8.7 Finite bags

bag T is the type (schema) of finite bags, or "multisets", of type T elements. A bag is a collection of elements with multiplicity. We define the concept using techniques similar to those of the last subsection:

type bag T **by** $Ebag$, **bag1** T ==
module
func $\emptyset : \longrightarrow Ebag$ (empty bag)
func $adb : \mathbf{bag} \times T \longrightarrow \mathbf{bag1}$ (add element)
genbas $\emptyset, adb$

func $mpc : \mathbf{bag} \times T \longrightarrow Nat$ (multiplicity)
def $mpc(b, x) ==$ **case** b **of** $\emptyset \to 0 \mid adb(b', y) \to$
                if $x = y$ **then** $\mathbf{S}\, mpc(b', x)$ **else**
                    $mpc(b', x)$ **fi fo**
func $\char94 \sqsubseteq \char94 : \mathbf{bag} \times \mathbf{bag} \longrightarrow Bool$ (bag inclusion)
def $b \sqsubseteq c ==$ **case** b **of** $\emptyset \to \mathbf{t} \mid adb(b', x) \to$
         $mpc(b', x) < mpc(c, x) \wedge b' \sqsubseteq c$ **fo**
lma $\forall b, c : \mathbf{bag} \bullet (b \sqsubseteq c) = \forall x : T \bullet mpc(b, x) \leq mpc(c, x)$

def $b =^{\mathbf{bag}} c == b \sqsubseteq c \wedge c \sqsubseteq b$
lma $\forall b : \mathbf{bag},\ x, y : T \bullet adb(adb(b, x), y) = adb(adb(b, y), x)$ (commutativity)
lma $\forall b, c : \mathbf{bag} \bullet (b = c) = \forall x : T \bullet mpc(s, x) = mpc(t, x)$ (**obsbas** mpc)

func sbb : **bag** $\times\, T \longrightarrow$ **bag**   (remove element)
def $sbb(b,x) ==$ **case** b **of** $\llbracket \rightarrow \bot \mid adb(b',y) \rightarrow$
$$\text{if } x = y \text{ then } b' \text{ else}$$
$$adb(sbb(b',x),y) \text{ fi fo}$$

func $\#\hat{} $: **bag** $\longrightarrow Nat$ (cardinality)
def $\#b ==$ **case** b **of** $\llbracket \rightarrow 0 \mid adb(b',x) \rightarrow \mathbf{S}\#b'$ **fo**

func set : **bag** $\longrightarrow$ **set** T (set of bag)
def $set(b) ==$ **case** b **of** $\llbracket \rightarrow \emptyset \mid adb(b',x) \rightarrow$
$$add(set(b'),x) \text{ fo}$$
lma $\forall b :$ **bag,** $x : T \bullet (x \,\epsilon\, set(b)) = (mpc(b,x) \neq 0)$

func $\hat{}\,\sqcup\,\hat{}$: **bag** $\times$ **bag** $\longrightarrow$ **bag**   (bag union)
def $b \sqcup c ==$ **case** c **of** $\llbracket \rightarrow b \mid adb(c',x) \rightarrow$
$$\text{if } mpc(b,x) < mpc(c,x) \text{ then}$$
$$adb(b \sqcup c',x) \text{ else } b \sqcup c' \text{ fi fo}$$
lma $\forall b,c :$ **bag,** $x : T \bullet$
$$mpc(b \sqcup c,x) = max(mpc(b,x), mpc(c,x))$$

func $\hat{}\,\sqcap\,\hat{}$: **bag** $\times$ **bag** $\longrightarrow$ **bag**   (bag intersection)
def $b \sqcap c ==$ **case** c **of** $\llbracket \rightarrow \llbracket \mid adb(c',x) \rightarrow$
$$\text{if } mpc(b,x) < mpc(c,x) \text{ then}$$
$$b \sqcap c' \text{ else } adb(b \sqcap c',x) \text{ fi fo}$$
lma $\forall b,c :$ **bag,** $x : T \bullet$
$$mpc(b \sqcap c,x) = min(mpc(b,x), mpc(c,x))$$

func $\hat{}\,+\,\hat{}$: **bag** $\times$ **bag** $\longrightarrow$ **bag**   (bag sum)
def $b + c ==$ **case** c **of** $\llbracket \rightarrow b \mid adb(c',x) \rightarrow$
$$adb(b + c',x) \text{ fo}$$
lma $\forall b,c :$ **bag,** $x : T \bullet mpc(b+c,x) = mpc(b,x) + mpc(c,x)$

func $\hat{}\,\dot{-}\,\hat{}$: **bag** $\times$ **bag** $\longrightarrow$ **bag**   (bag difference)
def $b \dot{-} c ==$ **case** c **of** $\llbracket \rightarrow b \mid adb(c',x) \rightarrow$
$$sbb(b \dot{-} c',x) \text{ fo}$$
lma $\forall b,c :$ **bag,** $x : T \bullet$
$$c \sqsubseteq b \Rightarrow mpc(b \dot{-} c,x) = mpc(b,x) \dot{-} mpc(c,x)$$

func $[\hat{}\,]$: $T \longrightarrow$ **bag1**   (singleton bag)
def $[x] == adb(\llbracket,x)$
func $[\hat{}\,,\hat{}\,]$: $T \times T \longrightarrow$ **bag1**   (doubleton bag)
def $[x,y] == adb(adb(\llbracket,x),y)$

$\vdots$

endmodule

All defined functions except *sbb* and $\div$ are total. Notice the difference between bag union and bag sum. Otherwise the bag operators are largely analogous to those of sets. The *set* function computes the set of elements that occur in a given bag.

Exercises

5.27 Prove the lemmas listed in the **bag** module.

5.28 Let $s, t : \textbf{set}\ T$. Prove the following equalities for $b, c : \textbf{bag}\ T$.
 1. $c \sqsubseteq b \Rightarrow b \sqcap c = b \div (b \div c)$
 2. $b \sqsubseteq c \Rightarrow b \sqcup c = b + (c \div b)$

5.29 Define a semantic subtype *CBag* of canonic bags analogous to the construct *CSet* of example 5.48. Identify and carry out the associated proof obligations.

5.8.8   Finite sequences

In this section a small set of tools for reasoning about finite sequences is presented. The concepts and definitions are primarily intended for the documentation of procedural programs and semi-mechanized reasoning, in particular about arrays and historic time sequences. Needless to say, more specialized concepts will be needed in order to reason efficiently about sequences in the context of specialized problem areas. Even so, the size of the present tool box suggests that it ought to be defined by compounding subspecifications.

Some of the notations introduced below have already been used in chapter 4. Others may be new to the reader, and in order to facilitate the understanding a few lemmas are provided about the less obvious ones. It is a general observation that recursive function definitions are not always easy to understand, or, in other words, some properties of the defined functions may be far from obvious. If so, theorems exhibiting such properties are useful for better acquaintance with the functions.

The type (schema) **seq** T is defined as the union of two basic subtypes, $Eseq$ (the type of the empty sequence) and **seq1** T (non-empty sequences). Several functions on sequences are ill-defined for the empty sequence, but total on **seq1** T:

type seq T **by** $Eseq$, **seq1** T ==
module

Generator basis

func $\varepsilon : \longrightarrow Eseq$ (empty sequence)
func $\hat{}\vdash\hat{}$: **seq** $\times \ T \longrightarrow$ **seq1**   (append right)
1-1 genbas ε, $\hat{}\vdash\hat{}$

This generator basis is chosen because it is one-to-one, and is otherwise motivated in section 4.9. If our style of defining functions by generator induction is viewed as an applicative programming language in its own right, then left append might be a more natural generator than right append. (Then evaluation of sequence expressions would correspond to "reading" sequence arguments and constructing sequence values from left to right, rather than right to left, as explained in section 4.9.)

Relative constants

func $\langle\hat{}\rangle : T \longrightarrow$ **seq1**   (singleton sequence)
func $\langle\hat{},\hat{}\rangle : T \times T \longrightarrow$ **seq1**   (doubleton sequence)

$\vdots$

func $\hat{}\uparrow\hat{}$: $T \times Nat \longrightarrow$ **seq**   (replication)
func $\langle\hat{};\hat{}\rangle$: $Nat1 \times Nat \longrightarrow$ **seq** $Nat1$ (interval by length)
func $\langle\hat{}..\hat{}\rangle$: $Nat1 \times Nat \longrightarrow$ **seq** $Nat1$ (interval by end point)

def $\langle x \rangle$ $\ \ == \varepsilon \vdash x$
def $\langle x, y \rangle == \varepsilon \vdash x \vdash y$

$\vdots$

def $x \uparrow n ==$ **case** n **of** $0 \to \varepsilon \mid Sn' \to (x \uparrow n') \vdash x$ **fo**
def $\langle i; n \rangle ==$ **case** n **of** $0 \to \varepsilon \mid Sn' \to \langle i; n' \rangle \vdash (i + n')$ **fo**
def $\langle i..j \rangle == \langle i; (Sj) \dot{-} i \rangle$

lma   S1: $\forall i, k : Nat1, \ j : Nat \bullet i \le k < i + j \Rightarrow (\langle i..j \rangle[k] == i + k - 1)$

Examples: $a \uparrow 3 = \langle a, a, a \rangle, \ \ a \uparrow 0 = \langle 1; 0 \rangle = \langle 1..0 \rangle = \varepsilon,$
              $\langle 2; 3 \rangle = \langle 2..4 \rangle = \langle 2, 3, 4 \rangle$

Composition

func $\hat{}\dashv\hat{}$: $T \times$ **seq** $\longrightarrow$ **seq1**   (append left)
func $\hat{}\vDash\hat{}$: **seq** $\times$ **seq** $\longrightarrow$ **seq**   (concatenate)

def $x \dashv q ==$ **case** q **of** $\varepsilon \to \varepsilon \vdash x \mid q' \vdash y \to (x \dashv q') \vdash y$
def $q \vDash r ==$ **case** r **of** $\varepsilon \to q \mid r' \vdash x \to (q \vDash r') \vdash x$

lma S2: $\varepsilon \dashv q = q$
lma S3: $q \dashv (r \dashv s) = (q \dashv r) \dashv s$
lma S4: $q \dashv (x \dashv r) = (q \vdash x) \dashv r$

Lemma S4 motivates the symmetric notation $q \vdash x \dashv r$ which may be justified by seeing $\hat{}\vdash\hat{}\dashv\hat{}$ as one ternary mixfix operator with the profile $\mathbf{seq} \times T \times \mathbf{seq} \longrightarrow \mathbf{seq}$. The notations $q \vdash x \vdash y$ and $x \dashv y \dashv q$ stand for $(q \vdash x) \vdash y$ and $x \dashv (y \dashv q)$ respectively, whereas $x \dashv q \vdash y$ and $q \dashv r \dashv s$ may be parsed either way.

Some observers

func $\#\hat{}\ :\ \mathbf{seq} \longrightarrow Nat$ (length function)
func $set :\ \mathbf{seq} \longrightarrow \mathbf{set}\ T$ (set function)
func $bag :\ \mathbf{seq} \longrightarrow \mathbf{bag}\ T$ (bag function)

def $\#q\ \ \ == \mathbf{case}\ q\ \mathbf{of}\ \varepsilon \to 0 \mid q' \vdash x \to \mathsf{S}\#q'\ \mathbf{fo}$
def $set(q) == \mathbf{case}\ q\ \mathbf{of}\ \varepsilon \to \emptyset \mid q' \vdash x \to add(set(q'), x)\ \mathbf{fo}$
def $bag(q) == \mathbf{case}\ q\ \mathbf{of}\ \varepsilon \to [\![\,]\!] \mid q' \vdash x \to addb(bag(q'), x)\ \mathbf{fo}$

lma S4: $\forall q : \mathbf{seq} \bullet \#set(q) \leq \#bag(q) = \#q$

Decomposition and modification

func $lt, rt :\ \mathbf{seq1} \longrightarrow T$ (left term, right term)
func $lr, rr :\ \mathbf{seq1} \longrightarrow \mathbf{seq}$ (left rest, right rest)
func $\hat{}[\hat{}] :\ \mathbf{seq1} \times Nat1 \longrightarrow T$ (indexing)
func $\hat{}[\hat{} \mapsto \hat{}] :\ \mathbf{seq1} \times Nat1 \times T \longrightarrow \mathbf{seq1}$ (term substitution)

def $lt(q \vdash x)\ \ \ \ \ == \mathbf{case}\ q\ \mathbf{of}\ \varepsilon \to x \mid \mathbf{others}\ \to lt(q)\ \mathbf{fo}$
def $rt(q \vdash x)\ \ \ \ \ == x$
def $lr(q \vdash x)\ \ \ \ \ == q$
def $rr(q \vdash x)\ \ \ \ \ == \mathbf{case}\ q\ \mathbf{of}\ \varepsilon \to \varepsilon \mid \mathbf{others}\ \to rr(q) \vdash x\ \mathbf{fo}$
def $(q \vdash x)[\mathsf{S}i]\ \ \ \ == \mathbf{if}\ i = \#q\ \mathbf{then}\ x\ \mathbf{else}\ q[\mathsf{S}i]\ \mathbf{fi}$
def $(q \vdash x)[\mathsf{S}i \mapsto y] == \mathbf{if}\ i = \#q\ \mathbf{then}\ q \vdash y\ \mathbf{else}\ q[\mathsf{S}i \mapsto y] \vdash x\ \mathbf{fi}$

lma S5: $\forall q : \mathbf{seq1} \bullet lt(q) \dashv rr(q) = lr(q) \vdash rt(q) = q\ \wedge$
               $q[1] = lt(q)\ \wedge\ q[\#q] = rt(q)$
lma S6: $\forall q, r : \mathbf{seq}\ T,\ i : Nat1 \bullet (q \dashv r)[i] == \mathbf{if}\ i \leq \#q\ \mathbf{then}\ q[i]\ \mathbf{else}\ r[i - \#q]\ \mathbf{fi}$
lma S7: $\forall q : \mathbf{seq1},\ i : Nat1,\ x : T \bullet i \leq \#q \Rightarrow (\#(q[i \mapsto x]) = \#q)$
lma S8: $\forall q : \mathbf{seq1},\ i : Nat1,\ x : T \bullet q[i \mapsto x] == q[1..i-1] \vdash x \dashv q[i+1..\#q]$
lma S9: $\forall q : \mathbf{seq},\ x : T,\ i, k : Nat1 \bullet$
               $i \leq \#q \Rightarrow (q[i \mapsto x][k] == \mathbf{if}\ k = i\ \mathbf{then}\ x\ \mathbf{else}\ q[k]\ \mathbf{fi})$

lma S10:$\forall q_1, q_2 : \mathbf{seq} \bullet q_1 = q_2 == \forall i : Nat1 \bullet q_1[i] == q_2[i]$

Lemma S7 is obvious but useful. S9 is a stronger version of the rule AMOD of section 4.3.3. S10 expresses the fact that the indexing operation forms an observation basis for sequences.

Indexing by sequence

func $\hat{}[\hat{}]$: $\mathbf{seq}\, T \times \mathbf{seq}\, Nat1 \longrightarrow \mathbf{seq}\, T$ (sequence subscript)
func $\hat{}[\hat{} \mapsto \hat{}]$: $\mathbf{seq}\, T \times \mathbf{seq}\, Nat1 \times \mathbf{seq}\, T \longrightarrow \mathbf{seq}\, T$ (sequence substitution)

def $q[r]$ $==$ **case** r **of** $\varepsilon \to \varepsilon \mid r' \vdash i \to q[r'] \vdash q[i]$ **fo**
def $q[r \mapsto s] ==$ **case** (r, s) **of** $(\varepsilon, \varepsilon) \to q$
                          $\mid (r' \vdash i, s' \vdash x) \to q[r' \mapsto s'][i \mapsto x]$
                          $\mid$ **others** $\to \perp$ **fo**

lma S11: $\forall q : \mathbf{seq}\, T, \; r : \mathbf{seq}\, \{1..\#q\}, \; i : Nat1 \bullet q[r][i] == q[r[i]]$
lma S12: $\forall q : \mathbf{seq}\, T, \; r : \mathbf{seq}\, Nat1, \; i : Nat1, \; j : Nat \bullet$
           $\#r = j + 1 - i \Rightarrow (q[\langle i..j \rangle \mapsto r] == q[1..i-1] \vdash r \vdash q[j+1..\#q])$

These functions overload the operators for single subscript and term substitution, respectively. For that reason they must be considered introduced and defined in a separate module. We simplify notations of the form $q[\langle \ldots \rangle]$ by omitting the angular brackets.

Sequence predicates
In order to enhance readability we use mixfix notation for predicates, mostly based on boldface script:

func $\hat{}\mathbf{in}\hat{}$: $T \times \mathbf{seq} \longrightarrow Bool$ (occurs in)
func $\mathbf{norep}\hat{}$: $\mathbf{seq} \longrightarrow Bool$ (no repetitions)
func $\hat{}\mathbf{sub}\hat{}$: $\mathbf{seq} \times \mathbf{seq} \longrightarrow Bool$ (subsequence of)
func $\hat{}\mathbf{head}\hat{}$: $\mathbf{seq} \times \mathbf{seq} \longrightarrow Bool$ (head sequence of)
func $\hat{}\mathbf{tail}\hat{}$: $\mathbf{seq} \times \mathbf{seq} \longrightarrow Bool$ (tail sequence of)
func $\hat{}\mathbf{segm}\hat{}$: $\mathbf{seq} \times \mathbf{seq} \longrightarrow Bool$ (segment of)
func $\hat{}\mathbf{perm}\hat{}$: $\mathbf{seq} \times \mathbf{seq} \longrightarrow Bool$ (permutation of)
func $\hat{}\mathbf{psub}\hat{}$: $\mathbf{seq} \times \mathbf{seq} \longrightarrow Bool$ (permuted subsequence of)
func $\hat{}\mathbf{isa}\,\mathbf{mrg}\hat{}$: $\mathbf{seq} \times \mathbf{seq} \times \mathbf{seq} \longrightarrow Bool$ (is a merging of)

def x **in** q $==$ **case** q **of** $\varepsilon \to \mathbf{f} \mid q' \vdash y \to x = y \vee x$ **in** q' **fo**
def   **norep** q $==$ **case** q **of** $\varepsilon \to \mathbf{t} \mid q' \vdash x \to \neg x$ **in** $q' \wedge$ **norep** q' **fo**
def q **sub** r $==$ **case** q **of** $\varepsilon \to \mathbf{t} \mid q' \vdash x \to$ **case** r **of** $\varepsilon \to \mathbf{f} \mid r' \vdash y \to$
                  if $x = y$ **then** q' **sub** r' **else** q **sub** r' **fi fo fo**

def q **head** r $==q=r \lor$ **case** r **of** $\varepsilon \to \mathbf{f} \mid r' \vdash x \to q$ **head** r' **fo**
def q **tail** r $==$ **case** q **of** $\varepsilon \to \mathbf{t} \mid q' \vdash x \to$
$\qquad\qquad\qquad$ **case** r **of** $\varepsilon \to \mathbf{f} \mid r' \vdash y \to x = y \land q'$ **tail** r' **fo fo**
def q **segm** r $==$ **case** r **of** $\varepsilon \to q = \varepsilon \mid r' \vdash x \to q$ **tail** $r \lor q$ **segm** r' **fo**
def q **perm** r $== bag(q) = bag(r)$
def q **psub** r $== bag(q) \sqsubseteq bag(r)$
def q **is** r_1 **mrg** r_2 $==$
$\qquad\qquad$ **case** q **of** $\varepsilon \to r_1 = r_2 = \varepsilon \mid q' \vdash x \to$
$\qquad\qquad\qquad$ **case** r_1 **of** $\varepsilon \to \mathbf{f} \mid r_1' \vdash y \to x = y \land q'$ **is** r_1' **mrg** r_2 **fo** $\lor$
$\qquad\qquad\qquad$ **case** r_2 **of** $\varepsilon \to \mathbf{f} \mid r_2' \vdash y \to x = y \land q'$ **is** r_1 **mrg** r_2' **fo fo**

lma S13: $\forall q : \mathbf{seq} \bullet \mathbf{norep}\, q = (\#q = \#sel(q))$
lma S14: $\forall q, r_1, r_2 : \mathbf{seq} \bullet$
$\qquad (q$ **is** r_1 **mrg** $r_2) \Rightarrow (r_1$ **sub** $q \land r_2$ **sub** $q \land \#q = \#r_1 + \#r_2)$

All the binary relations on sequences except ˆ**perm**ˆ are partial orders. The latter is an equivalence relation.

Exercise

5.30 Define the predicates ˆ**perm**ˆ and ˆ**psub**ˆ without using the bag concept, and prove the above defining equations for these predicates.

Projection

func ˆ$/$ˆ : $\mathbf{seq} \times \mathbf{set}\, T \longrightarrow \mathbf{seq}$ $\qquad\qquad$ (project into set)
func ˆ$\backslash$ˆ : $\mathbf{seq} \times \mathbf{set}\, T \longrightarrow \mathbf{seq}$ $\qquad\qquad$ (project away from set)

def $q/s ==$ **case** q **of** $\varepsilon \to \varepsilon \mid q' \vdash x \to$ **if** $x \,\epsilon\, s$ **then** $(q'/s) \vdash x$ **else** q'/s **fi**
def $q \backslash s ==$ **case** q **of** $\varepsilon \to \varepsilon \mid q' \vdash x \to$ **if** $x \,\epsilon\, s$ **then** $q' \backslash s$ **else** $(q' \backslash s) \vdash x$ **fi**

lma S15: $\forall q : \mathbf{seq}, s : \mathbf{set}\, T \bullet q$ **is** $(q/s)\mathbf{mrg}(q \backslash s)$

Domination

func ˆ**dom**ˆ : $\mathbf{seq} \times \mathbf{set}\, T \longrightarrow Bool$ $\qquad\qquad$ (is dominated by)
$\quad$**def** q **dom** $s ==$ **case** q **of** $\varepsilon \to \mathbf{t} \mid q' \vdash x \to$
$\qquad\qquad\qquad q'$ **dom** $s \land (\#(q'/s) = \#(q' \backslash s) \Rightarrow x \,\epsilon\, s)$ **fo**
lma S16: $\forall q, r : \mathbf{seq}, s : \mathbf{set}\, T \bullet q$ **dom** $s \land r$ **head** $q \Rightarrow \#(r/s) \geq \#(r \backslash s)$

Imagine walking from left to right along a sequence q. If q is dominated by the set s then, whenever you look back, at least half of the number of terms you see are occurrences of s elements.

EXAMPLE 5.57

Let q be a sequence of characters which constitutes a mathematical expression. q is well-formed with respect to the parenthesis structure if it contains the same number of left and right parentheses, and provided the "parenthesis skeleton", $q/\{`('`,`)'\}$, is dominated by left parentheses (where '(' and ')' denote character values):

$$\#(q/\{`('\}) = \#(q/\{`)'\}) \land (q/\{`('`,`)'\}) \text{ dom } \{`('\}$$

If in addition the following requirement holds, the depth of parenthesis nesting does not exceed n:

$$((`)' \uparrow n) \vdash q/\{`('`,`)'\}) \text{ dom } \{`)'\}$$

□

EXAMPLE 5.58

Let q be a time sequence of *put* and *get* operations on a communication buffer of n slots (empty initially), regarding the operations as time ordered atomic events. Then any possible sequence q of events must satisfy domination predicates corresponding to those of example 5.57, where *put*-events and *get*-events correspond to left and right parentheses, respectively.

□

Generic predicates

The following schematically defined predicates make use of an unspecified binary predicate $\hat{}\mathbf{R}\hat{}$ defined for the base type T. We use an *ad hoc* syntax reminiscent of APL, [22]:

func $\hat{}\mathbf{R}\hat{}$: $T \times T \longrightarrow Bool$	(unspecified relation)
func $/\mathbf{R}\hat{}$: seq $\longrightarrow Bool$	(sorted wrt. $\mathbf{R}$)
func $\hat{}*\mathbf{R}\hat{}$: seq $\times T \longrightarrow Bool$	(all are $\mathbf{R}$)
func $\hat{}\mathbf{R}*\hat{}$: $T \times$ seq $\longrightarrow Bool$	(is $\mathbf{R}$ all)
func $\hat{}*\mathbf{R}*\hat{}$: seq $\times$ seq $\longrightarrow Bool$	(all are $\mathbf{R}$ all)

def $/\mathbf{R}q$ == **case** q **of** $\varepsilon \rightarrow$ **t** $\mid q' \vdash x \rightarrow$
                case q' **of** $\varepsilon \rightarrow$ **t** $\mid q'' \vdash y \rightarrow /\mathbf{R}q' \land y\mathbf{R}x$ **fo fo**
def $q*\mathbf{R}x$ == **case** q **of** $\varepsilon \rightarrow$ **t** $\mid q' \vdash y \rightarrow q'*\mathbf{R}x \land y\mathbf{R}x$ **fo**
def $x\mathbf{R}*q$ == **case** q **of** $\varepsilon \rightarrow$ **t** $\mid q' \vdash y \rightarrow x\mathbf{R}*q' \land x\mathbf{R}y$ **fo**
def $q*\mathbf{R}*r$ == **case** r **of** $\varepsilon \rightarrow$ **t** $\mid r' \vdash x \rightarrow q*\mathbf{R}*r' \land q*\mathbf{R}x$ **fo**

The predicate schema $/\mathbf{R}$ is primarily intended for transitive $\mathbf{R}$. Clearly, $/\leq$ is an ordinary "sorted" predicate (called *ndec* in exercise 4.49, p. 129). If $\mathbf{R}$ is transitive several obvious lemmas hold, such as $q*\mathbf{R}x \land x\mathbf{R}*r \Rightarrow q*\mathbf{R}*r$ and $/\mathbf{R}q \land /\mathbf{R}r \land q*\mathbf{R}*r \Rightarrow /\mathbf{R}(q \vdash r)$.

endmodule

Monotonicity

A function is said to be *monotonic* if it is order preserving in some sense, such as preserving the order of well-definedness, as discussed earlier. More generally, if an ordering relation on the type of a given argument is mapped to some ordering relation on the function codomain, the function is said to be monotonic in that argument with respect to the two orderings. For instance, the *set* function for sequences satisfies

$$q \textbf{ sub } r \Rightarrow set(q) \subseteq set(r)$$

and is thus monotonic (in its only argument) with respect to the subsequence and subset orderings. For well-founded orderings it is not unusual that minimal elements correspond, as they do for the *set* function: $set(\varepsilon) = \emptyset$.

When reasoning about time sequences the **head** relation on sequence arguments is of particular importance and leads to what we call *historic monotonicity*. For a sequence-to-sequence function f, or a sequence predicate P, historic monotonicity is defined as follows:

$$f(\overline{x}, q, \overline{y}) \textbf{ hmon } q \triangleq \forall q, r : \textbf{seq } T \bullet q \textbf{ head } r \Rightarrow f(\overline{x}, q, \overline{y}) \textbf{ head } f(\overline{x}, r, \overline{y})$$
$$P(\overline{x}, q, \overline{y}) \textbf{ hmon } q \triangleq \forall q, r : \textbf{seq } T \bullet q \textbf{ head } r \Rightarrow (P(\overline{x}, q, \overline{y}) \Leftarrow P(\overline{x}, r, \overline{y}))$$

where q is by definition a bound variable in either left hand side, and $\Leftarrow$ stands for "is implied by".

The relevance of these definitions follows from looking at a "discrete automaton" DA receiving a time sequence of inputs of type T, and reacting to each individual input by immediately producing zero or more outputs of type U. Let $q : \textbf{seq } T$ be the sequence of inputs received so far, the "load", and let $r : \textbf{seq } U$ be the corresponding sequence of outputs, the "response". If DA is a deterministic device, it may be described completely by specifying the response as a function of the load:

$$r = F_{DA}(q), \text{ for } F_{DA} : \textbf{seq } T \longrightarrow \textbf{seq } U.$$

Since more input cannot change outputs already given, it is clear that F_{DA} must be historically monotonic. If certain loads can make the device misbehave and break, the function is partial. The well-definedness predicate is historically monotonic if the device, when broken, cannot be repaired by providing more input. Also, any invariant on the response alone must be historically monotonic. If there is no output initially, minimal elements correspond: $F_{DA}(\varepsilon) = \varepsilon$; and if DA is not broken initially, then $P(\varepsilon) = \textbf{t}$ which is the minimal element with respect to $\Leftarrow$.

Notice that we do not have to consider infinite sequences in order to describe a device which might go on for ever.

The following historic monotonicities exist for the sequence functions and predicates defined in this section:

$$x \dashv q \quad \textbf{hmon } q, \qquad q \vdash r \quad \textbf{hmon } r, \qquad rr(q) \quad \textbf{hmon } q,$$
$$q[r] \quad \textbf{hmon } r, \quad \textbf{norep } q \quad \textbf{hmon } q, \quad q \textbf{ sub } r \quad \textbf{hmon } q,$$
$$q \textbf{ head } r \quad \textbf{hmon } q, \quad q \textbf{ seg } r \quad \textbf{hmon } q, \quad q \textbf{ psub } r \quad \textbf{hmon } q,$$
$$q/s \quad \textbf{hmon } q, \qquad q \backslash s \quad \textbf{hmon } q, \quad q \textbf{ dom } s \quad \textbf{hmon } q,$$
$$/\textbf{R}q \quad \textbf{hmon } q, \quad q * \textbf{R} \, x \quad \textbf{hmon } q, \qquad x \textbf{ R} * q \quad \textbf{hmon } q,$$
$$q * \textbf{R} * r \quad \textbf{hmon } q, \quad q * \textbf{R} * r \quad \textbf{hmon } r.$$

EXAMPLE 5.59

The concept of "semaphores" was introduced by Dijkstra for the purpose of synchronizing concurrent processes. There are two kinds of operations associated with a semaphore: a V-operation corresponds to sending a signal, and a P-operations means waiting for a signal, unless it has already been sent. Thus, a semaphore may be seen as a communication buffer for the sending (V) and receiving (P) of "empty messages".

We may model a somewhat specialized version of the semaphore concept as a discrete automaton described by $F : \textbf{seq}\, T \longrightarrow \textbf{seq}\, T$, where $T = P{:}C + V{:}C$, and C is the type (set) of concurrent processes. An occurrence of $P(x)$ in the load q represents the event of the *initiation* of a P-operation by process x, and similarly for an occurrence of $V(y)$ in q. We may assume that no process issues more than one P or V operation, which implies that the events recorded in q are all distinct. The elements of the response represent *completions* of initiated operations. Since the number of received messages at no time can exceed the number sent, the response must be V-dominated (overloading the name V to denote the set of events of the form $V(x)$ for $x{:}C$, and similarly for the name P). If a given load contains more P-initiations than V's, then $\#(q/P) - \#(q/V)$ excess P's must queue up in a "waiting line". If the queuing discipline is FIFO, the waiting line is the sequence $(q/P)[\#(q/V){+}1 .. \#(q/P)]$, consisting of the most recent P-initiations.

The semaphore function F may be TGI defined as follows:

def $F(q) ==$ **case** q **of** $\varepsilon \to \varepsilon \mid q \vdash e \to$ **case** e **of** $P(x) \to$
$\qquad\qquad$ **if** $\#(q/P) < \#(q/V)$ **then** $F(q) \vdash e$ **else** $F(q)$ **fi** $\mid V(x) \to$
$\qquad\qquad$ **if** $\#(q/P) \leq \#(q/V)$ **then** $F(q) \vdash e$ **else**
$\qquad\qquad$ $F(q) \vdash e \vdash (q/P)[\#(q/V){+}1]$ **fi fo fo**

where the last alternative includes the completion of a delayed P operation. The function satisfies the following lemmas for arbitrary $q : \textbf{seq}\ (P{:}C + V{:}C)$:

lma L1: $F(q)/V = q/V$ $\qquad\qquad\qquad$ (V's are output immediately)
lma L2: $F(q)/P$ **head** q/P $\qquad\qquad\quad$ (P's are output in the right order)
lma L3: $\#(F(q))/P = min(\#(q/P), \#(q/V))$ (They are delayed as necessary)
lma L4: $F(q)$ **dom** V $\qquad\qquad\qquad\qquad$ (to make $F(q)$ V-dominated)
lma L5: $F(q)$ **hmon** q

where L5 expresses that the device cannot change past history (the variable q of L5 is bound locally and does not stand for a particular history).

☐

Exercise

5.31 Prove the lemmas L1–5. Prove also that L1–5 together define F completely.

5.8.9 Sequential files

An abstract type, **file** T, representing the concept of one-way sequential files of type T records, might have the following minimal set of associated functions:

func *new_file* : ⟶ **file** T	(empty file)
func *put* : **file** $T \times T$ ⟶ **file** T	(write record)
func *adv* : **file** T ⟶ **file** T	(advance reading head)
func *rewind* : **file** T ⟶ **file** T	(rewind file)
func *get* : **file** T ⟶ T	(read record)

Notice that a "read" operation from a file variable F to a receiving record variable x would correspond to simultaneous assignments to both variables:

$$x, F := get(F), adv(F)$$

where the *get* operation looks at the record under the reading head and does nothing to the file, whereas the *adv* operation advances the reading head and thus leaves the file in a different state, corresponding to a new abstract file value.

A generator basis would have to contain all four producer functions, and that would leave us with a many-to-one basis. For instance, the *rewind* operation is necessary in order to prepare a written file for subsequent reading, but the second of two consecutive *rewind* operations should have no effect, i.e an expression of the form $rewind(rewind(F))$ should be semantically equal to $rewind(F)$. There is also a difficulty with the *adv* function which is not naturally total.

We may, however, regard a file as a *pair of sequences*, (q, r), where the left component is that part of the file which has been passed by the reading head, and the right component is the part not yet read. This idea can be realized by defining the type **file** T as a Cartesian product **seq** $T \times$ **seq** T, or by introducing an explicit auxiliary function taking two sequences and producing a file value. The function constitutes a one-to-one generator basis all by itself:

> **func** *file* : **seq** $T \times$ **seq** T ⟶ **file** T (file generator)
> **1-1 genbas** *file*

Now all the above functions may easily be defined. We omit the **case**-construct since there would be only one branch:

> **def** *new_file* $==$ $file(\varepsilon, \varepsilon)$
> **def** $put(file(q, r), x)$ $==$ $file(q \vdash x, \varepsilon)$
> **def** $adv(file(q, r))$ $==$ $file(q \vdash lt(r), rr(r))$
> **def** $rewind(file(q, r))$ $==$ $file(\varepsilon, q \dashv r)$
> **def** $get(file(q, r))$ $==$ $lt(r)$

Notice that the *adv* and *get* functions are ill-defined in cases corresponding to reading off the end of the file. By introducing a special T value, *EOF*, both functions may be turned into total ones by redefining as follows:

> **func** *EOF* : $\longrightarrow T$ (end of file mark)

> **def** $adv(file(q, r))$ $==$ **if** $r = \varepsilon$ **then** $file(q, \varepsilon)$ **else** $file(q \vdash lt(r), rr(r))$ **fi**
> **def** $get(file(q, r))$ $==$ **if** $r = \varepsilon$ **then** *EOF* **else** $lt(r)$ **fi**

For the purpose of illustration we show another way of dealing with the file concept. If two selector functions *lp* and *rp* were defined giving the left and right abstract sequence parts of a file, it is clear that they would observe "all there is to see" in the file. Thus, rather than using an auxiliary generator function, we could use a many-to-one generator basis consisting of the four original producer functions, and then define the abstract file values indirectly through an observation basis consisting of the auxiliary defined observers *lp* and *rp*:

genbas $new\_file, put, adv, rewind$
func lp, rp : **file** $T \longrightarrow$ **seq** T (left part, right part)
def $lp(F)$ $==$ **case** F **of** $new\_file \rightarrow \varepsilon$
> | $put(F, x) \rightarrow lp(F) \vdash x$
> | $adv(F) \rightarrow$ **if** $rp(F) = \varepsilon$ **then** $lp(F)$
>   **else** $lp(F) \vdash lt(rp(F))$ **fi**
> | $rewind(F) \rightarrow \varepsilon$
> **fo**

def $rp(F)$ $==$ **case** F **of** $new\_file \rightarrow \varepsilon$
> | $put(F, x) \rightarrow \varepsilon$
> | $adv(F) \rightarrow$ **if** $rp(F) = \varepsilon$ **then** ε **else** $rr(rp(F))$ **fi**
> | $rewind(F) \rightarrow lp(F) \dashv rp(F)$
> **fo**

obsbas lp, rp
def $get(F)$ $==$ **if** $rp(F) = \varepsilon$ **then** *EOF* **else** $lt(rp(F))$ **fi**

Notice that the basic observers are the only functions defined by generator induction over files, therefore consistency is guaranteed. Furthermore, equality on files is in this case constructively defined through the observation basis, since both basic observers are unary functions, cf. section 5.5.2:

$\vdash F_1 = F_2 \ == \ lp(F_1) = lp(F_2) \land rp(F_1) = rp(F_2), \quad \text{for } F_1, F_2 : \textbf{file } T$

The latter system and the modified version of the former are interchangeable for the purpose of specification and reasoning. New observer functions may be defined in either system with no danger of losing consistency, provided generator induction is not used in the second one. For instance, we may define a file length function in either system:

func $\#\hat{\ } : \textbf{file } T \longrightarrow Nat$ (file length)

def $\#file(q,r) == \#q + \#r$ (first system)
def $\#F \qquad == \#lp(F) + \#rp(F)$ (second system)

Notice that the file length may decrease when writing before the end of a non-empty file. In the second system we could define the maximum file length, past or present, by generator induction:

func $maxl : \textbf{file } T \longrightarrow Nat$ (maximum file length)
def $maxl(F) == \textbf{case } F \textbf{ of } new\_file \rightarrow 0$
$\qquad\qquad\qquad\quad | \ put(F,x) \rightarrow max(maxl(F), \textbf{S}\#lp(F))$
$\qquad\qquad\qquad\quad | \ \textbf{others} \rightarrow maxl(F)$
$\qquad\qquad\qquad \textbf{fo}$

But now consistency is lost, as can be seen by considering the expressions

$$put(rewind(put(put(new\_file, a), b)), c) \quad \text{and} \quad put(new\_file, c)$$

which have different *maxl* values, although they are equal according to the observation basis. There is no way of defining a function such as *maxl* in the first system; the abstract file representation as a pair of sequences does not contain enough historic information.

5.8.10 Maps

We take the term "map" to mean a representation of a function $U \longrightarrow T$ defined at a finite set of arguments. The domain and codomain are arbitrary given types. The map concept may be defined as an abstract type as follows:

type $Map\{U,T\} \ ==$
module
func $init : \ \longrightarrow Map$ (empty map)
func $\hat{\ }[\hat{\ } \mapsto \hat{\ }] : Map \times U \times T \longrightarrow Map$ (update map)
genbas $init, \hat{\ }[\hat{\ } \mapsto \hat{\ }]$
func $\hat{\ }[\hat{\ }] : Map \times U \longrightarrow T$ (apply map)

def $M[x] ==$ **case** M **of** $init \to \perp \mid M'[y \mapsto z] \to$
            if $x = y$ **then** z **else** $M'[x]$ **fi fo**

obsbas $\hat{\ }[\hat{\ }]$

func   *defined* : $Map \times U \longrightarrow Bool$ (definedness test)

def   *defined*$(M, x) ==$ **case** M **of** $init \to$ **f**
                     $\mid M'[y \mapsto z] \to$
                  $x = y \vee defined(M', x)$ **fo**

endmodule

We use square brackets in the notation for map application in order to distinguish it from the (meta-)operation of applying an ordinary function. It should be noted, however, that when writing specifications at a high level of abstraction it is sometimes better not to distinguish between functions in the mathematical sense and maps; that distinction may belong to a less abstract level of design.

There is no one-to-one generator basis for maps. The observation basis may be shown to imply the following equalities on generator expressions:

$$M[u \mapsto t_1][u \mapsto t_2] = M[u \mapsto t_2] \qquad \text{(overriding)}$$
$$u_1 \neq u_2 \Rightarrow M[u_1 \mapsto t_1][u_2 \mapsto t_2] = M[u_2 \mapsto t_2][u_1 \mapsto t_1] \text{ (commutativity)}$$

The *Map* type schema satisfies the monotonicity requirement MONOTY of section 5.7 with respect to both parameters. The functions associated with an (implied) *Map* subtype are legal redefinitions of those associated with the supertype. In particular, the definedness test gives the correct result *defined*$(M, x) == d_{M[x]}$ for all x of type T, and is *ill-defined* (not false) for x outside T but belonging to a supertype, due to failing coercion of x.

Let M be of type $Map\{U_1, T_1\}$, and let $U_2 \preceq U_1$ and $T_2 \preceq T_1$. Then M is coercible to $Map\{U_2, T_2\}$ if and only if M is only defined at points in U_2 with "function" values in T_2. Therefore, the application operator $\hat{\ }[\hat{\ }]$ associated with the subtype $Map\{U_2, T_2\}$ can only produce values in T_2, or be ill-defined, even if applied to the map M belonging to a supertype.

It happens that functions are needed which cannot be associated with any type according to the rules given in section 5.7. An example of such a function is one corresponding to functional composition of maps (applying the left operand first):

     func $\hat{\ } * \hat{\ }$: $Map\{U, V\} \times Map\{V, T\} \longrightarrow Map\{U, T\}$

where all of U, V, T presumably are formal types. Three different *Map* schemas occur in the profile, but the function cannot be associated with any of them. It would have to belong to a function module, say one called *Mapping*$\{U, V, T\}$.

Exercises

5.32 Define a semantic subtype *CMap* of canonic maps, analogous to the construct *CSet* of example 5.48, p. 183. Identify and carry out the associated proof obligations.

5.33   Extend the *Map* module with an operator $\hat{} + \hat{} :$ *Map* $\times$ *Map* $\longrightarrow$ *Map* such that $M_1 + M_2$ is a map identical to M_2 wherever the latter is defined, and identical to M_1 elsewhere. Redefine the operator in the subtype *CMap* of the last exercise, taking advantage of canonic maps to obtain better evaluation efficiency. Prove the correctness of the latter and the consistency of the former.

5.34   Give a TGI definition of the $\hat{} * \hat{}$ operator introduced above. Prove the strong equality

$$(M_1 * M_2)[x] == M_2[M_1[x]]$$

for variables of compatible types.

Initialized maps

A useful alternative kind of map is one initialized to a specified default value for all type correct arguments. An initialized map can give values different from the default in at most a finite set of points. The concept is obtained from the one above by a slight change in the application operator. We also parameterize the initial generator by the chosen default value. Since an initialized map is well-defined on the entire declared domain, no definedness test is needed:

> **type** *Imap*$\{U, T\}$ $==$
> **module**
> **func** *init* : $T \longrightarrow$ *Imap*   (initialized map)
> **func** $\hat{}[\hat{} \mapsto \hat{}]$: *Imap* $\times U \times T \longrightarrow$ *Imap*   (update map)
> **genbas** *init*, $\hat{}[\hat{} \mapsto \hat{}]$
> **func** $\hat{}[\hat{}]$: *Imap* $\times U \longrightarrow T$ (apply map)
> **def** $M[x] ==$ **case** M **of** $init(x) \rightarrow x \mid M'[y \mapsto z] \rightarrow$
> $\qquad\qquad\qquad$ **if** $x = y$ **then** z **else** $M'[x]$ **fi fo**
> **obsbas** $\hat{}[\hat{}]$
> **endmodule**

In the special case where the domain of an initialized map is an interval type, say $\{1..n\}$, the concept may be represented somewhat more efficiently as a *sequence of length n*, $\{q : \text{seq } T \bullet \#q = n\}$. Cf. example 5.64. See also section 6.2.

5.9   Type Simulation

It has been mentioned already that the generator inductive style of specification can be seen as an applicative *programming language*. An implementation would consist of a mechanism for the evaluation of variable-free expressions based on user defined types and functions. It could be a conventional bottom up expression interpreter, except that a pattern matching mechanism is needed for the interpretation of **case**-constructs or, if all functions are TGI defined, a term rewriting system restricted as described in section 5.3.1. The expressions, i.e. the "main program" and the function bodies, may be represented internally as list structures or even directly as character strings. Notice that abstract values are themselves expressions (in generators).

From the point of view of programming, evaluation efficiency is more important than ease of reasoning, and a concept representation optimized with respect to one of these purposes is likely to be quite different from one designed for the other. Thus, if a type T is designed with the objective of achieving maximum ease of understanding and reasoning, its definition is as simple as possible and, in particular, the space of T-values should not have more structure than is essential for the concept at hand. The types *Int* and *Nat* defined in section 5.8.2 are good examples. It is clear, however, that these types, as defined, are entirely useless for the purpose of numerical computation.

In general, given a type T, good for reasoning, there may be a need for another type T' to substitute for T in computations. T' must have associated functions which mimic those of T, although the value space of T' may be entirely different from that of T. It is designed with the objective of achieving good computational efficiency and may even be adjusted to fit the peculiarities of a particular computer. Unfortunately reasoning in terms of T' is likely to be less convenient, involving aspects of data structure and algorithmic details that are logically irrelevant. In this sense T is "more abstract" than T', and the latter more implementation-such as or "concrete".

Faced with a choice between ease of programming and reasoning on the one hand, and computational efficiency on the other, there is fortunately a way of achieving both ends; we may program and reason in terms of T and compute in terms of T' after a mechanical program transformation. The price for this is to prove that T' *simulates* T in a certain formal sense or, expressed in other words, that T is a *formal specification of T'*.

We say that T' *strongly simulates* T if and only if the following criteria hold:

(a) For each function f associated with T (including $=^T$) there is a function, say f', associated with T', whose profile is obtained from that of f by replacing each occurrence of T by T'. (We assume here that this covers *all* functions whose profiles contain occurrences of T, and that subtypes of T count as T.)

(b) There is a total and strict function $\mathcal{A} : T' \to T$ such that for every $f \epsilon F_T$:

$$\forall w' : \text{domain of } f' \bullet \begin{cases} \mathcal{A}(f'(w')) & == & f(w), & \text{for } f \epsilon PRD_T \\ f'(w') & == & f(w), & \text{for } f \epsilon OBS_T \end{cases}$$

where the argument list w is obtained from w' by replacing any component $x' : T'$ in w' by $\mathcal{A}(x')$.

$\mathcal{A}$ is called the *abstraction function* since it maps concrete values on abstract ones (cf. [20]). Let $x = \mathcal{A}(x')$. Then the value x' is said to be a *concrete representation* of the abstract value x. Since $\mathcal{A}$ is total, all T'-values represent abstract values (not necessarily all different). And, since $\mathcal{A}$ is a function, distinct abstract values are necessarily represented by distinct concrete ones if they have representations at all.

In the following we assume that the abstract type T is *convex*. Then the (b)-criteria for the T-generators imply that the whole of T is represented. This follows by generator induction over T. Any abstract value x can be expressed as a basic T-expression, say $x = g(w)$. Let g' be the T'-function representing the T-generator g. If g is a relative constant (in which case the argument list w may be empty), we may take $x' = g'(w)$ since $g(w) = \mathcal{A}(g'(w'))$ where $w' = w$ in this case. Otherwise we may take $x' = g'(w')$, where w' is obtained from w by replacing each T-argument by a representative in T', which inductively may be assumed to exist. (Notice that convexity of T implies that the type of any abstract generator argument is either (included in) T or unrelated to T.)

According to criterion (a) the equality relation over T is represented by some relation over T', say $\hat{}\simeq\hat{}: T' \times T' \longrightarrow Bool$. The corresponding (b)-criterion, $x' \simeq y' == \mathcal{A}(x') = \mathcal{A}(y')$, shows that $\hat{}\simeq\hat{}$ is a total and strict function, which is in general an *equivalence relation* on T'. In the special case where $\mathcal{A}$ is one-to-one it is identical to the T'-equality.

Let $T \neq Bool$. Then for any formula P (expression of type $Bool$!) containing subterms of type T, a strongly equivalent formula P' may be obtained in which each such subterm of P has been replaced by a corresponding expression of type T'. Assuming for simplicity that no **case**-construct over T occurs textually in P, the formula P' may be obtained in a sequence of steps of one of the following forms:

1. Replace all applied occurrences of a variable x of type T by $\mathcal{A}(x')$, where x' is a new variable of type T'. If x is a bound variable change the quantifier accordingly.

2. Replace a subexpression of the form $f(w)$, where f is a T-function and all arguments of type T, if any, of the argument list w are of the form $\mathcal{A}(e)$, by $\mathcal{A}(f'(w'))$ if $f \epsilon PRD_T$ and by $f'(w')$ otherwise, where f' is the T'-function corresponding to f and w' is obtained from w by deleting all outermost applications of $\mathcal{A}$, if any.

(Notice that the steps of type 2 will ultimately remove all occurrences of $\mathcal{A}$ because P is an expression of type other than T.)

Since the abstraction function is total and all T-values have representations in T', any step of type 1 strongly preserves the meaning of the formula, provided that $x = \mathcal{A}(x')$ if the variable x is free in P. It follows from criterion (b) that any step of type 2 replaces a (sub-)expression by one that is strongly equal. This shows that the translation result P' is strongly equal to P provided that free variables of types T and T' correspond. *In this sense the type T is adequately simulated by T'.*

Let A be a **case**-free abstract axiom. Then its translation A$'$ should be a valid formula. Strictly speaking, if A is of the form $e_1 == e_2$, its main operator is not part of the formula language of our formal logic and is not immediately translatable. As stated earlier, however, a strong equality can be expressed in terms of definedness predicates and ordinary equality, as $d_{e_1} = d_{e_2} \wedge (d_{e_1} \Rightarrow e_1 = e_2)$. Now, e_i is adequately simulated by e'_i, $i = 1, 2$, provided the values of abstract and concrete free variables correspond. Thus, $d_{e_i} = d_{e'_i}$, which shows that A can be translated to $d_{e'_1} = d_{e'_2} \wedge (d_{e'_1} \Rightarrow e'_1 \simeq e'_2)$ if the strong equality is over T, and to $e'_1 == e'_2$ otherwise.

Let AX be the set of T-axioms, **case**-free versions, including those defining $=^T$. (If the method of section 5.5.1 has been used, this includes the equivalence axioms E1-3 of section 5.5, as well as the relevant instances of E4.) Let AX' be the corresponding set of translated formulas. It is possible to show that *proving the formulas AX' constitutes an indirect proof of criterion (b)*, provided that all T'-values represent abstract ones and T is not a restricted type.

We sketch a proof of this fact in the simple case where T has a one-to-one generator basis and all non-generators are explicitly defined.

Proof

Let the abstract generators and their representations be $g_1, \ldots, g_n$ and $g'_1, \ldots, g'_n$, respectively. Then the translations of the **case**-free abstract equality axioms are

$$
\begin{aligned}
\mathrm{A}'_{ij} : \quad & g'_i(w'_i) \simeq g'_j(w'_j) \quad == \quad \mathbf{f} \qquad \text{for } i, j \in \{1..n\},\ i \neq j \\
\mathrm{A}'_{ii} : \quad & g'_i(w'_i) \simeq g'_i(u'_i) \quad == \quad w'_i \approx u'_i \quad \text{for } i \in \{1..n\}
\end{aligned}
$$

where $w'_i \approx u'_i$ stands for $\mathbf{t}$ if the two argument lists are empty and otherwise for a conjunction of terms, one for each argument pair x, y, where a term is $x \simeq y$ if $x, y : T'$, and $x = y$ otherwise.

These formulas, which are valid according to assumption, are sufficient to show that an abstraction function exists. To do so we chose two abstract values (basic T-expressions), e_1, e_2. Assuming that they are different, $e_1 \neq^T e_2$, we must show that their translations are different too, $e'_1 \neq^{T'} e'_2$. As a first step we prove $e'_1 \not\simeq e'_2$. Referring to the abstract equality axioms there are two exhaustive cases:

- e_1 is $g_i(\ldots)$, e_2 is $g_j(\ldots)$, $i \neq j$: Then A'_{ij} shows $e'_1 \not\simeq e'_2$.
- e_1 is $g_i(\mathrm{args}_1)$, e_2 is $g_i(\mathrm{args}_2)$, where $\mathrm{args}_1 \neq \mathrm{args}_2$: Using induction with respect to the depth of nesting we may assume $\mathrm{args}'_1 \not\approx \mathrm{args}'_2$. A'_{ii} then gives $e'_1 \not\simeq e'_2$.

By a similar technique, using A'_{ii} inductively, we may prove $e'_1 \simeq e'_1$, which shows, by E4 applied to the second argument of $\simeq$, that $e'_1 \neq^{T'} e'_2$.

The strong equalities of A'_{ij} and A'_{ii} show that any translated basic T-expression is well-defined. Consequently, the (b)-criteria for the abstract generators may be proved inductively, using the translation relation as defined by steps 1 and 2 above.

The remaining (b)-criteria may be proved as follows. Consider an abstract function definition $f(x) == e$, where $x : T$ (the case where no argument is of type T is simpler). Assume that e, apart from recursive function applications, only contains functions considered earlier. We know now that any abstract value has a concrete representation, and according to assumption the converse is also true. Therefore we may write equivalently $f(\mathcal{A}(x')) == e^x_{\mathcal{A}(x')}$, where $x' : T'$. According to assumption the translated axiom, $f'(x') \approx e'$, is valid. If the definition is non-recursive, it follows by translation steps of type 2, using (b)-criteria already established, that $e' \approx e^x_{\mathcal{A}(x')}$. Consequently, $f'(x') \approx e^x_{\mathcal{A}(x')} == f(\mathcal{A}(x'))$. This shows $\mathcal{A}(f'(x')) == f(\mathcal{A}(x'))$ if f is a T-producer, and $f'(x') == f(\mathcal{A}(x'))$ otherwise.

If the definition of f is recursive the same result follows by induction on the recursion depth for a given argument (if the recursion is indirect the group of mutually dependent functions must be considered simultaneously). Also, a set of **case**-free inductive axioms may be similarly analysed. ∎

One might think that the validity of A$'_{ij}$ and A$'_{ii}$ for arbitrary translated basic T-expressions would imply the totality of the abstraction function, but counterexamples do exist, as shown in example 5.61 below. It is sufficient, however, to show that an arbitrary T'-value can be expressed in terms of abstract producer representations. It then follows by translated axioms that it can either be expressed in terms of generator representations, or that it is equivalent to one that can be so expressed. (An alternative is to rely on an explicit definition of a total abstraction function and then prove the (b)-criteria for the abstract generators, which amounts to showing by induction over T that $\mathcal{A}(e') = e$ for arbitrary basic T-expression e and its translation e'.)

If T is a semantic subtype, say $T = \{x : U \bullet R(x)\}$, U unrestricted, any **case**-free T-inductive axiom, LHS $==$ RHS, must be replaced by

$$\text{LHS} == \textbf{if B then RHS else} \perp \textbf{fi}$$

where B expresses that every generator expression of type T in the left hand side satisfies the restriction R.

The above discussion shows that the abstraction function may not have to occur at all in the proof that T' formally simulates T. Still, it is good design strategy to characterize it, at least informally. It will guide the construction of the various concrete functions in expressing and representing an ultimate goal of the simulation.

Let the abstraction function be defined constructively, and assume that the (b)-criteria have been proved for all abstract generators, given independently defined representations. Then, for any abstract non-generator f we may save the work involved in writing and proving an independent definition of the representation f', simply by taking the corresponding (b)-criterion as the defining axiom. Then the translated f-axioms will be trivially satisfied. The (b)-criterion provides a direct definition of f' for any observer f, including $=^T$, though not necessarily a very efficient one. For a producer the definition is in general non-constructive (unless $\mathcal{A}^{-1}$ exists and is defined constructively), and if $\mathcal{A}$ is many-to-one the definition is even incomplete. Still, it may be convenient for reasoning purposes, which is sufficient if mechanical interpretation of f' is not required.

Another way to save work is to take the translated axioms for a T-function as a definition of the concrete representation. Again, however, the definition will usually be unsuitable for mechanical interpretation, even if the abstract axiom is TGI.

EXAMPLE 5.60

Sets of T-values, **set** T, as defined in section 5.8.6, may be simulated by T-sequences. At the same time the subtypes *Eset* and **set1** T are simulated by *Eseq* and **seq1** T, respectively. The idea is that a sequence q represents the set of values which occur in q. See section 5.8.8 for the definitions of the sequence operators used:

> **func** $\mathcal{A}$: **seq** $T \longrightarrow$ **set** T
> **def** $\mathcal{A}(q) == set(q)$

We consider the **set** operators $\emptyset$, *add*, *sub*, $\hat{\epsilon}\hat{}$, and equality. For the purpose of the example we take the latter to be defined by **obsbas** $\hat{\epsilon}\hat{}$. The following function representations are chosen:

$\emptyset : \longrightarrow \text{set} T$	repr. by	$\varepsilon : \longrightarrow \text{seq } T$
$add : \text{set } T \times T \longrightarrow \text{set } T$	repr. by	$\hat{\vdash}\hat{} : \text{seq } T \times T \longrightarrow \text{seq } T$
$sub : \text{set } T \times T \longrightarrow \text{set } T$	repr. by	$sub' : \text{seq } T \times T \longrightarrow \text{seq } T$
$\hat{\epsilon}\hat{} : T \times \text{set } T \longrightarrow Bool$	repr. by	$\hat{}\text{in}\hat{} : T \times \text{seq } T \longrightarrow Bool$
$\hat{}=\hat{} : (\text{set } T)^2 \longrightarrow Bool$	repr. by	$\hat{}\simeq\hat{} : (\text{seq } T)^2 \longrightarrow Bool$

where

> **def** $sub'(q, x) ==$ **case** q **of** $\varepsilon \to \varepsilon \mid q' \vdash y \to$
> $\qquad\qquad$ **if** $x = y$ **then** $sub'(q', x)$ **else** $sub'(q', x) \vdash y$ **fi fo**
> **def** $q \simeq r$ $== \mathcal{A}(q) = \mathcal{A}(r)$

The concrete operators are as evaluation efficient as the chosen value representations permit. Notice that all occurrences of x in q have to be removed in order to simulate subtraction of x from the corresponding set.

The simulation may be validated by proving the following theorems, where the first two are (b)-criteria for the generator representations, and the rest are translated axioms for the abstract operators *sub* and $\hat{\epsilon}\hat{}$, respectively. Since all abstract and concrete functions involved are total all strong equalities could be replaced by strict relations:

$$
\begin{aligned}
\mathcal{A}(\varepsilon) &= \emptyset \\
\mathcal{A}(q \vdash x) &= add(\mathcal{A}(q), x) \\
x \text{ in } \varepsilon &= \mathbf{f} \\
x \text{ in } (q \vdash y) &= (x = y \vee x \text{ in } q) \\
sub'(\varepsilon, x) &\simeq \varepsilon \\
sub'(q \vdash y, x) &\simeq \text{if } x = y \text{ then } sub'(q, x) \text{ else } sub'(q, x) \vdash y \text{ fi}
\end{aligned}
$$

An alternative to proving the generator representations is to validate the translated abstract equality definition. (The totality of the abstraction function is obvious.)

$$(q \simeq r) \; = \; \forall x : T \bullet (x \operatorname{in} q) = (x \operatorname{in} r)$$

All the proofs indicated above are quite trivial, using the definitions of the concrete operators (including the *set* function). This is due to the fact that the abstract generators are represented by the generators of the concrete space, which makes the two generator universes structurally similar. For a type U with a many-to-one generator basis, such as **set** T, it is possible to view the generator universe of U as a "concrete" type simulating U. In a sense that is what we have done in the present example.

□

EXAMPLE 5.61

Assume for the sake of argument that we wish to simulate the type *Nat* by *Int*. The generators 0 and **S** are to be represented by 0 and **S**$'$, respectively, and $=^{Nat}$ by $\simeq$, where

> **def S**$'x \; == $ **if** $x \geq 0$ **then** $x+1$ **else** $x-1$ **fi**
> **def** $x \simeq y \; == \; abs(x) = abs(y)$

The translated equality axioms

$$0 \simeq 0 == \mathbf{t}, \quad \mathbf{S}'x \simeq 0 == \mathbf{f}, \quad 0 \simeq \mathbf{S}'y == \mathbf{f}, \quad \mathbf{S}'x \simeq \mathbf{S}'y == x \simeq y$$

hold for all $x, y : Int$. It follows that non-negative integers represent the corresponding natural numbers, and since every negative number is equivalent to its absolute value under the defined relation, the abstraction function is total: $\mathcal{A}(x) == abs(x)$.

It turns out that there is another choice of equality representation which satisfies the translated axioms: $x \simeq y == x = y$. If now -1 would map to a natural number a, we would have $\mathcal{A}(a) = a = \mathcal{A}(-1)$. The (b)-criterion for equality, $x \simeq y ==$ $\mathcal{A}(x) = \mathcal{A}(y)$, then gives $a \simeq -1$ which implies $a = -1$, a contradiction. Thus, the abstraction function is not total in this case.

□

It is often advisable to let the concrete type, T', be a semantic subtype of one defined inductively, T^*:

$$T' \triangleq \{t' : T^* \bullet R(t')\}.$$

For instance, if the concrete representations of the abstract generators only span the indicated subset of V_{T^*} this will save us the trouble of considering irrelevant concrete values when designing the abstraction function as well as the concrete representation functions. (The former should be total on T', but all these functions may be ill-defined outside T'.) The restriction R is sometimes referred to as the *representation invariant*.

The choice of representation invariant is a very important element in the design of a concrete value space. A well chosen one is sometimes of crucial importance for the efficiency of the simulation, with respect to the economy of data representation, as well as the efficiency of function evaluation. It plays a role not unlike that of a loop invariant during program design and verification.

Quantifiers ranging over T', restricted as above, are expressed in the usual way according to the rules ∀SUBEQ and ∃SUBEQ of section 5.6:

$$\forall t' : T' \bullet P \quad \text{as} \quad \forall t' : T^* \bullet R(t') \Rightarrow P$$
$$\exists t' : T' \bullet P \quad \text{as} \quad \exists t' : T^* \bullet R(t') \wedge P$$

Thus, the representation invariant may be assumed for any variable $t' : T'$ which is quantified universally, explicitly or implicitly, and must be proved for existentially quantified variables. Furthermore, it must be proved that the simulation f' of any abstract producer function, $f \in PRD_T$, respects the representation invariant: $\forall w' \bullet R(f'(w'))$, where R may be assumed to hold for any argument of type T'. (Automatic coercion to T' of the function value may be inhibited by means of the **qua**-notation as usual.)

EXAMPLE 5.62

We simulate the type **set** T as in example 5.60, but in order to improve the economy of the representation the concrete data space is chosen to be the set of T-sequences without repeated terms:

$$NorepSeq\{T\} == \{q : \text{seq } T \bullet \text{norep } q\}$$

The abstraction function and several concrete operators can be as before, but the representation of the abstract *add* must be a new function *add'* respecting the representation invariant. The function *sub'* may be simplified:

$$
\begin{aligned}
&\textbf{def } \; add'(q,x) \;\; == \;\; \textbf{if } x \, \textbf{in} \, q \textbf{ then } q \textbf{ else } q \vdash x \textbf{ fi qua } NorepSeq \\
&\textbf{def } \; sub'(q,x) \;\; == \;\; \textbf{case } q \textbf{ of } \varepsilon \rightarrow \varepsilon \mid q' \vdash y \rightarrow \\
&\qquad\qquad\qquad\qquad \textbf{if } x{=}y \textbf{ then } q' \textbf{ else } sub'(q',x) \vdash y \textbf{ fi fo} \\
&\qquad\qquad\qquad\qquad \textbf{qua } NorepSeq
\end{aligned}
$$

The equality representation may be given an independent, somewhat more evaluation efficient definition, cf. exercise 5.30 p. 211:

$$\textbf{def } \; q' \simeq r' == q' \textbf{ perm } r'$$

We now have to prove that the representation invariant is respected by all producers (the last two proofs are needed in order to justify inhibiting the coercion of the function values):

norep ε
norep $q \Rightarrow$ **norep** $add'(q, x)$
norep $q \Rightarrow$ **norep** $sub'(q, x)$

In addition proof of criterion (b) or of the translated abstract axioms must be carried out. The **norep** property may be assumed for sequence operands.

$\square$

Exercises

5.35 Prove the simulation indicated in example 5.62.

5.36 Assume that the type T is totally ordered, say by $<$. Design a simulation of **set** T as in example 5.61, but with the representation invariant $\not< q$ (repetition-free and sorted). Discuss the consequences of strengthening the representation invariant for the computational efficiency of the operations, including equality.

Discuss also the relative merits of introducing this simulation of **set** T on the one hand, and on the other using a semantic subtype of canonic sets as in example 5.48.

5.37 Show that the type $Stree\{T\}$ of example 5.52, extended with a suitably defined sub function, can be taken as a simulation of **set** T.

EXAMPLE 5.63
We may simulate natural numbers using sequences of bits, $\{0, 1\}$, interpreted as binary positional representations. We may thus achieve space and time efficiencies of logarithmic order. We express the simulation by first defining a subtype $BinPos$ of bit sequences, thereby also preparing for example 5.65 of the next subsection. ($BinPos$ itself, however, cannot be considered a correct simulation, because the defined abstraction function and equivalence relation are mutually inconsistent.)

For types $T, U \prec V$, where U is a syntactic subtype, we use the *ad hoc* notation T_U to denote that part of T which is contained in U:

type $BinPos$ $==$ **seq** $\{0, 1\}$
module
func $\mathcal{A}$: $BinPos \longrightarrow Nat$
def $\mathcal{A}(q) ==$ **case** q **of** $\varepsilon \to 0 \mid q \vdash d \to$
$\qquad\qquad$ **case** d **of** $0 \to 2 * \mathcal{A}(q) \mid 1 \to 2 * \mathcal{A}(q) + 1$ **fo fo**

func $\hat{} \simeq \hat{}$: $BinPos \times BinPos \longrightarrow Bool$
def $q \simeq r == q = r$

func $\mathbf{S}\hat{}$: $BinPos \longrightarrow BinPos_{\mathbf{seq1}}$

def   Sq ==   **case** q **of** $\varepsilon \to \langle 1 \rangle \mid q' \vdash d \to$
$\qquad\qquad$ **case** d **of** $0 \to q' \vdash 1 \mid 1 \to (\mathbf{S}q') \vdash 0$ **fo fo**

func $\hat{}+\hat{}$: $BinPos \times BinPos \longrightarrow BinPos$
def $q + r$ == **case** r **of** $\varepsilon \to q \mid r' \vdash d \to$
$\qquad\qquad$ **case** q **of** $\varepsilon \to r \mid q' \vdash c \to$
$\qquad\qquad\qquad$ **case** d **of** $0 \to (q' + r') \vdash c \mid 1 \to$
$\qquad\qquad\qquad\qquad$ **case** c **of** $0 \to (q' + r') \vdash 1$
$\qquad\qquad\qquad\qquad\qquad\qquad \mid 1 \to (\mathbf{S}(q' + r')) \vdash 0$ **fo fo fo fo**

func $\hat{}<\hat{}$, $\hat{}\leq\hat{}$, ... : $BinPos \times BinPos \longrightarrow Bool$
def $q < r$ == **case** r **of** $\varepsilon \to \mathbf{f} \mid r' \vdash d \to$
$\qquad\qquad$ **case** q **of** $\varepsilon \to \mathbf{t} \mid q' \vdash c \to$
$\qquad\qquad\qquad$ **case** (c, d) **of** $(0, 1) \to q' \leq r'$
$\qquad\qquad\qquad\qquad\qquad \mid$ **others** $\to q' < r'$ **fo fo fo**
def $q \leq r$ == $q < r \lor q = r$
$\quad \vdots$

endmodule

We may now define a complete (strong) simulation of *Nat* as a semantic subtype *BitNat* of *BinPos*. The representation invariant serves to optimize the usage of data space by avoiding leading zeros. Notice also that the restricted abstraction function is one-to-one. Thereby the defined representation of abstract equality is consistent in the subtype. The abstract subtypes *Zero* and *Nat1* are simulated by $BitNat_{Eseq}$ and $BitNat_{seq1}$, respectively:

type *BitNat* == $\{q : BinPos \bullet q \neq \varepsilon \Rightarrow lt(q) = 1\}$
module
lma $\mathbf{S}\hat{}$: $BitNat \longrightarrow BitNat_{seq1}$
lma $\hat{}+\hat{}$: $BitNat \times BitNat \longrightarrow BitNat$

The observer functions defined in *BinPos* may be inherited unchanged, whereas other producer representations, including constants, must be defined separately:

func P$\hat{}$: $BitNat_{seq1} \longrightarrow BitNat$ $\qquad\qquad\qquad$ (predecessor)
def   P$(q \vdash d)$ == **case** q **of** $\varepsilon \to \varepsilon \mid$ **others** $\to$
$\qquad\qquad\qquad$ **case** d **of** $0 \to (\mathbf{P}q) \vdash 1 \mid 1 \to q \vdash 0$ **fo fo qua** *BitNat*
func $0, 1, 2, \ldots :$ $\longrightarrow BitNat$
def $0 == \varepsilon$ **qua** *BitNat*
def $1 == \langle 1 \rangle$ **qua** *BitNat*
def $2 == \langle 1, 0 \rangle$ **qua** *BitNat*
$\quad \vdots$

endmodule

Notice that the representation invariant ensures that d is **1** in the case $q = \varepsilon$ in the definition of the predecessor operator. Compare the above definitions with those of example 5.65.

□

Exercises

5.38 Prove (semantically) the syntactic lemmas of type *BitNat*.

5.39 Define and prove efficient representations of the abstract operators $\hat{\;}\dot{-}\hat{\;}$ and $\hat{\;}*\hat{\;}$. Hint: The predecessor operator is useful for defining the former.

EXAMPLE 5.64
Define a type of sequences of given non-zero length:

> **type** $Seq\{n : Nat1,\ T\} == \{q : \textbf{seq1}\ T \cdot \#q = n\}$
>   **module func** $\hat{\;}[\hat{\;}] :\ Seq \times \{1..n\} \longrightarrow T$
>   **func** $\hat{\;}[\hat{\;} \mapsto \hat{\;}] :\ Seq \times \{1..n\} \times T \longrightarrow Seq$
>   (semantic definitions unaltered)
>   **endmodule**

(The syntactic redefinitions are illegal according to the rules laid down in section 5.7.1, in restricting the index argument to a subtype of *Nat1*; they may, however, be considered semantically acceptable because the original operators are ill-defined for indices greater than the length of the sequence argument.) We prove that the type $Seq\{n, T\}$ simulates a type of initialized maps, $Imap\{\{1..n\}, T\}$. Notice that the redefined domains of the two sequence operators are exactly those of the corresponding operators of these initialized maps. It follows from the original semantic definitions of the former that they are total on the restricted domains.

The abstraction function is not formally definable in terms of generator induction on sequences because the subtype considered is non-convex. We may, however, introduce a family of functions indexed by positive integers:

$$\mathcal{A}_n :\ Seq\{n, T\} \longrightarrow Imap\{\{1..n\}, T\}$$

The family may be defined by induction on n:

$$\mathcal{A}_1(\varepsilon \vdash x) \triangleq init(x)$$
$$\mathcal{A}_{\textbf{S}\#q}(q \vdash x) \triangleq \mathcal{A}_{\#q}(q)[\textbf{S}\#q \mapsto x], \qquad \text{for } q : \textbf{seq1}\ T$$

where the main operators of the right hand sides should be those of $Imap\{\{1..1\}, T\}$ and $Imap\{\{1..\textbf{S}\#q\}, T\}$, respectively.

   (Since $Imap\{\{1..\#q\}, T\} \prec Imap\{\{1..\textbf{S}\#q\}, T\}$, $\mathcal{A}_{\#q}(q)$ is an acceptable operand for the latter.)

It is fairly clear that $\mathcal{A}_n$ is a one-to-one function, which means that equality over $Imap\{\{1..n\}, T\}$ is simulated by equality over $Seq\{n, T\}$.

The textual translation rules shall be:

$$
\begin{array}{lll}
M = M' & \text{corresponds to} & q = q' \\
init(x) & \text{corresponds to} & x \uparrow n \\
M[i \mapsto x] & \text{corresponds to} & q[i \mapsto x] \\
M[i] & \text{corresponds to} & q[i]
\end{array}
$$

where $M = \mathcal{A}_n(q)$ and $M' = \mathcal{A}_n(q')$. It is easy to see directly that the concrete representations of the abstract generators span the whole concrete value space; we have for instance $q = (q[1] \uparrow n)[2 \mapsto q[2]] \ldots [n \mapsto q[n]]$ for arbitrary sequence q of length n. Thus the simulation is provable without using the formal definition of the abstraction function.

Equality over *Imap* is defined through an observation basis consisting of the map application operator $\char94[\char94]$:

$$ M = M' == \forall i : \{1..n\} \bullet M[i] = M'[i] $$

and this operator has the following **case**-free axioms:

$$
\begin{array}{ll}
init(x)[i] & == x \\
M[j \mapsto x][i] & == \textbf{if } i = j \textbf{ then } x \textbf{ else } M[i] \textbf{ fi}
\end{array}
$$

The translations are as follows, considering that all occurring functions are total:

$$
\begin{array}{ll}
(q = q') & = \forall i : \{1..n\} \bullet q[i] = q'[i] \\
(x \uparrow n)[i] & = x \\
q[j \mapsto x][i] & = \textbf{if } i = j \textbf{ then } x \textbf{ else } q[i] \textbf{ fi}
\end{array}
$$

where $q, q' : Seq\{n, T\}$, $i, j : \{1..n\}$, $x : T$. The first equation expresses the fact that the subscripting operation is an observation basis for sequences (cf. lemma S10 of section 5.8.8), and the second one is quite obvious. For the sake of demonstration we prove the last equation. Using the induction rules for **seq1** T and *Nat1* with respect to q, i and j, the following proof goal is obtained:

$$ (q \vdash y)[Sj \mapsto x][Si] = \textbf{if } i = j \textbf{ then } x \textbf{ else } (q \vdash y)[Si] \textbf{ fi} $$

for $q : \textbf{seq } T$, $i, j : Nat$. In view of the semantic subtype restrictions we may assume $i, j \leq \#q$. We use available axioms for rewriting the left and right hand sides:

$$
\begin{array}{rl}
\text{LHS} \;\; \xrightarrow{\char94[\char94]} & \textbf{if } j = \#q \textbf{ then } q \vdash x \textbf{ else } q[Sj \mapsto x] \vdash y \textbf{ fi}[Si] \\[4pt]
\xrightarrow{\;\textbf{if}\;} & \textbf{if } j = \#q \textbf{ then } (q \vdash x)[Si] \textbf{ else } (q[Sj \mapsto x] \vdash y)[Si] \textbf{ fi} \\[4pt]
\xrightarrow{\char94[\char94]} & \textbf{if } j = \#q \textbf{ then if } i = \#q \textbf{ then } x \textbf{ else } q[Si] \textbf{ fi else} \\
& \qquad \textbf{if } i = \#q \textbf{ then } y \textbf{ else } q[Sj \mapsto x][Si] \textbf{ fi fi} \\[6pt]
\text{RHS} \;\; \xrightarrow{\char94[\char94]} & \textbf{if } i = j \textbf{ then } x \textbf{ else if } i = \#q \textbf{ then } y \textbf{ else } q[Si] \textbf{ fi fi}
\end{array}
$$

where the lemma $\#q[k \mapsto x] = \#q$ has been used in the last LHS derivation step. We consider two exhaustive cases.

Case $q=\varepsilon$: Then $\#q=i=j=0$ and LHS=RHS=x.

Case $q\neq\varepsilon$: Then, according to SGIND$_{\textbf{seq1}}$ T, the induction hypothesis for q may be assumed, giving

$$\text{LHS} \xrightarrow{\text{IH}q} \text{if } j=\#q \text{ then if } i=\#q \text{ then } x \text{ else } q[\text{S}i] \text{ fi else}$$
$$\text{if } i=\#q \text{ then } y \text{ else if } i=j \text{ then } x \text{ else } q[\text{S}i] \text{ fi fi fi}$$

Now we can prove LHS = RHS by considering five exhaustive cases:

$$
\begin{array}{llll}
j=\#q, & i=\#q, & i=j & \text{give LHS} = \text{RHS} = x \\
j=\#q, & i\neq\#q, & i\neq j & \text{give LHS} = \text{RHS} = q[\text{S}i] \\
j\neq\#q, & i=\#q, & i\neq j & \text{give LHS} = \text{RHS} = y \\
j\neq\#q, & i\neq\#q, & i=j & \text{give LHS} = \text{RHS} = x \\
j\neq\#q, & i\neq\#q, & i\neq j & \text{give LHS} = \text{RHS} = q[\text{S}i]
\end{array}
$$

□

5.9.1 Weak simulation

Since computers are finite state machines, it is useful to introduce the idea of *weak simulation*, where only a subset of the possibly infinite abstract space is actually represented. We may choose to accomplish a weak simulation of T by T' in two steps:

1. defining a suitably restricted semantic subtype $\bar{T} = \{x : t \bullet R\}$, assumed to be convex, such that every T-function to be simulated is restricted by replacing any occurrence of T in its profile by $\bar{T}$,
2. simulating the type $\bar{T}$ by T' (strongly).

The semantic consequence of restricting a T-function f as in step 1, is as described in section 5.7.1, i.e. the original semantic definitions are retained, except that coercion to $\bar{T}$ is applied to the function values of producers (and to arguments if necessary). Thus the corresponding $\bar{T}$-function $\bar{f}$ is an approximation to the former, $\bar{f} \sqsubseteq f$. Notice that the defining T-axioms are not affected, in particular, applications of T-functions occurring in these axioms refer to the unrestricted functions. (If any intermediate T-results violating the restriction occurs during function evaluation, it should be regarded as a consequence of a particular constructive function realization and not as an intrinsic property of the function.)

As we shall see, the subtype $\bar{T}$ can itself be seen as a weak simulation of T, using the identity function for $\bar{T}$ as the abstraction function and the restricted T-functions as the concrete representations, provided that all applications of T-functions in the axioms for these functions are (or could be) replaced by applications of the restricted ones. Furthermore "simulates" is a transitive relation on types. More precisely: If T' simulates $\bar{T}$ strongly and $\bar{T}$ simulates T weakly, then T' simulates T weakly.

EXAMPLE 5.65

We sketch a weak simulation *TenBitNat* of *Nat* by 10-digit binary representations:

$$\textbf{type } TenBitNat == \{q : \textbf{seq1 } \{0,1\} \bullet \#q = 10\}$$

With the abstraction function $\mathcal{A}(q) = \sum\limits_{i \, \epsilon \, \{1..10\}} 2^{10-i} * q[i]$ (interpreting bits as the integers 0 and 1 respectively) the simulated subtype of *Nat* is the interval type $\{0 .. 1023\}$. Thus, our weak simulation of *Nat* may be seen as a strong simulation of that subtype with restricted arithmetic operators. The abstraction function is clearly total and one-to-one. The translated abstract restriction, $0 \le x \le 1023$, states that *TenBitNat* values should be less than or equal to $\langle 1,1,1,1,1,1,1,1,1, 1 \rangle$, which holds strongly. (Notice that the abstractly equivalent predicate $x < 1024$ would translate to an ill-defined expression.) We do not bother to define subtypes of *TenBitNat* corresponding to those of *Nat* (they would have to be semantic subtypes).

As planned in example 5.63 of the last section, we may define *TenBitNat* as a semantic subtype of *BinPos* defined there. In this case, however, the codomains of the operators $\textbf{S}\hat{\,}$ and $\hat{\,}+\hat{\,}$ must be explicitly restricted. It may be shown that these operators, restricted to arguments of length 10 return values of the same length, except if overflow occurs, in which case the result is of length 11. The test for overflow will thus be realized through implicit coercion of the function value. As in the above example, the observer functions of *BinPos* may be inherited unchanged, whereas other producer functions must be defined separately, including numerals. Notice the different **P**-operator (that of example 5.63 would return a sequence of length 9 for any power of 2 represented in 10 bits):

type *TenBitNat* == $\{q : BinPos \bullet \#q = 10\}$
module
func S$\hat{\,}$: *TenBitNat* $\longrightarrow$ *TenBitNat*
func $\hat{\,}+\hat{\,}$: *TenBitNat* $\times$ *TenBitNat* $\longrightarrow$ *TenBitNat*

func P$\hat{\,}$: *TenBitNat* $\longrightarrow$ *TenBitNat*
def Pq == **case** q **of** $\varepsilon \to \perp \mid q' \vdash d \to$
        case d **of** $0 \to (\textbf{P}q') \vdash 1 \mid 1 \to q' \vdash 0$ **fo fo qua** *TenBitNat*

func $0, 1, 2, \ldots, 1023 : \longrightarrow$ *TenBitNat*
def 0   == $\langle 0,0,0,0,0,0,0,0,0,0 \rangle$ **qua** *TenBitNat*
def 1   == $\langle 0,0,0,0,0,0,0,0,0,1 \rangle$ **qua** *TenBitNat*
def 2   == $\langle 0,0,0,0,0,0,0,0,1,0 \rangle$ **qua** *TenBitNat*

$\vdots$

def 1023 == $\langle 1,1,1,1,1,1,1,1,1,1 \rangle$ **qua** *TenBitNat*
endmodule

Notice that expressions of the abstract type *Nat* occur in the definition of *TenBit-Nat* (in the representation invariant). This indicates that one must be prepared to deal with programs containing more than one realization of the same concept.

□

Exercises

5.40   Carry out the proof obligations associated with the assertion that *TenBitNat* strongly simulates the type $\{n: Nat \bullet n \leq 1023\}$. Assume an abstract predecessor operator defined as follows:

> **func Pˆ** : *Nat1* ⟶ *Nat*
> **def   PS**x == x

5.41   Define and prove representations of the abstract operators ˆ∗ˆ and ˆ∸ˆ.

Weak simulation in two steps, as described above, provides full control of the definedness aspect of concrete representation functions. It happens, however, that one may have to settle for less, not knowing the exact definedness conditions for the concrete operators, and perhaps not the actual subset of abstract values simulated. The reason may be that these conditions are too expensive to define and prove, or that they are not even *expressible* in abstract terms.

As a trivially simple example of the latter situation, consider the **set** concept simulated as in example 5.65, but with sequences of length $n : Nat1$ or less. A "maximal" simulated set may have any number of elements between 1 and n. It is easy to think of cases where complete definedness control is impractical, even if possible in principle, for instance the condition that an arbitrary program in a given high level language, simulated on a given computer, would run out of available memory.

In such situations we cannot require that the concrete producers are representations in the strong sense. Thus, criterion (b) for simulation of T by T' (p. 220) is weakened as follows.

(b′)   There is a total function $\mathcal{A} : T' \to T$ such that for every $f \in F_T$:

$$\forall w' : \text{domain of } f' \bullet \begin{cases} \mathcal{A}(f'(w')) \sqsubseteq f(w), & \text{for } f \in PRD_T \\ f'(w') \sqsubseteq f(w), & \text{for } f \in OBS_T \end{cases}$$

where the argument list w is obtained from w' by replacing any component $x' : T'$ in w' by $\mathcal{A}(x')$.

As before, T is assumed to be convex. Assume for simplicity that T is also unrestricted, and that all of T' is reachable through abstract producer representations and is convex with respect to the generator representations. Then the abstraction function exists and is total, and generator induction over V_T carries over directly to the set $V_{T'} / \simeq^{T'}$.

Some abstract functions may be *strongly represented* for a given weak simulation, in the sense that the original (b)-criteria hold for them. In principle any observer function is strongly representable, and the same is true for certain producers, e.g. those computing subterms of given abstract values. It is reasonable to require the abstract equality to be strongly represented, which means that the representation $\simeq$ should be strict and total on $T' \times T'$.

Notice that the coercion function $\hat{} \, \mathbf{as} \, T$ may be represented by $\hat{} \, \mathbf{as} \, T'$, whereas the type membership test $\hat{} \, \mathbf{isa} \, T$ can only be represented by $\hat{} \, \mathbf{isa} \, T'$ if T' strongly simulates T. The meta-notation d_e is not translatable to $d_{e'}$ unless the expression e is strongly represented by e' (the notation stands for some ordinary formula, however, which will be translatable as usual). Since strong (non-strict) equality is expressed in terms of definedness, it cannot in general be directly translated.

Consider a translatable formula P containing subterms of type T. Let P' be the translation of P, obtained in a sequence of steps of types 1 and 2 above:

$$P = P_0 \rightarrow P_1 \rightarrow \cdots \rightarrow P_n = P', \quad \text{for } n \geq 1$$

If P_{i+1} is obtained from P_i by replacing x by $\mathcal{A}(x')$, then $P_{i+1} == P_i$, provided x is free in P and $x == \mathcal{A}(x')$, and if P_{i+1} is obtained by using the (b')-criterion for a function f, then $P_{i+1} \sqsubseteq P_i$, provided that all functions occurring further out in P_i are monotonic with respect to definedness (strong equality is not!). We may conclude by transitivity that P' approximates P:

$$P' \sqsubseteq P, \quad \text{i.e.} \quad d_{P'} \Rightarrow d_P \wedge P' = P$$

provided no T-quantification occurs in P, the values of free T- and T'-variables correspond, and all occurring functions are monotonic with respect to definedness. Since there may be T-values which have no representation in T', we may also conclude:

$$d_{\forall x':T' \bullet P'} \Rightarrow d_{\forall x:T \bullet P} \wedge ((\forall x : T \bullet P) \Rightarrow \forall x' : T' \bullet P'), \quad \text{and}$$
$$d_{\exists x':T' \bullet P'} \Rightarrow d_{\exists x:T \bullet P} \wedge ((\exists x' : T' \bullet P') \Rightarrow \exists x : T \bullet P)$$

for P, P' as before, and $y = \mathcal{A}(y')$ for any remaining free T-variable y. Notice that any formula containing quantifiers can be written in a form such that all quantifiers occur in an initial sequence. The above results can be generalized to formulas whose initial quantifier sequence contains any number of universal T-quantifiers or any number of existential ones (irrespective of quantifiers over other types). However, if the sequence contains a mixture of universal and existential T-quantifiers, then definedness of the translated formula in general only implies the definedness of the abstract formula.

Assume now, in addition to the assumptions above, that all abstract function definitions are constructive strong equalities, terminating if recursive (not necessarily in the TGI sense). Then, in order to verify all of the (b')-criteria, it is sufficient to prove the following "translation" of each abstract axiom $f(\text{args}) == e$:

$$d_{f'(\text{args}')} \Rightarrow d_{e'} \wedge (f'(\text{args}') \approx e'),$$

where $\approx$ as usual stands for $\simeq$ or $=$ depending on the type of the operands, and where the representation invariant, if any, may be assumed for any T'-term occurring among the left hand arguments.

This claim is justified by the following fact. Let $f(x) == e$ satisfy the above assumptions. Then any function f' satisfying $f'(x) \sqsubseteq e_{f'}^{f}$ is an approximation to f, $f' \sqsubseteq f$. This is provable for arbitrary argument x by induction on the depth of recursion. The argument may be generalized to account for inductive function definitions as well as the presence of an abstraction function.

If all functions occurring in the right hand side e are strongly represented, then proving

$$f'(\text{args}') == \textbf{if } d_{\text{indargs}'} \textbf{ then } e' \textbf{ else } \bot \textbf{ fi}$$

(for each **case**-free f'-axiom), where indargs' is the list of translated generator expressions in the left hand side, is sufficient to show that f is strongly represented as well.

Chapter 6

Classes and Objects

In the preceding chapter formulas and other expressions were primarily regarded as representations of values, subject to simplification by substitution of equals for equals and to other kinds of reasoning. The fact that the inductive definition style may be implemented directly as an applicative programming language was of secondary concern. Now we return to the paradigm of imperative programming which offers more direct control over computer resources, with respect to processing time and the use of storage space. In particular, we consider imperative techniques for the manipulation of data structures.

6.1 Object Classes

A typical imperative language contains an applicative sub-language which approximates the mathematical abstractions of "timeless" functions applied to "spaceless" values, where the actual operation sequences and use of storage space during expression evaluation are organized behind the scenes. In this setting, values are data structures of low volume, typically a few computer words or less, which means that an illusion of spacelessness can be realized by having intermediate results during expression evaluation stored at the discretion of the language implementation, and effecting parameter transmission and assignment operations through value copying.

It is clear, however, that values such as sequences and trees, whether implemented as basic expressions represented directly, or using less storage demanding techniques, are potentially high-volume data objects. In general therefore, one cannot afford to maintain the illusion of spacelessness when dealing with values of such kinds. In particular, the programmer must be given the opportunity, and responsibility, of controlling the introduction of these data objects and to refer to them by name as individuals. Such a name, often called a *pointer*, may be realized technically as a *memory address* identifying the storage area in which the object resides. Parameter transmission of objects and assignment operations can then be efficiently implemented through the copying of pointers, which are low-volume items.

It is impractical to insist that any high volume data object, once introduced, should remain an immutable value, to be thrown away whenever a change has to occur. It is usually possible to arrange computations in such a way that large data structures are updated *in small steps*. Thus, it is important that high-volume objects should behave as a kind of generalized *program variable* whose value, or "state", can be built up and changed by piecemeal incremental modification.

We therefore introduce a concept of *object class*, or simply "class", intended to be the analogue in the imperative paradigm of the applicative/mathematical concept of "value type". The corresponding analogue of a "typed value" is called a *class object*, or simply an "object" if confusion with the non-technical term is unlikely. Classes and types are intended to be exchangeable syntactic categories (but a few restrictions will be necessary). A variable or an expression is said to be "type-like" if it represents a typed value, and "class-like" if it represents a class object. A class declaration is similar to that of a type, except that the initial keyword is **class**, not **type**, and that imperative language constructs may occur in class modules.

The differences between values and objects may be summarized as follows:

- Values are mathematically defined entities realized through immutable data items (such as the number 3, which is a permanent, timeless concept).
- Objects are stored data structures subject to change, probably accessed indirectly through pointers, and transmitted and assigned through pointer copying. The generator functions introduce new objects and pointers to them.

It may be noticed that since values are immutable it does not matter to the logic of the program whether they are accessed and manipulated directly, or indirectly through pointers. On the other hand the combination of pointer copying and internal change may create very serious problems for the logic of assignment operations. This is due to problems of aliasing which are rather more difficult to combat than those considered in chapter 4.

Looking back to the example given at the beginning of chapter 5 it is reasonable to treat stacks of integers as objects subject to incremental updating by *push* and *pop* operations. For that reason the stack concept could be modelled as a class:

class *STACK{T}* **by** *ESTACK*, *STACK1* $==$
module
func *estack* : $\longrightarrow$ *ESTACK*
func *push* : *STACK* $\times$ *T* $\longrightarrow$ *STACK1*
1-1 genbas *estack*, *push*

func *top* : *STACK1* $\longrightarrow$ *T*
def $top(push(S, x)) == x$

func *pop* : *STACK1* ⟶ *STACK*
def *pop(push(S, x)) == S*
endmodule

Let **var** S : $STACK\{Int\}$ = $push(push(estack, 3), 5)$. The corresponding data configuration may be pictured as in figure 6.1. (An implementation could omit the *estack*-object and represent it by a "null-pointer". There can be no point in distinguishing between different occurrences of *estack*-objects; they are empty data structures.)

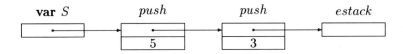

Figure 6.1

The operation $S := push(S, 17)$ changes the configuration to that of figure 6.2. Notice that only one *push*-object is generated. It is given copies of the two parameters, the value 17 and the pointer which resided in S. Any data structure pointed to from within an object is considered logically *part of the object*. Thus, the new *push*-object logically represents the entire extended stack, which contains the previous one as a sub-structure.

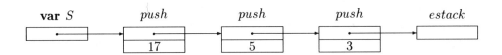

Figure 6.2

This example demonstrates a case where the required operations are realized with good efficiency through the use of pointers alone; there is no need so far to update objects internally. For instance, popping the stack S, $S := pop(S)$, requires two pointer accesses and one pointer assignment (plus a possible overhead for transmitting information to and from a function, and some for the retrieval of the storage space of a small data record left inaccessible.) The resulting configuration is shown in figure 6.3.

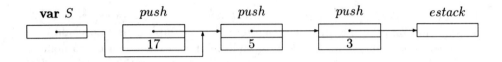

Figure 6.3

But see what happens if we have to append objects at the other end of the stack in order to implement a first in first out queuing discipline:

func enq : $STACK \times T \longrightarrow STACK1$
def $enq(S, x) ==$ **case** S **of** $estack \rightarrow push(S, x)$
                                    $\mid push(S', y) \rightarrow push(enq(S', x), y)$ **fo**

As a result of the recursion an extended *STACK*-object is recreated from scratch using new *push*-records. (Remember that *push* is a generator function, so every application of it results in the generation of a new record.) If the result is assigned back to S, the old stack becomes garbage.

We need a new mechanism in our programming language in order to enable object states to be updated internally. Our proposed mechanism is to define variables introduced in **case** discriminators to be *assignable program variables*, provided that the discriminand is a class-like variable, excepting formal **val** parameters. The purpose of the exception is to prevent "side effects" on class-like actual **val** parameters to procedures, implemented through pointer copying.

Thus, the assignment to Y in   **case** X **of** $g(\ldots, Y, \ldots) \rightarrow Y := e \mid \ldots$ **fo** updates the component Y of the object X, given that the latter is of the form $g(\ldots, Y, \ldots)$. In order to make sense logically, the assignment to an object component must be understood to have the side effect of a corresponding assignment to the object variable. Therefore, the assignment to Y should be interpreted as if followed immediately by the assignment $X := g(\ldots, Y, \ldots)$ to the discriminant (but since this does not actually happen, no new g-object will be generated). If X in turn is an object component introduced in a syntactically enclosing discrimination on a class-like variable, a succeeding assignment to the latter must be imagined, and so forth.

EXAMPLE 6.1
Let S be as in figure 6.1. The **case**-construct

   case S **of** $push(S', x) \rightarrow S' := push(S', 17) \mid \ldots$ **fo**

changes the stack S by inserting the number 17 as element number 2. This is achieved through updating the pointer sitting in the object containing the top element, 5. Thus, the result is as shown in figure 6.2, but with the numbers 5 and 17 interchanged.

□

With this new convention the enqueuing operation defined above can be realized more efficiently as an updating procedure:

proc *ENQ*(**var** $S : STACK$, **val** $x : T$) ==
    case S **of** *estack* $\rightarrow S := push(S, x)$ | $push(S', y) \rightarrow$ **call** $ENQ(S', x)$ **fo**

Here only one *push*-operation is needed, but it is necessary to search for the far end of the stack.

Consider the case where the stacked items are high-volume structures modelled as objects of a class C. Let **var** $S : STACK\{C\}$ and **var** $X : C$. (It is practical to allow the class $STACK$ to be parameterized by classes as well as types.) If, at some time, we push the object (pointed to by) X onto S, $S := push(S, X)$, then the resulting data configuration will be as shown in figure 6.4. Notice the two pointers converging on the leftmost C-object. They represent different access paths to that object, which implies that X and $top(S)$ are now *aliases*. Consequently, an operation such as **call** $upd(X)$, updating the state of the C-object X, has a *side effect on the variable* S; indeed the value of $obs(top(S))$, where *obs* is a C-observer, may change.

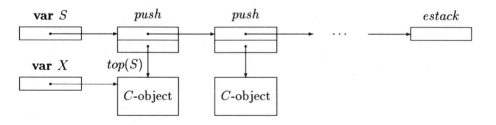

Figure 6.4

Pointer convergence occurs as the result of pointer assingment, explicit, or implicit through parameter passing. However, not all converging pointers in an implemented data structure are dangerous; they must also be *accessible* in order to lead to aliasing. For instance, the converging pointers in figure 6.3 are harmless since one of the two is inaccessible. As another example, consider a procedure p with an object parameter implemented through pointer copying. Let the formal parameter be X and let the variable V be the corresponding actual parameter of a call for p. Then, during the activation, V and X are stored pointers converging on the same object, but only the latter is accessible (provided that direct reference to non-local variables is not allowed in procedures).

The logic of internal object updating, which is sometimes mandatory for efficiency reasons, can be very complicated indeed if there is a danger of aliasing caused by converging object pointers. In order to make programming easier there is a need for styles which will prevent such aliasing, or at least reduce the resulting logical difficulties as much as possible. Unfortunately, in practice one has to reason about programs (formally or otherwise) which cannot be assumed to be error-free, for the purpose of debugging or in trying to prove correctness. This means that any programming style intended to simplify the logic of programs must be enforced by syntactic checks in order to be really useful; otherwise the general logic would in any event have to be pessimistic and cater for all the difficulties that might possibly be caused by object aliases. (Notice that strong typing contributes to reducing these difficulties: pointers are ensured to refer to objects of given classes, which means that expressions of disjoint classes can never be aliases.)

How then can one achieve the stacking of the C-object X onto S without creating an alias? A possible solution is to "forget" X while stacking it, by assigning another object to X simultaneously. A way to ensure that the second assignment does not in turn create an alias is to introduce a *new object*. Now, constant generators are cheap to implement (cf. the comment above on the possible implementation of *estack* activations), so if the assignment to X has no other purpose than to prevent aliasing, one might use a constant C-generator if there is one, say *nil*. Thus, the simultaneous assignments $S, X := push(S, X), nil$ achieve the stacking while causing no alias. Notice that the *push*-operation will not by itself create pointer convergence, provided that its two arguments are *disjoint data structures*, whereas, for instance, the result of $push(S, top(S))$ does contain two pointers to a substructure, as shown in figure 6.5.

Remark

It is not uncommon for the pointer concepts provided in programming languages to include an *ad hoc* null-value for pointers of all types, meaning "pointer to nothing". We have now seen two ways in which null-pointers are useful: to terminate recursion in data structures (such as *estack*), and to combat aliasing (such as *nil*). We may also add a third one: assigning null to a pointer variable is a safe way to get rid of data structures no longer needed, thereby freeing memory space for other usage, given that the language implementation includes a "garbage collection" mechanism. However, the possibility

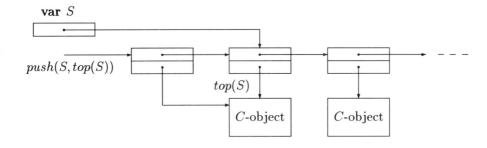

var S

$push(S, top(S))$

$top(S)$

C-object

C-object

Figure 6.5

of null-values for all pointers calls for a constant checking overhead (an implied **case**-test). In the present framework, constant generators can play the role of null-objects whenever needed. In those cases where null-objects are not needed there will be no checking overhead at all, and otherwise run-time checks can sometimes be replaced by textual type checking, by taking advantage of syntactic sub-classes (such as *STACK1*).

The notion of data disjointness referred to above is an important semantic relation on objects: two objects are disjoint if and only if no object is part of both. We also define a syntactic version of the concept, which applies to expressions:

1. Two variable occurrences are disjoint, except if both are class-like, and one is a component of the other or they are occurrences of the same variable. (This is a syntactic check, except possibly if the two occurrences are subscripted variables from the same sequence (array) and the subscripts are syntactically different.)

2. Let $\mathcal{CV}[e]$ be the set of variables occurring in the expression e, outside any type-like (sub-)expression of e, counting syntactically different subscripted variables as distinct members of the set. Then two expressions e_1 and e_2 are disjoint iff all pairs of variables, one from $\mathcal{CV}[e_1]$ and one from $\mathcal{CV}[e_2]$, are disjoint. (In particular, any two expressions are disjoint unless both are class-like.)

For programs satisfying certain syntactic checks, such as those listed below, it can be shown that any two disjoint class-like expressions at any time evaluate to objects which are semantically disjoint. Notice that the disjointness check on expressions is fully syntactic, except possibly when subscripted variables occur.

Consider now the operation of unstacking a class-object from $S : STACK\{C\}$ and naming it $X : C$, using the functions *pop* and *top*. As we have seen, the assignment to S causes no problem, but the assignment $X := top(S)$ must be considered illegal by itself since it leads to a configuration like that of figure 6.4 with convergent accessible pointers. Again the mechanism of simultaneous assignment offers a solution: The statement $S, X := pop(S), top(S)$ is safe, because the two right hand expressions denote disjoint objects.

In the present case a semantic analysis is required to prove the disjointness. It can, however, be made syntactically manifest by introducing the composite function *poptop*:

> **func** $poptop : STACK1\{C\} \longrightarrow STACK\{C\} \times C$
> **def** $poptop(push(s, x)) == (s, x)$

We shall assume inductively that the arguments to any application of *push* are disjoint; then the same is true for the components of the *poptop* result. Consequently the assignment $(S, X) := poptop(S)$ is alias-safe.

An assignment to a class-like variable X in general may produce convergent accessible pointers if the right hand side contains class-like variables other than X, such as for example $X := Y$, where Y is a variable. However, the occurrence of X or a component of X in the right hand side does not cause problems. For instance, the assignment to X in **case** X **of** $g(Y) \rightarrow X := Y \mid \ldots$ **fo** reduces the object by taking away a g-record. Neither can any assignment of the form $X := f(X)$ lead to alias, provided that the function f itself is alias-safe. This follows by observing that the only applicative basic operations available on objects are component selection and embedding in generators (whose arguments are assumed to be disjoint), and setting up a pointer to a newly generated object cannot cause aliasing.

It follows by inductive reasoning that the following requirements are sufficient to guarantee the absence of alias caused by pointers. It is assumed for simplicity that neither functions nor procedures refer directly to non-local class-like variables.

1. The arguments of any function application must be pairwise disjoint. The same is required of the components of any tuple and of the individual right hand sides of a multiple assignment statement.

2. Let LHS and RHS be the complete left and right hand sides of a possibly multiple assignment statement. Then the LHS variables must be pairwise disjoint and every member of $CV[\text{RHS}]$ must occur in the LHS or be a component of a variable occurring in the LHS. If the assignment occurs immediately prior to leaving the scope of a local variable or formal **val** parameter, that variable or parameter is also allowed to occur in $CV[\text{RHS}]$.

3. The parameters of a procedure call must in general be pairwise disjoint, and the **val** parameters may contain no class-like variables outside type-like (sub-)expressions. However, any variable whose scope is terminating (cf. requirement 2) may occur, as long as disjointness is not violated. If all **var** parameters are type-like no restriction at all is necessary.

These restrictions can be enforced by syntactic checks, except that the occurrence of subscripted variables (cf. section 6.2) may require semantic reasoning on subscript values. Notice that formal parameters of both kinds count as variables with respect to restriction 2, but since **var** parameters are aliases for non-local variables these should not count as local ones.

An assignment to an object component **case** X **of** $g(Y) \rightarrow Y := e \mid \ldots$ **fo** is subject to the same checks as any other assignment. (Notice that the imagined subsequent side effect, $X := g(Y)$, passes the checks since Y is a component of X.) If e contains X the statement is not acceptable, because X and Y are distinct variables and X is not a component of Y. The assignment $Y := X$ would actually create a pointer cycle accessible through X, and consequent aliasing. Any swap operation is harmless, however, even if the two variables are not disjoint; thus no restriction is called for. (Try it!)

Restriction 3 is explained by noting that the effect of a procedure invocation **call** $p(e, v)$, where e is the list of actual **val** parameters and v is the list of actual **var** parameters, is that of a simultaneous assignment of the form $v := f(e, v)$. The resulting right hand tuple is considered class-like if there are class-like components. If so, requirement 1 implies pairwise disjointness of all actual parameters, and requirement 2 restricts $\mathcal{CV}[e]$ as stated because all **var** parameters already occur as arguments to f. Notice that the effect function in general has the form of a tuple with one component for each **var** parameter. We may be assured that the component expressions are mutually disjoint in terms of the formal parameters on the assumption that the procedure body does not generate aliases. Then, since the actual parameters are disjoint, these component expressions must also be disjoint in terms of the variables occurring in the actual parameters.

The requirement on actual **val** parameters is very restrictive. For instance, an invocation of the procedure ENQ above, say **call** $ENQ(S, X)$, does not pass the check if X is a class-like variable (and it does cause pointer confluence!). It would therefore be useful to combine the call with an assignment statement performed "simultaneously", so that the combined multiple assignments will pass the alias preventing checks, say **call** $ENQ(S, X)$ **and** $X := nil$, using an *ad hoc* syntax.

The absence of aliasing implies that the pointers occurring in the implementation of programs containing classes are entirely transparent, in the sense that *the semantics of the program are exactly as if all classes were interpreted as types* (except that any assignment to a component of a variable would then be illegal and must be reinterpreted as an assignment to the latter). For that reason we use similar syntax for class-like and type-like entities.

The value space of a variable of a class C is the type T_C, called the *type equivalent* of C, obtained by replacing the initial keyword **class** of its definition by **type**, replacing any class occurring in the definition by its type equivalent, and replacing procedures by the corresponding strong effect functions. The right hand side of a class definition is allowed to be a type, say **class** $C == T$ (or T may occur as the module prefix of a class module). If so, T is the type equivalent of C. It is useful in that case to have automatic coercion from C to T. Coercion the other way is more problematic, and classes should not be allowed to occur in type definitions, nor as actual parameters in type expressions.

EXAMPLE 6.2
We define an imperative version of the search tree concept of example 5.52, with operations for the insertion and the removal of elements. The latter may be type-like as well as class-like:

> **class** $STREE\{T\} == Stree\{T\}$
> **module**
> **proc** $INS(\textbf{var } S : STREE, \textbf{val } x : T) ==$
>   **case** S **of** $nil \rightarrow S := tree(nil, x, nil) \mid tree(L, v, R) \rightarrow$
>   **if** $x < v$ **then call** $INS(L, x)$ **else**
>   **if** $v < x$ **then call** $INS(R, x)$ **else skip fi fi fo**
>
> **proc** $REM(\textbf{var } S : STREE, \textbf{val } x : T) ==$
>   **case** S **of** $nil \rightarrow$ **skip** $\mid tree(L, v, R) \rightarrow$
>   **if** $x < v$ **then call** $REM(L, x)$ **else**
>   **if** $v < x$ **then call** $REM(R, x)$ **else**
>   **case** R **of** $nil \rightarrow S := L \mid$ **others** $\rightarrow$
>   **call** $MOVMIN(R, v)$ **fo fi fi fo**
>
> **proc** $MOVMIN(\textbf{var } R : STREE1, \ v : T) ==$
>   **case** R **of** $tree(RL, Rv, RR) \rightarrow$
>   **case** RL **of** $nil \rightarrow R := RR; \ v :=: Rv \mid$ **others** $\rightarrow$
>   **call** $MOVMIN(RL, v)$ **fo fo**
> **endmodule**

Here $STREE1$ stands for the subtype of non-empty search trees. The swap operation $v :=: Rv$ is necessary in order to pass the alias checks if T is a class; logically the assignment $v := Rv$ would be sufficient.

All functions associated with the type $Stree$ are inherited by the $STREE$ class and may be applied to $STREE$ arguments (which may in fact be transmitted by pointer in an implementation without harming the program logic).

□

Exercises

6.1 Show that the procedure ENQ has the effect function enq, where both are defined above.

6.2 Define and validate effect functions for the procedures of $STREE$.

6.2   Arrays

The concepts arrays and subscripted variables are very important in imperative programming because the operation of subscripting (indexing) may be implemented with extreme efficiency on standard hardware. In fact, a random access memory *is* an array, and, provided user defined arrays have *fixed sizes*, the available memory can be fully utilized by means of simple storage allocation strategies for permanent data or last-in-first-out stacks of procedure and function invocations, as for programs in Algol-like languages.

There are several ways of formalizing the notion of arrays of n elements of type T. A very natural one would be to see it as a Cartesian product with n components, i.e. as T^n. This would, however, require the introduction of a fundamentally new operator on types: the exponentiation operator. We feel quite strongly about keeping the set of basic mechanisms of a formal language as small as possible, and therefore prefer to define new concepts in terms of existing ones if possible, and in the case of arrays there are already two good candidates. Notice that access to a tuple component in general must be by name in a strongly typed language, not by computed number, in order that its type be textually well-defined. Therefore T^n is not a simple generalization of the Cartesian product mechanism in our framework.

We may see an array as a *mapping* from a given integer interval to the element type, or as a *sequence* of the given length, and the choice between these views is to some extent a matter of taste. The former has the advantage that an assignment operation to a subscripted variable, $A[i] := e$, corresponds for reasoning purposes to an application of a generator, $A := A[i \mapsto e]$. But sequences have a one-to-one generator basis and therefore an equality relation better suited for manipulation by term rewriting. Yet, our main reason for choosing the latter view may be a feeling that the sequence concept corresponds well to the idea of an updatable data structure, whereas mappings are applicative by nature. Anyway, we have shown earlier that initialized maps from integer intervals may be strongly simulated by sequences, see example 5.64 p. 229.

Arrays should be considered class-like since they are incrementally updatable and potentially high-volume. For simplicity we require indexing with lower bound 1 for all arrays. Then the array concept can (almost) be defined in terms of the sequence type in a very simple way:

class array T $==$ **seq** T

Thus an array is an object whose state (or "contents") is a sequence value. Strictly speaking, the definition would imply that the operation of subscripting applied to an array A is nothing but an observer function providing access to element values, as defined in section 5.8.8. However, we wish nevertheless to treat $A[i]$ as an assignable individual variable for legal subscript i. Fortunately this piece of *ad hoc*'ery has no consequence for our applicative formula language. The consequences for the logic of assignments and procedure calls are discussed in sections 4.3.3 and 4.6. (Notice that predicates of the form $i \epsilon A.ix$ should be interpreted as $1 \leq i \leq \#A$ for any array A.)

Many traditional programming languages forbid assignments to an array as a whole; as a consequence the size of any array remains constant during its scope, as the language implementor would like it to. We comply with that tradition to the extent that assignments to array variables are forbidden in the programming language proper. In particular, although array variables are class-like, no assignment by pointer copying is available. Consequently, we may take the expression $\#A$, for array A, to be a constant by definition.

Our treatment of arrays requires any array variable to be initialized at the time of declaration. The mandatory initializing expression, which is of sequence type, will determine the size of the array as well as its initial contents. In the following examples only expressions of the form $e \uparrow n$, replicating the value of e n times, are used for array initialization. Some languages or language implementations may require the length of the initializing sequence to be textually manifest, others may not.

Example: The declaration **var** $A : $ **array** $Nat = 0 \uparrow 10$ corresponds to the more traditional notation **var** $A : $ **array** $1 : 10$ **of** Nat (as, for instance, in Pascal), except that all elements are initialized to 0.

Since arrays are class-like, all array parameters are transmitted by pointer. In analogy with other class-like parameters, the components of an array **val** parameter should not be updatable. Thereby, unwanted side effects are prevented. Notice that the length of any array is accessible through the #-notation. Thus, no additional parameters are needed for defining the set of legal indices for the array.

So far the only kind of array expressions provided are variable occurrences. It may be useful to introduce also a mechanism of "indirect" array with array segment as a special case. We may do so by overloading the subscript operator a second time:

func $\hat{}[\hat{}] : $ **array** $T \times \{q : $ **seq** $Nat1 \bullet $ **norep** $q\} \longrightarrow $ **array** T

defined semantically as before, see section 5.8.8, the subsection on indexing by sequence (with the sequence generators interpreted as array producers). Then, by providing an array expression $A[q]$ as an actual **var** parameter in a procedure call, where q is a repetition-free sequence of indices, assignments to components of the formal parameter should result in updating the array A at corresponding locations. Notice that aliasing would occur if the subscript sequence had repeated elements. Thus, let F be the formal parameter. If now $q = \langle 1, 1 \rangle$, then $F[1]$ and $F[2]$ would be aliases. Fortunately, any sequence of the form $\langle i..j \rangle$ is repetition-free and therefore directly acceptable if i and j are legal indices and $i \leq j+1$.

Although assignments to arrays may be forbidden in the programming language as such, the net effect of a procedure call with an actual array **var** parameter is nevertheless an assignment to the array, of a sequence value necessarily of the same length. Furthermore, if the actual parameter is an array segment, say $A[q]$, the effect must be seen as an assignment to the whole array, but the new sequence value is updated only at q: $A := A[q \mapsto f(\ldots)]$, where $f(\ldots)$ is the relevant component of the effect function (producing a sequence value). This fact is expressed by the following specialized adaptation rule for procedure calls, based on ADAP″, for the simple case of a procedure with a single **var** parameter of class **array** T (generalization is easy except notationally):

$$\text{AAPC}: \quad \frac{\vdash \{P\} \textbf{ call } p(A) \ \{Q\}}{\vdash \{(\forall A : \textbf{seq } T \bullet P \Rightarrow Q^A_{f(A)}) \Rightarrow R^B_{B[q \mapsto f(B[q])]}\} \textbf{ call } p(B[q]) \ \{R\}}$$

for $q : \textbf{seq } \textit{Nat1}$ and **norep** q.

EXAMPLE 6.3

We formulate a version of the well known quicksort algorithm as an annotated recursive procedure. This is based on the "partitioning" algorithm used in the program *FIND* of example 4.21, p. 123. Thus, the loop of the procedure *PARTIT* is identical to a section of the *FIND* program. It partitions the given array into three segments related as stated in the postcondition, where the middle one is either empty or a singleton:

```
proc PARTIT(var A : array Int, i : Nat1, j : Nat)  ==
    {1=i≤j=#A; const α := A} var r := A[(i+j)/2];
    loop while i ≤ j;
      loop while A[i] < r; i := i + 1 repeat
      loop while  r < A[j]; j := j − 1 repeat
      if i ≤ j then A[i] :=: A[j]; i, j := i + 1, j − 1 fi
    repeat
    {Split(A, α, i, j)}
```

where $Split(A, \alpha, i, j)$ stands for:
$$0 \leq j < i \leq \#A + 1 \wedge i \leq j + 2 \wedge A[1..j] *{\leq}* A[j+1..i-1] *{\leq}* A[i..\#A] \wedge A \textbf{ perm } \alpha$$

```
proc SORT(var A : array T)  ==
    {const α := A}
    if #A>1 then
      var i : Nat1 = 1; var j : Nat = #A {A=α ∧ 1=i≤j=#A}
      call PARTIT(A, i, j) {Split(A, α, i, j)}
      call SORT(A[1..j]) {Split(A, α, i, j) ∧ /≤ A[1..j]}
      call SORT(A[i..#A]) {Split(A, α, i, j) ∧ /≤ A[1..j] ∧ /≤ A[i..#A]}
    fi{/≤ A ∧ A perm α}
```

□

Exercises

6.3 Prove the correctness and normal termination of *PARTIT*. Hint: The proofs are similar to those of example 4.21. The loop invariants must be slightly adjusted.

6.4 Prove the correctness and normal termination of *SORT*. Hint: Use rule AAPC for adapting the assumptions about the recursive calls.

6.3   Object Orientation

A traditional style of "object orientation" has the block concept of Algol 60 as a starting point. An Algol block is a program text encapsulating a set of declarations of local variables and local procedures, the "block head", as well as a behaviour pattern expressed as a list of statements, the "block tail". Each activation of a block is a data structure whose components are (instances of) the local variables. It also has its own instances of the local procedure declarations and the block tail (at least conceptually), in the sense that, by definition, they refer to the variables of that particular block activation.

Many variants of the block concept exist. Emphasizing the operational aspect (the block tail) we can get procedures, coroutines, parallel processes, or complete programs. Stressing the "existential" aspect (the block head) we can get data structures with associated operators and various kinds of modules or "packages". The latter is typical for the object oriented style.

Consider then a block head as a pattern for data structures with associated operators. It can be seen as an object class in the sense of the last section, more precisely as a *labelled Cartesian product*, where the labelled components correspond to the local variables. In general, the object class corresponds to a subclass of the product restricted by a representation invariant, R, and having additional associated operators:

$$\text{class } OBJECT\{\ldots\} == \{v_1 : T_1 \times \cdots \times v_n : T_n \bullet R(v_1, \ldots, v_n)\}$$
$$\text{\textbf{module} associated functions and procedures \textbf{endmodule}}$$

In a strongly typed language it does not make much difference whether one associates a set of operators with a class or with the individual objects, since all objects of a class will have the same set of associated operators, or at least *similar ones*. There is one difference though: in the object oriented style the associated functions and procedures are regarded as being *local* to each object. This means that they are specialized so as to refer directly to the component variables of the object, rather than obtaining access through a **case** discriminator applied to an object parameter.

A traditional syntax for invoking an operator *op* belonging to an object X is the dot notation, $X.op(\ldots)$. In our framework we may see the X as a distinguished actual parameter to the operator *op* associated with the class of X, by definition a **val** parameter to functions and a **var** parameter to procedures. For operator definitions occurring in the above module a left hand side of the form $.op(\ldots)$ is understood as a shorthand for $(v_1,\ldots,v_n).op(\ldots)$ (which in turn is a standard shorthand for a **case**-construct with only one branch), and the same shorthand may be used for invoking local operators from "within" the object. For a procedure the implied parameters are assignable variables, since they are components of a class-like **var** parameter. In this way the labels of the Cartesian product, defined as component selector functions (in section 5.8.4) are made to play the roles of local program variables, sometimes called *representation variables* (or "instance variables"). It is also convenient to interpret $X.v_i$, for X of the above class as an assignable variable, thus permitting assignments to the components of X outside **case**-constructs.

It is neither practical nor desirable to check by coercion that individual component updates respect the representation invariant, they normally do not; and it is up to the programmer to show that the invariant will be maintained by updating procedures. It may be reasonable to restrict all component updates to occur textually within the associated class module, in order to provide a syntactic guarantee that no user of the class can violate the representation invariant. If the class is used to simulate a more abstract concept, there may be reason to prohibit all direct access to components from outside the class, in order to prevent the confusion of different levels of abstraction.

Notice that the rule of overloading given in section 5.7.1 is guaranteed to select the correct version of any overloaded operator when using the dot notation.

Since a Cartesian product has a single generator the latter is necessarily a *relative constant*. This means that, using this restricted class mechanism, recursive structures such as those shown in section 6.1 cannot be directly defined. To compensate for that, one may introduce a concept of *reference*, or "explicit pointer", pointing either to a data structure of a given type or class (or of a subtype/subclass of the given one) or to "nothing":

> **type** $Ref\{T\}$ **by** $Null,\ Obj\{T\}$ $\ ==$
> **module**
> **func** $null : \longrightarrow Null$ (pointer to nothing)
> **func** $\uparrow\hat{\ } : T \longrightarrow Obj$ (pointer to data)
> **1-1 genbas** $null,\ \uparrow\hat{\ }$
> **func** $\hat{\ }\downarrow : Obj \longrightarrow T$ (data pointed to)
> **def** $(\uparrow X)\downarrow\ == X$
> **endmodule**

Notice the coercion test inherent in the application of $\hat{\ }\downarrow$ to a *Ref*-item, for coercion to the subtype *Obj*.

A $Ref\{T\}$-variable, initialized to *null*, could simulate a variable of type T, undefined initially, if the operators $\uparrow\hat{}$ and $\hat{}\downarrow$ were treated as *ad hoc* coercions inserted automatically wherever needed (and $Ref\{T\}$ were treated as T with respect to overloading).

If we break the rule laid down at the end of section 6.1 by providing class parameters for the *Ref* type, it becomes possible to define recursive data structures directly as Cartesian products:

class $BINTREE\{T\} == L:Ref\{BINTREE\} \times v:T \times R:Ref\{BINTREE\}$

The consequences of instantiating the *Ref* type with a class parameter are quite drastic. Let R be a variable of type $Ref\{C\}$, equal to $\uparrow CO$, where C is a class and CO is a C object. Although the contents of R is itself a small immutable data structure, it does contain an object pointer and the object CO pointed to is not immutable. The result of updating the object would have to be interpreted logically as a new $Ref\{C\}$ value. Worse still, any assignment to R of a non-null value would entail the copying of a pointer, and would have to be checked for alias. This in fact means that the variable R, although type-like from an implementation point of view, must be regarded as *class-like* with respect to the program logic, including alias checks. Diluting the type concept in this way should be discouraged in general. In particular, type-like generator functions should not ordinarily be allowed to have class-like arguments.

A class C is said to simulate a type T imperatively, if the type equivalent T_C simulates T. A C-procedure, **proc** $.P(\textbf{var }x:U,\ \textbf{val }y:V)$, defined using the above syntactic convention, by definition has the effect function profile $T_C \times U \times V \longrightarrow T_C \times U$, where T_C is of the form $v_1:T_1 \times \cdots \times v_n:T_n$, even if only some of the components v_i are updated in P. This is because an internal update, as usual, must be considered an update of the object as a whole. An imperative simulation of T, where the effect functions are validated by Hoare Logic, can at best be partially correct, even if T_C simulates T strongly.

EXAMPLE 6.4

We define a class weakly simulating (imperatively) the type **set** T. A syntax for function declarations, analogous to that of procedures, is used by combining the profile and semantic definition and allowing an imperative function body.

An array segment, $A[1..n]$, where A and n are object components, is used to represent the abstract set value. Since the operators *Has*, *ADD*, and *SUB* all need to search the array A for an occurrence of its T parameter value, that mechanism is formulated as an auxiliary procedure *SRCH*. The assignment to $A[n+1]$ in that procedure serves to ensure normal termination of the search loop without complicating the loop test. It is also the reason for the strong inequality $n < \#A$ of the representation invariant. (The side effect which consequently occurs in the *Has* function is discussed below.)

class $SET\{T\} == \{A:\textbf{array } T \times n:Nat \bullet \ n < \#A \wedge \textbf{norep } A[1..n]\}$
module
func $Emp(N : Nat1, \ x : T) : SET == (x{\uparrow}(N+1), 0)$

func $.Eqv(S : SET) : Bool == A[1..n] \textbf{ perm } S.A[1..S.n]$

proc $.SRCH(\textbf{val } x : T, \textbf{ var } i : Nat1) ==$
    $\{\textbf{const } \alpha := A[1..n]\} \ i := 1; \ A[n+1] := x;$
    $\textbf{loop } \{i \le n+1 \wedge \neg x \textbf{ in } A[1..i-1]\} \textbf{ while } A[i] \ne x; \ i := i+1 \textbf{ repeat}$
    $\{i \le n+1 \le \#A \wedge \textbf{norep } A[1..n] \wedge \neg x \textbf{ in } A[1..i-1] \wedge A[i] = x \wedge A[1..n] = \alpha\}$

func $.Has(x : T) : Bool == \{\textbf{const } \alpha := A[1..n]\} \textbf{ var } i . Nat1,$
    $\textbf{call } .SRCH(x, i); \ Has := i \le n \ \{Has = x \textbf{ in } A[1..n] \wedge A[1..n] = \alpha\}$

proc $.ADD(x : T) ==$
    $\textbf{var } i : Nat1; \textbf{ call } .SRCH(x, i);$
    $\textbf{if } i > n \textbf{ then } n := n+1; \textbf{ if } n = \#A \textbf{ then abort fi fi}$

proc $SUB(x : T) ==$
    $\textbf{var } i : Nat1; \textbf{ call } .SRCH(x, i); \textbf{ if } i \le n \textbf{ then } A[i] := A[n]; \ n := n-1 \textbf{ fi}$
endmodule

Let the abstraction function be: $\mathcal{A}(A, n) == set(A[1..n])$. Then

    $\textbf{var } S : SET\{T\} = EMP(N, t)$

imperatively simulates a variable of the abstract type $\{s : \textbf{set } T \bullet \#s \le N\}$, initialized to $\emptyset$, for arbitrary $N : Nat1$ and $t : T$. The parameter t is needed to provide an initial value of the elements of $S.A$. (It is a nuisance though, since these values are logically redundant.) The standard simulation requirement for the representation of the constant $\emptyset$ must be adjusted to

    $\forall N : Nat1, \ t : T \bullet \emptyset == \mathcal{A}(EMP(N, t))$

The abstract functions $=$, ϵ, add, sub, and $\#$ are represented by Eqv, Has, Add, Sub, and n, respectively. Add and Sub are guarded effect functions of the corresponding procedures:

    func $\hat{\ }.Add, \ \hat{\ }.Sub : SET\{T\} \times T \longrightarrow SET\{T\}$
    def $(A, n).Add(x) == \textbf{if } x \textbf{ in } A[1..n] \vee n+1 < \#A \textbf{ then}$
          $(A[n+1 \mapsto x], \textbf{ if } x \textbf{ in } A[1..n] \textbf{ then } n \textbf{ else } n+1 \textbf{ fi})$
          $\textbf{else } \bot \textbf{ fi}$
    def $(A, n).Sub(x) == \textbf{if } x \textbf{ in } A[1..n] \textbf{ then}$
          $(A[n+1 \mapsto x][inv(A[1..n], x) \mapsto A[n]], \ n-1) \textbf{ else}$
          $(A[n+1 \mapsto x], \ n) \textbf{ fi}$

where the function *inv* represents "inverse indexing"

> **func** *inv* : **seq** $T \times T \longrightarrow$ *Nat*
> **def** $inv(q,x) ==$ **case** $\varepsilon \to 0 \mid q' \vdash y \to$
>   **if** $x=y$ **then** $\#q$ **else** $inv(q',x)$ **fi fo**
> **lma** $\forall q : $ **seq** $T, \ x : T \bullet x$ **in** $q \Rightarrow q[inv(q,x)] = x$

Based on these effect functions we may prove simulation in the strong sense of the subtype of **set** T, restricted as above. The proof obligations consist of:

1. validating the effect functions, as well as the given specification of *Has*,
2. showing that the representation invariant is established and preserved, and
3. proving the simulation relation, directly or by proving translated axioms.

As an example of the latter, we consider the following abstract axiom, modified so as to reflect the subtype restriction on abstract sets:

$$sub(add(s,x),y) == \textbf{if } d_{add(s,x)} \textbf{ then}$$
$$\qquad\qquad \textbf{if } x=y \textbf{ then } sub(s,y) \textbf{ else } add(sub(s,y),x) \textbf{ fi}$$
$$\qquad \textbf{else} \perp \textbf{ fi}$$

where the definedness predicate must be expressed as $x \epsilon s \vee \#s < N$, in order to be well-defined in the subtype. The translation is

$$(A,n).Add(x).Sub(y).Eqv(\textbf{if } (A,n).Has(x) \vee n < N \textbf{ then}$$
$$\qquad\qquad \textbf{if } x=y \textbf{ then } (A,n).Sub(y)$$
$$\qquad\qquad \textbf{else } (A,n).Sub(y).Add(x) \textbf{ fi}$$
$$\qquad \textbf{else} \perp \textbf{ fi})$$

where the representation invariant may be assumed for (A,n), and where the two arguments of *Eqv* must be shown equally defined. The definedness is easy to check. Then, after substitutions and some simplification, we obtain the left and right hand sides listed below to be compared. The simplifications are mechanical except for the formulation and use of the lemma

$$x \neq y \wedge y \textbf{ in } A[1..n] \Rightarrow x \textbf{ in } A[inv(A[1..n],y) \mapsto A[n]][1..n-1] = x \textbf{ in } A[1..n].$$

There are six cases to be considered, depending on the truth values of $x = y$, x **in** $A[1..n]$, and y **in** $A[1..n]$, respectively.

$$\text{LHS} = \begin{cases} (A[n+1 \mapsto x][inv(A[1..n],x) \mapsto A[n]], n-1) & \text{if } \textbf{t,t,t} \\ (A[n+1 \mapsto x][n+2 \mapsto x], n) & \text{if } \textbf{t,f,f} \\ (A[n+1 \mapsto y][inv(A[1..n],y) \mapsto A[n]], n-1) & \text{if } \textbf{f,t,t} \\ (A[n+1 \mapsto y], n) & \text{if } \textbf{f,t,f} \\ (A[n+1 \mapsto x][n+2 \mapsto y][inv(A[1..n],y) \mapsto x], n) & \text{if } \textbf{f,f,t} \\ (A[n+1 \mapsto x][n+2 \mapsto y], n+1) & \text{if } \textbf{f,f,f} \end{cases}$$

$$\text{RHS} = \begin{cases} (A[n+1 \mapsto x][inv(A[1..n],x) \mapsto A[n]], n-1) & \text{if } \mathbf{t,t,t} \\ (A[n+1 \mapsto x], n) & \text{if } \mathbf{t,f,f} \\ (A[n+1 \mapsto y][inv(A[1..n],y) \mapsto A[n]], n-1) & \text{if } \mathbf{f,t,t} \\ (A[n+1 \mapsto x], n) & \text{if } \mathbf{f,t,f} \\ (A[n+1 \mapsto y][inv(A[1..n],y) \mapsto A[n]][n \mapsto x], n) & \text{if } \mathbf{f,f,t} \\ (A[n+1 \mapsto x], n+1) & \text{if } \mathbf{f,f,f} \end{cases}$$

Five of the pairs are either syntactically equal or equal in the essential part of A. Only in the case $\mathbf{f,f,t}$ is there a difference in the essential parts, but they are permutations of one another, by interchanging the elements at positions $inv(A[1..n],y)$ and n. So the two objects are equivalent.

In the definition of the function Has we have violated the rule that functions should have no side effects; it does have one on A at position $n+1$ through the auxiliary procedure $SRCH$. (More precisely, we have violated the integrity of the implicit class-like **val** parameter A of Has by modifying a component of it in the $SRCH$ procedure.) The side effect may, however, be considered *innocent*, because the modified object is equivalent to the initial one. Thus, no side effect is seen on the abstract level. In [20] Hoare points to the fact that such innocent side effects may even be "benevolent", for instance by adjusting the representation of a set in such a way that elements searched for frequently are found early.

A conclusion of this discussion is perhaps that *ad hoc* language restrictions, although helpful in general, may be even more useful if the user is allowed to violate them at the cost of additional proof obligations.

□

Exercises

6.5 A FIFO queue shall be weakly and imperatively simulated by a class of the following form:

class $FIFOQ\{T\} == \{A : \textbf{array } T \times F : Nat1 \times L : Nat1 \times B : Bool \bullet$
$\qquad\qquad 1 \leq F, L \leq \#A \wedge \textbf{if } B \textbf{ then } L \leq F \textbf{ else } F \leq L \textbf{ fi}\}$
module
func $Emp(N : Nat1, \ t : T) : FIFOQ == (t \uparrow N, 1, 1, \mathbf{f})$
func $.Length : Nat == \cdots$
func $.First : T == \cdots$
proc $.ENQ(x : T) == \cdots$
proc $.POP == \cdots$
endmodule

with the abstraction function:

$$\mathcal{A}(A, F, L, B) == \textbf{if } B \textbf{ then } A[F..\#A] \dashv A[1..S-1] \textbf{ else } A[F..S-1] \textbf{ fi}$$

The concrete operators correspond to the following standard sequence functions: ε, $\#\hat{}$, lt, $\hat{}\vdash\hat{}$, and rr, respectively. Program and verify the concrete operators. Meaningless cases should lead to explicit $\perp$ or **abort**. The effect functions should be such that the subtype $\{q : \mathbf{seq}\ T \bullet \#q \leq N\}$ is simulated strongly if the array is initialized to length N.

6.4   Pointer Aliases

Programming with pointer aliases requires a drastic reinterpretation of the program. One has to allow for the possibility of arbitrary aliasing by making object pointers explicit as indices into sequences of objects of the same class. The reinterpretation can be explained by performing the following simultaneous alterations to the program text, assuming for simplicity that only objects of one class, C, may have accessible converging pointers to them. (The approach can be generalized to cater for more than one class, as well as subclasses.)

1. Introduce a global program variable **var** $\tilde{C} : \mathbf{seq}\ T_C$, where T_C is the type equivalent of the class. The purpose of this variable is to contain the states of all C-objects generated so far, in the order of generation.

2. Replace any occurrence of C in the domain of a function profile by T_C.

3. Replace any other occurrence of C by *Nat1*. Corresponding values will be used as indices to the sequence $\tilde{C}$.

4. Replace any C-expression e, which is an actual argument of a function or the discriminand of a **case** construct, by $\tilde{C}[e]$.

5. A class C generator expression $g(\ldots)$ has the *side effect* of extending the sequence $\tilde{C}$ by a corresponding T_C value. In order to represent such side effects, an assignment of the form $X := g(e_1, \ldots, e_n)$, where g is a C-generator, must be rewritten as
$$\tilde{C}, X := \tilde{C} \vdash g(e_1, \ldots, e_n),\ \#\tilde{C}+1,$$
   provided that no argument e_i contains a C-expression. In general $\tilde{C}$ must be extended by all C-expressions occurring in the right hand side, taken in the left-to-right, bottom up order, the expressions themselves replaced by $\tilde{C}$, correctly indexed, when used as arguments. (Strictness of functions is assumed.) Procedure calls must be treated similarly if actual parameter expressions have side effects. Unfortunately, functions and procedures which implicitly apply C-generators have implicit side effects as well.

6. An assignment to a component of a C-object must be interpreted as changing the T_C value of the corresponding element of the sequence $\tilde{C}$, which in turn must be interpreted as an assignment to the *whole sequence*. Thus,

   case X **of** $g(\bar{x}, y, \bar{z}) \rightarrow y := e\ |\ \ldots$ **fo**

for $X:C$, is changed to

$$\textbf{case } \tilde{C}[X] \textbf{ of } g(\bar{x}, y, \bar{z}) \rightarrow \tilde{C} := \tilde{C}[X \mapsto g(\bar{x}, e, \bar{z})] \mid \ldots \textbf{ fo}$$

where $g(\bar{x}, e, \bar{z})$ is seen as an expression of type T_C, and the expression e is treated as above. Notice that X remains unchanged in this logic.

The logic becomes somewhat more complicated if subclasses of C occur. Each subclass D must be associated with a corresponding subtype $Nat1_D$ of $Nat1$, and $\tilde{C}$ must be treated as a function satisfying the syntactic lemma $Nat1_D \longrightarrow D$ for every subclass D of C.

The above should make it clear that it is good policy to avoid aliasing if possible. Sometimes, however, a moderate amount of aliasing is necessary in order to achieve good efficiency in the processing of data objects.

EXAMPLE 6.5

In order to represent a FIFO queue as efficiently as possible by a list of class objects, we have to store pointers to both ends of the list, thereby causing an alias on the last *ELEM*-object of the list:

class $LIST\{T\}$ **by** *NIL*, *ELEM* $==$
module
func $nil : \longrightarrow NIL$
func $el : LIST \times T \longrightarrow ELEM$
1-1 genbas $nil,\ el$

func $seq : LIST \longrightarrow$ **seq** T
def $seq(ls) == $ **case** ls **of** $nil \rightarrow \varepsilon \mid el(nx, t) \rightarrow t \dashv seq(nx)$ **fo**
endmodule

class $FIFOQ\{T\} == \{first : LIST\{T\} \times last : LIST\{T\} \bullet$
$$\textbf{case } (first, last) \textbf{ of } (nil, nil) \rightarrow \textbf{t}$$
$$\mid \ (el(nx_1, t_1),\ el(nx_2, t_2)) \rightarrow$$
$$rt(t_1 \dashv seq(nx_1)) = t_2 \wedge nx_2 = nil$$
$$\mid \ \textbf{others } \rightarrow \textbf{f fo}\}$$
module
proc $.ENQ(x : t) ==$
$\quad$ **const** $new := el(nil, x);$
$\quad$ **case** $last$ **of** $nil \rightarrow first, last := new, new$
$\quad\quad\quad\quad \mid \ el(nx, t) \rightarrow last, nx := new, new$ **fo**

proc $.POP ==$
$\quad$ **case** $first$ **of** $nil \rightarrow$ **abort** $\mid el(nx, t) \rightarrow first := nx$ **fo**;
$\quad$ **if** $first = nil$ **then** $last := nil$ **fi**
endmodule

In modifying the program according to the above rules we shall make one short-cut. Since *nil*-objects are, and remain, indistinguishable in terms of contents, we do not regard *nil* as a *LIST*-expression, but as a *Nat1* constant, say 1, having initialized the variable $\widetilde{LIST}$, called $\tilde{L}$ for short, accordingly. Then $(X = nil) = (\tilde{L}[X]\ \textbf{is}\ NIL)$ holds for all $X : \{1..\#\tilde{L}\}$. There is consequently no need to distinguish syntactically between subtypes of *Nat1* corresponding to the subclasses of *LIST*:

var $\tilde{L}$: **seq** $T_{LIST} = \varepsilon \vdash nil$

class $FIFOQ\{T\}\ ==\ \{first : \times last : Nat1 \bullet$
$\qquad\qquad$ **case** $(\tilde{L}[first], \tilde{L}[last])$ **of** $(nil, nil) \to \textbf{t}$
$\qquad\qquad\qquad\qquad |\quad (el(nx_1, t_1), el(nx_2, t_2)) \to$
$\qquad\qquad\qquad\qquad\qquad rt(t_1 \dashv seq(\tilde{L}[nx_1])) = t_2 \wedge nx_2 = nil$
$\qquad\qquad\qquad\qquad |\quad \textbf{others} \to \textbf{f fo}$
module
proc $.ENQ(x : T)\ ==\ (\tilde{L}, first, last) :=$
$\qquad$ **case** $\tilde{L}[last]$ **of** $nil \to (\tilde{L} \vdash el(nil, x), \textbf{S}\#\tilde{L}, \textbf{S}\#\tilde{L}) \mid el(nx, t) \to$
$\qquad ((\tilde{L} \vdash el(nil, x))[last \mapsto el(\textbf{S}\#\tilde{L}, t)], first, \textbf{S}\#\tilde{L})$ **fo**

proc $.POP\ ==\ (first, last) :=$
$\qquad$ **case** $first$ **of** $nil \to \bot \mid el(nx, t) \to$
$\qquad\qquad$ **case** nx **of** $nil \to (nil, nil) \mid \textbf{others} \to (nx, last)$ **fo fo**
endmodule

It should be noted that, whereas the function *seq* is TGI defined and therefore total for convergence-free *LIST* structures, the same is not necessarily true otherwise. Thus, if pointer cycles occur the recursion may not terminate. Assuming, however, that *FIFOQ* is the only user of *LIST*, we may strengthen the representation invariant by

$$\forall k, nx : Nat1, t : T \bullet k \leq \#\tilde{L} \wedge \tilde{L}[k] = el(nx, t) \wedge nx \neq nil \Rightarrow k < nx \leq \#\tilde{L}$$

which shows that the structures are cycle-free, and that *seq* is well-defined. It also shows that $first \leq last$ always holds.

We prove that the procedure *ENQ* preserves the invariant in the interesting case that $\tilde{L}[last]$ is other than *nil*. Left construction gives the following verification condition:

case $(\tilde{L}[first], \tilde{L}[last])$ **of** $(el(nx, t), el(nx', t')) \to$
$\qquad\qquad rt(t \dashv seq(\tilde{L}[nx])) = t' \wedge nx' = nil \Rightarrow$
$\quad$ **case** $((\tilde{L} \vdash el(nil, x))[last \mapsto el(\textbf{S}\#\tilde{L}, t')][first],$
$\qquad (\tilde{L} \vdash el(nil, x))[last \mapsto el(\textbf{S}\#\tilde{L}, t')][\textbf{S}\#\tilde{L}])$ **of** $(el(nx_1, t_1), el(nx_2, t_2)) \to$
$\qquad rt(t_1 \dashv seq((\tilde{L} \vdash el(nil, x))[last \mapsto el(\textbf{S}\#\tilde{L}, t)][nx_1])) = t_2 \wedge nx_2 = nil$ **fo fo**

It follows from $last \leq \#\tilde{L}$ that $(nx_2, t_2) = (nil, x)$; therefore the consequent simplifies to:

case $(\tilde{L} \vdash el(nil, x))[last \mapsto el(\mathbf{S}\#\tilde{L}, t')][first]$ **of** $el(nx_1, t_1) \rightarrow$
$rt(t_1 \dashv seq((\tilde{L} \vdash el(nil, x))[last \mapsto el(\mathbf{S}\#\tilde{L}, t')][nx_1])) = x$ **fo**

Case $first = last$ gives $(nx_1, t_1) = (\mathbf{S}\#\tilde{L}, t')$, and thus the consequent reduces to $rt(t' \dashv seq(el(nil, x))) = x$, which holds.

In the case $first < last$ we may conclude $\tilde{L}[last \mapsto el(\mathbf{S}\#\tilde{L}, t')][first] = \tilde{L}[first]$, which shows $(nx_1, t_1) = (nx, t)$. The consequent thus becomes:

$$rt(t \dashv seq((\tilde{L} \vdash el(nil, x))[last \mapsto el(\mathbf{S}\#\tilde{L}, t')][nx])) = x$$

Now, the premise shows that the list in $\tilde{L}$ starting at nx has an element in position *last*. Since the modified $\tilde{L}$ is unchanged to the left of *last* the same must be true for the modified list. It follows from the modifications of $\tilde{L}$ that this list element is followed by the one in position $\mathbf{S}\#\tilde{L}$, which has the T-value x and has no *ELEM*-successor. Consequently x is the rightmost element of the sequence

$$seq((\tilde{L} \vdash el(nil, x))[last \mapsto el(\mathbf{S}\#\tilde{L}, t')][nx])$$

This together with the fact that $last < \mathbf{S}\#\tilde{L}$ shows that the strengthened representation invariant is preserved in the case considered.

By including access procedures to the T-values (or objects) occurring in a *FIFOQ* list, say to the first and last ones, and at the same time prohibiting access to the components *first* and *last*, any user of the *FIFOQ* class is fully protected against the aliases occurring locally in *FIFOQ* objects.

□

Exercises

6.6 Prove that the above procedure *POP* preserves the *FIFOQ* invariant.

6.7 Formulate an extension $SCANLIST\{T\}$ of the above class $FIFOQ\{T\}$ (a subclass in the sense of object orientation) with the additional component variable *scanp* : *LIST*, representing the current position of a pointer scanning the list, and the following user accessible mechanisms:

proc $.SCAN == scanp := first$
proc $.ADV ==$ **case** $scanp$ **of** $nil \rightarrow$ **abort** $\mid el(nx, t) \rightarrow scanp := nx$ **fo**
func $.Cur : Ref\{T\} ==$ **case** $scanp$ **of** $nil \rightarrow null \mid el(nx, t) \rightarrow \uparrow t$ **fo**

for initializing a scan, advancing to the next element, and accessing the current T-value if any, respectively.

Prove that the two procedures respect the invariant $seq(scanp)$ **tail** $seq(first)$. Propose reasonable additions to the mechanisms of *FIFOQ* in order to respect the new invariant.

Bibliography

[1] E.A. Ashcroft, M. Clint, C.A.R. Hoare: Remarks on "Program Proving: Jumps and Functions by M. Clint and C.A.R. Hoare". *Acta Informatica* vol. 6 (1976).

[2] R.J.R. Back: Invariant Based Programs and their Correctness. In *Automatic Program Construction Techniques* (Biermann, Guiho, and Kodratoff, eds.). Macmillan Publishing Company, 1983.

[3] G.M. Birtwistle, O.-J. Dahl, B. Myhrhaug, K. Nygaard: *Simula Begin.* Studentlitteratur. Auerbach Publ. 1973.

[4] C.-L. Chang, R.C.-T. Lee: *Symbolic Logic and Mechanical Theorem Proving.* Academic Press, 1973.

[5] M. Clint, C.A.R. Hoare: Program Proving: Jumps and Functions. *Acta Informatica* vol.1 (1972).

[6] O.-J. Dahl, C.A.R. Hoare: Hierarchical Program Structures. In O.-J. Dahl, E.W. Dijkstra, C.A.R. Hoare: *Structured Programming.* Academic Press 1972, pp. 175–220.

[7] O.-J. Dahl: Can Program Proving be Made Practical? In M. Amirchahy, D. Neel: *Les Fondements de la Programmation.* IRIA 1977, pp. 57–114.

[8] N. Dershowitz, J.-P. Jouannaud: Rewrite Systems. In J. van Leeuwen (ed.): *Handbook of Theoretical Computer Science,* Vol. B, Elsevier Science (1990), pp. 245–320.

[9] E.W. Dijkstra: *A Discipline of Programming.* Prentice Hall, 1976.

[10] R.W. Floyd: Assigning Meaning to Programs. *Mathematical Aspects of Computer Science*, XIX American Mathematical Society (1967), pp. 19–32.

[11] G. Gentzen: Untersuchungen über das logische Schliessen. *Mathematische Zeitschrift*, vol. 39 (1934), pp. 176–210.

[12] K. Gödel: On Undecidable Propositions of Formal Mathematical Systems. *Lecture notes*, Institute for Advanced Study, Princeton, N.J., 1934.

[13] J.A. Goguen, J.-P. Jouannaud, J. Meseguer: Operational Semantics of Order-Sorted Algebra. *Proc. 1985 Int. Conf. on Automata, Languages and Programming*, W. Brauer (ed.) Lecture Notes in Computer Science 194, Springer Verlag, 1985.

[14] J.V. Guttag: *The Specification and Application to Programming of Abstract Data Types*. Ph. D. Thesis, Computer Science Department, University of Toronto, 1975.

[15] J.V. Guttag, J.J. Horning: The Algebraic Specification of Abstract Data Types. *Acta Informatica*, vol. 10 (1978), pp. 27–52.

[16] A.G. Hamilton: *Logic for Mathematicians*. Cambridge University Press (1978).

[17] C.A.R. Hoare: An Axiomatic Approach to Computer Programming. *Comm ACM*, vol. 12 (1969), pp. 576–580.

[18] C.A.R. Hoare: Procedures and Parameters: An Axiomatic Approach. *Symposium on Semantics of Programming Languages*. Springer Verlag, 1971, pp. 102–116.

[19] C.A.R. Hoare: Proof of a Program: FIND. *Comm ACM*, vol. 11 (1971), pp. 39–45.

[20] C.A.R. Hoare: Proof of the Correctness of Data Representations. *Acta Informatica*, vol. 1, 1972.

[21] C.A.R. Hoare: *Communicating Sequential Processes*. Prentice-Hall, 1985.

[22] K. Iverson: *A Programming Language*. Wiley, New York, 1962.

[23] D.E. Knuth: *Fundamental Algorithms*, Addison-Wesley 1968.

[24] D.E. Knuth, P.B. Bendix: Simple Word Problems in Universal Algebras. *Computational Problems in Abstract Algebra*, pp. 263–297. J. Leech (ed.). Pergamon Press, Oxford 1970.

[25] J. von Neumann, H.H. Goldstine: Planning and Coding for an Electronic Computing Instrument Part 1, Vol. 1. In: *The Mathematic and Logical Aspects of an Electronic Computing Instrument,* Institute for Advanced Study, Princeton, N.J., 1947.

[26] O. Owe: Partial Logics Reconsidered: A Partial Approach. *Formal Aspects of Computing.* Springer International, 1992.

[27] O. Owe, O.-J. Dahl: Generator Induction in Order Sorted Algebras. *Formal Aspects of Computing* (1991), 3:2–20.

[28] D. Prawitz: *Natural Deduction.* Acta Universitatis Stockholmiensis 3, 1965.

[29] J.R. Schoenfield: *Mathematical Logic.* Addison-Wesley, 1967.

Index